The Theory of Economic Policy in a Strategic Context

In developing a new and highly innovative theory of economic policy, this book deals with conflicts between strategic actions by public and private agents. It builds on the Lucas critique, but also applies the tools introduced by Tinbergen and Theil to dynamic policy games and from there derives a new theory of economic policy. Its main propositions describe such properties in the models currently used for policymaking as neutrality and equilibrium existence, uniqueness, and multiplicity. These properties are key to understanding the impact of concepts such as rational expectations, time inconsistency, communication and the use of policy announcements. As the numerous examples show, they are useful both for model building and for devising optimal institutions. *The Theory of Economic Policy in a Strategic Context* is an essential but accessible tool for economic researchers involved in policy questions.

NICOLA ACOCELLA is Professor of Economic Policy at the University of Rome "La Sapienza."

GIOVANNI DI BARTOLOMEO is Associate Professor of Economics at the University of Teramo, where he is also the Director of the postgraduate course in Management and Business Communication.

ANDREW HUGHES HALLETT is Professor of Economics and Public Policy at George Mason University, and Professor of Economics at the University of St. Andrews. He is a Fellow of the Royal Society of Edinburgh.

The Theory of Economic Policy in a Strategic Context

NICOLA ACOCELLA

GIOVANNI DI BARTOLOMEO

ANDREW HUGHES HALLETT

CAMBRIDGE
UNIVERSITY PRESS

CAMBRIDGE UNIVERSITY PRESS
Cambridge, New York, Melbourne, Madrid, Cape Town,
Singapore, São Paulo, Delhi, Mexico City

Cambridge University Press
The Edinburgh Building, Cambridge CB2 8RU, UK

Published in the United States of America by Cambridge University Press, New York

www.cambridge.org
Information on this title: www.cambridge.org/9781107023864

First published 2013

Printed in Great Britain by the MPG Books Group

A catalogue record for this publication is available from the British Library

Library of Congress Cataloguing in Publication data
Acocella, Nicola, 1939–
The theory of economic policy in a strategic context / Nicola Acocella,
Giovanni Di Bartolomeo, Andrew Hughes Hallett.
pages ; cm
Includes bibliographical references and index.
ISBN 978-1-107-02386-4
1. Economic policy. 2. Rational expectations (Economic theory)
I. Di Bartolomeo, Giovanni, 1969– II. Hughes Hallett, Andrew. III. Title.
HD87.A286 2012
330.1–dc23
2012018814

ISBN 978-1-107-02386-4 Hardback

To Flavia, Elena and Viola, for being smart, sweet, and joyful. N.A.

To Daniela (wherever she might be) and Raffaele with love, as always. G.D.B.

To David, Jim and Nicky, who prefer controllability to stabilizability, but understand both. A.H.H.

Contents

List of figures — *page* ix
List of tables — x
Preface — xi
Common symbols — xiv
1 An overview: the realm of economic policy — 1

Part I ***The classical theory of economic policy*** — 15
2 Statics — 17
3 Dynamics — 45

Part II ***From the classical to the new theory of economic policy*** — 81
4 The Lucas critique — 83
5 Policy games: an introduction — 95

Part III ***The new theory of economic policy: statics*** — 123
6 A theory of strategic conflict: foundations — 125
7 From individual players to system controllability — 152
8 Conflicts and coordination among groups — 170
9 Announcements as a coordination mechanism — 197

Part IV ***The new theory of economic policy: dynamics*** — 225
10 Controllability in a strategic dynamic setting — 227

11 Dynamic policy games with rational expectations 250

12 Credibility, dynamic controllability and rational expectations 272

13 Expectations and target coordination: institutional aspects 307

14 A summary and round-up of the conclusions 322

References 326

Index 344

Author index 348

Figures

2.1	Fixed target approach	*page* 27
2.2	Iso-loss curves	28
2.3	Flexible target approach	29
2.4	Losses and optimization	30
3.1	A time line for dynamic policy problems	52
3.2	Relations among state controllability (C), null controllability (NC) and stabilizability (S)	65
3.3	A schematic view of the sequence of an optimal policy plan	78
5.1	Best response function	103
5.2	Quasi-reaction function	105
5.3	Stackelberg equilibrium	110
5.4	Nash equilibrium	111
6.1	A monetary and fiscal policy game	139
9.1	Announcement equilibrium vs. commitment	209
9.2	Multiple Nash equilibria	211
9.3	Announcement equilibria	213
9.4	Market shares and Δt	223

Tables

3.1	Summary of policy models	*page* 57
6.1	Properties of the model	147
9.1	Monetary and fiscal announcements	214
11.1	A complete taxonomy	266

Preface

Economics lost an important part of its foundations, and some would say of its *raison d'être*, when the theory of economic policy devised by Jan Tinbergen, Henry Theil, Ragnar Frisch and others was destroyed under the logical stringency of the Lucas critique. The idea of the government as influencing or even controlling a private sector with conflicting targets, but not fully informed and possibly inactive, was certainly short-sighted and correctly dismissed after Lucas' criticisms. However, the Lucas critique contributed to a widespread but often incorrect belief of policy irrelevance, time inconsistency in policy actions and the need to substitute government by markets.

This book recognizes Lucas' point of view and the idea that different agents – in particular, the government and private agents – can have fully or partially divergent goals and actively intervene in order to try to pursue them. But it distinguishes that idea from its implications, derived in specific context, by attempting to build, on the ashes of the Tinbergen–Theil contributions, a general approach to the theory of economic policy consistent with the Lucas critique and rational expectations. In our view, the proper general context where such active conflicts can be analyzed is to be seen in policy games. Then, by using a revised version of the tools introduced by Tinbergen, Theil and others in this context, we derive a new and more relevant theory of economic policy.

The main propositions of this new theory describe such properties of the models usually used for policymaking as neutrality or equilibrium existence, uniqueness, and multiplicity. These properties are also the key to understanding the impact of many concepts – such as rational expectations, time inconsistency, communication effectiveness, and policy announcements – currently used in macroeconomic theory and many other applications. These concepts are therefore useful both for model building and for devising proper institutions, and we hope that they will re-establish the theory of economic policy as part of mainstream economic thinking or make it an essential tool for any economic social science researcher interested in evaluating different policy issues. Finally, they may also contribute to putting public action into a more balanced and nuanced perspective: not blindly powerful as in the fifties and sixties, but also not powerless as it was presented to be in the following decades.

Whilst innovative, and the first comprehensive restatement of the theory of economic policy for several decades, our book should be accessible to every graduate or advanced undergraduate student of economic and social sciences familiar with the essentials of game theory, linear algebra and calculus; and should become a "vade mecum" for researchers in academia, think tanks or research institutes who lack an overview of the flaws and alternative approaches to the policy problems they are familiar with.

The book is based on the techniques and outlook of a number of papers published by the three of us over the past eight years. Those papers in turn build on earlier work by one of the authors, Andrew Hughes Hallett, who some time earlier had contributed to the theory of economic policy along the lines of Tinbergen and Theil.

This book would not have appeared without the support of a number of institutions and people. Nicola Acocella and Giovanni Di Bartolomeo acknowledge funding from Sapienza University of Rome and MIUR when the new theory was only in their minds. The Department of Geo-economics and that of Methods and Models for Economics, Territory and Finance (Memotef) at Sapienza have also provided them with a friendly and encouraging environment. Nicola Acocella is deeply indebted to Federico Caffè, who started his interest in the theory of economic policy some fifty years ago, suggesting that policymaking should be considered as the result of the interaction of "big government" with "big business" and "big labor" before the Lucas critique was stated and game theory applied to policy problems (Caffé, 1966: 14). Nicola Acocella has taught parts of the book to his students in the Doctoral School Program of Sapienza University and would like to thank them for all their suggestions, doubts and questions on some initial versions of the theory. Elisa Guglielminetti spotted some remaining typos in the last version of the manuscript. Giovanni Di Bartolomeo also acknowledges the University of Teramo and the Marie Curie Fellowship Program for funding, the University of Crete (Department of Economics), and the CORE at the Université

Catholique de Louvain for hospitality during his work on the very last part of the book.

We should also express our thanks to many colleagues for their comments and feedback, after many discussions on the issues investigated in the book during the last ten years, when we were developing the first concepts of our approach to the theory of economic policy. These were invaluable in giving us a better understanding of the subject matter. We are particularly grateful to Bas van Aarle, Guido Candela, Maria Chiarolla, Jacob Engwerda, Peter Flaschel, Douglas Hibbs, George Kouretas, Reinhard Neck, Stefano Papa, Wilfried Pauwels, Joseph Plasmans, Emanuela Randon, Patrizio Tirelli. We are also grateful to the anonymous referees of Cambridge University Press for their appreciation of our manuscript and their valuable remarks.

All the authors especially thank Paolo G. Piacquadio, a former student of the Sapienza Doctoral School, for his cooperation in a number of papers and his revision of the whole manuscript. His coauthorship in Chapters 8 and 9 is formally recognized, but his contribution of ideas as well as formal solutions to a number of issues goes well beyond that.

Veronica Fedeli has provided invaluable help in editing the many papers on which this book is based, as well as editing the many versions of the manuscript. Chris Harrison, of Cambridge University Press, provided us with valuable suggestions and has followed the various steps of the publication with care and efficiency. Thanks also to Elizabeth Spicer for her efficiency and patience.

Finally, we would like to thank our respective families without whom, it might be thought, the book would have been completed in half the time. In fact, the blame for that is entirely ours (although not perhaps in equal measure); as is the responsibility for any errors, omissions or views that the reader might not agree with.

Common symbols

Real number set	R
Matrix rank	r[.]
Matrix determinant	det(.)
Partial derivative of y with respect to x	$\partial y/\partial x$
Expectation operator	E[.]
Lag operator	L
Spectrum	σ[.]
The i-th element of vector y	$y(i)$
The i-th, j-th element of matrix B	$B(i,j)$
Identity matrix	I
Vector y at time t	y_t
Sequence of vectors x between time 1 and s	$X^S = \{x_i\}_1{}^S \in \Omega_X$
Endogenous (target) variables	y
(Exogenous) desired target values	$\bar{y}$
Exogenous (control) instruments	u
State variables	z
Number of quadratic targets	q
Number of linear targets	l
Number of instruments	m
Policymaker's preference matrices and vectors	Q, r, l
Endogenous (target) variable lags	p
Irrelevant endogenous variable lags	r
Exogenous (control) instrument lags	g
Economic system parameter matrices	A, B, C, D, E, F, G, H
Economic system parameter vectors	w, d
Policy multipliers	Π
Target interval	T
Policy lead	S
Information set	Ω

1 An overview: the realm of economic policy

Summary. The theory of economic policy has its roots in the contributions of Tinbergen and Theil, who solved the problem of a policymaker aiming to achieve certain policy targets by using the available policy instruments and considering the model of the economy as a given constraint. The theory developed by Tinbergen and Theil presented a theoretical framework for designing economic policy over a long time horizon. However, after Lucas raised the issue that the private sector could react to the policymaker's decisions, their theory lost its appeal and most policy problems have been discussed in terms of policy games, thus introducing the possibility of conflicts and externalities among different players. The new theory of economic policy continues with the policy game approach, and applies the concepts and tools introduced by Tinbergen and Theil to develop a theory of conflicts, and to be able to assert conditions for policy neutrality, equilibrium existence, and policy uniqueness or multiplicity.

1.1 The Tinbergen–Theil contributions

The theory of economic policy is an area of economic theory that focuses on the investigation of a policy problem "resulting from the interaction of a policy objective, representing some abstract policymaker's desires, with a policy model representing the feasible outcomes of policy actions" (Preston and Pagan, 1982).

The theory of economic policy has its roots in Jan Tinbergen's econometric models of the Dutch and the US economies (Tinbergen, 1936, 1939), and was developed by Tinbergen himself while serving as the first director of the Dutch Central Planning Bureau from 1945 onwards.[1] In the early 1950s, while considering the development of econometric models in a policymaking context, Tinbergen in fact

[1] See Magnus and Morgan (1987) and Hughes Hallett (1989).

derived the formal conditions to achieve given policy targets using a set of policy instruments in a linear representation of the economy. In other words, he was able to derive the formal conditions to "control" a linear economic system (Tinbergen, 1952, 1956). Tinbergen's results are summarized in the classical Golden Rule, which asserts that a policymaker can reach any given (fixed) set of independent target values if the number of independent instruments equals or exceeds the number of targets. A similar approach was developed by Bent Hansen in the same years (Hansen, 1958). Tinbergen deserves the credit for having raised the problem of policymaking in a consistent way. But he left many issues unresolved; not least, how to deal with systems in which the number of instruments is less than that of targets (hereafter called "non-Tinbergen" systems).

Later, Henri Theil provided a solution for many of the issues that had been left unsolved in the Tinbergen theory. He prescribed that the policymaker should minimize a loss (or maximize a utility) function defined on the relevant target variables, subject to constraints describing the responses of the economy. He thus solved the problem of how to pick policies when the policymaker is confronted with a non-Tinbergen system. In so doing, Theil arrived at a solution of the policy problem formally very similar to that proposed by Ragnar Frisch, who had first conceived of policy problems in terms of minimizing a social loss function to be derived by interviewing policymakers.[2] Theil also overcame Tinbergen's rigid distinction between targets and instruments, by allowing the latter to be relevant in their own right (for example, where policymakers have preferences over how the instruments should be used; or have strong views over whether their use should be restricted to certain "acceptable" values) and introducing them directly into the objective function. Theil, in addition, was the first to develop a theory of economic policy in a multi-period dynamic setting. Finally, he introduced uncertainty into the model of the economy and the policy process with an appeal to the principle of certainty equivalence (Theil, 1954, 1956, 1958, 1964).

Further improvements and advances in the theory as to the existence, uniqueness and design of economic policies are due to a number of authors: for example, Leontief (1964, 1976), Heal (1973), Preston (1974), Johansen (1977, 1978), Preston and Pagan (1982), Hughes

[2] See Frisch (1949, 1950, 1957, 1961).

Hallett and Rees (1983), Holly and Hughes Hallett (1989). The development of modern methods of control theory[3] has complemented this strand of literature to give a very powerful set of techniques for designing and implementing policies to achieve given social and economic targets.

Tinbergen, Frisch, Theil, and the other founding fathers of the theory of economic policy were mainly concerned with its normative aspects. They were less interested in analyzing the effectiveness of specific policy instruments, an issue that has been raised more prominently in the subsequent economics literature with reference to specific policy problems; particularly in monetary policy, in fiscal policy, and in other applications.

1.2 Rational expectations and the Lucas critique: a loss of control?

The Tinbergen–Theil theory of economic policy has been the theoretical foundation for macroeconomic policy[4] since the 1960s. In 1960, Paul Samuelson and Robert Solow published a celebrated article in the *American Economic Review* in which they argued that the Phillips curve could be considered as a long run structural equation and thus treated as a sort of menu of policy options (Samuelson and Solow, 1960). As a consequence, the flexible target approach was the way to face the trade-off between inflation and unemployment along the Phillips curve.

After the 1960s ended, however, the theory of economic policy became the object of fierce criticism for a number of reasons. The introduction of rational expectations (REs) led to an assertion of the ineffectiveness of monetary policy that was more forceful than even that most famously stated by Milton Friedman in his 1968 American Economic Association Presidential Address (Sargent and Wallace, 1975). In a similar way, with rational forward-looking expectations,

[3] See, for example, Bellman (1957, 1961), Kalman (1960), Pontryagin, Boltyanskii, Gamkrelidze and Mishchenko (1962), Athans and Falb (1966), Pindyck (1973), Chow (1975), Aoki (1976), Petit (1990).

[4] Note, however, that their contribution (and more generally, the whole theory of economic policy) can easily be made the basis of microeconomic applications too. This is particularly true for Theil's flexible target approach (see Theil, 1958, 1964).

fiscal policy was considered ineffective as an instrument for managing income levels (Barro, 1974). A proposition of policy neutrality or policy "invariance" was thus stated with regard to the two most widely used macroeconomic policy instruments.

Apart from critiques advanced with respect to the effectiveness of specific instruments, a more general argument was raised by Lucas (1976) according to which a Tinbergen-type decision model is inconsistent with the assumption of REs. The importance of this contribution lies in the fact that it denied the validity of the solution given by Tinbergen, Theil, and others; and with it the existence of an optimal policy vector, or a sequence of policy vectors, that can achieve policy targets or get close to them. The root of the problem is that this approach assumes the private sector behavior to be invariant to the policy vector itself. In other words, when the private sector has REs of future developments, the policymaker will lose control of the economic system, as those expectations deny the existence of an equilibrium of the kind postulated in the existing theory of economic policy.

The implication of this argument is easy to understand if one realizes that assuming REs amounts to an implicit change in the nature of the economic system confronting the policymaker: the private sector has objectives conflicting with those of the policymaker and can react (to a certain degree) to actions taken by the policymaker. The policymaker then faces a system that is no longer parametric; and this in itself leads, according to Lucas, to a loss of control. However, that implication might not survive an explicit account of the underlying conflict between the policymaker and the private sector (the underlying policy game posed in explicit form). Put differently, this critique might be true of the Tinbergen–Theil theory of economic policy. But that is not to say it is also true of a revised or new theory of economic policy. It all depends on whether the private sector reactions can be accommodated in the policymaker's decisions; or whether the private sector's reactions are strong enough to *exactly* offset, in their own self-interest, what the policymaker is trying to do. In general, private agents cannot offset those actions completely – nor would they try to do so, as we shall show.

1.3 Policy games: the conflict becomes explicit

In the 1980s, starting with Barro and Gordon (1983), a new approach to the analysis of economic policy was developed: that of policy games, exempt from the Lucas critique. As noted above, introducing REs amounts to implicitly assuming some kind of reaction of the system to the policy enacted, driven by conflicting objectives. This assumption, and the underlying conflict between policymaker and private sector which it reflects, can be made explicit if the issue facing the policymaker is framed in a context where the private sector's behavior is explicitly modeled as having been derived from its preferences and objectives. Strategic interactions between the private sector and the policymaker then ensure that the REs of both are satisfied.

At the time of Barro and Gordon (1983), the emphasis of the policy debate was still far from the search for conditions of existence of an instrument vector that could guarantee satisfaction of some fixed targets (Tinbergen's fixed target approach) or of an optimal policy that could minimize a given loss function (Theil's flexible target approach). In fact the Lucas critique was often deemed to negate the possibility that the policymaker could control the system at all. The discussion therefore concentrated instead on issues of the effectiveness, or neutrality, of specific instruments when the private sector has some specific target and instrument; thus continuing, in a new setting, the debate that had started in the previous two decades.

Barro and Gordon (1983) in fact studied a (Stackelberg) game between central bank and private sector, where the latter is leader and trades off real wages and employment when setting the nominal wage rate. They then delivered the well-known assertion of long run monetary neutrality as a result of the private sector expectations of discretionary monetary policy: the private sector forms REs and fully crowds out monetary effects on real output. A superior solution, for the public sector, would be to commit to a certain rule. But, having induced favorable private sector expectations, the policymaker would always be tempted to cheat and renege on his commitment, the classic time inconsistency argument (Kydland and Prescott, 1977), in an attempt to achieve yet better outcomes. However, being aware of this possibility, the private sector would (in self-defense) anticipate worse results; results that can be avoided only if the temptation to cheat is balanced by a fear that the policymaker might lose his reputation and no longer be able to act effectively if this game of interactions with the private sector is repeated.[5]

[5] See also Stokey (1989, 1991).

Thus, with Barro and Gordon (1983) we have a result of policy neutrality. But their result is specific to the assumptions of their model. We certainly do not have a general theory of policy neutrality. A part of the subsequent literature has tried to elaborate such a theory in different ways, without making any reference to Tinbergen's contribution.

In an influential article, Rogoff (1985) showed that uncertainty can break the neutrality mechanism, in terms of second moments, by creating a trade-off between the variances of inflation and output (or employment). Sargent (1999) also explored the short run trade-off between inflation and unemployment by focusing on uncertainty, specifically on imperfect knowledge and misperceptions by policymakers and/or private agents in a policy game with learning. He showed that the rise and fall of US inflation can be attributed to policymakers' changing beliefs about the natural rate hypothesis. In other words, he put forward a hypothesis that US inflation dynamics can be explained by the Federal Reserve discovering and subsequently abandoning the Phillips curve. In a similar manner, Orphanides and Williams (2002) attributed the volatility and failure of US anti-inflation policies in the 1970s to the Federal Reserve's misunderstanding of the natural rate of output, and hence output gap, on the basis of real-time data. Real-time data is, of course, the only data available to the policymakers when they have to make their decisions. So these volatility trade-offs will always be present; there is no point in supposing the policymakers used the ex post data they could not have had at the time.

By introducing nominal rigidities, the New Keynesian school has developed a more refined version of Rogoff's model, where uncertainty derives from the forward-looking behavior of the private sector.[6] It is worth noticing that, in an influential article, Clarida, Galì and Gertler (1999) explicitly mentioned the Tinbergen–Theil approach in illustrating their solution:

> This formulation is in many ways in the tradition of the classic Jan Tinbergen (1952)/Henri Theil (1961) (TT) targets and instruments problem. As with TT, the combination of quadratic loss and linear constraints yields a certainty equivalent decision rule for the path of the instrument.

[6] The New Keynesian approach is well illustrated by Woodford (2003) and Galì (2008).

The optimal feedback rule, in general, relates the instrument to the state of the economy.[7]

Another interesting line of investigation has followed the idea that neutrality depends on the preferences of the private sector. Simply adding other targets explicitly shared with the policymaker to the private sector's preferences could have avoided the neutrality result. Gylfason and Lindbeck (1994) suggested that monetary policy non-neutrality arises whenever the private sector (e.g., labor unions) explicitly shares the objective of price stability with the central bank, in addition to their usual targets for real wages and employment. Jerger (2002) likewise demonstrated that the traditional paradigm of neutrality does not hold if wage setters are inflation averse. Acocella and Ciccarone (1997) generalized that result by taking into consideration a concern for public debt. However, this way of ruling out policy neutrality seems to lose ground when imperfectly competitive markets are introduced into the story: Guzzo and Velasco (1999), Soskice and Iversen (2000), Cukierman and Lippi (2001), Lippi (2003), and Coricelli, Cukierman, and Dalmazzo (2006) all show that non-neutrality of monetary policy can also derive from the interaction between imperfectly competitive goods and labor markets even when unions do not explicitly share a common objective with the monetary authorities. Acocella and Di Bartolomeo (2004) then show that even the implicit addition of shared targets would have the effect of violating the neutrality result. Only in their conclusions do they hint at a possible explanation in terms of number of instruments and targets of the various players. So there are a great many ways in which this neutrality (the Lucas critique) can be overcome. Many of them are illustrated in the examples in Chapters 5 and 6. Chapter 12 develops a general theory of policy under REs that knits these different results together.

1.4 The new theory of economic policy: rediscovering Tinbergen

An advance in explaining the neutrality of the policy of a player was made when it was realized that neutrality might have to do with the

[7] However, as they correctly remark, in New Keynesian models "target variables depend not only on the current policy but also on expectations about future policy" (Clarida, Galì and Gertler, 1999).

existence of conflicts with the desired values of targets shared by other players and the possibility that the player in question does, or does not, have enough instruments for reaching its targets. This consideration led to a rediscovery of the requirements for controllability of an economic system as asserted by the Tinbergen theory of economic policy (Acocella and Di Bartolomeo 2005, 2006; Acocella, Di Bartolomeo and Hughes Hallett, 2007).

For purposes of illustration, let us consider a situation in which different players have at least one overlapping target but they conflict on the precise value preferred for that (those) target(s). Assume that one player, say player 1, can control his variables of interest, since he has at least as many linearly independent instruments as independent target variables: that is, the Tinbergen Golden Rule holds. It is then fairly obvious that no other player can have an influence on, or shift those shared targets if that player's target values (for the targets held in common) are different from those of player 1, and if that player does not have enough instruments to reach his own targets and hence control those shared with player 1. In this situation the conflict can be only solved to the benefit of the controlling player, and the other player's policies are neutral with respect to the shared objectives. This is the first fundamental proposition of the new theory of economic policy.

In the event, the new theory has proved to be a theory not only of neutrality, but also of game equilibrium existence, uniqueness, and multiplicity. A unique equilibrium arises when only one player or no player at all controls its targets. In the case when more than one player can control common targets, all the controlling players should be able to reach their objectives by assumption. However, if they have conflicting target values, none can actually do so as the system cannot admit different values for the same variable at the same time. But if there is no such conflict, that is, if the players capable of controlling the system share not only the same targets but also the same target values, there will be multiple combinations of the instruments controlled by different players capable of reaching those values and a coordination failure will arise. These results represent the second fundamental proposition of the new theory of economic policy.

Proceeding in this way amounts to using the Tinbergen and Theil theory of economic policy in a new setting – that of policy games – and involves a situation of conflicts among different agents. The possibility that one agent, the policymaker, might pursue his own objectives in a situation of conflict easily brings us to the conditions under which that conflict can (or cannot) be solved to his benefit; or, if another player also controls the system, to the conditions where no equilibrium will exist. From this point of view, the new theory of economic policy can be regarded as a theory of conflict resolution. Neutrality, policy effectiveness and the non-existence, uniqueness or multiplicity of equilibrium are all key aspects of such a theory.

The most important implication of the new theory is that all the results concerning the properties of a policy game can be stated in terms of simple rules about the number of (linearly independent) instruments compared with (linearly independent) targets for each player. These characteristics can therefore be determined without solving the game, which appears to be of relevance from a methodological point of view for a researcher in the process of building a model. To design a model of a "viable" policy process, we need a check on the mutual consistency between the optimal decisions of the agents involved. This must exclude controllability of the same targets by more than one player. In addition, if we want to ensure some important feature of the policy game we are going to analyze, in the form of a certain action to be taken by a certain player, we need that player only (and no other player) to satisfy the Golden Rule of economy policy.

Economic models obviously have an institutional counterpart. Important implications of the new theory for institution building have first been derived when looking at a game from the perspective of groups of players or of all the players. From the former point of view, there may be situations involving no conflict among some players, leading to implicit coalitions between them; and also cases where conflicts between groups of players lead to the same results in terms of neutrality and equilibrium existence as we have derived for single players (Acocella, Di Bartolomeo and Piacquadio, 2009). So, for example, when looking at the system as a linear quadratic (LQ) policy game with overlapping preferences, if the total number of instruments available for all the players exceeds the total number of targets of all the players, multiple equilibria will arise and conditions for existence are unlikely to be satisfied. This implies the existence of a fundamental asymmetry in institutional solutions: if an economic system is over-determined (i.e., the total number of instruments is higher than the number of targets), it can always be solved by some "social planner" by setting the excess instruments, over targets, at arbitrarily fixed values. Meanwhile the decentralized solution might fail to exist and, in case of existence, problems of coordination in setting instruments always emerge. Thus the advantages of centralization that derive from an abundance of instruments are lost in the decentralized solution and indeterminacy arises. This raises again a problem of coordination failure that can be solved in various ways: e.g., by voluntarily giving up the use of its instrument by some country; or by resorting to a hegemon; or by imposing some kind of centralized solution (Hughes Hallett, Acocella, and Di Bartolomeo, 2011) or by introducing announcements (Acocella, Di Bartolomeo, Hughes Hallett and Piacquadio, 2009).

Another institutional implication of the new theory that deserves a mention at this point derives from an extension of the Tinbergen–Theil analysis to dynamic problems in a context where a policymaker interacts with the private sector and REs hold. In fact REs, rather than implying ineffectiveness of policies, will typically help the policymaker to pursue his targets if he makes proper announcements, when a weaker condition involving the possession of sufficient instruments is satisfied. If this is the case, the policy problem is no longer a matter of finding institutions guaranteeing a credible commitment; but of how the necessary policy changes should be announced (Hughes Hallett, Di Bartolomeo and Acocella, 2012).

The importance of this new theory of economic policy can therefore be summarized in four points.

First, its two fundamental propositions (on policy neutrality and equilibrium existence) appear to be essential for model building, as they state the conditions under which the effectiveness of policy instruments, as well as consistency of the optimal strategies of all the players (and thus the existence of the equilibrium of the game), are guaranteed.

Second, the theory has important applications for devising proper institutions.

Third, REs are not necessarily an obstacle to policy effectiveness. On the contrary, they can enhance it and make debates on time inconsistency and the need for commitment irrelevant when the policymaker and the private sector share the same information on the working of the economic system. That again carries important implications for the design of institutions and how they work.

Finally, from the perspective of the history of economic thought, it may be important that the theory of economic policy, in going back to the tools devised by Tinbergen and Theil and applying them to a context of policy games, has become a theory of conflict resolution, precisely because it states the properties of the game both in terms of whose instruments are effective and in terms of the conditions for the existence, uniqueness and multiplicity of solutions to policy games.

1.5 Overview of the book

The book is divided into four parts. The first two parts cover known concepts, whereas Parts III and IV illustrate the new theory of economic policy. Part I describes the theory of economic policy as developed by Tinbergen, Theil and others. Part II presents the implications of the Lucas critique and the approach of policy games. Part III illustrates the new theory of economic policy in a static setting. Part IV develops our approach in a dynamic context. The reader who wants to know the essentials of the new theory of economic policy can limit himself or herself to Chapters 6 and 7 of Part III. The context of each part is described in more detail as follows.

Part I traces the essentials of the theory of economic policy as developed by Tinbergen, Theil and others. Specifically, Chapter 2 sketches the basics of the two main static approaches to the theory – the fixed target approach devised by Tinbergen and Hansen, and the flexible approach used by Frisch and Theil – together with their main extensions to cover uncertainty, implicit targets, and instrument costs. Chapter 3 introduces the main developments of this theory for a dynamic context, working from two basic representations of the economy: the structural or reduced form and the state space or final form. From here, different concepts of policy multipliers, controllability and stabilizability, and different kinds of control rules in a dynamic setting are also defined.

Chapter 4 in Part II presents the harmful implications of the Lucas critique for the Tinbergen–Theil approach and introduces the concept of REs. The following chapter, Chapter 5, deals with policy games, which are the natural way to discuss policy issues in a context designed to overcome the Lucas critique. The framework of policy games – in terms of losses (or utilities), the model of the economic system and different solution concepts (Nash and Stackelberg) – is introduced there together with a first clarification of the relations between REs and policy games. Some examples are presented to illustrate the policy game approach.

Part III is devoted to the presentation of the new theory of economic policy in a static, but strategic setting. Chapter 6 lays the first foundations of that theory, deriving the main propositions on policy neutrality and existence, uniqueness or multiplicity of equilibria in a two-player game on the basis of Tinbergen controllability in a system with a single player (policymaker). It then extends these propositions to the case of *N* players with instrument costs, and checks the validity of the simple rules for devising the properties of the game without solving it. Chapter 7 presents some developments of the conditions under which unique, multiple or no equilibria exist. These developments are derived by taking the perspective of all players in the economic system, and have implications in terms of institutions and applications to important issues of international economics. Further institutional implications are drawn in Chapter 8 from still another perspective, namely that of groups of players, as there may be symbiosis and implicit coordination among some players but conflicts between different groups of them. This chapter also derives conditions for policy effectiveness, equilibrium existence and Pareto efficiency – drawing on a concept, decisiveness, which generalizes Tinbergen controllability. Finally, Chapter 9 applies the tools of this new theory of economic policy for finding a closed form solution to the issue of choice among multiple equilibria through credible announcements (cheap talk).

Part IV develops the new theory in a dynamic context. Chapter 10 derives the conditions for policy neutrality and equilibrium existence in terms of the concepts of controllability in a strategic setting described by difference games. The solutions explored are those of open loop, Feedback Nash and Stackelberg non-cooperative games. The two following chapters further extend the results of neutrality and equilibrium existence in the presence of REs. In Chapter 11 the context is that of a policy game, whereas in Chapter 12 a single policymaker is confronted by a private sector expressing REs. It is important to note that introducing REs does not change the conditions for the neutrality of the economic system. If neutrality emerges under exogenous expectations, it will also appear when the model contains REs. In Chapter 12 it is also shown that expectations of this kind can improve the controllability of the system, under certain conditions that include proper announcements of future policies. Chapter 13 takes the perspective of institution building in a dynamic setting where issues of inflation, sustainable growth and debt control arise. Chapter 14 concludes by tracing the main achievements of the new theory of economic policy, its limitations and possible future developments.

Apart from the examples explicitly mentioned in this overview, practically all chapters illustrate their content by examples drawn mainly, but not exclusively, from the macroeconomics literature. Specific appendices develop either some technical passages of the main text or some mathematical tools that go beyond a basic knowledge of those presupposed for readers of the book.

PART I

The classical theory of economic policy

2 Statics

Summary. This chapter sets the scene by defining a policy problem in terms of policy targets and instruments, the constraints that must be satisfied between them, and the preferences we may have in case there are conflicts between targets. We then start to analyze the question of whether we can reach those targets with the instruments at our disposal. We review first the fixed target approach (we achieve them exactly on average), and then the flexible target approach (we come as close as possible to them, on average, in a well-defined sense). We then give a brief introduction to how uncertainty may be handled, the difference between bounded and unbounded targets, and whether policy instruments need to be restrained.

2.1. Introduction

Chapter 1 noted that the founders of the theory of economic policy stated their theory in two main versions. Jan Tinbergen addressed the issue in terms of the *controllability* of a fixed set of independent targets by a policymaker endowed with a given set of policy instruments and facing given constraints representing the economy. Later, Henri Theil prescribed that the policymaker should minimize a loss function under the economy's constraints, which can solve the problem of how to pick policies when the policymaker has fewer policy instruments at his disposal than the number of targets he wishes to reach.

In line with Tinbergen and Theil, in this chapter we start by assuming that a single decision maker (from now on, and without loss of generality, the government) aims to achieve certain given target values exactly. This is Tinbergen's *fixed target approach*. If this should not be possible, then we can consider minimizing the inevitable deviations from those target values in the form of a quadratic objective function (Theil's *flexible target* or *optimization approach*). Following Preston and Pagan (1982), we illustrate how the two approaches can be merged together, the former being a particular case of the latter. In other words, we can always state the policy selection process in terms of an optimization problem. The outcome will be either that the government can reach its target values; or, if the fixed target approach should fail, it can always achieve its second best outcomes. Although the flexible approach is not the only alternative to a fixed target approach (as we show below), flexible targets are in line with the reformulation of the theory of economic policy within a strategic context that we shall be discussing from Chapter 6 onwards.

The rest of the chapter is organized as follows. The next section introduces the fixed target approach and possible alternatives to it. Section 2.3 outlines those alternative approaches. Section 2.4 considers the flexible target approach in greater detail and shows its more general character. Sections 2.5 and 2.6 illustrate these approaches using geometric analysis. Section 2.7 discusses three further important issues: (a) uncertainty; (b) bounded and unbounded first best solutions and (c) instrument costs. Finally, Section 2.8 concludes by introducing some drawbacks of the approach which will be developed further in the chapters that follow. Some technical issues are relegated to appendices in order to preserve the readability and accessibility of the main text.

2.2. The fixed target approach

The economic relationships between variables are defined by the following general linear algebraic system:

$$\mathbf{A}Y = \mathbf{B}Z + \mathbf{k} \quad \text{(full structural form)} \tag{2.1}$$

where $\mathbf{A}$ and $\mathbf{B}$ are coefficient matrices, Y and Z are the vectors of *possible* target and instrument variables respectively, and $\mathbf{k}$ is a vector of (linear combinations of) other exogenous variables and/or white noise shocks, the expectations of which the rest of the economy and the government have to take as given.[1]

[1] For the sake of simplicity, the exact stochastic nature of $\mathbf{k}$ is not made explicit in this chapter since we will be invoking the certainty equivalence principle to handle additive uncertainty. For more complex cases, we can appeal to first-order approximations of certainty equivalence, as advocated by Theil (1964). We review this issue in Section 2.7.

Thus, in order to consider the government's problem in the context of the Tinbergen–Theil approach, we shall concentrate our attention first and foremost on the following linear sub-system of the equations from (2.1):[2]

$$Ay = Bu + k \quad \text{(condensed structural form)} \tag{2.2}$$

where $y \in R^q$ is the vector of relevant economic variables (the government's target variables) whose generic entry is denoted by $y(i)$, extracted from Y; $u \in R^m$ is the vector of the government's policy instruments, whose generic element is denoted by $u(j)$, extracted from Z; A and B are appropriately parameterized target and instrument coefficient matrices; and k is an appropriate vector of constants, each component of which is a linear combination of constants, exogenous variables and white noise shocks.

We assume that A and B are full rank matrices: i.e., all targets and instrument variables are linearly independent of each other (an independence assumption).[3] There are q distinct targets and m distinct instruments to be chosen and set, respectively, by the government.

The linear *reduced form* model can be written in matrix terms as

$$y = A^{-1}Bu + A^{-1}k = Cu + \bar{c} \quad \text{(reduced form)} \tag{2.3}$$

provided that A is nonsingular, as it is from our rank assumptions. Matrix C is a matrix of multipliers and is sometimes called the *Jacobian matrix*. Element $C(i, j)$ indicates the effect, on target i, of changes in instrument j; that is, $\partial y(i)/\partial u(j)$.

At this stage it will be useful to define policy effectiveness and policy neutrality in terms of a reduced form model such as (2.3). We start by introducing the concept of effectiveness and then use this concept to define neutrality.

Definition 2.1 (*effectiveness*). An instrument is effective with respect to a target variable if changes in the instrument determine changes in the target variable. Otherwise it is ineffective.

[2] The relationship between these two equation systems is explained in Appendix 2A.

[3] The full rank assumption is always assured by an appropriate manipulation of the original system (2.1), i.e., by removing any linearly dependent, and hence redundant, target and instrument variables.

Definition 2.2 (*exogenous policy neutrality*). Economic policy is neutral with respect to a target variable if *all* the instruments are ineffective with respect to that target variable.

In the present case, each zero in matrix C implies the ineffectiveness of one instrument with respect to one target. Specifically, element $C(i, j) = 0$ implies that the instrument $u(j)$ is ineffective with respect to target $y(i)$. Exogenous neutrality with respect to target $y(i)$ therefore emerges if the row entries of matrix C are all zeros. Our rank assumptions rule out neutrality.[4]

The aim of the government is to control the economic system (2.2). That will involve finding values of the instruments that enable it to reach certain desired values of the target variables, $\bar{y} \in R^q$ (*target values*), in their economy.

More formally we define controllability as follows.

Definition 2.3 (*controllability*). A system is controllable if the government can reach the values of the target variables for any possible vector of desired targets by choosing an appropriate policy (vector of policy instruments). We can also say that it is weakly controllable if the government can reach a *given* (specific) vector of target values.

Formally, *controllability* implies that the government can always find the vector u that solves the equation $\bar{y} = Cu$, for all possible desired values of $\bar{y}$. Controllability can also be defined in weaker terms: a system is *weakly controllable* if, given a vector of desired targets, the government can reach particular values of $\bar{y}$, but not necessarily any value of $\bar{y}$, by choosing an appropriate policy vector. Controllability clearly implies weak controllability, but not conversely. Moreover, it should be noted that controllability is in fact an existence condition for suitable policy instrument values (*existence* problem). But it assures neither the uniqueness of the policy (*uniqueness* problem) nor how best to determine it (the *policy design* problem). Note also that controllability clearly implies policy non-neutrality, but the converse is not true.

[4] It is trivial to show that, when only one instrument is available, effectiveness corresponds to non-neutrality and neutrality corresponds to ineffectiveness. However, in multi-instrument cases this is not generally true.

Existence conditions for a solution are easily found by applying standard mathematical techniques. Usually these are rank conditions on certain coefficient matrices or transformations of those matrices.[5]

Theorem 2.1 (*controllability*). The system $y = Cu + \bar{c}$ is controllable for any vector of desired targets if and only if $\mathrm{r}[C] = q$. It is weakly controllable, for a given vector of targets values $\bar{y}$, if and only if $\mathrm{r}[C:\bar{y}] = \mathrm{r}[C]$.

Having $\mathrm{r}[C] \leq \min\{q, m\}$, $\mathrm{r}[C] = q$ implies that $q \leq m$. Thus controllability embodies the famous Tinbergen precepts about the number of instruments and targets.

Theorem 2.2 (*the Tinbergen theorem, or static controllability*). The government can achieve any vector of independent targets by an appropriate vector of instruments if and only if the number of independent instruments is equal to, or greater than, the number of targets.

Formally, the Tinbergen theorem comprises two conditions (Preston and Pagan, 1982):

1. a counting rule, according to which the number of instruments should be greater than the number of targets, i.e., $q \leq m$;
2. an independence rule, stating that the (linearly) independent instruments are at least q in number, if this is the number of independent targets.

The theorem can be qualified to impose uniqueness. This requires $\mathrm{r}[C] = q = m$; the number of independent targets must be equal to that of the independent instruments. In such a case, the optimal policies for the original system are

$$u = B^{-1}(A\bar{y} - k) \tag{2.4}$$

since $C = A^{-1}B$, and the inverses are unique. Henceforth, we will say that an equation system is controllable (statically controllable, or controllable in the sense of Tinbergen and Theil) if the number of independent instruments equals that of independent targets. This result is also known as the *Golden Rule*.

[5] Formal proofs of the statements in this section are not given since they summarize well-known results; in Appendix 2B and 2C we only report some useful references to linear algebra. For a more extensive discussion we refer to Preston and Pagan (1982) or Hughes Hallett and Rees (1983).

Now, assuming that the policy model fails to satisfy the appropriate weak or strong existence criterion of controllability, the first best policy cannot be achieved. The failure to find a solution for the fixed target problem in those cases generates the need for some alternative, which we discuss in the next section.

2.3 The flexible target approach

The flexible target approach is based on the minimization of a *loss function* (or maximisation of preferences). A useful formalization of the government's cost for deviations of the relevant variables from their target values is the following quadratic form:

$$L = (y - \bar{y})' Q(y - \bar{y}) \tag{2.5}$$

where Q is an appropriate symmetric,[6] positive definite matrix of relative priorities between the target variables. In Equation (2.5) we do not explicitly consider instrument costs.[7] We refer to $\bar{y}$ and Q as the parameters of the government's preferences.

Quadratic functions are used not only for their mathematical tractability but also for their useful economic properties. In fact, deviations from the target in either direction are associated with increasing costs. The marginal rate of substitution between any two target variables is therefore never constant, but depends on the values of the two variables at the point at which it is computed. In addition, quadratic forms can be obtained as second-order Taylor approximations of more complex functions.[8] In detail, "quadratic cost functions are of particular interest in game theory, firstly because they constitute second-order approximations of other types of nonlinear functions, and secondly because they are analytically tractable, admitting in general closed form equilibrium solutions which provide insights into the properties

[6] Later in the book, we will often consider simple diagonal Q matrices, which imply that the preferences are separable in their arguments. Assuming non-separable preferences would not affect any of our results, but their economic interpretation is less natural than quadratic deviations if we do not have a specific model in mind as a reference point.

[7] See Section 2.7.4 for the extension.

[8] An explicit demonstration will be found in Hughes Hallett (1979). For more recent examples, see Woodford (2003) and also Section 2.7.2.

and features of the equilibrium solution concept under consideration" (Başar and Olsder, 1995: 197).[9]

The flexible target policy is obtained by minimizing Equation (2.5) with respect to the vector of instruments, subject to Equation (2.3). The corresponding first-order condition is

$$C'QCu = C'Q(\bar{y} - \bar{c}) \qquad (2.6)$$

where $\bar{c} = A^{-1}k$ and $C = A^{-1}B$ were defined in (2.3).

As in the previous case, existence of a solution is ensured if $r[\Phi : k_\Phi] = r[\Phi]$: that is, if Φ is left-invertible,[10] where $\Phi = C'QC \in R^{m\times m}$ and $k_\Phi = C'Q(\bar{y} - \bar{c}) \in R^m$. Uniqueness, however, requires, in addition, the nonsingularity of Φ. It is worth noticing that, as Q is positive definite, $r[\Phi] = r[C]$. Thus, C being of full column rank, $r[\Phi] = m$ which means that Φ is of full rank too.[11] It follows that (2.6) has a unique solution.

The policy design problem therefore implies the following *optimal* policies:

$$u = \Phi^{-1}k_\Phi = (C'QC)^{-1}C'Q(\bar{y} - A^{-1}k). \qquad (2.7)$$

If $q = m$, the above policy selection reduces to $u = B^{-1}(A\bar{y} - k)$ – the same expression as found in the fixed target case (2.4) – which implies $y = \bar{y}$ when inserted in (2.2).

Before leaving this section, we need to emphasize that, when considering the flexible approach, any policy is endogenous and depends on the policymaker's preferences. For this reason, we find it convenient to redefine neutrality as follows.

Definition 2.4 (*endogenous policy neutrality*). Economic policy is neutral with respect to a target variable if the optimal value of such a variable is not affected by any change in the policymaker's preferences.

Definition 2.4 generalizes Definition 2.2 in the same way as the flexible target approach to policymaking nests the fixed target one. In the following pages of this book, we focus on strategic contexts where policies are always endogenous; and when speaking of neutrality we will

[9] Matrix and vector derivations and the properties of quadratic forms are surveyed in Appendix 2B.

[10] On the concept of a left-inverse matrix and the Moore-Penrose left-inverse see Appendix 2C.

[11] If Q is a positive definite matrix, then $r[C'QC]=r[C]$ for any conformable matrix C.

always refer to the concept of endogenous policy neutrality, instead of the concept of exogenous neutrality.

2.4 Target priorities

The government may fail to meet the conditions for controllability and therefore to achieve its targets exactly. In such a case, as shown in Section 2.3, the government's action can be determined by invoking the flexible targets approach. However, there are also some other possible alternative solutions: (i) searching for additional instruments (independent of those already available; that is, for instruments having an impact on at least one target that is different from the impact of any possible linear combination of existing instruments); (ii) dropping a set of targets equal in number to the existing excess of targets over instruments. After that there is only one alternative to the fixed target approach, and that involves (iii) defining some relative priorities over targets. The flexible target approach (incorporating suggestion (iii)) would be superior to dropping some of the targets altogether, unless closer inspection of the policymaker's priorities reveals that those targets had in fact zero priority relative to the others. Similarly, in a second best policy based on the flexible target approach, target priorities imply that the government's action can still be effective in the sense that the government has the possibility to improve its objectives by getting as close as possible (as defined by the priorities and preferences embodied in Equation (2.5)) to the unreachable target values by using direct optimization techniques. That is, at the optimum, (2.5) will have minimized the (weighted) sum of squared failures to reach the government's ideal values for its target variables.

Expressing priorities over targets means that the policymaker may choose the preferred target(s) he wants to reach or get close to a certain value, sacrificing the other target(s) for which he will achieve only a loose approximation to their target values. Obviously, putting a very high priority on certain targets, and a low or zero priority on others, will get us arbitrarily close to the ideal values for the former – but more or less uncontrolled outcomes for the latter. This produces a lexicographic ordering over the target variables.

This flexible approach is an alternative to setting fixed values for all targets when the policymaker has a smaller number of independent instruments than target variables; and also when he does not know exactly what constraints he is likely to face. The latter case can be expressed as a relationship linking one target to another: a kind of transformation curve. For example, for two targets, $y_2 = f(y_1) \pm \varepsilon$, where ε denotes a disturbance. In both cases, it may be more appropriate to specify priorities in reaching objectives.

As an example of this transformation curve idea, consider a policymaker who wishes to ensure a certain volume of income in the less developed area of the country (let us say the South), and then seeks to maximize income in the more advanced area (the North). Assume further that the feasible alternatives of producing income in the two regions can be expressed as a relationship linking one target variable to the other (a transformation curve): say $Y_S = f(Y_N)$, where Y_N (Y_S) is the income of North (South). This approach would require putting a priority on producing income in the South which can be expressed by setting $Y_S = \bar{Y}_S$; and then maximizing Y_N subject to $Y_S = f(Y_N)$.[12]

To take another example, if price stability and employment are the objectives and the policymaker wishes to give priority to the former, he will set a certain inflation rate as his target value, $\dot{p} = \bar{\dot{p}}$, and then seek to minimize the unemployment rate given the actual position of the transformation curve describing the economic system – in this case a Phillips curve $\dot{p} = f(u)$.

As a general proposition, this approach therefore involves minimizing the deviation of the non-priority target from its target value, subject to the desired value of the prioritized target and the constraint of the transformation curve between them (that is, a model which defines the feasible responses of the economy).

2.5 Geometric representation of a problem with fixed targets

We can now give an example of the geometric representation of the problem of fixed targets. Consider an aggregate demand–aggregate supply (AD-AS) representation of the economy, taken from Hansen (1968) and reproduced by Preston and Pagan (1982):

$$\begin{cases} AD: p = bq + au_1 & \text{with } b<0 \\ AS: p = dq + cu_2 & \text{with } d>0. \end{cases} \tag{2.8}$$

[12] Indeed this example, and the other that follows, can be seen as a special case of the flexible target approach where lexicographic losses or preferences are introduced.

This can be expressed in its matrix structural form as follows:

$$\begin{matrix} p - bq = au_1 \\ p - dq = cu_2 \end{matrix} \rightarrow \underbrace{\begin{bmatrix} 1 & -b \\ 1 & -d \end{bmatrix}}_{A} \underbrace{\begin{bmatrix} p \\ q \end{bmatrix}}_{y} = \underbrace{\begin{bmatrix} a & 0 \\ 0 & c \end{bmatrix}}_{B} \underbrace{\begin{bmatrix} u_1 \\ u_2 \end{bmatrix}}_{u}. \tag{2.9}$$

It is worth noticing that the above system is controllable since $\mathrm{r}[A^{-1}B] = 2 = q = m$.

The conventional reduced form of system (2.9) is

$$y = A^{-1}Bu \rightarrow \begin{bmatrix} p \\ q \end{bmatrix} = \begin{bmatrix} -\dfrac{ad}{b-d} & \dfrac{bc}{b-d} \\ -\dfrac{a}{b-d} & \dfrac{c}{b-d} \end{bmatrix} \begin{bmatrix} u_1 \\ u_2 \end{bmatrix}. \tag{2.10}$$

This can be rewritten as

$$\begin{bmatrix} p \\ q \end{bmatrix} = \begin{bmatrix} -\dfrac{ad}{b-d} \\ -\dfrac{a}{b-d} \end{bmatrix} u_1 + \begin{bmatrix} \dfrac{bc}{b-d} \\ \dfrac{c}{b-d} \end{bmatrix} u_2; \tag{2.11}$$

or more generally as $y = C_1u_1 + C_2u_2$, where we have written $C = A^{-1}B = [C_1 | C_2]$. We can say that, in their reduced form, these targets can be expressed in terms of the column vectors of matrix C, weighted by the values of instruments u_1 and u_2, respectively. Differentiating Equation (2.11) with respect to u_1, we get the per unit impact (multipliers) of the first instrument on the two targets (p and q). The ratio of those two multipliers then gives the gradient (representing the marginal rate of transformation) of the p to q transformation as a result of changes in u_1. With reference to the AD-AS model, this is positive since $d > 0$ in the following expressions:

$$\frac{\partial p}{\partial u_1} = -\frac{ad}{b-d} \quad \text{and} \quad \frac{\partial q}{\partial u_1} = -\frac{a}{b-d} \Rightarrow \frac{\partial p / \partial u_1}{\partial q / \partial u_1} = \frac{ad}{b-d} \cdot \frac{b-d}{a} = d > 0. \tag{2.12}$$

Differentiating p and q with respect to u_2, we get the multipliers of the second instrument with respect to the two targets. The ratio of those

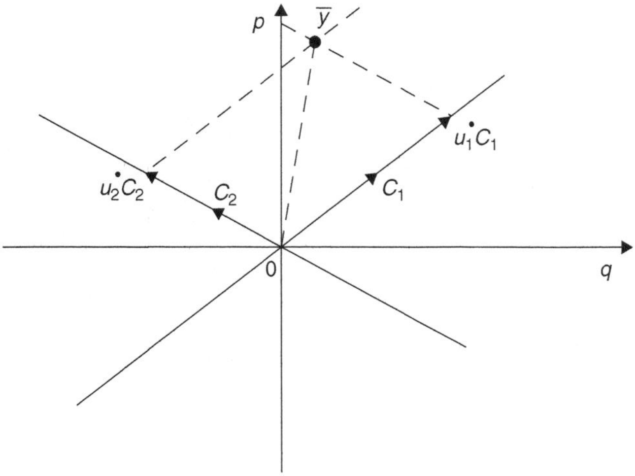

Figure 2.1 Fixed target approach

multipliers gives the gradient of the p/q ratio as a function of changes in u_2, which is negative since $b < 0$ in the following expressions:

$$\frac{\partial p}{\partial u_2} = -\frac{bc}{b-d} \quad \text{and} \quad \frac{\partial q}{\partial u_2} = -\frac{c}{b-d} \Rightarrow \frac{\partial p / \partial u_2}{\partial q / \partial u_2} = \frac{bc}{b-d} \cdot \frac{b-d}{c} = b < 0. \tag{2.13}$$

We can now represent any changes in the target values geometrically in (q, p) space. If the system (2.11) is linear with no constant terms, it is immaterial whether we represent the problem in the absolute levels of the targets and instruments (as we do in Figure 2.1) or in terms of their changes.

In this figure $[\bar{p},\bar{q}]' = \bar{y}$ indicates the policymaker's desired targets; C_1 represents the vector of the p/q ratio as a function of u_1 (all p and q combinations that can be reached by varying u_1, given u_2). Similarly, C_2 represents the vector of the p/q ratio as a function of u_2.

Thus, the solution of the problem of how to reach the ideal values $\bar{y} = [\bar{p},\bar{q}]'$ is given by the parallelogram law, which can be thought of as a geometric equivalent of the interpretation of the reduced form (2.11) where targets are expressed in terms of the column vectors of matrix C, weighted by the values of instruments u_1^* and u_2^*.

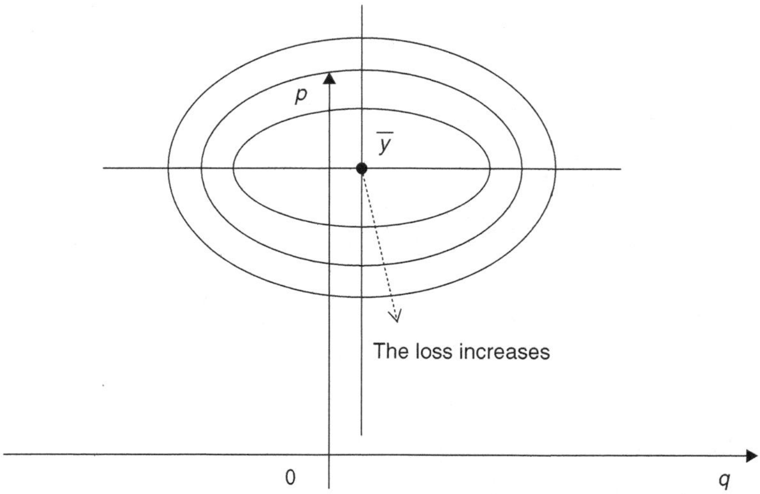

Figure 2.2 Iso-loss curves

2.6 Geometric representation of a problem with flexible targets

Let us consider the same problem as in the previous section, except for the fact that the government now wants to minimize (2.5), where $y = [p,q]'$, subject to Equation (2.11), but has only a single instrument available. Let us say it uses u_1, with u_2 set at zero. In this case, only the C_1 line appears in (q, p) space. We can still represent the targets in the same space. Figure 2.2 depicts the case when Q in Equation (2.5) is a diagonal matrix with $q_1 \neq q_2$. In the figure, the penalty weight, or priority, on p is higher than that on q as can be seen by the smaller distance to each line in the p-plane then in the q-plane. Thus $q_1 > q_2$, in the elements of Q. Price stability therefore has a higher priority than quantity stabilization.

Concentric ellipses, around the first best point, indicate a sequence of loss levels which diminish as we go toward the center of the ellipses. If $Q = I$, these ellipses will become concentric circles. From these ellipses we can draw inferences about the marginal rate of substitution between the targets. These marginal rates will vary according to the exact starting position. In the upward sloping segments of the ellipses (or circles) one target represents a "good" and the other is a "bad," whereas in the descending parts both targets are either good (if convex) or bad (if concave).

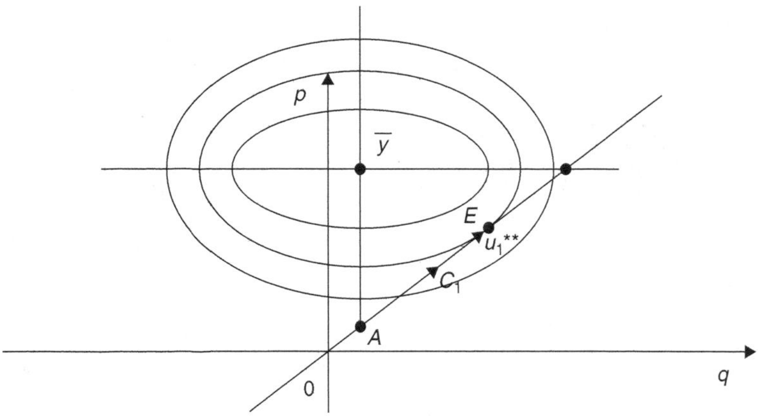

Figure 2.3 Flexible target approach

Of course, reaching the center of the ellipses or circles would represent the solution in the case where the system is actually Tinbergen controllable. In contrast to that, we need to consider the case where only one instrument is available, as described in Figure 2.3.

If only one instrument is available, the policymaker cannot achieve his first best target value, $\bar{y}$. But his instrument can still be set to achieve either the desired value for the quantity (point *A*), or prices (point *B*), or for a range of points in between. Clearly both *A* and *B* are sub-optimal since they fail to find the lowest possible loss, given the constraint. The optimal policy, marked as u_1^{**} here, corresponds to the point of tangency between the innermost reachable ellipse and the line defined by the slope C_1. That leaves us at point *E*. This optimal policy is clearly second best to the non-achievable solution defined by the case when the system is Tinbergen controllable. At point *E*, the marginal rate of substitution is equal to the policy multiplier (in substance, the marginal rate of transformation of q into p) and thus the policymaker's marginal benefit equals his marginal cost.

Figure 2.4 shows the optimal policy in two cases associated with different marginal rates of substitution, all else being equal.

The ellipses in panel (a) represent a policymaker giving a higher relative weight to p (price stability) than to q (output or employment). This describes the preferences of a classic "conservative central banker." The opposite applies to the ellipses in panel (b), which could be referred to as a case of a populist central banker. Different

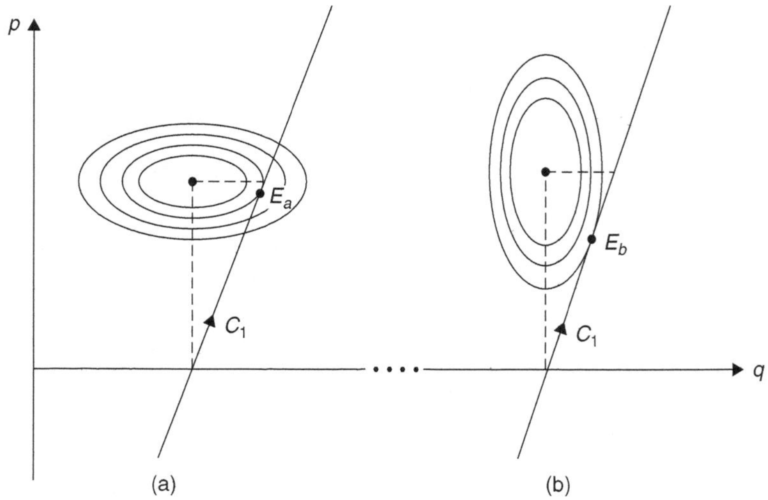

Figure 2.4 Losses and optimization

preferences clearly imply different second best outcomes.[13] It is worth noticing that, in the example presented, when a policymaker dislikes inflation losses more than output losses, his policies become more aggressive toward inflation. Looking at the figure, if the policymaker becomes more conservative, he changes his preferences from those represented in panel (b) to those of panel (a), his marginal rate of substitution changes and thus in order to equalize it to the policy multiplier (which is given), the equilibrium point must shift from E_b to E_a, where the inflation loss is lower and the output loss higher. Those differences evidently vanish if the government can control the system independently of its preferences.

2.7 Extensions: uncertainty, LQ preferences, instrument costs

2.7.1 Additive uncertainty and certainty equivalence

We examine the impact of uncertainty on policy choice. Consider a policy transmission mechanism where the government is not sure about

[13] This problem has been studied in detail by Rogoff (1985), who considers the optimal policy of the central bank after an unexpected shock by the private

the effect of its instruments (u) on the outcomes for its targets (y) as uncertainty about the non-controllable variables is present. Formally,

$$y = Cu + \bar{c} + \varepsilon \tag{2.14}$$

where ε is a vector of stochastic terms, with $E[\varepsilon] = 0$ and $E[\varepsilon\varepsilon'] = \Sigma$.

In this situation, as the outcomes achieved after setting the policies cannot be known in advance, the government will minimize the following expected loss:

$$E[L] = E\left[(y - \bar{y})'Q(y - \bar{y})\right]. \tag{2.15}$$

As before, we can compute (in expected terms) the first-order condition that solves the government problem:

$$E\left[C'QCu - C'Q(\bar{y} - \bar{c}) + C'Q\varepsilon\right] = 0. \tag{2.16}$$

Since $E[\varepsilon] = 0$, Equation (2.16) does not differ from (2.6) – i.e., the optimal policy under certainty. Thus we can state that, if the only source of uncertainty is an additive error vector (*additive uncertainty*) then the optimal policy of the government is to behave "as if" everything was known with certainty given the expectation. This proposition is known as the certainty equivalence principle.[14] It is worth noticing that this principle can also be easily extended to a dynamic setting (Appendix 3A: Multi-period certainty equivalence).

To see what is going on, note that the equivalence of (2.6) and (2.16) means that when we want to solve the stochastic problem of minimizing the *expected* loss function (2.15) subject to the constraints (2.3), we obtain exactly the same policies as we would have obtained by solving the deterministic problem of minimizing the underlying loss function (2.5) subject to the *expected* constraints from (2.3). That is what certainty equivalence means: faced with the stochastic problem in (2.15), we can solve it by optimizing the equivalent deterministic problem – replacing the stochastic terms by their "certainty equivalents" or expected values. Put formally:

sector. In such a case, the problem can be reduced to a Theil problem where private sector expectations are given when the central bank sets its instrument.

[14] The result was first proposed by Tinbergen (1952) and Theil (1958).

$$\begin{aligned}\min_u \{E(L) \mid y - Cu - \bar{c} - \varepsilon\} &= \min_u \{u'C'QCu - 2u'C'Q(\bar{y} - \bar{c}) \\ &\quad + 2u'E[C'Q\varepsilon] + E[(\bar{y} - \bar{c})'Q\varepsilon] + E[\varepsilon'Q\varepsilon]\} \\ &= \min_u \{u'C'QCu - 2C'Q(\bar{y} - \bar{c}) + (\bar{y} - \bar{c})'Q(\bar{y} - \bar{c}) + trQE[\varepsilon\varepsilon']\} \\ &= \min_u \{L \mid y - Cu - \bar{c} - E(\varepsilon)\} + trQE[\varepsilon\varepsilon']\end{aligned} \tag{2.17}$$

since $E(\varepsilon) = 0$. From this we see that the decisions will be the same either way; from the original stochastic problem, or from the underlying deterministic (certainty equivalent) one. But the final utility or loss function outcomes will be different by a factor which is independent of those decisions:

$$\mathrm{tr}[QE(\varepsilon\varepsilon')] = \min\{E(L^*)\} - \min\{L^{CE}\} \tag{2.18}$$

where $E(L^*)$ denotes the minimized value of (2.15) evaluated at (2.16), and L^{CE} that of (2.5) evaluated at the certainty equivalent solution (2.6). This difference is composed of a preference-weighted average of the variances and covariances of the random shocks in the problem. Hence $\mathrm{tr}[QE(\varepsilon\varepsilon')]$ allows us to measure the importance of uncertainty in our problem, relative to the deterministic components – as well as to trace the source of the greatest, or most dangerous of those uncertainties (Hughes Hallett, 1981). But at the same time, the decisions reached under certainty equivalence will be independent of the degree of uncertainty (or risk) in the problem. In view of (2.18), that is a consequence of the form of objective function, not of certainty equivalence per se.

A key point in this analysis is that certainty equivalent decisions require no knowledge of the distribution functions of the random variables, beyond their conditional means. That is their chief advantage. To make assumptions on the form and higher moments of those distributions might be very difficult in many economic policy problems, and it might be dangerous (at the risk of missing some "black swans") to make inaccurate estimates for want of better knowledge. However, the larger the dispersion of stochastic terms for a given mean, the greater the risks about the realized target values. Hence certainty equivalent decisions reflect a risk-neutral attitude: they are unaffected by risk aversion, or indeed by any term reflecting the *degree* of uncertainty$E(\varepsilon\varepsilon')$. That is their chief disadvantage: they do not react to risk; or the degree, skew or possibility of catastrophic outcomes (fat tails) in the random variables. This raises the question of whether the first moment of the objective function's distribution can be justified as the sole optimization criterion under uncertainty. If this distribution is affected by whatever decisions are taken, then higher order moments may need to be considered as well (Holly and Hughes Hallett, 1989). That gives rise to a series of "risk sensitive" or robust decision rules that differ from those studied in this book.[15]

2.7.2 *Multiplicative uncertainty and certainty equivalence*

Certainty equivalence, in fact, no longer holds for more complex specifications of uncertainty. Specifically, if there is uncertainty about the parameters of the model, then the government cannot behave as if uncertainty does not exist. The key difference is that uncertainty about a parameter is multiplicative rather than additive in the decision rule: the more a policy is used, the more the uncertainty is *multiplied* into the system (Brainard, 1967). As a result, under multiplicative uncertainty, policymakers will usually tend to be more cautious in the exercise of policy and express a less vigorous response to disturbances.

In view of (2.16), the decisions that minimize $E[L]$ would actually be

$$u^* = \left[E(C'QC)\right]^{-1} E\{C'Q(\bar{y} - \bar{c})\} \tag{2.19}$$

since $E(\varepsilon) = 0$. By analogy with the certainty equivalence strategy, we write the simpler *first-order certainty equivalence* solution:

$$u^{FOCE} = \left[E(C)'QE(C)\right]^{-1} \{E(C)'Q(\bar{y} - E(\bar{c}))\}, \tag{2.20}$$

where we have replaced the uncertain (stochastic) parameter matrix C by its expectation $E(C)$, and the vector of random shocks and exogenous variables by its expectation $E(\bar{c})$. The decisions in u^* and u^{FOCE} differ by Jensen's inequality. In fact, writing $dC = C - E(C)$ and $d\bar{c} = \bar{c} - E(\bar{c})$, those differences turn on the term $E[dC'QdC]$ since

$$E\left[C'QC\right] = E(C)'QE(C) + E\left[dC'QdC\right]; \tag{2.21}$$

and on $E[dC'Qd\bar{c}]$ since

$$E\left[C'Q\bar{c}\right] = E(C)'QE(\bar{c}) + E\left[dC'Qd\bar{c}\right]. \tag{2.22}$$

[15] See Hughes Hallett (1984), Whittle (1982), Hansen and Sargent (2007), Sims (1998, 2003, 2006).

Hence, only if the weighted variances and covariances of the uncertain parameters (and the covariances of those parameters with exogenous shocks) are small do the first-order certainty equivalent decisions coincide with the optimal decisions for this case. Otherwise they are an approximation, but a useful approximation because the true "certainty equivalents" to be inserted into (2.20) to make $u^{FOCE} = u^*$ are extremely difficult to determine; and because to evaluate the expectations in (2.19) directly without a detailed knowledge of the joint probability distributions of C and $\bar{c}$, at least up to the first two moments, is typically too expensive (and often impossible).[16] On the other hand, (2.20) is a genuine first-order approximation to u^*, since it involves ignoring the second terms on the right of (2.21) and (2.22), respectively, as being second-order small.

Note also that the existence of first-order certainty equivalent policies u^{FOCE} requires $r[E(C)'QE(C)] = m$. This condition may not always be satisfied, even when optimal policies u^* do exist because $r[C'QC] = m$ by (2.21). In other words, all the available instruments may be needed to combat uncertainty, even in cases where there are fewer targets to be reached than instruments to reach them.

We do not consider the stochastic structure of the policy problem beyond the certainty equivalence principle in this chapter.[17] Nevertheless, the tools that we develop in the next chapters can often be adapted to more complex kinds of uncertainty.[18] A full generalization of our theory in this direction is beyond our scope.[19]

[16] These probability distributions are of reduced form parameters, and hence known only asymptotically. Numerical integration or Monte Carlo simulation techniques are the only way to evaluate them in practice.

[17] In Chapter 3, after introducing the dynamic policy problem, we briefly discuss the extension to multi-period certainty equivalence (see Appendix 3A).

[18] In particular, multiplicative uncertainty can be easily dealt with in our LQ strategic approach (see, e.g., Beetsma and Jensen, 1998, 2003; Lawler, 2007; James and Lawler, 2009, 2011; Di Bartolomeo, Giuli and Manzo, 2009; and Di Bartolomeo and Giuli, 2011). Similarly, robust control is strategic by nature because it invokes strategic interactions between the government and a fictitious "evil" player; see Giannoni (2002), Leitemo and Söderström (2008), Dennis, Leitemo, and Söderström (2009), and Ellison and Sargent (2011) for some examples in a LQ context.

[19] For a full formal description of uncertainty and risk in a wider context, see Holly and Hughes Hallett (1989). For an advanced illustration of robust control methods, see Hansen and Sargent (2001, 2007).

2.7.3 Bounded and unbounded first best positions

In this section we consider loss functions that also contain linear terms. LQ losses generalize the quadratic deviations from target values that we normally use. Although quadratic deviations are the most natural and clearest way to represent the policymaker's desires, as they correspond to his target values, the inclusion of linear terms is useful in many situations. For instance, linear terms are often introduced in preference functions, as a result of second-order approximations of complex utility functions (Hughes Hallett, 1979) or around distorted steady states under small perturbations (e.g., Benigno and Woodford, 2005, 2006, 2012), whereas pure quadratic deviations are used instead for small deviations around efficient steady states.

The main difference between quadratic deviations and LQ losses is twofold. First, when LQ losses are considered, the policymaker's first best are no longer represented by his target values. Second, in the case of LQ losses the policymaker's first best may even fail to exist as losses may be unbounded. This section formally describes these issues.

A general representation of the government loss can be written as follows:

$$L = \frac{1}{2}(y - \bar{y})'Q(y - \bar{y}) + y'r + \tilde{y}'l. \qquad (2.23)$$

Equation (2.23) also includes linear effects. In this expression, $y \in R^q$ is now the vector of target variables that enter the equation in a quadratic manner (second-order); $\bar{y} \in R^q$ is the corresponding vector of target values; $\tilde{y} \in R^l$ is the vector of target variables that enter only linearly;[20] Q is an appropriate positive diagonal matrix; and r and l are appropriate vectors. Note that Q is a full rank square matrix by assumption. We refer to $\bar{y}$, Q, r and l as the parameters of the government's preferences. Equation (2.23) is defined over $t = q + l$ variables.

Equation (2.23) encompasses three possible cases. In each, the associated first best (or *optimum optimorum*) has a different nature.

[20] The reader should note a little abuse of notation as we use l for both the vector of weight of the linear targets and for its dimension. The difference is clear, however, from the context in which they are used.

1. The case $r = l = 0$ clearly nests Equation (2.5). In such a case, the first best of the government corresponds to its target values and its first best outcome is thus bounded.
2. The first best is also bounded if some linear terms are added to the quadratic variables (i.e., $r \neq 0$ and $l = 0$), but now the first best is no longer given by their target values. The first best is $\bar{y}(i) + \frac{1}{2}\frac{r(i)}{Q(i,i)}$ for the i-th target variable in y.
3. Finally, if at least one target variable enters the preferences only linearly (i.e., $l \neq 0$), the first best is not bounded, since for this variable an infinite value is optimal, whereas for the other q variables the *optimum optimorum* is reached as above.

Theorem 2.2 applies to cases 1 and 2 and controllability is ensured if $m = q = t$. However, in case 2, if Theorem 2.2 is satisfied, the policymaker achieves a first best that does not correspond to his quadratic target values. By contrast, in case 3, when $l \neq 0$, if the Golden Rule is satisfied, then $t = m > q$, but a finite solution for the policymaker's problem does not exist, since achieving the first best would imply setting at least one instrument at an infinite value in order to get an infinite value of the target (in this case, preferences are not satiated or satiable). We can define a weaker concept of controllability, that of Q-controllability, when $m = q \leq t$. In this case the policymaker can achieve his first best for all his quadratic variables. Of course, when $l = 0$, Q-controllability coincides with controllability as stated in Section 2.2.

We illustrate LQ preferences by a simple example. Consider an all-encompassing monopoly trade union. Its utility (or loss function) can be written as

$$U = -L = a_{\omega}\omega - \frac{1}{2}a_n(n - \bar{n})^2 - a_{\pi}\pi, \tag{2.24}$$

where ω is the real wage (the degree of distortion in the economy), n is employment, π is inflation; a_{ω}, a_n, a_{π} are the weights assigned to the different target variables and $\bar{n}$ is the union's target value (i.e., full employment). The union aims to obtain full employment and a high real wage; moreover, we assume that the union may be interested in reducing inflation as inflation affects its members who are retired and who earn transfers defined in nominal terms.[21]

[21] Note that in this representation ω is a "good" whereas π is a "bad."

The underlying economy is described by two equations:

$$\omega = -\eta(n - \bar{n}), \text{ and} \tag{2.25}$$

$$\pi = w + m. \tag{2.26}$$

The former is a simple labor demand; the latter makes inflation dependent on nominal wages ($w = \omega + \pi$) and a measure of the monetary stance (m).[22]

Equation (2.25) implies that n and ω are not independent target variables. Then Equation (2.24) can be written as

$$\begin{aligned} U &= -L = a_\omega \omega - \frac{1}{2} a_n \left(\frac{\omega}{\eta}\right)^2 - a_\pi \pi \text{ or} \\ U &= -L = -a_\omega \eta(n - \bar{n}) - \frac{1}{2} a_n (n - \bar{n})^2 - a_\pi \pi \end{aligned} \tag{2.27}$$

which clearly illustrates its LQ nature, considering independent target variables.

It is easy to verify that the utility (2.27) is unbounded if $a_\pi \neq 0$. By deriving it for ω (or n) and π, in fact, we get that the *optima optimorum* (first best) are

$$\omega = \frac{a_\omega \eta^2}{a_n} \text{ or } n = \bar{n} - \frac{a_\omega \eta}{a_n}, \text{ and} \tag{2.28}$$

$$\pi = -\infty \text{ if } a_\pi \neq 0. \tag{2.29}$$

Equation (2.28) describes the trade-off for the union, which is associated with the non-independence of real wage and employment. The different effect of the linear terms in (2.27) is clear: only first-order target variables (π) imply unbounded first best, while linear terms in second-order target variables (ω or n) just imply an *optimum optimorum* different from the target value ($\bar{n}$). To avoid unbounded preferences one can either introduce a quadratic preference for inflation (targeting a zero rate) or a lower bond at zero.

2.7.4 *Instrument costs*

Instrument costs will play an important role in our approach when we consider strategic interactions. It is useful to introduce them now since

[22] We will discuss models of this kind extensively in Parts II and III.

instrument costs can, in fact, be incorporated easily without modifying our setup. Each instrument can be decoupled into two variables by considering the possible double nature of an instrument: as a means to achieve the optimal policy (influencing the economic system), and as a variable of possible interest per se to the policymaker (the instrument has a target value too).

For instance, consider a problem of the kind described by Equations (2.2) and (2.5). If, in addition, the use of the m instruments is associated with quadratic costs, we can represent this problem by introducing the instruments into the preference functions or alternatively by adding m auxiliary equations, $y_U = u$, to the system (2.2) and an additional quadratic term, $y'_U H y_U$, in (2.5), where H is a matrix measuring the relative cost of using each of the instruments.[23] Formally, we consider:

$$\min L = (y - \bar{y})' Q (y - \bar{y}) + y'_U H y_U \tag{2.30}$$

subject to

$$\begin{bmatrix} y \\ y_U \end{bmatrix} = \begin{bmatrix} C \\ I \end{bmatrix} u + \begin{bmatrix} A^{-1}K \\ 0 \end{bmatrix}. \tag{2.31}$$

Equations (2.30) and (2.31) clearly have the same form as (2.2) and (2.5). This formulation is of course artificial. However, its usefulness as an analytic device will become clear in subsequent chapters. It is also worth noticing that, if quadratic costs are associated with any or all the instruments, the system (2.31) is never controllable by the government as the total number of targeted values is now always greater than the number of instrument variables available.

The decoupling process described above can be used to introduce linear costs (adding a linear term to Equation (2.5)); and for subgroups of instruments, in order to consider costs on the use of some instruments while leaving the others free.

[23] For the sake of simplicity we consider a case where the cost of using the instruments is considered with respect to the policy inaction, i.e., it is optimal to set all them to zero. However, this assumption can be easily generalized considering the cost of deviation from some (exogenous) preferred values.

2.8 Conclusions

The key feature of the Tinbergen–Theil approach to economic policy is its encompassing vision of policy problems. This is important, given the need to consider the differential effects of maneuvering each instrument; effects that influence the outcomes for not just one target but a number of targets, or even all of them. This approach gives the idea that the policymaker could determine the course of economic events and calculate precise solutions to policy problems in a straightforward way.

The proponents of the approach were conscious of some of its limitations. As to the problems associated with the cost and the political or administrative feasibility of the solutions generated by this approach, certain refinements of the model are possible – for example, by introducing costs related to the use of instruments (such as those dealt with in Section 2.7.4). Among the main limitations, however, the static nature can be generalized by re-specifying the model in an appropriate way. We will examine this issue in the next chapter.

Other criticisms are of a more logical nature and derive from a lack of consideration of the private sector's expectations. Insofar as those expectations are of an adaptive nature, the assertion of the ineffectiveness of some policy action, such as for monetary policy (Friedman, 1968), could be limited to the long run. However, when forward-looking expectations are introduced, this critique of the Tinbergen–Theil theory of economic policy becomes more radical and may lead to more forceful assertion of policy ineffectiveness. We examine this critique in Chapter 4.

Appendix 2A. Extracting a sub-set of target variables

Assume that relevant target variables are $y \in R^q$ and policy instruments are $u \in R^m$; we can rewrite the full structural form of the model (2.1), $AY = BZ + \mathbf{k}$, as follows:

$$\left[\bar{A} \; \vdots \; \bar{C}\right]\begin{bmatrix} y \\ \cdots \\ y_N \end{bmatrix} = \left[\bar{B} \; \vdots \; \bar{D}\right]\begin{bmatrix} u \\ \cdots \\ u_N \end{bmatrix}, \tag{2A.1}$$

where $y_N \in R^r$ and $u_N \in R^j$ are irrelevant endogenous variables and constants; $\bar{A} \in R^{(q+r)\times q}$, $\bar{B} \in R^{(q+r)\times m}$, $\bar{C} \in R^{(q+r)\times r}$, $\bar{D} \in R^{(q+r)\times j}$ are obvious coefficient matrices.

For the sake of brevity, we have assumed that the policymaker is interested only in the first q variables. If this is not the case, it is trivial to reorder the equations (and hence endogenous variables) in such a way as to put relevant variables in the first q positions. To simplify the analysis, we also assume k = 0. By using suitably partitioned matrices we can isolate the first q equations of system (2A.1) from the others, obtaining

$$\bar{A}_1 y + \bar{C}_1 y_N = \bar{B}_1 u + \bar{D}_1 u_N \tag{2A.2}$$

$$\bar{A}_2 y + \bar{C}_2 y_N = \bar{B}_2 u + \bar{D}_2 u_N \tag{2A.3}$$

where $\bar{A}_1 \in R^{q\times q}$, $\bar{B}_1 \in R^{q\times m}$, $\bar{C}_1 \in R^{q\times r}$, $\bar{D}_1 \in R^{q\times j}$, $\bar{A}_2 \in R^{r\times q}$, $\bar{B}_2 \in R^{r\times m}$, $\bar{C}_2 \in R^{r\times r}$, $\bar{D}_2 \in R^{r\times j}$ are obtained from $\bar{A}$, $\bar{B}$, $\bar{C}$, $\bar{D}$ as row-partitioned matrices; for example, $\bar{A}_1 \in R^{q\times q}$ corresponds to the matrix formed by the first q rows of A, whereas $\bar{A}_2 \in R^{r\times q}$ is the matrix formed by the last r rows of A (similarly for the others; sub-index 1 refers to the first q rows, while sub-index 2 refers to the last r rows). It follows that Equations (2A.2) and (2A.3) represent the first q and the last r equations of system (2A.1).

If $\bar{C}_2$ is invertible, we can solve (2A.3) with respect to y_N:

$$y_N = \bar{C}_2^{-1}\bar{B}_2 u + \bar{C}_2^{-1}\bar{D}_2 u_N - \bar{C}_2^{-1}\bar{A}_2 y. \tag{2A.4}$$

Plugging (2A.4) into (2A.2), we get

$$\bar{A}_1 y + \bar{C}_1 \bar{C}_2^{-1}\left[\bar{B}_2 u + \bar{D}_2 u_N - \bar{A}_2 y\right] = \bar{B}_1 u + \bar{D}_1 u_N, \tag{2A.5}$$

which is (2.2) in the main text, where $A = \bar{A}_1 - \bar{C}_1\bar{C}_2^{-1}\bar{A}_2$, $B = \bar{B}_1 - \bar{C}_1\bar{C}_2^{-1}\bar{B}_2$, $k = (\bar{D}_1 - \bar{C}_1\bar{C}_2^{-1}\bar{D}_2)u_N$.

Appendix 2B. Basic matrix algebra

2B.1 Simple derivatives with respect to vectors

A linear multi-variable relationship can be easily expressed in matrix terms, i.e., $y = Ax$, where $y \in R^m$ and $x \in R^n$ are vectors and $A \in R^{m\times n}$ is a matrix. Then vector y can be differentiated with respect to x, to obtain all the first-order partial derivatives of a vector with respect to another vector. These derivatives are given by a matrix A, which is sometimes called a *Jacobian matrix* or the *Jacobian*,[24] whose generic term $A(i,j)$ is $\partial y(i)/\partial x(j)$. We can thus write $\partial y/\partial x = \partial Ax/\partial x = A$.

Linear forms,[25] e.g., $y'b$, where $b \in \mathrm{R}^m$ is a vector of parameters, can also be derived with respect to a vector. The result now is a vector, as we are deriving a scalar term with respect to a number of variables. Formally, $\partial y'b/\partial y = b$. Similarly, $\partial b'y/\partial y = b$.

Finally, quadratic forms,[26] e.g., $y'Ax$, can be derived with respect to vectors. If we want to find the derivative of this form with respect to x, we simply follow the differentiation rule of vectors and thus we have $\partial(y'Ax)/\partial x = (y'A)' = A'y$. Similarly, if we want to find the derivative of the same form with respect to y', we have $\partial(y'Ax)/\partial y' = Ax$. In order to find the derivative of particular quadratic forms such as $x'Bx$ where $B \in \mathrm{R}^{n \times n}$ is symmetric, we can exploit the property that for them $B = B'$ holds. Thus we have $\partial(x'Bx)/\partial x = 2Bx$.

2B.2 Positive and negative (semi-)definite matrices

A real matrix B is positive definite if $x'Bx > 0$ for all nonzero vectors x with real entries. Instead, a real matrix B is negative definite if $x'Bx < 0$ for all nonzero vectors x with real entries.[27] Operationally, if B is also symmetric, it is positive (negative) definite if and only if all its eigenvalues are positive (negative).

Similarly, a real matrix B is positive semi-definite if $x'Bx \geq 0$ for all nonzero vectors x with real entries; it is negative semi-definite if $x'Bx \leq 0$ for all nonzero vectors x with real entries. Operationally, if B is also symmetric, it is semi-positive (semi-negative) definite if and only if all its eigenvalues are non-negative (non-positive).

[24] In general the Jacobian is the first derivative of any mapping from m to n. The Jacobian of a function thus describes the orientation of a tangent plane to the function at a given point. In this way, it generalizes the gradient of a scalar-valued function of multiple variables that itself generalizes the derivative of a scalar-valued function of a scalar.

[25] A linear form is a homogeneous polynomial of degree 1 in a number of variables.

[26] A quadratic form is a homogeneous polynomial of degree 2 in a number of variables. It is worth noticing that here also we are deriving a scalar-valued function with respect to a number of variables.

[27] If B is a complex matrix, B is positive definite if the real part of x^1Bx is greater (smaller) than zero, where x^* is the conjugate transpose of x.

2B.3 Maxima and minima

Consider a vector $x \in R^n$ and let $f : R^n \rightarrow R$, then the derivative of f with respect to x is

$$\nabla f(x) = \left(\frac{\partial f}{\partial x(1)}, \frac{\partial f}{\partial x(2)}, \ldots \frac{\partial f}{\partial x(n)} \right) \tag{2B.1}$$

where $\nabla f(x)$ is the gradient of $f(x)$.

By taking account of the second partial derivatives we can instead define the Hessian matrix $H(f(x))$, which is a square matrix of order n:

$$H(f(x)) = \begin{pmatrix} \frac{\partial^2 f}{\partial x(1)^2} & \frac{\partial^2 f}{\partial x(2)x(1)} & \cdots & \frac{\partial^2 f}{\partial x(n)x(1)} \\ \frac{\partial^2 f}{\partial x(2)x(1)} & \cdots & \cdots & \cdots \\ \cdots & \cdots & \cdots & \frac{\partial^2 f}{\partial x(n)x(n-1)} \\ \frac{\partial^2 f}{\partial x(n)x(1)} & \cdots & \frac{\partial^2 f}{\partial x(n)x(n-1)} & \frac{\partial^2 f}{\partial x(n)x(n)} \end{pmatrix}, \tag{2B.2}$$

where the mixed derivatives of $f(x)$ are the entries off the main diagonal.

If the gradient is zero at some point $x = x_0$, then f has a critical point at x_0. The determinant of the Hessian at x_0 is then called the discriminant. If this determinant is zero, then x_0 is called a degenerate critical point of $f(x)$. Otherwise it is non-degenerate.

For a non-degenerate critical point x_0:

1. If the Hessian is positive definite at x_0, then $f(x)$ attains a local minimum.
2. If the Hessian is negative definite at x_0, then $f(x)$ attains a local maximum.
3. If the Hessian has both positive and negative eigenvalues, then x_0 is a saddle point for $f(x)$ (this is true even if x_0 is degenerate).
4. Otherwise the test is inconclusive.

Consider the quadratic function $x'Bx + b'x$. A minimum requires $\nabla f(x)' = 2Bx + b = 0$ and that $H(f(x))$ is positive definite in the value of x that solves the previous expression. It is worth noticing, however, that in our quadratic case the positive or negative definiteness of $H(f(x))$ is independent of x since $H(f(x)) = 2B$.

Appendix 2C. Pseudo-inverse matrix

2C.1 Definitions

A generalized inverse matrix of the matrix A is any matrix A^- such that:

$$AA^-A = A. \tag{2C.1}$$

The matrix A^- is not unique. Of particular importance among the possible alternative definitions is the *pseudo-inverse* (or *Moore–Penrose inverse*). Formally, the pseudo-inverse of a matrix A is the matrix A^+ that fulfils the following four properties: (i) $AA^+A = A$; (ii) $A^+AA^+ = A^+$; (iii) AA^+ is symmetric; (iv) A^+A is symmetric.[28] The matrix A^+ is unique and always exists.

Regarding the construction of A^+ we have to distinguish two cases.

(1) Assume that A has full rank, then there are three possibilities:
  (a) $A \in R^{n\times n}$ and $r[A] = n$ (square matrix), $A^+ = A^{-1} \in R^{n\times n}$.
  (b) $A \in R^{n\times m}$ and $r[A] = n$ (broad matrix), $A^+ = A'(AA')^{-1} \in R^{m\times m}$.
  (c) $A \in R^{n\times m}$ and $r[A] = m$ (tall matrix), $A^+ = (A'A)^{-1} A' \in R^{n\times n}$.
  It is easy to check that: in case (a) $A^+A = AA^+ = I \in R^{n\times n}$ (A^+ is the *regular inverse*); (b) $AA^+ = I \in R^{m\times m}$ (A^+ is the *right-inverse*); (c) $A^+A = I \in R^{n\times n}$ (A^+ is the *left-inverse*).[29]
(2) Assume A does not have full rank (rank-deficient matrix), i.e., $A \in R^{n\times m}$ and $r[A] = r < \min(n,m)$. Then a pseudo inverse, A^+, can be constructed from the *singular-value decomposition.* See Golub and Van Loan (1996: 257–258) or Ben-Israel and Greville (2003) for details.

2C.2 Linear equation system and matrix inversion

Assume $A \in R^{n\times m}$ and consider the linear system

$$Ax = b \tag{2C.2}$$

[28] Note that in case of complex matrices, the symmetric condition is substituted by a condition of being Hermitian.

[29] A full rank square matrix which admits both a right and left-inverse is the unique regular inverse A^{-1}.

where $x \in R^m$ is a vector of unknowns and $b \in R^n$ is a vector of known parameters.

Conditions for the existence of a solution are then obtained by considering the augmented matrix $B = [A : b]$.

(a) If $r[A] = r[B] = m$, there is a unique solution.
(b) If $r[A] = r[B] < m$, there are many solutions.
(c) If $r[A] < r[B]$, there is no solution.

The solution of the equation system (2C.2) is obtained by using the matrix inversion. Formally, by pre-multiplying by A^+, we obtain

$$A^+Ax = A^+b. \tag{2C.3}$$

If A admits a left-inverse, the solution is trivial:

$$x = A^+b. \tag{2C.4}$$

Consider the case of a full rank matrix. (i) If A is square, then $x = A^{-1}b$ as A has an inverse. (ii) If A is full column rank, then $x = A^+b = (A'A)^{-1} A'b$ as A has a left-inverse. (iii) Finally, if A is full row rank, then a solution does not exist as A^+A cannot be defined ($A^+ \in R^{m\times m}$ and $A \in R^{n\times m}$). Now consider the case of $A \in R^{n\times n}$ but with rank $r < n$. The system (2C.3) is still solved by (2C.4), where A^+ is the pseudo-inverse of the rank-deficient matrix, constructed as described above (Section 2C.1: point 2).

3 *Dynamics*

Summary. This chapter sets out the general modeling framework to be used in Part IV, where the new theory of economic policy is developed in a dynamic context. As such it forms a technical bridge to the models, analytic techniques and concepts as they were used in the economic literature in the era before policy announcements, expectations of future behavior, or strategic interactions became important. It also constitutes a connection to the analysis and concepts used by control theorists in the engineering literature. The concepts covered are: (a) reduced form representations, and final and state space forms for dynamic economies; (b) a differentiation of policy objectives – path objectives, (multi-period) static objectives, and dynamic point objectives; (c) stability properties, the impact of policy actions over different intervals of time and the associated cyclical behavior; and (d) the distinctions between different types of control rules, their error reduction characteristics and "reachability."

3.1 Introduction

We start by reviewing structural and reduced form models; also the final and state space forms for models with multiple lags. At this stage we do not deal with models that have policy interactions (endogenized policy variables) or forward-looking expectations (endogenous lead variables). We introduce those aspects later in Chapters 5 and 6 in a static framework, and again in Part IV for the dynamic case. In those places we will revisit and extend the material of this chapter to cover strategic interactions and expectations; and associated material on the saddle point property for stability, multipliers, and the limits to time-inconsistent behavior and the Lucas critique.

Along the way, we first illustrate two basic, equivalent representations of dynamic economies: the structural or reduced form (already introduced in the static analysis) and the state space or final form.

We then show how an economy's behavior can be broken down into its component cycles and how we can use different notions of controllability (static, dynamic, path) as well as different types of control rules (proportional, integral and differential or derivative) and different types of information in those rules to give open loop, feedback and closed loop controls. Finally, stabilizability and error reduction analysis allow us to focus on the error-correcting properties of a model/economy under control, and hence the "reachability" of certain policy targets.[1]

The chapter is structured as follows. The next section describes the standard representations of a dynamic economy in both the structural and reduced forms. Section 3.3 introduces the dynamic policy multipliers. Section 3.4 informally illustrates the policy problem in a dynamic setup, while Section 3.5 formally discusses different concepts of controllability and the related conditions to achieve them in terms of the rank of policy multiplier matrices. Sections 3.6 and 3.7 describe the alternative representation of the economy by using state space forms and show the equivalence between these different representations. Sections 3.8 and 3.9 revise the issues of observability and stabilizability, respectively. In particular, Section 3.8 reviews the different control rules that will be later used in Part IV. Section 3.10 concludes the chapter.

3.2 Dynamic structural and reduced forms

3.2.1 A simple dynamic setting

The simplest dynamic representation of an economy, in the form of a model, is as a linear difference equation system:[2]

$$\hat{A}_0 y_t = \hat{A}_1 y_{t-1} + \hat{B}_0 u_t + \hat{C}_0 w_t \quad t = 1,\ldots,T \qquad \text{(structural form)} \qquad (3.1)$$

where y_t is the vector of endogenous variables and potential policy targets in the system; u_t the vector of policy instruments available; and w_t

[1] This chapter draws heavily on classical contributions to the theory of economic policy, mostly from Preston and Pagan (1982) and Hughes Hallett (1989).

[2] We use difference, rather than differential, equations to represent the economy's dynamics. Given the discrete nature of economic data, this is the conventional approach in economics. Petit (1990) provides an analysis in continuous time.

are random shocks and other exogenous influences or variables, which also affect this economy's outcomes. The matrices $\hat{A}_0$, $\hat{A}_1 \in R^{q\times q}$, $\hat{B}_0 \in R^{q\times m}$ and $\hat{C}_0 \in R^{q\times q}$ represent parameters and may also be the identity matrix. These matrices are all nonzero, meaning that they all contain at least one, or some, or many nonzero elements.

Equation (3.1) displays the model in *structural form*, just as we would specify it equation by equation from economic theory. It is a dynamic version of the structural form introduced in Chapter 2, albeit with only one lag term to provide the dynamics. It is easy to generalize to multiple lags in both y_t and u_t, and in w_t for that matter, as we show next. But in fact, with an appropriate shift in notation, for many purposes we will not need to use that more complicated specification.

It is also easy to transform system (3.1) to its *reduced form*, equivalent to the reduced form models of Chapter 2:

$$y_t = A_1 y_{t-1} + B_0 u_t + C_0 w_t \qquad \text{(reduced form)} \tag{3.2}$$

where $A_1 = \hat{A}_0^{-1}\hat{A}_1$, $B_0 = \hat{A}_0^{-1}\hat{B}_0$ and $C_0 = \hat{A}_0^{-1}\hat{C}_0$. This reduced form model takes account of all the contemporaneous simultaneity in the model, and always exists so long as there are no redundant equations (equations linearly dependent on other equations).[3] If that is the case, $\hat{A}_0$ is of full rank, $r[\hat{A}_0] = q$ and $\hat{A}_0^{-1}$ will exist.

3.2.2 *A dynamic setting with multiple lags*

To allow for multiple lags in the impact or use of the instruments, we can write the model in structural form as

$$\hat{A}_0 y_t = \sum_{i=1}^{p} \hat{A}_i y_{t-i} + \sum_{i=0}^{g} \hat{B}_i u_{t-i} + \sum_{i=0}^{r} \hat{C}_i w_{t-i} \qquad \text{(structural form)}, \tag{3.3}$$

where p, g and r denote the maximum lags observed in y_t and u_t, and w_t. This can be transformed to a reduced form model:

$$y_t = \sum_{i=1}^{p} A_i y_{t-i} + \sum_{i=0}^{g} B_i u_{t-i} + \sum_{i=0}^{r} C_i w_{t-i} \qquad \text{(reduced form)} \tag{3.4}$$

where, in obvious notation, $A_i = \hat{A}_0^{-1}\hat{A}_i$ for $i \geq 1$; and $B_i = \hat{A}_0^{-1}\hat{B}_i$, $C_i = \hat{A}_0^{-1}\hat{C}_i$ for $i \geq 0$.

[3] From now on, we will assume that any such equations have already been substituted out.

At this point, it may be easier to simplify notation by introducing the lag operator L: $L^v y_t \equiv y_{t-v}$ for $v \in \{0,1,\ldots\}$. The dynamic structural form (3.3) can then be written as

$$\hat{A}(\mathrm{L})y_t = \hat{B}(\mathrm{L})u_t + \hat{C}(\mathrm{L})w_t, \tag{3.5}$$

where $\hat{A}(\mathrm{L}) \equiv I - \sum_{i=1}^{p} \hat{A}_i L^i$; $\hat{B}(\mathrm{L}) \equiv \sum_{i=0}^{g} \hat{B}_i \mathrm{L}^i$; $\hat{C}(\mathrm{L}) \equiv \sum_{i=0}^{r} \hat{C}_i \mathrm{L}^i$ are coefficient matrices in the lag operator. The associated reduced form, (3.4), is then

$$y_t = A(\mathrm{L})y_t + B(\mathrm{L})u_t + C(\mathrm{L})w_t, \tag{3.6}$$

where $A(\mathrm{L}) = \sum_{i=1}^{p} A_i \mathrm{L}^i$, $B(\mathrm{L}) = \sum_{i=0}^{g} B_i \mathrm{L}^i$ and $C(\mathrm{L}) = \sum_{i=0}^{r} C_i \mathrm{L}^i$.

For use below, and to show the dynamic relationships between individual targets and instruments, we can also rewrite the structural form (3.5) as

$$\hat{A}(\mathrm{L})y_t = \hat{B}(\mathrm{L})u_t + d_t \quad \text{where} \quad d_t = \sum_{i=0}^{r} \hat{C}_i w_{t-i}. \tag{3.7}$$

Notice that, assuming stability, every dynamic structure embodies a static, steady state model as a special case: $\hat{A}(1)y = \hat{B}(1)u + \hat{C}(1)w_t$.

3.3 Policy multipliers

A policy multiplier describes the incremental impact, on a target variable, of a change in the policy instruments, either contemporaneously, or after a certain delay, or cumulated since the change was made. We can also distinguish between one-off policy changes (the instrument reverts to its original value/path after one period) vs. sustained policy changes (the instrument remains at/on its new value/path for a number of periods). For ease of explanation, we will use a single lag reduced form model (3.2) in this section.[4]

[4] We generalize to the multiple-lags case, (3.4), in Section 3.5. But it turns out that the multiple-lags case is not interesting analytically, however important computationally. So the results we need in this book come from this section.

The *impact multiplier* measures the effect of a change in one specific instrument at the current time t on one specific target at the same time. Formally the effect of the j-th instrument on the i-th target is given by the (i, j)-th element of B_0, i.e.,

$$\Pi_0(i,j) \equiv \frac{\partial y(i)_t}{\partial u(j)_t} = B_0(i,j), \quad i = \{1,\ldots,q\}, j = \{1,\ldots,m\}. \tag{3.8}$$

It is trivial that we can express all the impact multipliers (i.e., for $i = 1,\ldots,q$ and $j = 1,\ldots,m$) in a matrix form Π_0, which is equal to B_0.

The impact multipliers are the equivalent of the policy multipliers introduced in the previous chapter. But the instruments also exhibit delayed effects through the model's dynamic structure. A change of an instrument in the past also affects a target variable at the current time (or equivalently current changes affect future targets). We can thus define the *v-period delay* multiplier for the incremental effect of a one-off policy change at $t - v$ on the target variables at time t:

$$\frac{\partial y(i)_t}{\partial u(j)_{t-v}} \equiv \Pi_v(i,j) = \left[A_1^v B_0\right]_{i,j} \tag{3.9}$$

for any value of $v = 1,\ldots,\infty$. In matrix form we can express the *v-period delay* multipliers as $\Pi_v = A_1{}^v B_0$, with impact multipliers from $v = 0$ (no delayed effects) as a special case. Putting these multipliers into matrix form, we now have a full set of *impact* and *v-period delay* multipliers for the incremental effects of a one-off policy change:

$$\begin{aligned}\frac{\partial y_t}{\partial u} &= \left[\frac{\partial y_t}{\partial u_t}, \frac{\partial y_t}{\partial u_{t-1}}, \ldots, \frac{\partial y_t}{\partial u_{t-v}}\right] = \{\Pi_0, \Pi_1, \ldots, \Pi_v\} \\ &= \left[B_0, A_1 B_0, A_1^2 B_0, \ldots\ldots, A_1^v B_0\right]\end{aligned} \tag{3.10}$$

for any value of $v = 1,\ldots,\infty$.

The instant and delayed multipliers, defined in (3.10), capture the direct effect on current targets of a change in the current or past instruments. We can finally define *dynamic multipliers* as the cumulative effects produced by impact and delayed multipliers. For instance, the one-period dynamic multiplier ($\Pi_1{}^D(i, j)$) measures all the impacts of a sustained change in $u(j)_{t-1}$ and $u(j)_t$ on $y(i)_t$, which is the sum of two effects: (1) the direct effect of a change of $u(j)_t$ at t on the target variable $y(i)_t$ at t; plus (2) the one-period indirect or lagged effect of a change of $u(j)_{t-1}$ at $t-1$ on $y(i)_t$ at t, which is given by the impact of $u(j)_{t-1}$ on y_{t-1} and transmitted to $y(i)_t$ through the model's dynamics, i.e.,

$$\Pi_1^D(i,j) \equiv \frac{\partial y(i)_t}{\partial u(j)_t} + \frac{\partial y(i)_t}{\partial y_{t-1}}\frac{\partial y_{t-1}}{\partial u(j)_{t-1}} = \Pi_0(i,j) + \Pi_1(i,j) = \left[B_0(i,j) + A_1 B_0(i,j)\right] \tag{3.11}$$

for $i = \{1,\ldots,q\}$, $j = \{1,\ldots,m\}$. In matrix form, $\Pi_0^D \equiv \Pi_0 + \Pi_1 = B_0 + A_1 B_0$.

Generalizing, we can define in matrix form the v-period dynamic, *cumulative* multiplier effects so far for a sustained policy change, as

$$\Pi_v^D \equiv \sum_{v=0}^{t} \frac{\partial y_t}{\partial u_{t-v}} = B_0 + \sum_{i=1}^{v} A_1\,\Pi_{v-i} = B_0 + \sum_{i=1}^{v} A_1^i B_0 \quad v \in \{0,1,\ldots\}, \tag{3.12}$$

which is the sum of the direct effect on current targets, and lagged effects transmitted to current targets through the model's dynamics.

Thus the effects of a policy change (or changes) are distributed over time and can be written as

$$\left[\frac{\partial y}{\partial u}\right] = \begin{bmatrix} \dfrac{\partial y_t}{\partial u_t} & \cdots & \dfrac{\partial y_{t-v}}{\partial u_t} \\ \vdots & \ddots & \vdots \\ \dfrac{\partial y_t}{\partial u_{t-v}} & \cdots & \dfrac{\partial y_{t-v}}{\partial u_{t-v}} \end{bmatrix} = \begin{bmatrix} B_0 & 0 & \cdots & \cdots & 0 \\ A_1 B_0 & B_0 & & & \vdots \\ A_1^2 B_0 & A_1 B_0 & B_0 & & \vdots \\ \vdots & & \ddots & \ddots & 0 \\ A_1^{v-1} B_0 & \cdots & \cdots & A_1 B_0 & B_0 \end{bmatrix} \tag{3.13}$$

for any $v = 1,\ldots,\infty$.

The cumulative effect of any changes in the instruments, on targets in period t, is automatically obtained by matrix multiplication along row-block v and down a stacked vector of the given (zero and non-zero) instrument changes $du = [du_1',\ldots,du_t']'$. The total effect, on all targets, of all instrument changes is therefore given by $dy = (\partial y/\partial u)du$ using (3.13), where dy is the stacked vector of total target changes $[dy_1,\ldots,dy_t]'$.

Next we consider the model's *long term* multipliers. The values of the targets in period t, with policy instruments set at arbitrary values, are given by the model's *final form* – row t from (3.13):

$$y_t = A_1^t y_0 + \sum_{i=0}^{t-1} A_1^i B_0 u_{t-i} + \sum_{i=0}^{t} A_1^i w_i \qquad \text{for any } t = 1,\ldots,\infty. \tag{3.14}$$

This raises the interesting question of whether the economy is stable; that is, returns to a steady state after a shock, dw_t in period $t = 1$, say, or after a change in the instruments, du_t in the same period. Evidently this turns on $\lim_{t\to\infty}(A_1^t) = 0$ so that (i) the first term on the right of (3.14) vanishes for large enough values of t *and* (ii) the multipliers in the bottom row of (3.13) eventually die out, given that the only changes are in du_1 (or dw_1). At that point there would be no further effects on y_t from the change in u_1, although the steady state value of y_t will have changed from its starting point. This limit value, $\lim_{t\to\infty}(A_1^t) = 0$, holds if and only if the roots of A_1 all lie within the unit circle: i.e., if A_1 has spectral radius less than 1. If that is the case, we can talk of the *final multipliers*

$$\frac{\partial y_\infty}{\partial u_1} = \sum\nolimits_0^\infty A_1^i B_0 = (I - A_1)^{-1} B_0 \tag{3.15}$$

as representing the long term effect of a policy change on the target or other endogenous variables.

Of course, it would also be possible to talk of the impact or longer-term effects of external events on the target variables by replacing B_i with C_i throughout Equations (3.8) to (3.15). But we do not need to deal with that case until we come to strategic interactions and policy games in Chapter 6. Similarly, we can easily generalize all these different model representations and multiplier forms to the case of more complicated dynamics (multiple lags in endogenous variables or policy instruments) by means of the generalized lag and state space forms in Section 3.5. Finally, we can also generalize to the case where forward-looking expectations (or where the instruments set by others anticipate our own policy choices) play a role by filling out the upper triangle in (3.13), currently occupied by zeros, with the appropriate anticipation effects on current behavior. We deal with that case in detail in Chapters 11 and 12.

3.4 Dynamic policy problems

If there are dynamic relationships describing how the economy evolves, there are likely to be dynamic objectives, which policymakers would like to reach. There are four possible types:

1. Static objectives: hitting desired target values from any initial condition.

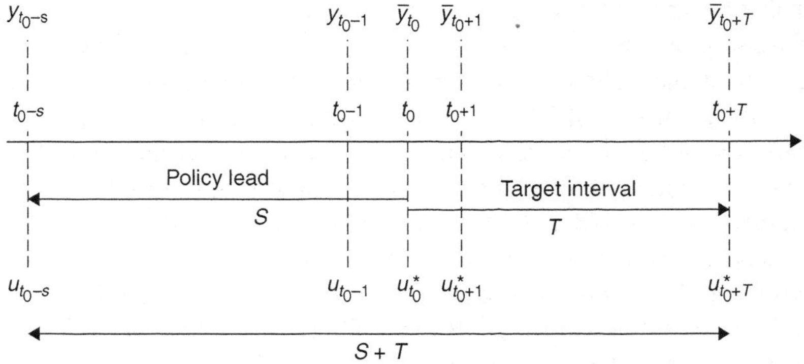

Figure 3.1 A time line for dynamic policy problems

2. Multi-period static objectives: hitting and holding desired target values across a certain time interval, if necessary by changing instrument settings.
3. Target point objectives: fixed targets to be reached at some specific point in time in the future.
4. Target path objectives: hitting certain target values at a certain point of time, and then holding a sequence of arbitrary point objectives for a certain interval thereafter.

Formally, the above problems can be illustrated in terms of four parameters. Assuming that the policymaker aims to reach his desired targets from t_0 (current period), or from t_0 on, the policymaker should act at least from the current period and anticipate his future policy changes. The relevant parameters can then be defined as follows:

(a) The degree of anticipation or policy lead $S \in \{0,1,\ldots\}$.
(b) The target interval $T \in \{0,1,\ldots\}$.
(c) The number of targets per period (q).
(d) The instruments per period (m).[5]

This leaves us with a four-parameter theory of dynamic policy: S, T, q, m. A time line for policy problems in a dynamic setting can then be depicted as in Figure 3.1. The line describes the policy interval

[5] Normally we assume that we have a fixed number of targets and instruments in each period (i.e., q and m do not vary in each period). In Chapter 10 we will show some effects of relaxing this assumption.

(between $t_0 - S$ and $t_0 + T$) where the policymaker is active, where t_0 is the "current period."

In the case of static objectives, the policymaker aims to achieve his target vector in the current period by setting his instruments in the current period. This corresponds to Tinbergen's static fixed objective problem since the policymaker aims to achieve his target vector under linear constraints augmented by the given initial conditions. Multi-period static objectives imply a natural extension of the Tinbergen idea of fixed targets to a dynamic context as, in this case, the policymaker aims at achieving a configuration of desired targets ($\bar{y}$) during a time interval between t_0 and $t_0 + T$. When there are target point objectives, the policymaker wants to reach his targets at a certain time (i.e., in S periods) anticipating his action by S periods. In this case, one can also define the policy problem of endogenizing S by interpreting it as the smallest time interval needed to achieve the target vector. Finally, target path objectives imply that the policymaker aims to reach, after S periods, a certain dynamic path for the economy that is then held for T successive periods thereafter.[6]

Before we come to calculate specific policy measures, we need to generalize the above representation of the policy problem to models with multiple lags. We will then be ready to consider certain qualitative characteristics: existence, uniqueness, and strategic design.

3.5 Multi-lag model representations, multipliers and state space forms

3.5.1 Multi-lag representations

How do we incorporate multi-lag versions of our model, (3.4) or (3.7) say, into our multiplier and final form representations so far? Our approach is to replace the q different p-th order difference equations in the reduced form (3.4), which are hard to manipulate, by a first-order difference equation system of dimension k in the same variables, where $k = qp$. To do that, we will use the stacking technique introduced in Section 3.3.

[6] We can also think of endogenizing the policy lead S in this case too.

Let us start from the reduced form model at (3.4):

$$y_t = \sum_{i=1}^{p} A_i y_{t-i} + \sum_{i=0}^{g} B_i u_{t-i} + d_t \quad \text{with} \, d_t = \sum_{i=0}^{r} C_i w_{t-i}. \tag{3.16}$$

We can now write (3.16) as a stacked equation system consisting of the q original equations plus $q(p - 1)$ extra identities:

$$\begin{bmatrix} y_t \\ y_{t-1} \\ \vdots \\ \vdots \\ y_{t-p+1} \end{bmatrix} = \begin{bmatrix} A_1 & A_2 & .. & .. & A_p \\ I & 0 & .. & .. & 0 \\ 0 & I & \ddots & & \vdots \\ \vdots & \ddots & I & \ddots & \vdots \\ 0 & .. & 0 & I & 0 \end{bmatrix} \begin{bmatrix} y_{t-1} \\ y_{t-2} \\ \vdots \\ \vdots \\ y_{t-p} \end{bmatrix} + \begin{bmatrix} B_0 & B_1 & \cdots & B_q \\ 0 & .. & .. & 0 \\ \vdots & \ddots & & \vdots \\ \vdots & & \ddots & \vdots \\ 0 & .. & .. & 0 \end{bmatrix} \begin{bmatrix} u_t \\ u_{t-1} \\ \vdots \\ u_{t-g} \end{bmatrix} + \begin{bmatrix} d_t \\ 0 \\ \vdots \\ \vdots \\ 0 \end{bmatrix}, \tag{3.17}$$

where the first q rows just reproduce the model (3.16); and the next $q(p - 1)$ rows are identities of the form $y_{t-j} = y_{t-j}$ for $j = 1,\ldots, p - 1$. Equation system (3.17) can be rewritten as

$$\tilde{y}_t = A\tilde{y}_{t-1} + B\tilde{u}_t + \tilde{d}_t, \tag{3.18}$$

where $\tilde{y}_t$ is the column vector on the left of (3.17), $\tilde{u}_t$ is the stacked vector of instruments and $\tilde{d}_t$ that of the error terms; and A and B are the expanded $qp \times qp$ and $qp \times mg$ matrices defined in terms of the sub-matrices A_i and B_i, respectively. But system (3.18) is in exactly the same form as the reduced form model at Equation (3.2). Hence we can write, and calculate, the policy multipliers exactly as we did in Section 3.3, Equations (3.8)–(3.15), including the final form model (3.14), by using the same formulae with A replacing A_1 and B replacing B_0.

Moreover, because matrix A in (3.18) is a partitioned companion matrix, taking the leading term on the right after the model has reached steady state ($\tilde{y}_t \simeq \tilde{y}_{t-1}$), and inverting the resulting coefficient matrix $(I - A)$, we obtain

$$\tilde{y}_t = (I - A)^{-1} B\tilde{u}_t + error. \tag{3.19}$$

Then permuting the rows and columns of $\tilde{y}_t$, $(I - A)^{-1}B$ and $\tilde{u}_t$ to reverse the order of the variables in Equation (3.19),[7] and differentiating, we get the final form of the model with the impact, interim,

[7] Pre-multiply (3.19) by the *anti-diagonal* permutation matrix P, and insert $P^{-1}P = I$ between B and u_i.

and final multipliers, and dynamic multipliers, exactly as set out in Equation (3.14).

3.5.2 *State space representations*

As an alternative to the approach developed above, we can represent the system in a *state space form* that is often employed for analytical tractability since it reduces an q-th order system of linear difference equations, like (3.2) and (3.4), to a larger, but easier to handle, first-order difference equation system.

There is, however, no unique procedure for computing a state space representation. There are many different state space representations of the same dynamic system, each characterized by coefficients that differ depending on the technique chosen to construct it.[8]

3.5.2.1 A simple model

We begin by defining a new set of equations in $p + g$ state variables z_t:

$$\begin{array}{ll} y_t \equiv z_{1,t} & u_t \equiv z_{p+1,t} \\ y_{t-1} \equiv z_{2,t} = z_{1,t-1} & u_{t-1} \equiv z_{p+2,t} = z_{p+1,t-1} \\ y_{t-2} \equiv z_{3,t} = z_{2,t-1} & u_{t-2} \equiv z_{p+3,t} = z_{p+2,t-2} \\ \vdots & \vdots \\ \vdots & \vdots \\ y_{t-p+1} \equiv z_{p,t} = z_{p-1,t-1} & u_{t-g+1} \equiv z_{p+g,t} = z_{p+g-1,t-1} \\ y_{t-p} = z_{p,t-1} & u_{t-g} = z_{p+g,t-1} \end{array} \quad . \tag{3.20}$$

We can now generate the *state space* model in Chow (1972, 1973) or Turnovsky (1973, 1974):

$$\begin{bmatrix} y_t \\ y_{t-1} \\ \vdots \\ y_{t-p+1} \\ --- \\ u_t \\ u_{t-1} \\ \vdots \\ u_{t-g+1} \end{bmatrix} = \left[\begin{array}{cccccc|cccc} A_1 & A_2 & \dots & \dots & & A_p & B_1 & \dots & \dots & B_q \\ I & 0 & & & & 0 & 0 & \dots & \dots & 0 \\ & & \ddots & & & & \vdots & & & \vdots \\ 0 & 0 & & & I & 0 & 0 & \dots & \dots & 0 \\ \hline 0 & 0 & \dots & & 0 & 0 & 0 & & & 0 \\ 0 & 0 & \dots & & 0 & 0 & I & \ddots & & 0 \\ \vdots & \vdots & & & \vdots & \vdots & \vdots & \ddots & \ddots & \vdots \\ 0 & 0 & & & 0 & 0 & 0 & \dots & I & 0 \end{array}\right] \begin{bmatrix} y_{t-1} \\ y_{t-2} \\ \vdots \\ y_{t-p} \\ - \\ u_{t-1} \\ u_{t-2} \\ \vdots \\ u_{t-g} \end{bmatrix} + \begin{bmatrix} B_0 \\ 0 \\ \vdots \\ 0 \\ - \\ I \\ 0 \\ \vdots \\ 0 \end{bmatrix} u_t + \begin{bmatrix} I \\ 0 \\ \vdots \\ 0 \\ - \\ 0 \\ \vdots \\ \vdots \\ 0 \end{bmatrix} d_t, \tag{3.21}$$

[8] For a more general discussion we refer the reader to Petit (1990: section 2.3).

i.e., $z_t = Fz_{t-1} + Gu_t + Ed_t$, which is an expanded form of our stacked equation system (3.17), together with the *de-stacking equation*:

$$y_t = \begin{bmatrix} I & 0 & \cdots & 0 & \vdots & 0 & \cdots & 0 \end{bmatrix} \begin{bmatrix} y_t \\ y_{t-1} \\ \vdots \\ y_{t-p+1} \\ u_t \\ \vdots \\ u_{t-g+1} \end{bmatrix}, \text{ i.e., } y_t = Hz_t. \tag{3.22}$$

The whole state space model can therefore be written as

$$\begin{cases} z_t = Fz_{t-1} + Gu_t + Ed_t \\ y_t = Hz_t \end{cases} \text{with } z_0 = a \in \mathrm{R}^{pq+gm}, \tag{3.23}$$

where F, G, E are defined by the coefficient matrices in (3.21).

3.5.2.2 A more compact state space representation

With a slightly different definition of the state variables, we can create a more compact form of the state space representation traditionally used in control theory. Each endogenous vector is now defined as *net* of the contemporaneous control variable u_t. Thus $\hat{y}_k \equiv y_k - B_0u_k$ for $k = t - p,\ldots,t$; and $\hat{B}_k = B_k + A_kB_0$ for $k = 1,\ldots,g$ with $A_k = 0$ for $k \in \{p + 1, \ldots,g\}$, $B_k = 0$ for $k \in \{g + 1, \ldots, p\}$.

The definition of the state variables is then:

$$\begin{array}{ll} \hat{y}_t \equiv \hat{z}_{1,t} & u_{t-1} \equiv \hat{z}_{p+1,t} \\ \hat{y}_{t-1} \equiv \hat{z}_{2,t} = \hat{z}_{1,t-1} & u_{t-2} \equiv \hat{z}_{p+2,t} = \hat{z}_{p+1,t-1} \\ \vdots & \vdots \\ \vdots & \vdots \\ \hat{y}_{t-p+1} \equiv \hat{z}_{p,t} = \hat{z}_{p-1,t-1} & u_{t-g+1} \equiv \hat{z}_{p+g-1,t} = \hat{z}_{p+g-2,t-1} \\ \hat{y}_{t-p} \equiv \hat{z}_{p,t-1} & u_{t-g} \equiv \hat{z}_{p+g-1,t-1} \end{array} . \tag{3.24}$$

This allows us to define a state space model form with $p + g - 1$ variables:

$$\begin{cases} \hat{z}_t = \hat{F}\hat{z}_{t-1} + \hat{G}u_t + \hat{E}d_t \\ y_t = \hat{H}\hat{z}_t + \hat{D}u_t, \end{cases} \text{with } \hat{z}_0 = a \in \mathrm{R}^{pq+(g-1)m}, \tag{3.25}$$

Table 3.1 *Summary of policy models*

Static	Dynamic
Structural form:	**Structural form:**
$Ay = Bu + d$	$\hat{A}(L)y_t = \hat{B}(L)u_t + \hat{d}_t$
Reduced form:	**Reduced form:**
$y = A^{-1}Bu + A^{-1}d$	$y_t = A(L)y_t + B(L)u_t + d_t$
	State space forms (3.23) and (3.25):
	$\begin{cases} z_t = Fz_{t-1} + Gu_t + Ed_t \\ y_t = Hz_t \end{cases}$
	$\begin{cases} \hat{z}_t = \hat{F}\hat{z}_{t-1} + \hat{G}u_t + \hat{E}d_t \\ y_t = \hat{H}\hat{z}_t + \hat{D}u_t \end{cases}$

where, in addition to the definition of $\hat{y}_k$, $\hat{F}$ differs from F because, in $\hat{F}$, the $(p + 1)$-th row and column blocks of F are deleted; and $\hat{B}$ replaces B. Similarly for $\hat{G}$, $\hat{E}$, $\hat{H}$, $\hat{D}$.

Table 3.1 summarizes the representation for static[9] and dynamic policy models.

3.6 The equivalence of different state space model forms

Consider the linear system (3.25)

$$\begin{cases} z_t = Fz_{t-1} + Gu_t + Ed_t \\ y_t = Hz_t + Du_t \end{cases}, \quad \text{with } z_0 = a \in \mathrm{R}^{pq+(g-1)m}, \tag{3.26}$$

where, for simplicity, hats have been deleted. By backwards induction and substitution in the upper equation of (3.26), we have:

$$z_t = F^t z_0 + \begin{bmatrix} G \\ FG \\ \vdots \\ F^{t-1}G \end{bmatrix}' \begin{bmatrix} u_t \\ u_{t-1} \\ \vdots \\ u_0 \end{bmatrix} + \begin{bmatrix} E \\ FE \\ \vdots \\ F^{t-1}E \end{bmatrix}' \begin{bmatrix} d_t \\ d_{t-1} \\ \vdots \\ d_1 \end{bmatrix} \quad t \in \{1, 2, \ldots\}. \tag{3.27}$$

[9] See Chapter 2.

Substitution of (3.27) into the lower equation of (3.26) now yields

$$y_t = HF^t z_0 + \begin{bmatrix} HG \\ HFG \\ \vdots \\ HF^{t-1}G \end{bmatrix}' \begin{bmatrix} u_t \\ u_{t-1} \\ \vdots \\ u_0 \end{bmatrix} + \begin{bmatrix} HE \\ HFE \\ \vdots \\ HF^{t-1}E \end{bmatrix}' \begin{bmatrix} d_t \\ d_{t-1} \\ \vdots \\ d_1 \end{bmatrix} \quad t \in \{1, 2, ...\}$$

or, in a compact form,

$$y_t = HF^t z_0 + R_t U_t + W_{t-1} L^{-1} D_{t-1}, \tag{3.28}$$

where R_t is a $q \times (t+1)m$ matrix.

Theorem 3.1 (*reduced form and state space model equivalence*). The reduced form model, (3.2) or (3.18), and the state space model in (3.26), are equivalent only if the following instrument multiplier equivalence holds:

$$\frac{\partial y_t}{\partial u_t} \equiv \Pi_0 = B_0 = D. \tag{3.29}$$

$$\frac{\partial y_t}{\partial u_{t-v}} \equiv \Pi_v = B_v + \sum_{i=1}^{v} A_i \Pi_{v-i} = HF^{v-1}G, \quad v \in \{1, 2, ...\}. \tag{3.30}$$

The dynamic multiplier sequence $\{\Pi_0, \Pi_1, \Pi_2, ...\}$ converges if, as for the reduced form model (3.6), the characteristic equation $|A(L) - \lambda I_q| = 0$ has all its roots inside the unit circle. In terms of Equation (3.28), stability requires convergence of the sequence $\{HF^iG\}_{i=0}^{\infty} = \{HG, HFG, HF^2G, ...\}$. For this to be true, it is *sufficient* that F is stable, or that $|F - \lambda I| = 0$ has all roots inside the unit circle. The two conditions for convergence are equivalent: $|F - \lambda I| = 0$ has roots inside the unit circle if and only if $|A(\mathrm{L}) - \lambda I_q| = 0$ has roots inside the unit circle.[10]

As indicated earlier, the stability property discussed here is an asymptotic concept. If it holds, then the multiplier sequence $\{\Pi_0, \Pi_1, \Pi_2, ...\}$ defined above, or at (3.10), (3.12) and (3.13), converges asymptotically to zero – meaning that the impact of any policy change or external shock on the target variables eventually dies out. However, in some cases, it is also possible to get exact convergence after a finite (possibly large) number of steps if the multiplier sequence goes to zero after s

[10] Preston and Pagan (1982).

terms: $\{\Pi_0, \Pi_1, \ldots, \Pi_s, 0, \ldots\}$, $\{D, HG, HFG, \ldots, HF^{s-1}G, 0, \ldots\}$, or $\{A_1, A_1^2, \ldots, A_1^s, 0, \ldots\}$.

This will happen if A_1 or F is a nilpotent matrix of order s, implying $A_1^s = 0$, $F^s = 0$ and that the roots of A_1 (or $A(L)$ or F in the case of multiple lags) are all zero. That is unlikely, though not impossible.

3.7 Are the instruments capable of achieving arbitrary desired targets?

As in the static case, the existence of policies capable of achieving certain defined objectives is related to the concept of controllability. However, as shown in Section 3.4, the policy problem may have become more complex with the introduction of dynamics. Moreover, it has to be handled in different ways depending on the form of the model: that is, on whether it is written in reduced form, in final form or in state space form. In this section we first define the concepts of controllability for each form in a loose way (Section 3.7.1); and then introduce formal definitions, as well as conditions that ensure that controllability of the type appropriate for dynamic policy problems actually holds (Sections 3.7.2 and 3.7.3).

3.7.1. Concepts of controllability in reduced or final form

The problems illustrated in Section 3.4 imply that there are four types of controllability in a dynamic policy environment. Formal definitions, and conditions for those forms of controllability to hold in practice, are analyzed in detail in Part IV. The conceptual definitions are as follows.

1. *Static controllability:* policy instruments have the ability to reach any specified set of target values, from an arbitrary initial position, *in expectation*, within a single decision period.
2. *Multi-period static controllability:* policy instruments have the ability to reach any specified sequence of desired target values (from an arbitrary initial position), in expectation, at every point within an interval containing an arbitrary number of consecutive decision periods.
3. *Dynamic controllability:* policy instruments have the ability to achieve an arbitrary set of target values, in expectation, at a single

point a certain number of periods in the future, given an arbitrary starting point and without concern for what values those targets or other variables might take along the way or after the target values have been achieved.

4. *Path controllability:* policy instruments have the ability to achieve an arbitrary set of target values a given number of decision periods after an arbitrary start; and then either hold those values or follow some pre-specified path of target values, again in expectation, at each decision point for an arbitrary period of time thereafter.

Formally, in the terms of our four-parameter theory of dynamic policy – given q and m – these concepts of controllability define the capacity to reach the desired targets over an interval of length T, i.e., $[t_0, t_0 + T]$, starting the policy actions in period $t_0 - S$:

1. Static controllability: $S = 0, \quad T = 0$.
2. Multi-period static controllability: $S = 0, \quad T > 0$.
3. Dynamic controllability: $S > 0, \quad T = 0$.
4. Path controllability: $S > 0, \quad T > 0$.

It is obvious that the conditions necessary to ensure controllability are going to involve having a matrix of policy multipliers of sufficient rank – that is, instruments with sufficient independent impacts on the target variables to move those targets from their starting point to their desired values within the prescribed time frame. Thus static controllability will require the impact multiplier matrix in (3.16) or (3.4) to have $\mathrm{r}[B_0] = \mathrm{r}[\Pi_1] = q \leq m$; and multi-period static controllability requires the same for all t, rather than in a single period (which is not obvious if the list of targets or instruments available changes over time). Dynamic controllability requires $r[A_1^{t-1}B_0, \ldots,] = r[\Pi_{t-1}, \ldots, \Pi_0] = q$, so that the target variables in the t-th row of (3.13) can be controlled: see Corollary 3.1 below. Finally, path controllability requires static controllability as a necessary condition. We will expand on this in Section 3.7.3.

These controllability concepts have several features in common:

(a) They all ignore the instrument costs of achieving the targets: that is, the costs or discomfort of having the policy instruments vary as much as may be required from their initial values, or from the policymaker's preferred values, in order to achieve their targets. This is a problem that we take into account later.

(b) It will become obvious, if it is not already, that static controllability (1) is necessary and sufficient for (2); and sufficient but not necessary for (3). It turns out that (1) is also necessary and sufficient for (4): see the discussion following Theorem 3.8 below. For that reason we do not follow that case further in this book.

(c) Given uncertainty, all controllability properties are defined in terms of achieving *expected* target values; not in terms of actual outcomes that will be subject to uncontrollable (and unknowable) shocks or errors that occur after the policy program is initiated. Since we are working with linear models, the expectations are mathematical expectations or "certainty equivalents." However, if we go to nonlinear models, the appropriate certainty equivalents would, by Jensen's inequality, no longer be mathematical expectations of the individual random terms or the coefficients in the model. And where there is parameter uncertainty, these expectations would only be first-order certainty equivalent at best; that is, mathematical expectations derived from a linearization of the "expected" model. Chapter 12 takes this point further.

3.7.2 Controllability in state space notation

Here, and in the next sub-section, we are concerned only with dynamic behavior with reference to models in state space systems. In this context, the control theory literature traditionally speaks of three forms of dynamic controllability: state controllability, null state controllability, and asymptotic state controllability.

3.7.2.1 State controllability

State controllability is the equivalent of dynamic controllability in conventional policy models, as we show below. Conditions that guarantee state controllability will therefore also guarantee dynamic controllability.

Consider the state space form (3.26):

$$\begin{cases} z_t = Fz_{t-1} + Gu_t + Ed_t \\ y_t = Hz_t + Du_t \end{cases} \quad \text{with } z_0 = a \in \mathrm{R}^k. \tag{3.31}$$

We define a sequence of instruments between 0 and s as $U^s = \{u_i\}_1^s \in \Omega_U$ and a sequence of the d terms is similarly defined as $D^s = \{d_i\}_1^s \in \Omega_D$.

Note that, if we know the sequence of u and d from 0 to s and the initial condition a, by solving system (3.31), we can obtain the value for state variable z at s. We can indicate this value as $z_s(a, U^s, D^s)$. We can now define state controllability as follows.

Definition 3.1 (*state controllability*). The state space form (3.31) is state controllable if and only if $\forall a, \bar{z} \in R^{pq+(g-1)m}$ and $\forall D^s \in \Omega_D$, $\exists U^s \in \Omega_U$, and a finite $s \geq 1$ such that $z_s(a, U^s, D^s) = \bar{z}$, where $\bar{z}$ is the desired outcome for this system at s.

This means that system (3.31) is controllable whenever there exists a sequence of instrument values, U^s, capable of moving that system from initial state a to some terminal state $\bar{z}$ within at least s periods, given D^s. The reasoning is that, by Equation (3.28), we know the solution, at any s, is

$$z_s\left(a, U^s, D^s\right) = F^s a + \begin{bmatrix} G \\ FG \\ \vdots \\ F^{s-1}G \end{bmatrix}' \begin{bmatrix} u_{s-1} \\ u_{s-2} \\ \vdots \\ u_0 \end{bmatrix} + \begin{bmatrix} E \\ FE \\ \vdots \\ F^{s-1}E \end{bmatrix}' \begin{bmatrix} d_s \\ d_{s-1} \\ \vdots \\ d_1 \end{bmatrix},$$

or in obvious notation,

$$z_s\left(a, U^s, D^s\right) = F^s a + Q_{s-1} U_{s-1} + V_{s-1} L^{-1} D_{s-1}. \tag{3.32}$$

Next we need the *Cayley–Hamilton theorem*: If F is $k \times k$ and $|\lambda I - F| = 0$ defines its characteristic roots as λ, then $p(F) = 0$ has roots $p(\lambda)$. The implication for (3.32) is that either $F^k = 0$ (F is nilpotent of order $s \leq k$); or F^k is a non-trivial linear combination of the preceding powers of F.

Using the above result, we can state Theorem 3.2.

Theorem 3.2 (*state controllability*). The state space form (3.31) is state controllable if and only if $Q \equiv [G\ FG\ \ldots\ F^{k-1}G]$ has rank k, i.e.,

$$r[Q] = r[G\ FG\ \ldots\ F^{k-1}G] = k \equiv qp. \tag{3.33}$$

Notice, for those who like to read ahead, that (3.33) is precisely the condition (in state space notation) that guarantees dynamic controllability in a conventional model. Thus, the following corollary holds.

Corollary 3.1. Theorem 3.1 shows the conventional model represented by (3.13) is equivalent to the state space model (3.31) if the rows corresponding to the identities within the stacked state vector are deleted, since the multiplier matrix equalities defined in (3.29) and (3.30) then hold. In that case, we can write the controllability condition, (3.33), in the notation of conventional models as $r[Q] = r[B_0, \ldots, A_1^{t-1}B_0] = r[\Pi_0, \ldots, \Pi_{t-1}] = q$. That was shown in Section 3.7.1. Notice, however, that this condition does not say how quickly an economy will transfer from a to b; only that it will do so within q periods or less. We return to this point, and a more general representation of dynamic controllability, in Part IV.

As can be seen by inspecting the state space form (3.31), state controllability, and thus the rank of Q, have to do with the natural dynamics generated by F (as expressed by its eigenvalues). That gives us the possibility of trying to control/modify those eigenvalues by introducing a policy rule for u, whose impact is transmitted via G, that superimposes a new dynamic pattern on the model's behavior. In effect, this changes the original eigenvalues into new ones subject to our choice.

We can use this idea to generate a theorem that will prove to be useful when we come to discuss the conditions for an economy's stabilizability (Section 3.9 below).

Theorem 3.3 (*state controllability*). The state space form (3.31) is state controllable if and only if every characteristic root of F, λ_i, is also controllable: that is, if $r[Q] = k$ implies and is implied by $r[F - \lambda_i I, G] = n$, $\forall \lambda_i \in \sigma[F]$, i.e., the set of eigenvalues of matrix F.

Since we have already established that state controllability in state space models is equivalent to dynamic controllability for conventional (reduced form) models, Theorem 3.3 implies the same result applies to the reduced form models (3.2) or (3.16)–(3.18): i.e., (3.2) or (3.18) is dynamically controllable if and only if every characteristic root of A_1 or A, respectively, is also controllable.

3.7.2.2 Null state controllability

Null state controllability can be defined as follows.

Definition 3.2 (*null state controllability*). System (3.31) is null state controllable if and only if $\forall a \in \mathrm{R}^k$ and for $D = \{0, \ldots, 0\}$, $\exists U^s \in \Omega_U$ and a finite $s \geq 1$ that imply $z_s(a, U^s) = 0$.

Notice that this leads to a relaxation of state controllability because it no longer implies "implicit costs" on the use of the instruments ($D = 0$ is no longer in the choice set, meaning that y_t is less constrained); *and* because, with a suitable redefinition of H, it can be made to apply to just a small number of targets (a sub-set of the endogenous/state variables in y_t) since the instruments can now be used without regard to their impact on the other variables in y_t. Thus the following theorems hold.

Theorem 3.4 (*state controllability and null state controllability*). For discrete time systems, state controllability implies, but is not implied by, null state controllability. Null state controllability is more widely applicable or realizable.

Theorem 3.5 (*null state controllability*). The state space form (3.31) is null controllable if and only if $\exists s \in \{0, m - 1\}$ implies $r[G, FG, \ldots, F^s G, F^{s+1} G] = r[G, FG, \ldots, F^s G]$; or if and only if every nonzero eigenvalue $\lambda \in \sigma[F]$ is controllable, i.e., $r[F - \lambda I, G] = k$.

Thus, null state controllability is the equivalent of controllability of the condensed system discussed in greater detail in Part IV.

3.7.2.3 Asymptotic state controllability

This property, known also as *stabilizability*, is the asymptotic version of the capacity to bring the economy back to its equilibrium path (the zero state, say) after any shock or other disturbance; i.e., $\exists U^s \in \Omega_U$ such that $\lim_{s \to \infty} z_s(a, U^s) = 0$.

Theorem 3.6 (*stabilizability*). System (3.31) is stabilizable if and only if every eigenvalue $\lambda \in \sigma[F]$, stable and unstable, is controllable; or, equivalently, if and only if $r[F - \lambda I, G] = k$. Thus, state controllability (C) implies null controllability (NC), which in turn implies stabilizability (S). But the reverse is not true.

The theorem is illustrated by Figure 3.2.

3.7.3 The existence of target path controllability conditions

Path controllability refers to the most complicated policy strategy and emphasizes the importance of hitting and then holding the economy to an arbitrary desired target path or stationary point thereafter. That involves finding target/instrument pairs that create a steady state equilibrium path with a dynamic model. Holding to a stationary point or

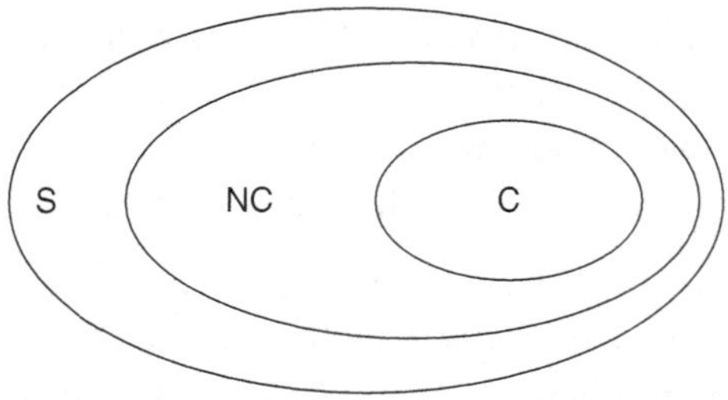

Figure 3.2 Relations among state controllability (C), null controllability (NC) and stabilizability (S)

to a certain target path fairly obviously depends on the model (economy) having the static controllability property, whereas hitting that point or path in the first place depends on having dynamic controllability properties (state controllability).

Path controllability thus is fully contained in our four-parameter policy problem, involving parameters S, T, q and m. Recall that below (3.7) we noted that every dynamic reduced form model of the economy, $\hat{A}(L)x_t = \hat{B}(L)u_t + \hat{d}_t$, has embedded within it a *static* model, $\hat{A}(1)y = \hat{B}(1)u + \hat{d}$, which describes its steady state or steady state equilibrium path behavior. Note that a steady state target path does not imply stationarity: i.e., the existence of an equilibrium point with no dynamic motion beyond t.

Theorem 3.7 (*stationarity and static controllability*). All points in target space can become stationary points, or a steady state path, for $[\hat{A}(L),\hat{B}(L)]$ where $r[\hat{A}(1)] = q$, if and only if $[\hat{A}(1), \hat{B}(1)]$ implies static controllability. The rank condition $r[\hat{A}(1)] = q$ precludes redundant equations.

The path of economic development in this case is defined by the multiplier sequences derived by stacking the equations from (3.12), the model's final form with the equation ordering reversed:

$$\begin{bmatrix} y_{T+S} \\ \vdots \\ y_{S+2} \\ y_{S+1} \end{bmatrix} = \left[\begin{array}{cccc|ccc} \Pi_0 & \Pi_1 & \cdots & \Pi_T & \Pi_{T+1} & \cdots & \Pi_{T+S} \\ & \ddots & \ddots & \vdots & \vdots & & \vdots \\ & & \ddots & \Pi_1 & \Pi_2 & \cdots & \Pi_{S+1} \\ 0 & & & \Pi_0 & \Pi_1 & \cdots & \Pi_S \end{array}\right] \begin{bmatrix} u_{T+S} \\ \vdots \\ \vdots \\ u_{S+1} \\ u_S \\ \vdots \\ u_1 \end{bmatrix} + errors, \tag{3.34}$$

where the multiplier sub-matrices Π_i are as defined in (3.10), or by (3.10) derived from (3.18), or by (3.29) and (3.30) in state space, depending on which model we are using.

Given that, we can state the following theorem.

Theorem 3.8 (*target path controllability*). The dynamic policy model $[\hat{A}(L), \hat{B}(L)]$ is target path controllable with lead S and interval T if and only if the multiplier matrix in (3.34), with dimensions $q(T + 1) \times m(T + S + 1)$, is of full rank; i.e.,

$$r[R_{T,S}] = r\begin{bmatrix} \Pi_0 & \Pi_1 & \cdots & \Pi_T & | & \Pi_{T+1} & \cdots & \Pi_{T+S} \\ & \ddots & \ddots & \vdots & | & \vdots & & \vdots \\ & & \ddots & \Pi_1 & | & \Pi_2 & \cdots & \Pi_{S+1} \\ 0 & & & \Pi_0 & | & \Pi_1 & \cdots & \Pi_S \end{bmatrix} = q(T+1). \quad (3.35)$$

This condition is necessary and sufficient. The corresponding counting rule for target path controllability, a necessary condition, is therefore $m(T + S + 1) \geq q(T + 1)$, as shown in Theorem 3.11 below.

The proof is fairly obvious because we need dynamic controllability to get from an arbitrary starting point to the first steady state or equilibrium path point at the end of the S periods of lead time: Figure 3.1. But we need multi-period static controllability thereafter to complete the T periods on the target path. It is clear that static controllability with m independent instruments and q targets, and $q \leq m$, will be sufficient for both parts. The only issue is whether static controllability is necessary as well. Buiter and Gersovitz (1984) provide a formal proof for that proposition.[11]

Consequently, we have Theorem 3.9:

Theorem 3.9 (*static and path controllability equivalence*). Consider the dynamic system $[\hat{A}(L), \hat{B}(L)]$. The following statements are equivalent:

(i) $[\hat{A}(L), \hat{B}(L)]$ is statically controllable.
(ii) $[\hat{A}(L), \hat{B}(L)]$ is path controllable for all S and T.

[11] Earlier, Buiter and Gersovitz (1981) noted that static controllability is sufficient for path controllability and argued that the necessary condition was $q \leq (2-1/q)m$. That result was later revised.

(iii) $r[R_T] = q(T+1)\ \forall T$.
(iv) $r[D] = r[\Pi_0] = r[B_0] = q \leq m$.

Condition (3.35) allows for the possibility that we may use different numbers of instruments or targets in each period, since, if we had equal numbers of targets and instruments, the problem would simply decompose into one of multi-period static controllability. We would be able to get onto the target path in the first period, and stay on it thereafter.

Theorem 3.10 (*target path controllability, minimum lead*). For the case where different (fewer) instruments are used in different (earlier) periods, some positive lead time $S > 0$ is needed. The minimum lead $\hat{S}$ is defined as follows:

$$r\left[R_{T,S}\right] < q(T+1) \qquad S = 0, 1, \ldots, \hat{S} - 1.$$
$$r\left[R_{T,\hat{S}}\right] = q(T+1)$$

Only with complete static controllability is anticipation unnecessary.

Theorem 3.11 (*target path controllability, necessary conditions*). The dynamic system $[\hat{A}(L), \hat{B}(L)]$ is target path controllable over the S lead periods only if the expanded counting rule $m(S+T+1) \geq q(T+1)$ is satisfied. But it is controllable over the T policy periods only if $q \geq m$ and the instruments are linearly independent.

In view of Theorems 3.8 and 3.11, any further elaboration of the path controllability property is unnecessary. It is implied if static controllability holds.

3.8 Uniqueness and observability

An economic system is said to be *observable* if every initial state z_0 can be determined from the observations on y_t, $t \geq 1$, over a finite number of periods. The system is therefore completely observable if every transition of the state eventually affects every element of the output vector. The connection to uniqueness is that, if the controllability property had led to a unique desired outcome, then if the system were also observable we would be able to determine a unique value for z_0. But if controllability had led to a multiplicity of possible outcomes, then it would not be possible to determine a unique value for z_0 from the y_t values. The system could no longer be said to be observable. Hence a test for observability is a test for uniqueness of the policies derived for an economy under control.

Controllability therefore reflects the existence of policies to achieve certain objectives. Observability instead asks the related question: is there a unique transfer available from the current state to the desired target values? This question may be of some importance in its own right for political economy reasons, but normally we discriminate between non-unique alternatives by taking that with the lowest instrument costs. Observability is thus of greater significance for control theorists who wish to minimize the number of state variables and ensure their stability. But it is usually a property with limited importance in economic policymaking. However, if instruments are set in a decentralized way, as occurs in a strategic context, observability becomes directly relevant.[12]

Formal conditions for observability are stated in the following theorem.

Theorem 3.12 (*observability*). The compact state space system (3.25) has $D = 0$, and implies

$$\begin{bmatrix} y_0 \\ y_1 \\ \vdots \\ y_{t-1} \end{bmatrix} = \begin{bmatrix} H \\ HF \\ \vdots \\ HF^{t-1} \end{bmatrix} y_0 + \begin{bmatrix} 0 & \cdots & \cdots & 0 \\ HG & \ddots & & \vdots \\ \vdots & \ddots & \ddots & \vdots \\ HF^{t-2}G & \cdots & HG & 0 \end{bmatrix} \begin{bmatrix} u_0 \\ \\ u_{t-2} \\ u_{t-1} \end{bmatrix}. \tag{3.36}$$

Observability requires the solution for y_0 from (3.36), and is therefore a property of this system, if and only if the matrix

$$M = \begin{bmatrix} H \\ HF \\ \vdots \\ HF^{t-1} \end{bmatrix}$$

is of full rank (possesses an inverse), i.e., $r[M] = k = qp$.

[12] For instance, the lack of observability could create coordination problems, as anticipating other agents' policies may become impossible because the other agents choices are no longer unique.

3.9 Stabilizability and control rules

So far our review of controllability has not considered explicitly what particular control path for the instruments is needed to reach a given set of dynamic objectives, or explored what the dynamics of that path might look like. The accent has been on whether those policies actually exist, possibly uniquely, and what conditions need to hold if they are to exist.

This is a natural state of affairs. Existence (and uniqueness) is a prior question before we come to the exact numerical values needed to reach certain targets, or the dynamics of the path leading to those targets. A good part of this book is devoted to the existence of such policies and the existence of economic and policy equilibria for the economy under study. Nevertheless, there is a natural interest in the characteristics and consequences (stability, path of outcomes, speed of convergence, size of policy interventions) of the instrument path. The rest of the book is concerned with those questions under a variety of different circumstances.

Consequently, at this point it is important to review the different kinds of policy rules that could be applied to an economy operating under uncertainty and shifting sets of information. The differences between them depend largely on how they react to or incorporate changes in the available information; and how successfully they eliminate errors made in the past, or allow for new expectations of future developments.

3.9.1 Dynamic control rules under changing information

It would be most sensible to control an economy, or any other dynamic system, in its reduced form since that describes the target outcomes period by period. We therefore take the economy to be defined by (3.2) for the single lag case, or by (3.4)–(3.7) for multiple lags and rewritten as (3.18), as may be needed.

Most texts assume that the economy is best controlled using a linear feedback rule, for the policy instruments, of the form

$$u_t = K_t y_{t-1} + k_t, \quad \text{for } t = 1, 2, \ldots, T \tag{3.37}$$

if (3.2) applies; or more generally of the form $u_t = K_t(\mathrm{L})y_t + k_t$, where $K_t(\mathrm{L}) = K_{t1}\mathrm{L} + \cdots + K_{tp}\mathrm{L}^p$, when (3.7) applies.

Rule (3.37) is taken from the idea of a servo-mechanism in engineering, and says that the next period's control action (policy instrument) should be set as a suitable function of the last observed value of the targets and endogenous variables determined within the system; or as the last observation of the p previous targets/endogenous values if there are multiple lags. It allows each policy setting to adjust to the latest information and the extent that past outcomes differ from what may have been expected and/or planned earlier due to unexpected shocks, random errors, changing expectations, implementation errors, or changing economic behavior. And it is optimal, in the sense of minimizing a loss function over the target variables, if the feedback matrix, K_t, and feedback gain, k_t, are expectations derived from the backward recursions of dynamic programming (or Pontryagin's approach) based on Bellman's Principle of Optimality.

Normally we take model coefficients and planners' preferences (priorities and target values) to be fixed and known, at least at each t, even if they are updated between each t and $t + 1$. But the external information, i.e., past errors and past external variables, plus the expectations for future errors and external variable values, which appear in the feedback gain term k_t (but not K_t), are stochastic and may change between periods (both in past realizations and in revised expectations for future realizations). Thus we should rewrite (3.37) with $K_{t/t}$ replacing K_t and $k_{t/t}$ replacing k_t, where $y_{t/t} = E_t(y_t) = E_t(y_t|\Omega_t)$ denotes the expectation of variable y conditional on the information set Ω_t. We define Ω_t to be the information set available to policymakers (but not necessarily to private agents) at *the start* of period t. Thus, in the language of Chapter 2 and Appendix 3A, (3.37) if properly used will display multi-period certainty equivalence with respect to $k_{t/t}$, and first-order certainty equivalence with respect to $K_{t/t}$.

Note the qualification "if properly used." This is important given the shifting information with respect to revisions to the values of past variables and updating of expectations for future variables. The same applies to our understanding of how the economy works, and of our understanding of the policymakers' priorities and target values. There is no guarantee that the policymakers will use all the available opportunities to update their information and expectations of the future when deciding on their policies in each period (or that they will use the same expectations as we do).

Hence, three types of dynamic policy rules are possible.

Definition 3.3 (*open loop policy rule*). An open loop policy rule is one that can be calculated, optimally or not, at the first planning period and then implemented irrespective of how the economy actually develops thereafter:

$$u_t = h_{t/1}(\Omega_1) = K_{t/1}(L)E_1\left[y_t \mid A(L), B(L), d_t\right] + k_{t/1} \quad \text{for each } t = 1,\ldots,T. \tag{3.38}$$

Open loop policies are therefore a function of the information available at the start of period $t = 1$, and are not updated or revised as new information becomes available. Nor do they react to, or use information on, the latest measured state of the economy: i.e., use $E_t(.)$ as opposed to $E_1(.)$. This is in contrast to both *feedback* and *closed loop policy rules* defined below.

Definition 3.4 (*feedback policy rule*). A feedback policy rule reacts to the latest information on past realizations of variables in the model; but not to changes in expectations or probabilistic information on future variables, or improved coefficients in the model (an improved understanding of the economy's behavior) going forward. The decisions depend only on the past evolution of the system:

$$u_t = h_{t/1}(\Omega_t) = K_{t/1}(L)E_t\left[y_t \mid E_1\{A(L), B(L)\}, E_t(d_t)\right] + k_{t/1} \quad \text{for } t = 1,\ldots,T. \tag{3.39}$$

In other words, the above definition says that feedback policy rules use the latest information on the state of the economy, but unrevised decision rule parameters and unrevised expectations for the future.

Definition 3.5 (*closed loop policy rule*). A closed loop policy rule takes account of all the latest information available at each t, including probabilistic information on disturbances, any revised expectations for future variables, and any revisions made to the model or our understanding of the policymakers' preferences and priorities. All of this in the same feedback rule form. Thus:

$$u_t = h_{t/t}(\Omega_t) = K_{t/t}(L)E_t\left[y_t \mid E_t\{A(L), B(L), d_t\}\right] + k_{t/t} \quad \text{for } t = 1,\ldots,T. \tag{3.40}$$

A closed loop rule therefore reacts to all current information, including *currently* expected future events or outcomes, current target values and priorities, and our current understanding of the economy (model). Thus, at each t, it uses what is presently known about information that will be obtained with certainty later, and anticipates continuing to do so at each future date. Hence the rule (3.40) anticipates "closing the loop" by using currently expected future measurements of the system – and knows that it will continue to do so in the future. By contrast, a feedback rule uses the latest measurements from the past, but fails to anticipate future measurements or the closing of the loop implied by recomputing $h_{t/t}(.)$ with each new information set. The decisions will be inferior unless nothing happens to change our expectations for the future.

Of course, it is always possible to manufacture various hybrids such as the Athans, Kuh, Papademos, Pyndick, Ozan and Wall (1976) sequentially updated open loop rule, $u_t = h_{t/j}(\Omega_j)$ for $1 < j < t$; or where the variable values are updated by a feedback rule, but not in the model: i.e., the rule at (3.39) with $k_{t/t}$ in place of $k_{t/1}$. But these are simple variations. More important are the cases where not all agents (players in a policy game; or government vs. private sector) use the same information. These are cases of asymmetric information, and need to be treated separately when we get to models with multiple policymakers (Chapter 10). Similarly, we will have to extend these ideas when the economy's current behavior depends jointly on the model's expectations/projections of future outcomes, and current outcomes that affect those future outcomes through the economy's natural dynamics. That is, the REs formulation introduced in Chapter 11.

3.9.2 *Stabilizability*

As noted above, the traditional approach to controlling a dynamic system is to introduce a servo-mechanism, which endogenizes the policy instruments as a function of past outcomes of the system. Then the parameters of that function – the control rule in effect – can be chosen to give the *controlled system* certain desirable characteristics. In a linear discrete-time context, there are three types of rule to consider (Phillips 1954, 1957):

(a) Proportional rules: $u_t = K_t y_{t-1} + k_t$, say.

(b) Integral rules: $u_t = \sum_{i=1}^{p} K_{t,i} y_{t-i} + k_t = K_t(\mathrm{L}) y_t + k_t$.

(c) Differential (or derivative) rules: $u_t = K_t \Delta y_{t-1} + k_t$.

Obviously the proportional rule is the same as our feedback rule for a single-lag model, though it can be generalized to a multi-period integral rule for use in a multi-lag model. In that sense the proportional and derivative rules are just special cases of the integral rule.

We also noted above that the distinction between a feedback rule and a closed loop rule is that a feedback control is essentially backward-looking and is designed to take account of any innovations and unexpected disturbances $d_{t-1} - E_{t-1}(d_{t-1})$ in the error terms and exogenous variables (and hence in the targets) that have appeared since the last decision was made. Conventionally k_t is conditioned on Ω_1 even though the feedback mechanism itself responds to Ω_t in (3.39). This contrasts with (3.40) where policies respond to a combination of feedback from unanticipated disturbances in the past *and* feedforward terms from any anticipated disturbances in the future.

With this distinction in mind, we can now consider the effect of a simple feedback rule, $u_t = K_t y_{t-1} + k_t$, on the behavior of the targets of the reduced form economy (3.2). Substituting that rule into (3.2) shows that the economy, under control, would behave as

$$y_t = \left[A_1 + B_0 K_t\right] y_{t-1} + B_0 k_t + C_0 w_t. \tag{3.41}$$

The effect is to change the matrix controlling the dynamics of the system from A_1 to $A_1 + B_0 K_t$. This changes the stability of the system; including the characteristic roots and underlying cycles exhibited in the economy. The general case with multiple lags is very similar: substitute the integral control rule $u_t = K_t(\mathrm{L}) y_t + k_t$ into (3.6) to show the economy under control as

$$u_t = \left[A(\mathrm{L}) + B(\mathrm{L}) K_t(\mathrm{L})\right] y_t + B(\mathrm{L}) k_t + d_t. \tag{3.42}$$

In either case, we see that the effect of the control rule is to attenuate the effects of shocks or unexpected disturbances and change the economy's dynamics and degree of inherent stability at the same time. In fact, since the control rule parameters (K_t, k_t) are subject to choice, we can choose them to get the dynamic characteristics, degree of smoothing or degree of stability that we want. Specifically, we can invoke Theorem 3.6 to show that, given dynamic (state) controllability, we can choose K_t to deliver an arbitrary set of eigenvalues for the controlled system (3.41) or (3.42); that is, to control the choice of eigenvalues of the composite matrix $(A_1 + B_0K_t)$, or $[A(L) + B(L)K_t(L)]$, to deliver the cycles, the stability and degree of smoothing that we want. That is the importance of Theorem 3.6: the economy is stabilizable.

Since Theorem 3.6 was stated exclusively in terms of the state space models of Sections 3.5, 3.6 and 3.7, it will be useful to restate it here in terms of a conventional reduced form model (3.2); or in terms of (3.6) if there are multiple lags.

Theorem 3.13 (*stabilizability in a reduced form model*). An economy represented by the system (3.2), or (3.6), is stabilizable in the sense that a policy rule of the form $u_t = K_t y_{t-1} + k_t$ (or $u_t = K_t(L)y_t + k_t$) can be found that will stabilize that economy, up to an arbitrary set of eigenvalues, if the economy is dynamically controllable in the sense of rank $[A_1^{t-1}B_0, \ldots, B_0] = q$; or of rank $[A^{t-1}B, \ldots, B] = qp$ from (3.18) if we are using the dynamic system (3.6).

Proof. See Wonham (1974). ■

Comment 3.1. Theorem 3.13 implies that policies can always be found to guarantee that the economy will return to a suitable path after unanticipated shocks or changes in the information sets appear, if the economy itself is dynamically controllable.

3.9.3 Cyclical control

Can we go any further? It is a standard result that the dynamic properties of a system such as (3.41), our economy under control, are fully determined by the roots of that difference equation. Write those roots, the eigenvalues of $(A_1 + B_0K_t)$, as

$$\lambda_i = a_i \pm b_i\sqrt{-1} = r_i\left(\cos\theta_i \pm \sqrt{-1}\sin\theta_i\right), \text{ where } i = 1,\ldots,q. \quad (3.43)$$[13]

[13] If the roots are not all complex, some imaginary parts, b_i, will be zero; implying a geometrically declining/increasing trend with infinite cycle length.

Then the economy under control has q elementary cycles with amplitude $r_i = \sqrt{a_i^2 + b_i^2}$ and damping factor $1/r_j$ per period; and cycle length $2\pi/\theta_i$, where θ_i is computed from $\cos\theta_i = a_i/r_i$. Since we can choose to have any roots we wish by choice of K_t, all these characteristics – including guaranteed stabilizability – are within our control by choice of suitable feedback policy rule parameters.

However, that is as far as we can go by choice of K_t. If $(A_1 + B_0K_t)$ has a matrix of eigenvectors Y, and diagonal matrix of eigenvalues $\Lambda = diag\{\lambda_1, \ldots, \lambda_q\}$, then we have $Y Y = I$ as a property of the eigenvector matrix and we rewrite $(A_1 + B_0K_t)Y = \Lambda Y$ as

$$(A_1 + B_0K_t) = \Lambda YY' = \sum \lambda_i y_i y'_i. \tag{3.44}$$

This shows that, while we can choose the dynamics, degree of stability and cyclical characteristics of our economy under control via K_t, we cannot choose the relative importance of those component cycles or how they combine to produce the outcomes or pattern of growth in each target variable. Hence we cannot choose the outcomes we want. This is because K_t is of dimension $q \times m$ and, unless $q = m$, we cannot choose K_t to yield an arbitrary set of elements in $(A_1 + B_0K_t)$, and hence whatever eigenvectors (in addition to eigenvalues) we need to deliver the exact dynamic or cyclical outcomes we want in each individual target variable. Evidently, that will only be possible in cases with static controllability: when $q = m$.

3.9.4 *Error reduction properties and "reachability"*

An interesting question is how fast a policy error, that is a discrepancy between a target variable and its desired value, can be eliminated. Evidently an approximate answer from (3.43) is that such deviations will be reduced by r_1 of their original size, or by $(r_1)^t$ after t periods, where r_1 is the size (spectral radius) of the largest eigenvalue in the economy under control: (3.41) or (3.42).

However, this is rather an approximate measure as it ignores the influence of the other roots of the system and derives from a series of inequalities $\|x_t\|_\infty \le \|x_t\|_2^{1/2} < r_1 \|x_{t-1}\|_2^{1/2}$ in the vector of deviations $x_t = y_t - \bar{y}_t$, when $\bar{y}_t$ contains the set of desired values at t.

On the other hand, it is obvious that an integral control rule of a certain order will do better in reaching the given target values than a control rule of a lower order (or control rule of a different type). Salmon (1982) shows this formally. To eliminate the discrepancy between the current state y_t and its target value $\overline{y}_t$ at some future date, we need that state to be determined by a difference equation system of at least an *error correction* form of order p:

$$(I - L)^p y_t = D(L)y_{t-p}, \tag{3.45}$$

where $D(L) = [A(L) + B(L)K_t(L)]$ is a matrix polynomial in the lag operator L, and where $p - 1$ is the order of the difference equation determining $\overline{y}_t$. Thus, if y_t and $\overline{y}_t$ follow difference equations of equal order, then the "policy errors" $x_t = y_t - \overline{y}_t$ will tend to a (nonzero) constant. If y_t follows a system of lower order than that of $\overline{y}_t$, the policy errors will eventually explode. But if y_t follows a difference system of higher order, the errors will eventually be eliminated.

How can we use that information here? Taking the general case and realizing that the initial conditions, y_0 and earlier, are not available for choice, the general feedback decision rule $u_t = K_t(L)y_t + k_t$ is of order zero at most in period $t = 1$, of order 1 in period $t = 2$, and of order $t - 1$ in period t and so on. Since the underlying economy has p lags, the controlled economy at t will follow a difference equation system of order $\max\{t - 1, p\}$. Hence for t large enough, and assuming the existence of sufficient instruments and that $\overline{y}_t$ follows a system of order $p - 1$ or less, we can be sure that our policy rule will be powerful enough to reach its targets (eliminate any policy failures: x_t). Hence, for $t > p$:

(a) An integral control rule is necessary in general to ensure convergence on the target values.
(b) The big policy adjustments will occur in the early periods ($t < p$) because the control rule lacks sufficient power (is of too low an order) at that stage. Thus, other things equal, policy "failures" tend to increase in the early stages of a policy problem, but get smaller later on. However, this result can be overridden when forward-looking (market) expectations play a role and policymakers make suitable announcements of policy actions to be taken in the future.[14]
(c) Smoother policy adjustments will appear in later periods ($t > p$) when the control rule has gained sufficient power.

[14] See Chapter 12 for a detailed analysis of this possibility.

Thus any target is reachable, given appropriate instruments, if the lead time is long enough and the control rule is of sufficient order.

3.10 Conclusions

The evolution of an economy is typically formulated in terms of a structural model whose equations describe the behavior of markets, activities, and behavioral or institutional responses to particular events or variables. But to understand the impacts of a policy change, or to make forecasts of possible future behavior, the model has to be solved as a system: either via its reduced form (to account for the simultaneity and interactions between its components) or in final form (to show how those interactions, direct and indirect, will impact over time).

In this chapter we have shown how such an analysis naturally leads to a consideration of policy multipliers: the immediate, dynamic and cumulative impacts of policy changes on the policy targets on other endogenous variables. Then, given the positive properties of the system as represented by the multipliers, the normative question arises: will we be able to find policies that can move the economy from its current position to some pre-specified and more desirable state, either immediately or within a specified period of time?

To that end, we have considered three forms of controllability and derived the conditions under which each is available: static controllability (the targets can be reached immediately, in expectation); dynamic controllability (the targets can be reached by a given time period in the future); and path controllability (the targets can be achieved at a given time in the future, and then held to a pre-specified path thereafter). If none of these conditions for controllability is satisfied, there may be no solution for the policymaker's problem. Since the conditions concerned are all rank conditions on the associated multipliers matrices, the advantage of this approach is that we can confirm the existence of appropriate policies in general, and without having to solve the whole system or evaluate the likely policies on a trial-and-error basis for all the possible scenarios on all information sets of interest.

In addition to controllability, we have investigated the related (and possibly more important) property of stabilizability: under what conditions can we find policies or policy rules that guarantee that the economy will return to a stable path after any unanticipated shocks or changes (errors) in the information set?

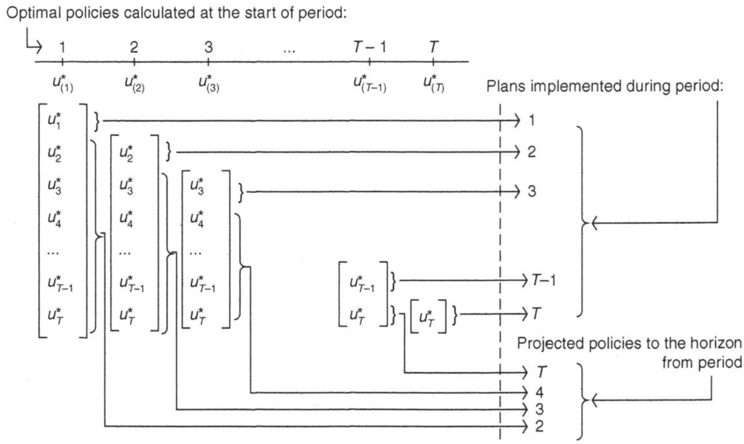

Figure 3.3 A schematic view of the sequence of an optimal policy plan

The conditions for stabilizability are essentially the same as for dynamic controllability. But it is of interest to extend these results to show the extent to which we can control or change the cycles operating in the economy, or the speed with which errors (the distance between the target variables and their intended values) can be reduced. In the latter context, we have drawn a sharp distinction between open loop, feedback and closed loop policies, which will prove extremely important later when we come to consider how to accommodate forward-looking expectations and strategic behavior into the range of possible policies.

Appendix 3A. Multi-period certainty equivalence

In Chapter 2, we introduced certainty equivalence by assuming a single information set to express the expectations. That is correct for a static framework. In a dynamic setup, we have changing information sets, Ω_t, one for each period. So whether we calculate the policies required for each period sequentially for $t = 1,\ldots,T$, or jointly from a stacked vector using a final form model like (3.17), or a state space model like (3.21), those calculations will have to be conditioned on the latest information available. But they can be recalculated for the remaining decisions for $t,\ldots,T$ based on each subsequent information set Ω_t. Each recalculation will involve a new initial condition, new expectations for the uncertain variables/parameters *and* for future shocks and future exogenous variables. Each time we do this, we will generate a new evaluation of the appropriate policies for period t, and new forecasts of what we currently expect future policies to be in the periods $t - 1,\ldots,T$, as shown in Figure 3.3.

Thus, since we are updating each time to take into account changes that may have occurred in past outcomes, in current parameters and exogenous events, and in future expected shocks, this sequence of multi-period certainty calculations takes us from a set of open loop policies to closed loop policies (including feedback terms).

PART II

From the classical to the new theory of economic policy

4 *The Lucas critique*

Summary. The most powerful objection leveled at the Tinbergen–Theil approach has been the Lucas critique: every policy introduced into an economy generates a reaction by the private sector or other policymakers that invalidates the premise upon which the original policy interventions were calculated. Taken literally, this means that all policies designed in a parametric context are in vain because they will have different effects than intended and perhaps no effect at all. This chapter illustrates the critique and shows that it reflects strategic interactions between rational players/policymakers, often implicitly modeled by using REs. Finally, it emphasizes that the resolution of the critique is to take the underlying policy game into account explicitly.

4.1 The essence of the critique

Policy evaluation exercises using econometric models in the tradition of Tinbergen and Theil's approach assume that private agents' behavior rules remain fixed while the government considers variations of its policy rules.[1] Lucas noted that if private agents solve optimization problems, then their actions depend on the government's policy rule: if the policy rule is changed, agents will adjust their behavior. Because the traditional theory of economic policy misses this dependence, it will not give reliable policy advice.

In other words, in the decision models presented in earlier chapters, the behavior of private agents is assumed to be predictable on the basis of a given specification of the behavioral functions and the identification of the fixed parameters. Policy decisions are determined by setting certain objectives and taking into account the relationships between these objectives and policy instruments based on the behavior of

[1] We can refer to these (either static or dynamic) contexts as parametric policy problems.

private agents. However, this approach ignores the feedback effect of government decisions on the behavioral *functions* of private agents.

For instance, we can assume: (a) that government influences national income (through government spending G on consumption and investment), or disposable income (through taxes and transfers in addition to government consumption and investment); (b) that private consumption will be affected by fiscal policy: if $C = c(Y - T + TR)$, where C is consumption, c is the marginal propensity to consume, Y is national income, T is tax revenues and TR is transfers to households; (c) that fiscal policy will affect C through G (which acts on Y), as well as T and TR (which act on C). This model would account for consumers' reactions to government action. However, we may also wish to account for the fact that changes in policy regimes (or the rules by which government policy choices are made) can influence the *parameters* of private behavioral functions: in our example, the marginal propensity to consume. If this were to happen, it would affect the sensitivity of private sector decisions to government decisions and/or the *functional form* of private agents' behavior. This is the substance of the critique advanced by Lucas (1976) against the Tinbergen–Theil model of economic policy.

The analytical models used as a basis for decision models are normally the product of a combination of theory and econometric analysis that establishes the exact specification and numerical form of the behavioral functions and independent variables, as well as the values of the parameters. Econometric assessments are based on the available data about the relevant variables in past situations (characterized by the presence of certain external shocks, or certain types of policy). After testing, the model is used to forecast the consequences of particular policy changes; e.g., an increase in government spending, an optimal monetary policy design. This is, however, accomplished by taking as given and invariant the estimated values of the parameters and the form of the behavioral functions of private agents (e.g., the propensity to consume, the form of consumption function) in the new situation. But there is no guarantee that those values or functional forms would remain constant. Suppose that government spending had not been adjusted in previous years, or that any adjustment in the past had involved different forms of spending: e.g., investment in place of government consumption and transfers; or had involved certain types of government spending (teachers' salaries) rather than others (student canteens). A change in the volume and/or content of public expenditure may give rise to new forms of private behavior. For example, a program to increase the number of student canteens might change students' propensity to consume so that it differed from that estimated in econometric models based on data collected before the number of canteens was increased.

If model parameters do change, reflecting a change in the behavior of the system, but the "old" model is taken as a constraint in government decision making, the ensuing policies will not be optimal at all. They would be so only if private behavior did not change. In other words, the constraint underlying the design of government action is not a guaranteed constraint but is likely to change as government behavior itself changes.

4.2 A formal exposition

Following Cuthbertson and Taylor (1987), let us assume the following description of the private agents' behavior at time *t*:

$$y_t = \alpha x_t + \beta E(z_{t+1} \mid \Omega_t) + \eta_t, \tag{4.1}$$

where y_t, the dependent variable, is a function of some other variable, x_t, as well as the expected value at time $t + 1$ of a third variable z_{t+1} (conditioned on the information set Ω_t available at t) and a stochastic disturbance, $_t$.

Assume also that each z_t is stochastically dependent on the values of z in the previous two periods, i.e., it follows a second-order autoregressive process:

$$z_t = \phi_1 z_{t-1} + \phi_2 z_{t-2} + \varepsilon_t, \tag{4.2}$$

where ε_t is white noise, with $E(\varepsilon_t|\Omega_{t-i}) = 0$, $0 < i < t$. The RE of z_{t+1} is then

$$E(z_{t+1} \mid \Omega_t) = \phi_1 z_t + \phi_2 z_{t-1}. \tag{4.3}$$

Substituting (4.3) into (4.1), we have the true model of the economy if (4.2) holds as specified:

$$y_t = \alpha x_t + \beta(\phi_1 z_t + \phi_2 z_{t-1}) + \eta_t. \tag{4.4}$$

The econometrician will actually estimate a function of the form:

$$y_t = \alpha x_t + \gamma_1 z_t + \gamma_2 z_{t-1} + \eta_t, \tag{4.5}$$

which is equivalent to the *true* model of the economy.[2]

The policymaker takes an estimate of (4.5), and from that determines an optimal policy. This policy remains valid if implementing it does not change the form of Equation (4.2). That may not be the case, especially if changes are made in the *rules* of government decisions. For example, imagine that the intermediate target of monetary policy is changed from money supply to the interest rate. This may alter the nature of the autoregressive process that generates z_t – which might be better represented in some other way. For example, assume that z_t represents the money supply. If the intermediate target of monetary policy is the money supply, we can show z_t as being affected by the values of z in the previous two periods. If, however, the intermediate target is the interest rate, the money supply at time t can be better represented by a *random walk* process, which is a specific *autoregressive process* of order 1:

$$z_t = z_{t-1} + \varepsilon_t. \tag{4.6}$$

If this is the case, the description of the economy's behavior given by (4.5) is no longer accurate. In order to obtain an appropriate policy, (4.5) needs to be replaced by another relationship – in this case obtained by substituting (4.6) into (4.1):

$$y_t = \alpha x_t + \beta z_t + \eta_t. \tag{4.7}$$

However, the choice between (4.5) and (4.7) as the constraint on the optimization process leading to the policy decision (and therefore the selection of the intermediate target) obviously cannot be made if we do not already know the outcome of the decision, since the behavior of the economy changes in response to the government decision. We are thus faced with a situation where we do not know the right model.

[2] Estimates of γ_1 and γ_2 are in fact estimates of nonlinear functions of the "deep parameter" β and the historically contingent, possibly policy dependent, parameters ϕ_1 and ϕ_2, since $\gamma_1 = \beta\phi_1$ and $\gamma_2 = \beta\phi_2$.

4.3 Deep parameters and rational expectations: a resolution?

Acknowledging the Lucas critique, there are a number of ways to redefine the public decision process in a more satisfactory fashion, at least at the theoretical level. One way to circumvent Lucas' critique is to focus directly on *deep parameters*, such as β in Equation (4.4), which can ensure the stability of the relation. Deep parameters are those that appear in the functions describing consumer tastes and technology, which should not change in any systematic way as a result of changes in economic circumstances and the countercyclical policies.[3]

A shortcoming of the approach based on fixed deep parameters concerns the tendency of these parameters to drift. Lucas raised his critique at a time when Keynesian macroeconometric models were highly respected as tools for quantitative policy evaluations. Despite this, he stressed that the methods used in econometric forecasting were often found to contradict the assumption that agents' behavioral rules were fixed and, as a result, the coefficients in the more important forecasting equations were frequently adjusted.[4] Lucas left this drift process in the coefficients unexplained. Neither macroeconomic theory nor the RE econometric models constructed after Lucas' critique explain this drift phenomenon. And, although the econometric forecasting literature has taken the issue of coefficient drift increasingly seriously, it still offers no economic explanation of it. Parameter drift is therefore a key piece of evidence that government's beliefs about the economy and its policies toward inflation and stabilization have evolved over time.

A way to derive a consistent relationship between economic targets and instruments based on deep parameters is by introducing REs. This solution is, however, just a way to circumvent the main argument against the Tinbergen–Theil theory of economic policy: the existence of strategic interactions between the policymaker and other agents. It is nevertheless convenient because it implies an implicit consideration of the strategic interactions between government and private sector as REs can be introduced into the decision maker's constraints formulated in term of deep parameters only after introducing and solving

[3] For an opposing view, see, e.g., Vercelli (1991), who argues that even tastes and technology are not really invariant to changes in economic policy rules.

[4] His interpretation of these adjustments was that the models are typically only approximations of the economy, with the relationships changing over time: that is, with arbitrarily drifting coefficients.

the private sector's optimization problem.[5] In a simple static context, as we shall see in the next chapter, doing this is typically equivalent to solving a Stackelberg game.

This chapter argues that drift can better be explained by formulating public decision making in an explicitly strategic manner. This means considering the strategic interactions between policymakers, or between policymakers and private agents, extended perhaps to include learning and the possibility of model misspecifications.

4.4 Overcoming the critique

The Lucas critique is undoubtedly well founded and raises both practical and theoretical problems. At a practical level, the amount by which parameters change in response to the change in economic policies is important. If the change is small, designing policy on the basis of previously estimated values will be broadly reliable. Obviously, reliability also depends on the data set used to estimate the parameters: the larger the set and the more it encompasses situations in which different policies were in use, the less the parameters will vary and the greater is the reliability of the model's determination of optimal policies. In the 1970s many macroeconomic relationships broke down as a consequence of major changes in the policy regime (for example, the Phillips curve) as agents adjusted their behavior and future expectations to fit the new environment.

From a theoretical point of view, the Lucas critique underscores the presence of reciprocal interactions between the behavior of private agents and that of the government. In particular, the private sector plays an active rather than passive role, changing its behavior as expectations about government behavior change.[6] The critique is a response to the fact that the traditional approach to the economic policy does not admit this sort of interaction. Once we recognize the fact that the behavioral functions of private agents can themselves change in relation to public choices, we have to accept that both government

[5] In Section 4.5 we formally show the link between REs and strategic behavior in a dynamic model.

[6] Leeper's (1991) distinction between active and passive monetary policies is a powerful example of this.

and private agents must consider the reciprocal responses to their decisions. This suggests we need a change of approach, to move from a parametric to a strategic context. The usual and easy solution is to introduce REs. However, the most natural way to tackle the problem is to make use of game theory, since dynamic games are specifically structured to model strategic interactions between agents and in any case nest RE models as a particular case – as we show in the next section. The rest of this book is about this strategic view of economic policy management.

Questions raised by the Lucas critique have a specific relevance for the evolution of agents' conduct and market performance since the 1980s. The spread of economic knowledge, liberalization and international opening of markets, the rising importance of financial markets and the speed of changes in those markets all imply the formation and spread of forward-looking expectations. By their nature, these features mean that sudden changes are possible, but follow rules that are difficult to detect.

There are at least two consequences relevant for economic policy:

(a) First, economic trends are more often the outcome of conventions and "fads." In this situation only public policy can move the economy out of a liquidity trap, unemployment, and, more generally, undesired or undesirable equilibria.
(b) Public policy must take account of the active nature of private agents' conduct as well as the effects policy has on the formation of market expectations. Hence, public action should not breed expectations that make it ineffective. On the contrary, it should try to create expectations that generate desirable outcomes. How to do that is investigated in detail in Chapter 12. It reflects some necessary features of public policy that may limit the range of feasible policy, but that if used in combination with announcements ("forward guidance" in Federal Reserve language[7]) of future policies can actually enhance their power.

[7] See Woodford (2007, 2008) or Williams (2011). Forward guidance strategies have also been adopted by the Reserve Bank of New Zealand, the Norges Bank and the Riksbank, who publish forecasts of their future interest rates in an attempt to enhance their ability to steer market expectations.

In summary, the evolution of economic systems, while making public intervention more necessary, may also impose some restrictions on the range of effective policies.

The importance of financial markets in these conclusions cannot be overstated. They are the main mechanism for channeling the influence of expectations and, hence, for creating limits to or enhancements of the effectiveness of public policy. This is because expectations in financial markets change more rapidly or more sensitively than in other markets. Since financial instruments are promises rather than physical objects, by their very nature they express evaluations of the future to a larger extent than physical assets do. Nevertheless, financial assets, like physical assets, have a value in the present. At different points in the subsequent analysis we will underscore the interaction between public action and private agents' behavior through the influence of public action on private expectations.

4.5 The link between rational expectations and strategic behavior

This section establishes a formal link between models with forward-looking RE terms and strategic behavior by multiple players, when those players (one of whom may be the private sector or a representative agent) have objectives well-defined in terms of the endogenous variables of the model. Those objectives will be the normal goals of economic policy in the sense of, say, (2.15) if the player is a policymaker. But more generally the objectives might be to achieve a particular wage or price level in the economy as a whole if the player is the private sector; or certain interest rates in the financial markets; or (more likely) to forecast as accurately as possible what the government's policies and outcomes are likely to be. Again, the objective function will be of the form (2.15).

Given that, and at the risk of notational complication, consider a policy game between two players over two periods $(t, t+1)$. The two objective functions are[8]

$$L^{(i)} = (y - \bar{y}^{(i)})' Q^{(i)} (y - \bar{y}^{(i)}) = \tilde{y}^{(i)\prime} Q^{(i)} \tilde{y}^{(i)} \quad \text{for } i = 1,2, \tag{4.8}$$

[8] Note that here we are using a different notation (superscripts) to index players, since the sub-index refers to time.

where $y = \begin{bmatrix} y_t \\ y_{t+1} \end{bmatrix}$ are the target variables in the problem, and $\bar{y}^{(i)} = \begin{bmatrix} \bar{y}_t^{(i)} \\ \bar{y}_{t+1}^{(i)} \end{bmatrix}$ are the target values assigned to those variables by player i.

We define the preference weights accordingly: $Q^{(i)} = diag(Q_t^{(i)}, Q_{t+1}^{(i)})$. The underlying economic model could be described by a two-period stacked final form similar to (3.13): $y = \begin{bmatrix} B_0 & 0 \\ A_1 B_0 & B_0 \end{bmatrix} u + d$ say. Partitioning the instruments, u, between players, and allowing the players to have different target variables and target values (deleting non-target rows), the model from player i's perspective becomes

$$\tilde{y}^{(i)} = R^{(i,i)} u^{(i)} + R^{(i,j)} u^{(j)} + c^{(i)} \text{ for } i, j = 1,2 \text{ and } i \neq j, \tag{4.9}$$

where $R^{(i,i)} = \begin{bmatrix} R_{t,t}^{(i,i)} & R_{t,t+1}^{(i,i)} \\ R_{t+1,t}^{(i,i)} & R_{t+1,t+1}^{(i,i)} \end{bmatrix}$ describes player i's responses to his own policies $u^{(i)} = \begin{bmatrix} u_t^{(i)} \\ u_{t+1}^{(i)} \end{bmatrix}$; $R^{(i,j)} = \begin{bmatrix} R_{t,t}^{(i,j)} & R_{t,t+1}^{(i,j)} \\ R_{t+1,t}^{(i,j)} & R_{t+1,t+1}^{(i,j)} \end{bmatrix}$ his target's responses to player j's decisions $u^{(j)} = \begin{bmatrix} u_t^{(j)} \\ u_{t+1}^{(j)} \end{bmatrix}$; and $c^{(i)} = d - \bar{y}^{(i)}$. In other words, the matrix $[R^{(1,1)}, R^{(1,2)}]$ and symmetrically $[R^{(2,1)}, R^{(2,2)}]$ can be obtained by picking out the appropriate columns from the matrix of dynamic multipliers in (3.13) when $v = 2$.

Player 1 can substitute (4.9) into (4.8) for $i = 1$ to obtain his optimal policy reaction function:

$$u^{(1)} = -[R^{(1,1)\prime} Q^{(1)} R^{(1,1)}]^{-1} R^{(1,1)\prime} Q^{(1)} (c^{(1)} + R^{(1,2)} u^{(2)}). \tag{4.10}$$

Similarly, player 2 can substitute (4.9) into (4.8) for $i = 2$ to obtain a corresponding reaction function for $u^{(2)}$. In a compact form, both reaction functions can be described by[9]

$$\begin{bmatrix} I & -D^{(1)} \\ -D^{(2)} & I \end{bmatrix} \begin{pmatrix} u^{(1)} \\ u^{(2)} \end{pmatrix} = \begin{pmatrix} F^{(1)} c^{(1)} \\ F^{(2)} c^{(2)} \end{pmatrix}, \tag{4.11}$$

[9] Note that solving (4.11) yields the Nash (non-cooperative) equilibrium for this game (see Chapter 10).

where $F^{(i)} = -[R^{(i,i)\prime}Q^{(i)}R^{(i,i)}]^{-1}\, R^{(i,i)\prime}Q^{(i)}$ and $D^{(i)} = F^{(i)}R^{(i,j)}$ for $i,j = 1,2$ and $i \neq j$.

Now, take the top sub-vector out of (4.9) for player 1, and substitute $u^{(2)}$ out using the lower equation in (4.11); we get (in obvious notation)

$$\begin{aligned}\tilde{y}_t^{(1)} &= \left(R_{t,t}^{(1,1)} \quad R_{t,t+1}^{(1,1)}\right)u^{(1)} + \left(R_{t,t}^{(1,2)} \quad R_{t,t+1}^{(1,2)}\right)[D^{(2)}u^{(1)} + F^{(2)}c^{(2)}] + c_t^{(1)} \\ &= \{R_{t,t}^{(1,1)} + R_{t,t}^{(1,2)}D_{t,t}^{(2)} + R_{t,t+1}^{(1,2)}D_{t+1,t}^{(2)}\}u_t^{(1)} + \{R_{t,t+1}^{(1,1)} + R_{t,t}^{(1,2)}D_{t,t+1}^{(2)} \\ &+ R_{t,t+1}^{(1,2)}D_{t+1,t+1}^{(2)}\}u_{t+1}^{(1)} + [R_{t,t}^{(1,2)} : R_{t,t+1}^{(1,2)}]F^{(2)}c^{(2)} + c_t^{(1)},\end{aligned} \tag{4.12}$$

which we can rewrite as

$$\tilde{y}_t^{(1)} = G_{t,t}u_t^{(1)} + G_{t,t+1}u_{t+1}^{(1)} + g_t. \tag{4.13}$$

Now take the second sub-vector from (4.9) for $i = 1$, and again substitute $u^{(2)}$ out:

$$\begin{aligned}\tilde{y}_{t+1}^{(1)} &= \left\{R_{t+1,t}^{(1,1)} + R_{t+1,t}^{(1,2)}D_{t,t}^{(2)} + R_{t+1,t+1}^{(1,2)}D_{t+1,t}^{(2)}\right\}u_t^{(1)} \\ &+ \left\{R_{t+1,t+1}^{(1,1)} + R_{t+1,t}^{(1,2)}D_{t,t+1}^{(2)} + R_{t+1,t+1}^{(1,2)}D_{t+1,t+1}^{(2)}\right\}u_{t+1}^{(1)} \\ &+ \left[R_{t+1,t}^{(1,2)} : R_{t+1,t+1}^{(1,2)}\right]F^{(2)}c^{(2)} + c_{t+1}^{(1)},\end{aligned} \tag{4.14}$$

which we rewrite, to match (4.13), as

$$\tilde{y}_{t+1}^{(1)} = H_{t+1,t}u_t^{(1)} + H_{t+1,t+1}u_{t+1}^{(1)} + h_{t+1}. \tag{4.15}$$

It is always possible to use a generalized inverse for $H_{t+1,t+1}$ in order to renormalize (4.15) on $u_{t+1}{}^{(1)}$ and then eliminate it from (4.13); or a unique inverse if player 2 has at least as many instruments as targets in the second period ($m_{t+1} = q_{t+1}$). Thus

$$u_{t+1}^{(1)} = H_{t+1,t+1}^{+}[\tilde{y}_{t+1}^{(1)} - H_{t+1,t}u_t^{(1)} - h_{t+1}], \tag{4.16}$$

where "+" denotes a generalized (Moore–Penrose) left-inverse.[10] Inserting (4.16) into (4.13) eliminates $u_{t+1}^{(1)}$ and yields a conventional RE model where current endogenous variables depend on domestic policy instruments and expectations of future outcomes, plus other external factors. Specifically,

$$y_t = [G_{t,t} - G_{t,t+1}H_{t+1,t+1}^{+}H_{t+1,t}]u_t^{(1)} + G_{t,t+1}H_{t+1,t+1}^{+}y_{t+1}^{e} + k_t, \tag{4.17}$$

[10] See Appendix 2C.

where $k_t = [g_t + \bar{y}_t^{(1)}] - G_{t,t+1} H^{+}_{t+1,t+1} [h_{t+1} + \bar{y}_{t+1}^{(1)}]$, and $y_{t+1}^e = E(y_{t+1} \mid \Omega_t)$ is a conventional RE term.

4.6 What we have learned about how the Lucas critique works

The material of this chapter has shown that the Lucas critique should indeed be expected to apply in a world of rational private agents and/or rational policymakers. It is easy to see that each (rational) policy reaction function will depend on the policies or decisions made by others; *and vice versa*. See, for example, Equations (4.11) and (4.10) above. Consequently, as soon as one policymaker adjusts his policies, or his policy rule, the other policymakers whose decisions depend on the first policymaker's decisions will have to adjust their decisions – thus invalidating the premise of constant decision values by others that must have underlain the first policymaker's original calculations.[11] Hence the critique is clearly true and needs to be taken into account. But the obvious way to overcome it is to solve the implied policy game explicitly. Equation (4.11) is one such example among many possibilities.

Second, we have shown that a dynamic game between two or more players (including the private sector) can always be transformed, although not always uniquely, into a conventional single-player RE model. This is convenient; the implication is that a forward-looking RE term can represent not only the strategic behavior of the private sector but also the implicit shifting responses of the private sector to any policy changes or interventions by the policy authorities. This covers the case where the private sector's chief concern is to forecast the outcomes of the economy or government policy (i.e., to set expectations) accurately. It also means that the Lucas critique can be overcome if we learn to control a RE model correctly without time-inconsistent policies. Chapters 5, 10 and 11, and Chapter 12 in particular, show how to do that – both through explicit policy games, and indirectly through single-player RE models.

[11] Unless the first policymaker is a Stackelberg leader. But, even then, if the leader's decision causes the follower to adjust his policy rule, as opposed to his choice of policy values, the leader will want to revise his decision if he is to continue to choose the best policies for his objectives.

Third, since the RE representation of strategic behavior is typically not unique, in practice it needs to be tied down by specifying a theoretical model of the underlying economy or by estimating the parameter coefficients directly.

Fourth, the strategic behavior in the Lucas critique, as modeled in the previous section to show the link with REs of the outcomes, can come from any kind of policy game. We used a Nash game concept in Section 4.5, but that was for convenience and illustration. We could have done it for a Stackelberg game: $D^{(1)} = 0$ if player 1 is the leader. Alternatively, we could have introduced a conjectural variations game, with a contraction mapping designed to create Pareto improvements over the simple Nash solution, by replacing each $D^{(i)}$ by[12]

$$D_{s+1}^{(i)} = -[(R^{(i,i)} + R^{(i,j)}D_s^{(j)})'Q^{(i)}R^{(i,i)}]^{-1}(R^{(i,i)} + R^{(i,j)}D_s^{(j)})'Q^{(i)}R^{(i,j)} \quad (4.18)$$

for $i, j = 1, 2$ and $i \neq j$ in turn. The analysis of this chapter remains the same, but the conjectural variations formulation, if the iterations take time to complete, shows how the Lucas critique can also be represented as a sequence of reactions by the private sector followed by adjustments by government or other policymakers. The same would be true if the matrix on the left of (4.11) had spectral radius inside the unit circle, so that its inverse can be represented by a power series expansion of the original matrix. But there is no guarantee of that. These remarks show that the Lucas critique is just a reflection of the steps in an extensive form game, and can be overcome by computing the final solution of that game.

In fact, the only games that do not belong in this analysis are cooperative games. Such games are solved by appointing a "social planner" and therefore have no strategic interactions at the policy level, as opposed to what may happen between the policymakers at the negotiating stage beforehand.[13] Hence, policies derived from such cooperative games are Lucas critique-proof.

[12] See Başar and Olsder (1995) and Hughes Hallett (1986a) for these game representations.

[13] For alternative bargaining solutions in a multiplayer policy context, see Hughes Hallett (1986b).

5 *Policy games: an introduction*

Summary. This chapter sets up and explains the basic ingredients of policy games that provide the framework for studying strategic interactions between players and their policies. In particular, it lists the components essential for modeling policy games in an economy, defines simultaneous (Nash) and sequential (Stackelberg) solution concepts, and illustrates the ideas of sub-game perfection and time inconsistency. The relationship between the policy game approach and REs is then discussed further, along with definitions of policy neutrality and equilibrium (non)existence. Many examples of policy games describing some standard policy problems that are popular in the literature conclude the chapter.

5.1 Introduction

The main limit of the Tinbergen and Theil approach – emphasized by Robert Lucas, and as we saw in the previous chapter – is that it ignores the reaction of the private sector to government policies. The Tinbergen–Theil theory assumed that the economic system faced by the policymaker was invariant to alternative policy actions or the policy regime followed by that policymaker. This assumption is unrealistic because the *rational* private sector can always anticipate, and react to, the policymaker's actions. That would change not just the outcomes, but also the way the system itself behaves.

Evidently, one way to deal with Lucas' objection is to introduce REs. In formal terms, this breaks the independence of the policy multipliers from the instrument variables; the multipliers would become endogenously determined and conditioned on predictable responses by the private sector. In general, a more natural way to cope with the problem is to explicitly consider the strategic interactions between the government and the private sector or other policymakers. We refer to this as the policy game approach since it is extensively based on game theory, which is precisely concerned with the actions of decision makers who are conscious that their actions affect each other (Rasmusen, 1989).

An explicit representation of strategic interactions, however, is not a trivial issue. What actions will be chosen by the agents in a strategic context? In line with the Tinbergen–Theil theory of economic policy in previous chapters, we continue to assume that each agent behaves as a rational decision maker; that is, each player will choose the best action available to him, given all the information at his disposal. Unfortunately, and in contrast to the Tinbergen–Theil approach, the best action for any given agent now depends on the actions of other agents. So, when choosing any action, each agent must form a belief about the others' behavior. That means each policymaker must have in mind an evaluation of the actions the other players will choose. On what basis can such a belief be formed?

In a policy game, loosely speaking, a solution concept is a description of how those beliefs are formed. It specifies a formal rule for predicting how the game will be played. If rationality is assumed, beliefs satisfy REs. The predictions that follow are called solutions and describe the strategies that will be adopted by each of the players. This makes it possible to *predict* the results and outcomes of the game. The most commonly used solution concepts are those that ensure equilibrium. Among them, the most famous is the Nash equilibrium.[1]

Apart from the rationality assumption, a policy game contains four main ingredients, which are collectively known as the *rules of the game*.

1. A *set of players*, each endowed with at least one instrument variable, and interested in one or more target variables. Their interests and priorities are defined by *loss* (or *utility*) *functions*.[2]

[1] Many solution concepts, for certain games, will result in more than one solution. It is then uncertain which solution will be realized or adopted in practice. However, a refinement can be applied in order to narrow down the solutions by eliminating implausible equilibria, and to obtain clearer predictions about likely outcomes. Each refinement thus attempts to define some equilibria as "more likely," or "more robust" than the others to deviations by players. Governments may also try to select their preferred equilibrium by making announcements that influence expectations. We examine these possibilities later: in Section 5.2.2 for refinements of the Nash equilibrium and in Chapters 9 and 13 for a theory of policy announcements.

[2] Sometimes it is useful to include in the model certain individuals called pseudo-players whose actions are taken in a purely mechanical way. Among them, *Nature* is a pseudo-player who takes random actions at specified points in the game with specified probabilities.

2. A *description of the underlying economy*: the relationship between the target variables and the policy instruments, which makes it possible to assess the impact of instrument choices on losses or preferences.
3. A *solution concept*: the rule used by the players to form their beliefs about the others' actions. As we assume that agents behave rationally, the solution concept must correspond to the information sets they use in determining their decisions.
4. The *information sets* available to each player: these may differ across players, though for simplicity we usually assume that all players have access to the same information.

In practice, the above is an informal description of a strategic game adapted for economic policy applications.[3] In this book, we are more interested in the applications of game theory than in its foundations. Moreover, in our context, it is natural to define the players' preferences not over action profiles but over their consequences. The predictions for the economy then become dependent on the assessment of the consequences of actions on the preferences. As pointed out by Osborne and Rubinstein (1994: 12):

> The fact that the model is so abstract is a merit to the extent that it allows applications in a wide range of situations, but is a drawback to the extent that the implications of the model cannot depend on any specific features of a situation. Indeed, very few conclusions can be reached about the outcome of a game at this level of abstraction; one needs to be much more specific to derive interesting results.

This chapter mainly discusses one-shot or static policy games; i.e., the strategic context in which each decision maker chooses his plan of action once and for all, and not necessarily in a simultaneous manner.[4] In the next section we adapt the model described in Chapter 2 to a strategic

[3] A strategic game is a model of interactive decision making in which each decision maker chooses his plan of action given his information set. Formally, it consists of a finite set of agents N (the set of players); plus, for each player $i \in N$, a non-empty set A_i (the set of actions, x_i, available to player i); and for each player $i \in N$, a preference relation $\succ_i$ on $A = \times_{j \in N} A_j$ (the preference relation of player i). See Osborne and Rubinstein (1994: Definition 11.1).

[4] They may in fact play a sequential or Stackelberg game, where there is a sequence of single decisions by the different players. Mixed cases are also possible in n-player games, where some players play simultaneously and others sequentially. The rules of the game determine the equilibrium concept to be

context. That is, we explicitly consider a multiple decision maker world. Then Section 5.2 informally discusses the issue of the solution concept and illustrates the problem of time consistency. Section 5.3 considers the relationship between the policy games and the REs. Finally, Section 5.4 presents some examples drawn from policy games in the context of central banking management and, specifically, monetary policy neutrality.

5.2 The basic framework

5.2.1 Preferences and the economy

We consider a simple economy where n players interact. We assume that each player minimizes a LQ criterion. More formally, if player i's criterion is defined over $t(i) = q(i) + l(i)$ variables, where $l(i)$ is the number of those that enter only linearly and $q(i)$ is the number of other target variables, the LQ criterion can be written as[5]

$$L_i = \frac{1}{2}(y_i - \bar{y}_i)' Q_i (y_i - \bar{y}_i) + y_i' r_i + \tilde{y}_i' l_i \quad \forall i \in N, \tag{5.1}$$

where N is the set of the n players; $y_i \in R^{q(i)}$ is a vector of target variables that enter Equation (5.1) at least in a quadratic manner (second order); $\tilde{y}_i \in R^{l(i)}$ is a vector of target variables that enter *only* linearly (first-order); $\bar{y}_i \in R^{q(i)}$ is a vector of target values; Q_i is an appropriate positive diagonal matrix;[6] and r_i and l_i are

used to solve the game. However, note that the difference between games is not formally related to the actual sequence of the decisions but to the players' information sets, which may or may not be related to that sequence. For instance, if two players have to communicate their decisions in sequence in a closed envelope, the game is not sequential unless the second player can read the decisions of the other one before making his choice (thus changing his information set). For a more accurate description of the issue, see, e.g., Rasmusen (1989).

5 In principle a decision maker may also be interested in the values taken by instruments per se (i.e., instrument use may have a cost). However, in order to distinguish their different natures, we keep targets and instruments formally separate. It is worth noticing that to take account of the instrument costs, we can simply introduce additional targets into Equation (5.1) as well as equality constraints between them and the instruments into Equation (5.2) below (see Section 2.7.4 for details). This is not without implications for the properties of the game, as we will see in Part III of this book.

6 Assuming non-separable preferences does not change our exposition and formal results at all. Note also that Q_i is a full rank square matrix by assumption.

appropriate vectors.[7] We refer to $\bar{y}_i$, Q_i, r_i and l_i as the parameters describing player *i*'s preferences. Notice that player *i*'s first best (or *optimum optimorum*) corresponds to his target values only if $r_i = 0$.[8]

Each player *i* sets $u_i \in \mathrm{R}^{m(i)}$, which is a sub-vector of $u \in \mathrm{R}^M$. Of course, $\Sigma_{i \in N} m(i) = M$, since by definition no policy control can be set by more than one player. All the target variable vectors, y_i, are sub-vectors of $y \in \mathrm{R}^K$, but players can share some target variables. Thus $\Sigma_{i \in N} t(i) \geq K$. For the sake of simplicity, we also assume that each player cannot control more instruments than his targets, i.e., $m(i) \leq t(i)$.

The K target variables and M instruments are linked together by the following linear equation system:

$$y = Au + f. \tag{5.2}$$

Each line of the above system represents a linear relation between one target and the entire instrument set u. Vector $f \in \mathrm{R}^K$ is a vector of given constants (exogenous variables or expected shocks) outside the players' control. Thus:[9]

$$y_i = A_{ii}u_i + A_{ij}u_j + f_i \qquad \forall i, j \in \mathrm{N} \text{ with } j \neq i. \tag{5.3}$$

To keep things simple, we assume that the basis of A is the identity matrix, which means that system (5.2) cannot be reduced to several independent sub-systems.

5.2.2 *Solution concepts*

A one-shot strategic game is a model of interactive decision making in which each decision maker chooses his plan of action once and for all. In such a case the most often used solution concept is the Nash equilibrium. This describes a situation where no policymaker has any

[7] We must underline that while Q_i is positive definite, the coefficients of the linear targets can be positive or negative, according to whether targets are *bads* or *goods* (respectively) in our representation of preferences in terms of a loss function. See Equation (2.24) in the example of Section 2.7.4.

[8] See Section 2.7.3.

[9] It can also contain stochastic terms. In this case, our results hold in expected terms by the certainty-equivalence principle (see Section 2.7.1).

incentive to change, unilaterally, his own policy (strategy) given the policies of others.[10]

In principle, a policy game could have any number of Nash equilibria. In an LQ context, however, policy games can have only one of three possible outcomes: unique Nash equilibrium, no equilibrium, or an infinite number of equilibria. Moreover, when there are infinite combinations of different agents' strategies (players' instruments) that represent Nash equilibria, we can distinguish two cases: (1) strong multiple equilibria, where different strategies support different outcomes for the targets; and (2) weak multiple equilibria, where the strategies all support the same values for the vector of target variables.

The Nash equilibrium may sometimes appear irrational if assessed from a third-person perspective. This may happen if a Nash equilibrium is not Pareto optimal. However, the basic assumption supporting it is that agents (individually) act in a rational manner with respect to their own (private) preferences and objectives, even if the outcomes appear sub-optimal with respect to the community as a whole.

The Nash equilibrium may also lead to surprising (and unrealistic) results when choices are not made simultaneously; that is, in a Stackelberg game. It may, in fact, have nonrational consequences because players may *threaten* each other with irrational moves. In other words, timing matters. Outcomes usually differ in otherwise identical economies when the assumptions about the timing of the government's policy choices are altered.

Consider, for example, a timing variation in the well-known game of the battle of the sexes,[11] assuming that the husband chooses first. Although there are two Nash equilibria in this case, we will probably never see our couple at the ballet since the husband can rationally think that if he goes to the boxing match his wife will follow him because her alternative Nash equilibrium cannot be played.[12] A similar

[10] For games in which players randomize (mix) their strategies, the expected or average payoff must be at least as large as that obtainable by any other strategy.

[11] Recall, in the battle of the sexes, that "the story concerns a husband and wife who are trying to decide how to spend an evening. The man would like to attend a boxing match; the woman, the ballet. [...] But each would rather attend an entertainment with the other than not, and this is more important to each than attending his or her preferred form of entertainment" (Kreps, 1990).

[12] Formally, backward induction, which we are going to introduce shortly, recovers different outcomes in these two different games. Though they share the same choice sets and payoffs, these are different games.

example can be drawn from the game of chicken.[13] If one driver commits to not swerve, by tying his hands to the seat for example, the possible outcomes for the other driver are either to crash or to swerve. Of those two options, the more cowardly clearly gives a higher payoff.

In sequential games, a more meaningful analytic tool is the concept of sub-game perfect Nash equilibrium, which is a refinement of a Nash equilibrium. In addition to the Nash equilibrium, it requires that the strategy is also a Nash equilibrium in every sub-game. This eliminates all non-credible threats.

Sub-game perfect Nash equilibria are found by backward induction, which is the process of reasoning backward to determine a sequence of actions from each point going forward. In Stackelberg games, we proceed by first considering the last player who has to move. We consider the best decision that could be made by choosing his best action, *in any situation* at that step, i.e., given the choice of the other players. Using this information, one can then determine what the second-last player should best do, considering the last player's optimal action, just computed, and taking as given the actions of the others. This process continues backward in time until one has determined the best action for every player at each point in time.

As an example of backward induction and the sub-game perfect Nash equilibrium, consider a well-known two-player ultimatum game. One player (the proposer) suggests a division of 10 dollars between him and another player (the respondent). He can propose to donate any integer between 1 and 10, keeping the rest for himself. The respondent is then given the option either to accept the split or to reject it. If he accepts, both get the amount suggested by the proposer. If he rejects, he does not receive anything.

Formally, the game is played in two stages: in the first stage, the proposer suggests a division (his strategy is to choose an integer between 1 and 10); in the second stage, the respondent can either accept or reject the proposal (his strategy is to choose "yes" or "no").

Reasoning backward, to find the perfect sub-game Nash equilibrium, we begin from the second stage; thus we consider the actions

[13] In this game, two drivers drive towards each other on a collision course: one must swerve, or both may die in the crash. But if one driver swerves and the other does not, the one who swerved will be called a *chicken*, meaning a coward.

of the respondent, who is the last player to move, given an arbitrary nonzero proposal by the first player. Since the only choice the second player has *at each point* in the game is to choose between something and nothing, one expects that the second will accept (his optimal strategy is always "yes"). As a consequence, in the first stage, the proposer ought to suggest giving him as little as possible – i.e., 1 dollar. It follows that 9 dollars for the proposer and 1 dollar for the respondent are the payoffs for the unique sub-game perfect Nash equilibrium of the game.[14]

It is worth noticing that the sets of sub-game perfect Nash equilibria and Nash equilibria coincide in a simultaneous game with perfect information. We thus refer to the Nash equilibrium as the sub-game perfect Nash equilibrium when players act simultaneously. By contrast, we refer to the sub-game perfect Nash equilibrium as a Stackelberg equilibrium if players act sequentially. In such a case, when there are two agents, the first player to move is called the game leader and the other is the follower.

5.2.3 Reaction and quasi-reaction functions

The fundamental tool used to define a Nash equilibrium is a player's best response, or reaction function, which relates the best policy for each player to any choices that may be made by each of his opponents. Specifically, the best response is the strategy that produces the most favorable outcomes for a particular player, taking all other players' strategies as given.[15]

A player's *reaction function* can be easily found by minimizing (5.1) subject to (5.3). For instance, consider the two-player case where, for the sake of exposition, $y_i = y$ and $r_i = l_i = 0$ for both players. The M reaction functions are then defined by the following equations:

$$\frac{\partial L_i}{\partial u_i} = A_{ii}'Q_i A_{ii} u_i + A_{ii}'Q_i \left(A_{ij} u_j + f_i - \bar{y}_i\right) = 0 \qquad (5.4)$$

$$\text{with } i = \{1,2\} \text{ and } j \neq i.$$

This collapses to just two equations if each player is endowed with only one instrument variable ($M = 2$); then the reaction functions can

[14] However, the ultimatum game does have several other Nash equilibria, which are not sub-game perfect.

[15] See Fudenberg and Tirole (1991) or Gibbons (1992).

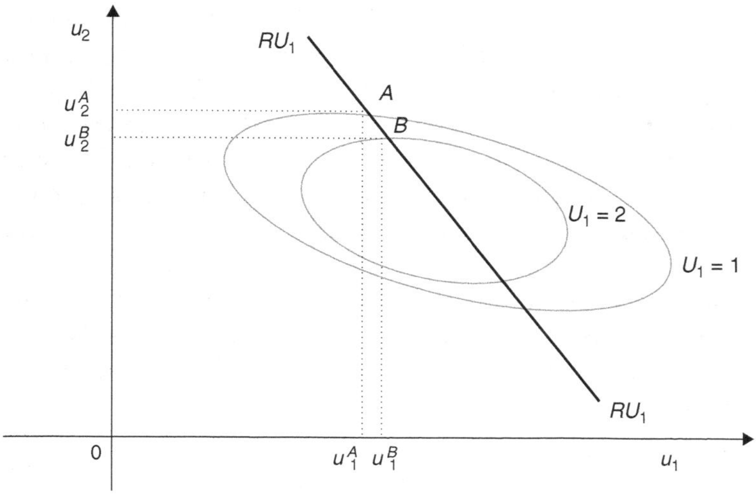

Figure 5.1 Best response function

be drawn in the space of the instruments, u.[16] For instance, consider Figure 5.1. If player 2 were to play u_2^A, the best response for player 1 is u_1^A, to which corresponds the lowest possible loss for player 1. A is thus a point on player 1's reaction function. In a similar way, a corresponding point B, for some lower loss level, can be found and player 1's reaction function, which is linear, can then be drawn between them.

Insofar as a best response function produces the most favorable outcome for a particular player, given the other players' strategies, if that player is on his best response line he has no incentive to change his current policy or deviate from it. Similarly, if the other players are also on their best response lines, they have no incentive to change their policies. Hence, if these conditions are simultaneously met for all players, we are, by definition, at a Nash equilibrium.

In other words, the intersection of the best response functions is a Nash equilibrium.[17] The Nash equilibrium itself can therefore be found by solving the system of M optimal reaction functions obtained by minimizing (5.1) subject to (5.2) for each player in turn. The set of

[16] As in the classic textbook example of a Cournot equilibrium.

[17] As we anticipated, in LQ games either the Nash equilibrium, if it exists, is unique or there will be an infinite set of combinations of policies that are Nash equilibria. Now the reason should be clear: as in the LQ context, the best responses are linear.

equations in (5.4) therefore defines a Nash equilibrium. We can informally refer to it as the *Nash equilibrium in terms of strategies*; in this case, the optimal policy of the players: u_1^* and u_2^*. This equilibrium can be depicted geometrically if we draw player 2's reaction function, in addition to that for player 1 which has already been drawn in Figure 5.1. Then, by inserting u_1^* and u_2^* plus any exogenous information into (5.2), optimal values for the target variables can also be found. These values represent an *equilibrium in the space of outcomes*.

Best responses can also be depicted in the *dual space* of target outcomes. In such a case we can talk of *quasi-reaction functions*. Formally, the M quasi-reaction functions are defined by the following equations:

$$\frac{\partial L_i}{\partial u_i} = A_{ii}' Q_i \left(y_i - \bar{y}_i \right) = 0 \quad \text{with } i = \{1,2\}. \tag{5.5}$$

Note that if $K = 2$, quasi-reaction functions can be drawn in the 2-dimensional space of target variables, y. This simple case is represented in Figure 5.2.

We might think of Figure 5.2 as an AD-AS diagram, where y_1 is output and y_2 is the price level. Player 1 can shift the aggregate demand (via monetary policy), whereas player 2 controls the supply schedule (via nominal wages). Point A represents the first best for player 1. It clearly lies on that player's quasi-reaction function since, if aggregate demand and supply cross there (in the case of AD^A and AS^A), player 1 has no incentive to shift the AD schedule. By contrast, if the policy of player 2 were to shift the aggregate supply schedule to AS^B, the best response for player 1 would be to shift the aggregate demand schedule to AD^B. Hence the points along the straight line passing through A and B represent player 1's optimal quasi-reaction function.

In this example we have considered two target variables and two instruments. However, in general, M differs from K. This implies that the number of equations and number of unknowns can differ in (5.5), which will typically lead to an over- or under-determined system. By contrast, system (5.4) is always uniquely determined. Indeed, condition (5.4) constitutes a necessary and sufficient condition for a Nash equilibrium to exist in terms of the underlying strategies (and associated outcomes via (5.2)). Condition (5.5), by contrast, is only necessary. In other words, the outcomes associated with the solution of a

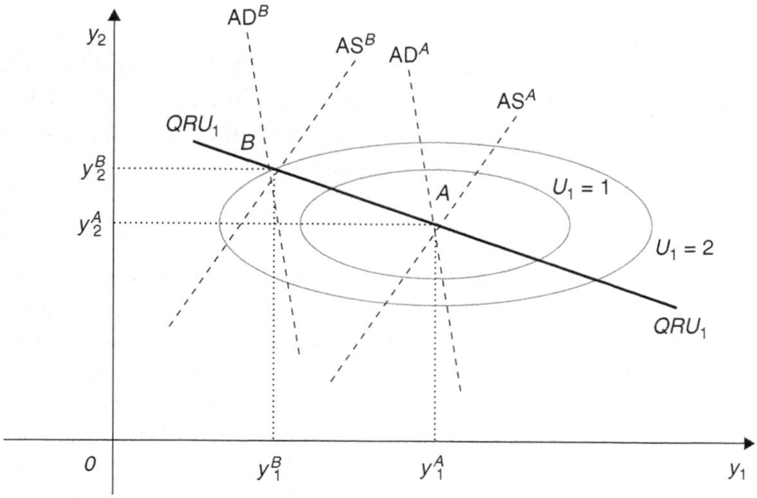

Figure 5.2 Quasi-reaction function

set of optimal reaction functions (5.4) will also solve the system of optimal quasi-reaction functions (5.5). But the contrary is not necessarily true.[18]

The corresponding Stackelberg equilibrium is found by backward induction. First we need to solve the problem of the last mover or follower, as in the Nash case, by minimizing (5.1) subject to Equation (5.2) to find that player's reaction function. Then we need to solve the second-last mover's problem by minimizing (5.1) subject to both (5.2) and the last mover's reaction function; and so on until all players (including the leader) have been considered.

Section 5.3 will show how to solve the Nash and Stackelberg game graphically. Section 5.4 will further clarify the solution procedure with some examples.

[18] The set of outcomes given by (5.5) is, in fact, larger than the set of the outcomes associated with the solution of (5.4) because the former may also contain some infeasible solutions; i.e., outcomes that cannot be obtained for any possible combination of instruments. Put more precisely, there is full duality between the two systems (5.4) and (5.5) *only* if the total number of instruments available to all players equals the sum of the number of their target variables; that would hold only if $K = 2$ in the example in this section. We will discuss this particular issue in more detail in Chapter 7.

5.2.4 Time inconsistency

In a one-shot game, a time inconsistency problem[19] may arise when Stackelberg games are under consideration. Time inconsistency is, in fact, directly related to the different incentives the leader faces for his own policy before and after the follower plays.

For instance:

> imagine a government that controls the money supply of a particular country. For political reasons, the government wishes to run the economy so as to maximize its growth. Assume that anticipated inflation is deleterious to growth, but that unanticipated inflation (fuelled by an unanticipated increase in the money supply) enhances growth. Taking the first effect into account, the government might wish to promise not to inflate the money supply at more than a given rate. But ex post the government may well wish to pump money into the economy, to take advantage of the second effect. The horns of this dilemma are that the government's ex ante promise not to inflate is incredible insofar as the general public recognize that, ex post, it will be both in the government's best interests and in its power to inflate the money supply. Hence, the public will anticipate high inflation, which depresses growth. (Kreps, 1990: 51)

The above policy promises are described as a Stackelberg game between the private sector (the follower, setting expectations) and the government (the leader, setting the growth in the money supply); time inconsistency would arise because the Stackelberg equilibrium is not defined by mutual best responses. This implies that the follower uses a best response in reaction to the leader's action, but that the leader's action is not itself a best response to the follower's. This asymmetry is crucial: it opens the door to a re-optimization by the leader once the follower has played. Thus, a government that *announced* that it will implement a Stackelberg solution would not be credible.[20]

In order to ensure credibility, and avoid potential time inconsistencies, Stackelberg games need to be supported by some commitment mechanism that makes the leader's action irreversible and hence

[19] The time inconsistency problem has been treated extensively in the monetary policy literature following Kydland and Prescott (1977) and Barro and Gordon (1983).

[20] There are important qualifications to this result, which we consider in more detail in Chapter 12 below. But, for now we will continue using the conventional propositions.

credible. Credibility may be introduced by adding assumptions that ensure the irreversibility of the leader's actions, such as a constitutional law forbidding money creation in excess of some limit, giving control of monetary policy to an independent central bank, legislating a target that is a stock rather than a flow (for example, a debt target instead of a deficit target in fiscal policy), or creating a regime of cyclically repeated games.[21] By contrast, the situation we described above would be correctly depicted as a Stackelberg game only if we implicitly or explicitly assumed that a commitment technology exists to support the outcomes.

5.3 Rational expectations and policy games revisited

This section clarifies the relationship between the RE assumption and policy games; in particular, between the former and the various different concepts we might use to solve policy games. We provide a simple informal discussion to stress the main relationship and describe the terminology used in this book.[22]

As shown in Chapter 4, REs can be introduced as follows. Assume that an agent is interested in predicting a future (unknown) value of a certain variable or vector of variables, z. We refer to the agent's forecast or expectation as $\varepsilon(z)$. The RE hypothesis then implies that $\varepsilon(z)$ is said to be rational if

$$\varepsilon(z) = E\left[z|\Omega\right], \tag{5.6}$$

where $E[z|\Omega]$ is the mathematical expectation of z conditional on the information set Ω available at the time the forecast is made. In other words, the RE hypothesis requires that, conditional on information available at the time the forecasts were made, the predictions made by the forecaster be unbiased and consistent with the equilibrium value generated by the model (z^*). Definition (5.6) implies

[21] Several options to ensure credible solutions have been considered in the literature. See McCallum (1997) for a review in the monetary policy context. A theory of cyclically repeated games, where the policy interventions are asynchronous and may imply credibility, is given in Libich, Hughes Hallett and Stehlik (2012).

[22] For a more formal description of this relationship and its derivation, see Brandsma and Hughes Hallett (1984) and Petit (1990: chapters 8–10).

$$\varepsilon(z) = z^* + \varepsilon, \tag{5.7}$$

where ε is a purely random shock (forecast error) with zero mean. In a deterministic model, such as those considered here, this implies $\varepsilon(z) = z^*$; that is to say, perfect foresight. In a stochastic model with additive uncertainty, the RE of z is its certainty equivalent.

REs can be introduced explicitly into our model by noting that the equations describing the economy depend also on the private sector's forecast of economic variables (and thus of policy variables) which are themselves rational. In models with explicit REs, the meaning and the effects of private agent or private sector REs are therefore clear. In those models, the action of the government is constrained by REs; the traditional decision problem is simply augmented with this further constraint. In that case, a RE equilibrium can be informally described by an outcome of the model augmented with expectations containing the following two elements:

1. *Expectations are rational.* Thus, expectations should be self-fulfilling at least on average.
2. *Agents act consistently with their expectations*; i.e., when they minimize their losses, they take account of their beliefs about the actions of the other players.[23]

There is, however, an alternative but equivalent way to incorporate REs through the interactions implied by a policy game. According to this approach, the underlying strategies of the private sector are "determined simultaneously" with those of the government.[24] Doing it this way, where the game is explicit, the relationship between the players' actions and the RE hypothesis becomes obscured. However, as we now show informally, the policy game approach, while accounting for REs, provides a richer and more general way to express interactions since it allows us to take account of different information structures – specifically, cases with asymmetric information across players. This in turn extends our traditional RE theory to a broader context.

[23] Recall Section 4.5 above.

[24] Notice that here when we use the expression "determined simultaneously" we do not necessarily mean that the private sector and the government play simultaneously, but only that the private sector's actions are explicitly modeled in addition to those of the government.

Our aim now is to show that the solution of a policy game under different assumptions about the players' information structure is always an RE equilibrium.

In policy games with perfect information, forecasts typically refer to the actions of the other agents.[25] The next step is to explain how a policy game equilibrium incorporates REs. In order to ensure that expectations are rational, a policy game needs to guarantee that the decision maker who holds REs is modeled as a player who "perfectly" anticipates the actions of the other player (that is to say, with no predictable errors) given the information he has.[26] Let us see how, and in what sense, this can be guaranteed by the concept of Nash sub-game perfect equilibrium (for example, in the equilibrium of a Stackelberg two-player static game).

In a game between two players (U and W), who have two policy instruments, u and w respectively, the time protocol associated with the Stackelberg equilibrium implies that the game leader (player W) moves first without knowing the value of the instrument set by his rival (player U). In setting w, the leader must form an expectation for the value u; or at least for the rule by which u will be set. It is also assumed that both players know both the rules of the game and the other player's preferences.

The Stackelberg game is described by Figure 5.3 in the space of instrument strategies. In the figure, *RU* is the reaction function of the follower, whereas ellipses are the leader's indifference curves. Point S (u_1, w_1) represents the Stackelberg equilibrium of the game.

The Stackelberg equilibrium is an RE equilibrium. The explanation is as follows. The leader, when setting his instrument, needs to form an expectation about the follower's strategy. However, since he knows that the follower plays after having observed his choice (and having taken account of it), his expectation is conditional on the follower's choice.[27] For instance, if the leader plays w_2, he knows the follower

[25] A Stackelberg leader, for instance, in choosing his policy must clearly form an expectation for the policy of his opponent (at least the rule that his opponent will be following), in order to anticipate the opponent's actions with the information that he (the leader) has. By contrast, in the Nash equilibrium, both agents have to form expectations about their opponents' actions.

[26] See, e.g., Mas-Colell, Whinston and Green (1995: 439) for a clear example.

[27] Otherwise his expectations will not be rational, since the leader does not use all the information he has.

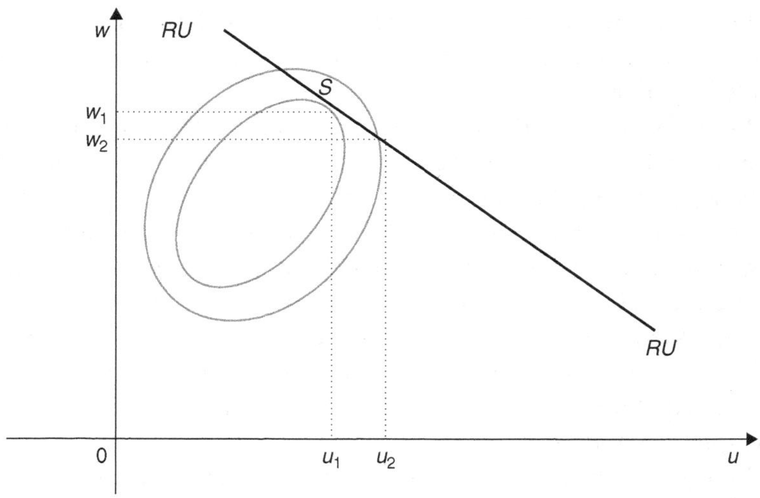

Figure 5.3 Stackelberg equilibrium

will observe w_2 and react to it by attempting to achieve the lowest possible loss. The follower would therefore play u_2. It then follows that, if the leader decides to play w_2, he should conjecture $\varepsilon(u) = u_2$. More generally, the leader can conjecture that, for each of his actions, the follower's choice will be that indicated by the point corresponding to that action on the follower's reaction function *RU*. Thus the leader's forecasting rule is $\varepsilon(u) = f(w_i)$, where w_i is a given action of the leader and $f(w)$ is the follower's reaction function. All such beliefs would be self-fulfilling. However not all of them would be RE equilibria. In fact, among all the possible strategies open to the leader, the rational leader will choose to play w_1, anticipating $\varepsilon(u) = f(w_1) = u_1$, since, given his forecasting rule, w_1 is the only strategy consistent with minimizing his own loss function.

Now consider the Nash equilibrium, point *N* in Figure 5.4. The time protocol associated with this solution implies that both players will move without knowing the value of the instrument being set by their rival. Moreover, as in the previous case, we assume that each player knows the rules of the game and the other player's preferences. In such a situation, to set their own instruments they both need to form expectations of the other player's choice. The reaction function of the leader, choosing w, is *RW*.

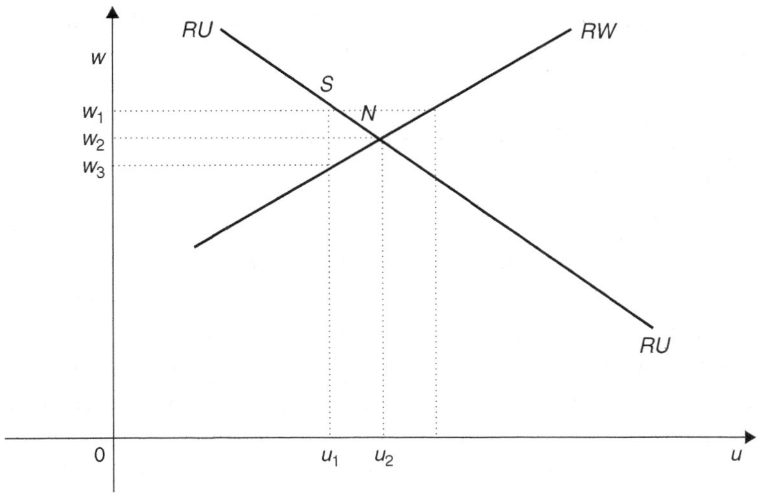

Figure 5.4 Nash equilibrium

As in the Stackelberg case, when W sets w he cannot observe u and has to make a conjecture. However, now also U has to form expectations about the policy of W, who knows this and must take it into account – his information set is thus different from that in the Stackelberg game. Point S (the Stackelberg equilibrium) is no longer an RE equilibrium from W's point of view. If W plays w_1, expecting $\varepsilon(u) = u_1$, and simultaneously U plays u_1, conjecturing that W will play w_1 (i.e., $\varepsilon(w) = w_1$), the expectations will still be self-fulfilling at point S. But why would U expect w_1? Such a choice by W would no longer be consistent with his expectations about U's choices (i.e., would not be rational). In fact, if W expects that U will play u_1, he should play w_3 instead of w_1 to minimize his loss since *RW* defines his best response.

Only if both players play the strategies associated with point N (u_2, w_2), and expect the rivals do the same (i.e., $\varepsilon(u) = u_2$ and $\varepsilon(w) = w_2$), are the actions consistent with loss minimization by both players and only then will the expectations be fulfilled. Thus, the Nash equilibrium is an RE equilibrium. In other words, the Nash equilibrium can be interpreted as the result of a situation in which both rational players form REs of the other player's policy decision since, *in equilibrium*, each player's conjecture of their rival's behavior will be realized. A

Nash equilibrium is supported by self-confirming beliefs and can be seen as the outcome of a two-sided RE assumption.[28]

5.4 Some examples: policy games and central bank management

This section provides some examples of policy games drawn from the debate about monetary policy neutrality. Its aim is twofold. First, we illustrate how the equilibrium concepts described above may be implemented in practice. Second, we aim to set up some cases where, depending on the parameter values, policies may be neutral or not, and an equilibrium may or may not exist, ready for the material of the next chapter.

As to policy neutrality, it is useful to recall the definition of policy effectiveness given in Section 2.3. However, in a strategic context, the ineffectiveness of a policy must be reformulated in endogenous terms, consistently with Definition 2.4, as the policies of all the players are now endogenous.

Definition 5.1 (*endogenous policy neutrality*). In a policy game context, player *i*'s policy is neutral or ineffective with respect to one (or more) of its target variable(s) if the equilibrium value of that (those) variable(s) is never affected by changes in the parameters of the player's criterion.

In other words, we refer to neutrality focusing on the outcome of the game: neutrality arises when a player cannot influence the equilibrium value of some variable. We call this *endogenous neutrality*, to differentiate it from the *exogenous* policy neutrality – defined in Chapter 2 in a parametric context. However, from now on we will just refer to neutrality or ineffectiveness, since it will be clear from the context which kind of neutrality applies.

The purpose of the examples that follow is to verify if and when monetary policy has any real effects on the economy, mainly on employment and output, according to different models of the policy game. This is an old debate, but, as we will show in the next chapter,

[28] Alternative interpretations can be derived by assuming a sort of adjustment mechanism or learning (in this case REs correspond to Nash equilibrium when the adjustment is instantaneous). See Sargent (1999) and Di Bartolomeo and Pauwels (2006) for some examples in a LQ context.

one that is easily resolved using our techniques. The section is structured as follows. After presenting the celebrated Barro–Gordon model, where the monetary authorities cannot affect real variables, we present three sources of monetary policy non-neutrality: a trade union's inflation aversion, and open economy or monopolistic competition in labor markets. Finally, we also discuss the issue in terms of fiscal and monetary policy interactions. Note that in the examples that follow, all parameters are assumed to be strictly positive unless stated otherwise.

5.4.1 Barro and Gordon's monetary policy game

The most celebrated policy game is probably that introduced by Barro and Gordon (1983). A simplified version of this model can be represented as follows:[29]

$$G = -\frac{a_1}{2}(n - n_G)^2 - \frac{a_2}{2}(p - p_G)^2, \tag{5.8}$$

$$P = -\frac{1}{2}(n - n_P)^2, \tag{5.9}$$

where G is the government's preferences, depending on the deviations of employment (n) and prices (p) from their targets.[30] P is the corresponding function for the private sector, depending only on employment. Note that the government and private sector preferences are here defined in terms of "utility" rather than loss. However, as we noted in Chapter 2, this does not affect our problem. In the examples that follow, we will sometimes use the two terms (loss and utilities) interchangeably, bearing in mind the equivalence of the two solution procedures (minimization and maximization).

The structure of the economy is simply described by two equations. The government directly sets the quantity of money, m, moving the demand schedule,

$$n = m - p, \tag{5.10}$$

[29] See, e.g., Cubitt (1992) and Sargent (1999). See also Stokey (1989, 1991), Neiss (1999) for more general and micro-founded representations.

[30] Note that in this static model, inflation and the price level coincide since the previous period's price level is given exogenously and, without loss of generality, is assumed to be zero.

and the private sector sets the nominal wage, w, varying the supply schedule,

$$n = p - w. \tag{5.11}$$

An often used and equivalent variation of the model assumes that the government sets the price level or inflation directly, and the private sector sets price expectations, both constrained by a description of the economy represented by a Phillips curve augmented by expectations:

$$n = \left(p - p^e\right) + n_P. \tag{5.12}$$

The Nash solution for either version of this model is[31]

$$n = n_P, \tag{5.13}$$

$$p = p_G + \frac{a_1}{a_2}\left(n_G - n_P\right). \tag{5.14}$$

The model illustrates an equilibrium with monetary policy neutrality or ineffectiveness. The real economy is, in fact, independent of the government's preferences, whereas any attempt to obtain an employment level greater than that desired by the private sector results in an inflation bias. It is easy to verify that if $a_1 = 0$, the equilibrium does not exist unless $n_G = n_P$.[32]

5.4.2 *A model with trade union aversion to inflation*

Gylfason and Lindbeck (1994) make a further step by considering the private sector's distortion as endogenous.[33] These authors consider the economic structure (5.10)–(5.11) and assume that a monopoly union directly controls the nominal wage, w, to maximize

$$P = -\frac{b_1}{2}\left(w - p - \omega_P\right)^2 - \frac{b_2}{2}\left(n - n_P\right)^2 - \frac{b_3}{2}\left(p - p_P\right)^2, \tag{5.15}$$

[31] It is easy to check that the same solution is found if the private sector is the leader in a Stackelberg game.

[32] In such a case, in fact, the quasi-reaction function of the private sector implies $n = n_P$, whereas that of the government is $n = n_G$; these are clearly not compatible.

[33] Similar approaches are used by, among others, Acocella and Ciccarone (1997), Cubitt (1995, 1997), Guzzo and Velasco (1999), Lawler (2000, 2001), and

where ω_p is the union's desired real wage. It is worth noting here that Gylfason and Lindbeck (1994) allow for inflation aversion ($b_3 \neq 0$) in the union's preferences. The government's objective function remains (5.8).

The Nash equilibrium of the above game turns out to be

$$n = \frac{(a_1 n_G + a_2 p_G) b_3 + a_2 (b_1 \omega_P + a_2 n_p - b_3 p_P)}{a_1 b_3 (b_1 + b_2) + a_2}. \tag{5.16}$$

$$p = \frac{(a_1 n_G + a_2 p_G)(b_1 + b_2) + a_1 (b_2 \omega_P - b_1 n_P + b_3 p_P)}{a_1 b_3 (b_1 + b_2) + a_2}. \tag{5.17}$$

This model produces monetary policy neutrality and no real effects, as in the previous example, if the trade union's inflation aversion is ignored. But inflation aversion by the trade union eliminates monetary policy neutrality since, if b_3 is not zero, employment also depends on the government's preferences.

5.4.3 *The wage-wedge in a small open economy*

A different way to obtain the non-neutrality of monetary policy is to open up the economy, as in Acocella and Di Bartolomeo (2004). Consider the supply Equation (5.11) together with the following logarithmic demand function instead of Equation (5.10):[34]

$$n = m - p - (\mu - 1)(p - e - p^*), \tag{5.18}$$

where e and p^* are the exogenously given nominal exchange rate and the foreign price level, respectively, and $(\mu - 1)$ is the real exchange rate elasticity of output.[35] For the sake of brevity, and without loss of generality, we assume (the log values) e and p^* are equal to zero. That implies a (perhaps temporarily) fixed exchange rate regime.

Di Bartolomeo and Pauwels (2006). See also Di Bartolomeo, Acocella and Tirelli (2012) and Acocella, Di Bartolomeo and Tirelli (2012a, 2012b) for a micro-founded approach based on non-LQ setups.

34 Here we use a simplified version of Acocella and Di Bartolomeo (2004) to which the reader may refer for more details. See also Gylfason and Lindbeck (1990), Jensen (1993, 1994), Lane (2000), Cavallari (2001), Di Bartolomeo (2005), Cuciniello (2011).

35 By assuming $h = 0$ and $\mu = 1$, we have the traditional closed economy model already analyzed.

In this economy, the policymakers set the nominal money supply and the union sets the nominal wage. The government's preferences are derived from Equation (5.8):

$$G = -\frac{\beta}{2}p^2 - \frac{1}{2}\left(n - n_G\right)^2, \tag{5.19}$$

where $\beta = a_2/a_1$ and $p_G = 0$ from (5.8). The union's preferences are a generalization of Equation (5.15):[36]

$$P = \alpha_1\left(w - cpi\right) - \frac{\alpha_2}{2}\left(w - cpi - \omega_P\right)^2 - \frac{1}{2}\left(n - n_P\right)^2 - \frac{\vartheta}{2}p^2, \tag{5.20}$$

where $cpi = (1 - h)p + hp^*$ is the consumer price index, and h is the weight of foreign goods in the consumption basket of wage earners. In this model, the real wage relevant for firms can differ from the real wage relevant for the union. The relevant real wage rate for firms, $w - p$, is expressed in terms of producer prices, while that for the union, $w - cpi$, is defined in terms of the consumer price index.

The Nash equilibrium levels of output and the price level are

$$n = \frac{\beta\mu n_P - \beta\left(\mu + h\right)\left(\alpha_2\omega_P + \alpha_1\right) + \left[h\left(\mu + h\right)\alpha_2 + \vartheta\right]n_G}{\left(\beta + h\right)\left(\mu + h\right)\alpha_2 + \left(\beta\mu + \vartheta\right)}, \tag{5.21}$$

$$p = \frac{\left(\mu + h\right)\left(\alpha_1 + \alpha_2\omega_P\right) - \mu n_P + \left[\left(\mu + h\right)\alpha_2 + \mu\right]n_G}{\left(\beta + h\right)\left(\mu + h\right)\alpha_2 + \left(\beta\mu + \vartheta\right)}. \tag{5.22}$$

By assuming that the union is the leader, and solving the game by backward induction, the Stackelberg outcomes are found to be

$$n = \frac{\beta^2 n_P - \beta\left(\beta + h\right)\left(\alpha_2\omega_P + \alpha_1\right) + \left[h\left(\beta + h\right)\alpha_2 + \vartheta\right]n_G}{\left(\beta + h\right)^2\alpha_2 + \left(\beta^2 + \vartheta\right)}, \tag{5.23}$$

$$p = \frac{\left(\beta + h\right)\left(\alpha_1 + \alpha_2\omega_P\right) - \beta n_P + \left[\left(\beta + h\right)\alpha_2 + \beta\right]n_G}{\left(\beta + h\right)^2\alpha_2 + \left(\beta^2 + \vartheta\right)}. \tag{5.24}$$

In both the Nash and the Stackelberg equilibria, non-neutrality holds. The result is not surprising at all as we know that the union's inflation

[36] Notice that both Equations (5.19) and (5.20) are now normalized by the employment weight, a_1, without loss of generality.

aversion implies effectiveness of the government's policies. However, in this framework, even if this assumption is removed (i.e., $\vartheta = 0$), non-neutrality still holds. In this model the open economy assumption is the key factor that permits the monetary authorities to have some real, as well as nominal, policy power. In fact, assuming also $h = 0$, the result vanishes; the model becomes the traditional Barro–Gordon model, in its Gylfason and Lindbeck variant, where workers are not inflation averse.

5.4.4 Monopolistic competition and wage setters

Recent contributions in the policy game literature stress a further channel of monetary non-neutrality. Among many innovative results directly related to the non-neutrality of monetary policy, Soskice and Iversen (1998, 2000) show that, if there is a multiplicity of unions and the product markets are monopolistically competitive, a Barro–Gordon framework delivers policy non-neutrality even if wage bargainers/unions are not inflation averse.[37]

In this type of economy,[38] N unions and a central bank are active. The central bank seeks to maximize the following quadratic objective function:

$$B = -\frac{\beta}{2}p^2 - \frac{1}{2}u^2, \tag{5.25}$$

where p is the price level and u is the unemployment rate. Each union, on the other hand, seeks to maximize a LQ preference function with the membership's (log) real wage, $w_i - p$, and unemployment rate, u_i, as arguments:

$$U_i = b_1(w_i - p) - \frac{1}{2}u_i^2 \quad i \in \{1, 2, ..., N\}. \tag{5.26}$$

The economy itself consists of three equations:[39]

[37] See also Cukierman and Lippi (2001), Jerger (2002), Coricelli, Cukierman and Dalmazzo (2004, 2006), Lawler (2005), Acocella, Di Bartolomeo and Hibbs (2008), Gnocchi (2009); and Cukierman (2004) for a survey of these results.

[38] Here we follow Acocella, Di Bartolomeo and Hibbs (2008).

[39] Equation (5.27) refers to the (micro) disaggregated equilibrium conditions, whereas Equations (5.28) and (5.29) refer to the (macro) aggregate ones. In detail: Equation (5.27) is the union's employment function stemming from a traditional labor demand derived by real profit maximization where each firm

$$u_i = \frac{\eta}{\alpha + \eta(1-\alpha)}(w_i - p) - \frac{1}{\alpha + \eta(1-\alpha)}(m - p), \tag{5.27}$$

$$p = \alpha w + (1-\alpha)m, \tag{5.28}$$

$$u = -\frac{1}{1-\alpha}(w - p), \tag{5.29}$$

where w_i is the wage set by the i-th union; $\eta > 1$ is the degree of monopolistic competition; $\alpha \in (0,1)$ is the elasticity of labor coefficient in the production function; and $w = \sigma w_i + (1-\sigma)w_{-i}$ is the average wage and w_{-i} is the average wage of the unions other than union i and where the general level of prices is defined according to the Dixit–Stiglitz aggregator: $p = \int_0^1 p_{ij}dj$. After some manipulation, the model's reduced form turns out to be

$$\begin{pmatrix} p \\ u \\ u_i \end{pmatrix} = \begin{pmatrix} 1-\alpha & \sigma\alpha & (1-\sigma)\alpha \\ 1 & -\sigma & (\sigma - 1) \\ -1 & \frac{\eta - \alpha\sigma(\eta-1)}{\alpha+\eta(1-\alpha)} & -\frac{\alpha(1-\sigma)(\eta-1)}{\alpha+\eta(1-\alpha)} \end{pmatrix} \begin{pmatrix} m \\ w_i \\ w_{-i} \end{pmatrix}. \tag{5.30}$$

Notice that the three target variables are independent of each other.

Solving the model for the Stackelberg equilibrium (with the unions as leaders) implies the following outcomes:

$$p = \frac{(1-(\alpha - \phi + \alpha\phi)\sigma)(\alpha - \phi + \alpha\phi)(\alpha + (1-\alpha)\eta)}{\{\eta(1-\sigma(\alpha - \phi + \alpha\phi)) + \alpha\sigma(1+\phi)\}(1+\phi)} b_1 \geq 0, \tag{5.31}$$

$$u = \frac{(1-(\alpha - \phi + \alpha\phi)\sigma)(\alpha + (1-\alpha)\eta)}{\eta(1-(\alpha - \phi + \alpha\phi)\sigma) + \alpha\sigma(1+\phi)} b_1 > 0, \tag{5.32}$$

where $\phi = [\alpha(1 - \alpha)\ \beta - 1]/[(1 - \alpha)^2\ \beta + 1]$. In order to evaluate possible non-neutrality, note that ϕ is the only parameter containing the

faces a Blanchard and Kiyotaki (1987) demand function. Equations (5.28) and (5.27) are the price level and the union's unemployment rate in equilibrium, respectively.

central bank's preference parameters. Clearly, Equation (5.32) shows that non-neutrality holds.

As in some of the previous cases, unemployment is affected by the government's preferences. In this case too, monetary policy has real effects. However, non-neutrality is now the result of a lack of coordination among the wage-setters. It is easy to verify that under full wage centralization the model collapses to the standard Barro–Gordon case.

However, solving the model for the Nash equilibrium, we obtain

$$p = \frac{(1-\alpha\sigma)(\eta-\alpha(\eta-1))(\alpha-\phi+\alpha\phi)}{(\eta-\alpha\sigma(\eta-1))(1+\phi)} b_1 \geq 0, \tag{5.33}$$

$$u = \frac{(1-\alpha\sigma)(\eta-\alpha(\eta-1))}{\eta-\alpha\sigma(\eta-1)} b_1 > 0. \tag{5.34}$$

Now, Equation (5.34) surprisingly shows that neutrality holds.

In the next chapter we will show that a close relationship exists between the different models that exhibit non-neutrality; and that monetary neutrality in the Barro–Gordon model is just one particular case. We will also show the rationale for the different results delivered by the different models.

5.4.5 *Fiscal and monetary interactions*

It is also useful to discuss a further application, consisting of a class of policy games between the government and central bank introduced by Dixit and Lambertini (2001, 2003a, 2003b).[40] In a game of this kind, the policymakers aim to stabilize output and inflation around their desired targets after a shock. They minimize quadratic preferences constrained by an aggregate demand equation and by an inflation adjustment equation. The model is formally defined by three elements: the policymakers' losses, the structure of the economy, and the solution

[40] See also Andersen and Schneider (1986), Buti, Roeger and In't Veld (2002), Hughes Hallett and Weymark (2004, 2007), Beetsma and Debrun (2007); and for interactions in a different kind of setup, Beetsma and Jensen (2005), Libich, Hughes Hallett and Stehlik (2012).

concept (we assume here that policymakers play simultaneously, i.e., we consider the Nash equilibrium).

The policymakers' expected losses depend on deviations of inflation p and real output y away from target values, p_i^* and y_i^* (subscripts identify policymakers). The government's (L_G) and central bank's (L_B) loss functions are

$$L_i = E\left[\frac{1}{2}(p - p_i^*)^2 + \frac{\theta_i}{2}(y - y_i^*)^2\right] \quad \text{for } i \in \{G, B\}, \tag{5.35}$$

where E denotes the expectation operator; and θ_G and θ_B are the marginal rates of substitution between the deviations of inflation and real output from their target values. We assume a conservative central banker (i.e., $\theta_B \leq \theta_G$).

The economy consists of a Lucas-type supply equation and a simple demand equation:

$$y = \bar{y} + b(p - p^e) + ax, \tag{5.36}$$

$$p = \varepsilon p_0 + \mu cx, \tag{5.37}$$

where p^e is the inflation expected by the private sector, and x and p_0 are the fiscal and monetary policy instruments, respectively. As usual, due to distortions in the goods markets, the natural level of real output ($\bar{y}$) is considered too low from a social point of view. Therefore, $y_G^* > \bar{y}$. Real output can deviate from the natural level because of the supply effect of surprise inflation ($p - p^e$), and because of the direct effect of fiscal policy on real output, which can be either positive for Keynesian demand effects, or negative for crowding out effects. The algebra of the model is, however, the same in both cases. Both the fiscal and the monetary policy instruments affect the level of inflation.[41] Without loss of generality, we therefore assume $b > 0$, $c > 0$ and $a > 0$.[42]

[41] This may be due to the fact that, in practice, the central banks are forced to accommodate fiscal expansions to some extent; or because of changes in the equilibrium price of goods which depend on the balance between the effects of fiscal policy on aggregate demand and the costs produced by changes in tax distortions or in public investment. Thus c can be either positive or negative.

[42] See Dixit and Lambertini (2003a, 2003b) for an extensive discussion about this model and its derivation.

By minimizing the government's and central bank's losses with respect to the fiscal and monetary instruments, respectively, subject to Equations (5.36) and (5.37), we can obtain the following first-order conditions:

$$E\left[\mu c\left(p-p_G^*\right)+\left(a+\mu c b\right)\theta_G\left(y-y_G^*\right)\right]=0, \tag{5.38}$$

$$E\left[\varepsilon\left(p-p_B^*\right)+\varepsilon b\theta_B\left(y-y_B^*\right)\right]=0. \tag{5.39}$$

These first-order conditions show that, in general, both policymakers affect both target variables according to their preferences. However, in particular cases the outcomes may be different. Dixit and Lambertini (2003b) show that, if the shocks are perfectly observed by both policymakers, these equations may imply fiscal policy neutrality for inflation; or the non-existence of an equilibrium, depending on the parameter values in the two loss functions. Both results are easy to verify, and are left as an exercise for the reader. More generally, however, as Demertzis, Hughes Hallett and Viegi (2004) show, there will be an equilibrium between the two policy settings in which, in the presence of an independent central bank, the outcomes are typically driven away from either player's preferred position by an endogenized electorate demanding more from fiscal policy (which it can influence) than it does from the conservatism in monetary policy (which it cannot).

5.5 A look ahead

Now that policy games have been introduced, we have an analytical technique to deal with multiple rational policymakers in a consistent framework. Our theory will develop from this analytic approach, to which we will apply the tools derived from the Tinbergen–Theil theory of economic policy – notably that of controllability.

The rest of the book is divided in two parts. In Part III we concentrate again on the static framework, whereas in Part IV we have a dynamic context, i.e., we assume that the economy evolves according to a difference equation system. Specifically, in the next chapter we derive propositions about both policy neutrality and equilibrium existence by applying the concept of controllability to specific players. In Chapters 7 and 8, we will focus on controllability at the level of the system or of groups of players, instead of the controllability by one or some of the players, and derive conditions for the existence of the Nash equilibrium that extend those required in Chapter 6. Chapter 9 will present an application of the new theory to the case of multiple equilibria. In the chapters of Part IV, we will move on to the dynamic context.

PART III

The new theory of economic policy: statics

6 *A theory of strategic conflict: foundations*

Summary. This chapter and the next form the core of our approach. Here we look at a general policy game, first in a simple two-player version but later generalized to N players, through a Tinbergen–Theil lens. We derive our main theorems for equilibrium existence and policy neutrality based on the concept of controllability. We discuss the role played by the assumption of instrument costs included in the loss functions of the players. Moreover recognizing that, in contrast to the case of pure quadratic deviations, some preferences may be non-satiated, we generalize our results to the case when additional linear terms appear in the players' objective functions. Finally, we illustrate the importance of our methodology by considering some of the standard models in economics – covering monetary policy, wage bargaining, monopolistically competitive markets, the wage-wedge problem, and fiscal–monetary interactions – and show how the existence of an equilibrium and the characteristics of that equilibrium can be investigated without solving the entire game.

6.1 The extension of the Tinbergen–Theil approach to policy games

The first purpose of this chapter is to show how we can build a theory of economic policy that, while based on many tools developed by the Tinbergen–Theil theory, is robust to the criticisms raised against it, in particular by the Lucas critique, and is still in line with the evolution of economic analysis in terms of REs and micro-foundations.

Unlike the Tinbergen–Theil approach, the new theory of economic policy is not centered around the problem of a single policymaker, but is concerned with the more general issue of the interactions of different (public, private, or both public and private) policymakers.

As we saw in the previous chapter, specific issues of policy effectiveness and neutrality can be handled in such a strategic context using the framework of policy games. In this chapter, we show that, in such contexts, it is possible to state general conditions for policy effectiveness and neutrality that exploit the properties of the Tinbergen–Theil theory. In addition, we give the necessary and sufficient conditions for the existence of an equilibrium for these interactions; that is to say, the conditions according to which the optimal choices of each policymaker are mutually compatible.

Thus, the new theory of economic policy accomplishes a number of tasks. First, it settles an old issue (that of policy invariance) in a setting (policy games) where it can be consistently applied to overcome the Lucas critique, while also linking us back to the propositions of the Tinbergen–Theil theory. Second, it asserts propositions useful for model building that state the conditions for the consistency of the optimal strategies of all the players (and thus the existence of the equilibrium of the game) as well as for the effectiveness of the policy instruments. Third, the theory is useful as it helps us to show the conditions under which a decentralized equilibrium may fail to exist. In this chapter, we deal with the first two aspects of the theory in a static context. The next chapter will deal with the third issue.

In accomplishing these tasks, our theory offers the tools for dealing with situations of conflict which are only too common in reality: for example, where people share targets, but are in opposition over the specific values that those targets should take; or where they have different instruments available to reach those targets. Using our theory, general rules can be derived for assessing whether an equilibrium can be reached, or whether there is a possibility of multiple equilibria and indeterminacy. Also, in cases where a unique equilibrium is reached, the theory allows us to see which or whose instruments are going to be ineffective.

In the next section, we lay down the main blocks of the theory with reference to a simple situation where two players with *quadratic loss functions* and overlapping target variables face linear constraints (LQ setting). Section 6.3 discusses the issue of instrument costs. Section 6.4 generalizes our analysis to the case of *LQ loss functions*. In Section 6.5, we show the usefulness of the theory for drawing general propositions about policy neutrality and the existence of an equilibrium. Section 6.6 concludes the chapter.

6.2 A simple illustration of the theory: neutrality and existence

6.2.1 A two-player policy game

We consider two players: the public sector (*government*), indexed by 1, and the private sector (*agent*), indexed by 2. They minimize the following quadratic loss functions:

$$L_i = \tfrac{1}{2}(y_i - \bar{y}_i)' Q_i (y_i - \bar{y}_i) \quad i = \{1,2\}, \tag{6.1}$$

where $y_i \in R^{q(i)}$ is a vector of target variables; $\bar{y}_i \in R^{q(i)}$ is a vector of target values; and Q_i is an appropriate positive definite diagonal matrix. Note that Q_i is a square matrix of full rank by assumption. Player *i*'s first best (or *optimum optimorum*) corresponds to his target values.

In this set-up, all the target variable vectors are sub-vectors of $y \in R^K$. Since the players may share some target variables, we also have $q(1) + q(2) \geq K$. The K target variables are linked together by the following linear equation system:

$$y = Au + f, \tag{6.2}$$

where $u \in R^M$ is the vector of the controls set by the two players; vector $f \in R^K$ is a vector of given constants that are outside the players' control.[1] Each row of the above equation system corresponds to a linear relationship between one target and the full instrument vector u. Again, to keep things simple, we will assume that the basis of A is the identity matrix.[2] All the players' control vectors, i.e., $u_i \in R^{m(i)}$, are sub-vectors of $u \in R^M$. We also assume that $m(1) + m(2) = M$ since a policy control, by definition, cannot be set by more than one player at a time. For the sake of simplicity, we also assume that each player cannot control more instruments than the number of targets under that player's supervision: i.e., $m(i) \leq q(i)$.

We consider three kinds of interactions (solution concepts) based on different information sets. In the non-cooperative *Nash equilibrium*, both decision makers play simultaneously and each of them has to

[1] It can also contain zero-mean shocks. In this case, our results hold in expected terms by the certainty equivalence principle.

[2] It means that system (6.2) cannot be reduced to many independent sub-systems. However, our results stand even without this assumption by using the concept of decisiveness as in Section 8.4. For a more detailed discussion, see Acocella and Di Bartolomeo (2005).

form expectations of the opponent's policy choices. In the case of a *commitment equilibrium*, the government is a Stackelberg game leader who forms expectations of the opponent's behavior. The government can commit itself to a policy rule, optimal or otherwise, and hence to a policy that is not contingent on that formulated by the other player. The follower (agent) can then choose, given whatever the government has chosen. The decisions are sequential across players. Finally, in a *discretionary equilibrium*, the government is a Stackelberg follower and cannot pre-commit to a particular policy, although the agent forms expectations for the government's policy.

6.2.2 Policy games in terms of the Tinbergen–Theil framework

We will operate in four steps:

(a) We first distinguish three different sub-vectors of target variables for each of the two players – one for each player that contains the variables of their own specific interest; and one that is common to both players and includes their overlapping targets.
(b) We then rearrange the matrix equation representing the economic system (6.2) in terms of these three sub-vectors.
(c) Next we decompose the representation of the economic system into two parts, in order to show the relations between the targets of interest for the two players and their policy instruments separately.
(d) Finally, we solve the game according to the specific equilibrium notion chosen.

Step (a): Players' target variables

We first distinguish the three sub-vectors of target variables.

1. The vector of variables of interest to the government only: $y_1^n \in \mathrm{R}^{n(1)}$.
2. The vector of shared target variables of interest to both players: $y^s \in R^s$.
3. The vector of variables of interest to the agent only: $y_2^n \in \mathrm{R}^{n(2)}$, with $n(1) + s = q(1)$ and $n(2) + s = q(2)$.

Regarding the instruments:

1. The vector of the instruments controlled by the government is u_1.
2. The vector of the instruments controlled by the agent is u_2.

Step (b): Players' constraints

From Equation (6.2), we can extract each y_i using the reordering procedure discussed in Chapter 2 (see also Equation (5.2)), to obtain the relevant sub-system for player i:

$$y_i = C_i u_i + E_i u_j + f_i \quad j \neq i, \tag{6.3}$$

where $C_i \in R^{q(i)\times m(i)}$, $E_i \in R^{q(i)\times m(j)}$, and $f_i \in R^{q(i)}$ are appropriate matrices and vectors.

Step (c): Controllability check

Equation (6.3) allows us to express the policy game approach in terms of the Tinbergen-Theil paradigm. For $i = 1$, it represents the constraints faced by the government when solving its own optimization problem, given the agent's decisions. For $i = 2$ it shows the corresponding constraints for the agent's problem, i.e., where the agent solves his problem by considering the government's instruments as given. According to Theorem 2.2, the system represented by Equation (6.3) is controllable by the government (or agent) if the number of government (agent) instruments is greater than or equal to the number of government (agent) targets.

Step (d): Players' optimization problems

Next, we consider three non-cooperative solution concepts: the *Nash equilibrium* (N); *Commitment* (C) or "Ramsey" policy; and *Discretion* (D) or the RE solution. Formally, the outcomes associated with the different equilibria can be obtained by solving the following optimization problems with respect to u_1 and u_2:

$$\begin{aligned} N \triangleq &\{\min_{u_1} \text{Eq.}(6.1)\text{s.t.Eq.}(6.3)\} \\ &\text{and } \{\min_{u_2} \text{Eq.}(6.1)\text{s.t.Eq.}(6.3)\} \end{aligned} \tag{6.4}$$

$$C \triangleq \{\min_{u_1} \text{Eq.}(6.1)\text{s.t.Eq.}(6.3) \mid \{\min_{u_2} \text{Eq.}(6.1)\text{s.t.Eq.}(6.3)\}\} \tag{6.5}$$

$$D \triangleq \{\min_{u_2} \text{Eq.}(6.1)\text{s.t.Eq.}(6.3) \mid \{\min_{u_1} \text{Eq.}(6.1)\text{s.t.Eq.}(6.3)\}\} \tag{6.6}$$

where (6.5) and (6.6) show that the leader will make optimal choices conditioned on the expectation that the follower will make the best decisions available to him at that point. The leader's decisions will then be optimal conditional on the follower's best reaction function.

Summarizing, a decision problem in a two-player strategic context has been reduced, in four steps, to two separate optimization problems that can be studied and solved individually with the tools used in the traditional approach to economic policy. In our decoupled representation of the policy game, a straightforward condition for neutrality can be stated as follows. If equilibrium exists, the government's policy is neutral with respect to the targets shared with the agent, if the sub-system (6.3) is controllable by the agent. It is worth noticing here that controllability by one player (e.g., the agent) implies that that player will always achieve his target values since his decisions correspond to his *optimum optimorum*.[3]

Although intuitive, the above conditions may appear to contain a contradiction, since controllability by the agent does not exclude the possibility that the government can also Tinbergen–Theil control its own sub-system. However, we will show that this contradiction is in fact only apparent. Indeed, were it more than just apparent, a policy equilibrium would not exist. The issue of equilibrium existence is therefore crucially related to that of controllability and neutrality, as the following theorem states more formally.

Theorem 6.1 (*existence of an equilibrium and the government's policy neutrality*). (i) The equilibrium of the game in target space exists if the intersection of the players' controllable sets is empty, or if the players share the same target values for the variables contained therein. (ii) The government's policy is neutral for all the government's target variables contained in the agent's controllable target set. (iii) Symmetrically, the agent's decisions are neutral for all the agent's target variables in the government's controllable target set.

Deriving necessary and sufficient conditions formally for the existence of Nash equilibrium is not a simple task.[4] However, our LQ context simplifies the discussion. Here the existence problem is related to the solution of a linear equation system and can therefore be reduced

[3] Formally, this is due to two assumptions: (a) the losses are defined in terms of deviations from the desired targets; (b) target variables are independent. Cases that are more complex will be introduced later in this chapter, after a generalization of our approach to non-satiated preferences. In the last section, we examine the role played by the independence of target variables in detail.

[4] After Nash (1951), the existence of Nash equilibria has been studied by, among others, Debreu (1952), Glicksberg (1952) and Dasgupta and Maskin (1986). See also the textbook treatment by Rasmusen (1989), Friedman (1991) and Fudenberg and Tirole (1991).

to certain rank conditions. A proof of the above theorem *in target space* runs as follows.[5]

Proof. Nash equilibria are usually computed by inverting the coefficient matrices in the players' reaction functions, which is to work in instrument space. But, as we saw in Section 5.2, they can also be derived directly in target space (the dual problem) by solving the following system of first-order conditions simultaneously:

$$\frac{\partial L_i}{\partial u_i} = C_i' \, Q_i \left(y_i - \bar{y}_i \right) = 0 \quad i = \{1,2\}. \tag{6.7}$$

Since both C_1 and C_2 are of full rank by assumption, $r[C_1] = \min\{q(1), m(1)\}$ and $r[C_2] = \min\{q(2), m(2)\}$. Moreover, for this theorem, we can restrict ourselves to just the relevant cases: $m(1) \leq q(1)$ and $m(2) \leq q(2)$.[6]

With the assumption that both players can perfectly control their own sub-systems, the matrices $C_1' \, Q_1$ and $C_2' \, Q_2$ are square of full rank and of order $m(1) = q(1)$ and $m(2) = q(2)$, respectively. Hence, $y_1 = \bar{y}_1$ and $y_2 = \bar{y}_2$ follow. But this result can only hold in the special cases of either the non-existence of shared targets or if $\bar{y}_1 = \bar{y}_2$, in which case a solution without conflict exists.[7] In all other cases, if both players control their sub-systems, the system formed by the two equations in (6.7) is over-determined: i.e., $m(1) + m(2) = n(1) + n(2) + 2s$ independent equations are being used to define $n(1) + n(2) + s$ independent unknowns.[8]

Once the first part of the theorem is obtained, the proof of the second part is intuitive. If the agent is able to control his sub-system, he can reach all his targets, including the shared target variables. Hence, the government's policy is neutral with respect to the shared

[5] See Section 6.4 for a formal proof in *instrument space*, done for the general case of a LQ loss function.

[6] The discussion can easily be generalized to the case of a number of instruments greater than that of the target variables.

[7] It is straightforward to verify that, in a solution without conflicts, neutrality as we defined it would hold even if the government were able to achieve its targets. In fact, changes in government preferences either do not affect the equilibrium outcomes (if there are changes in the weights of the targets) or imply the non-existence of an equilibrium (when the target values of shared variables change).

[8] The same inconsistency can also emerge in the case of sub-controllability (Acocella and Di Bartolomeo, 2005).

target variables, as claimed. If the government also controlled its own sub-system, the intersection of the government and the agent's controllable target sets would be not empty, and the equilibrium would not exist. Thus, the theorem is verified. ■

Corollary 6.1 (*extensions to Stackelberg equilibria*). The same potential inconsistencies can emerge naturally in Stackelberg equilibria. In fact, by applying the same argument, if one player has controllability in his sub-system (is able to achieve one or many target variables independently of the action of the other), Theorem 6.1 is clearly not affected by the timing; that is, when his opponent actually executes his actions, all of which are perfectly observed or anticipated.[9]

The reason why an issue of existence might arise in our context can also be usefully discussed in terms of the conditions required by a Nash equilibrium existence theorem with bounded strategies (for example, with instrument costs) due to Dasgupta and Maskin (1986).[10] In one-shot games, a Nash equilibrium always exists if (i) the space of strategies of each player is convex and compact; (ii) the payoff function of each player is a definite, bounded, and continuous function for each strategic combination; (iii) player *i*'s payoff function is concave with respect to each player's strategy for all possible strategic combinations and for all players.

In our case, condition (i) is not met since the players' controls are unbounded. Hence, equilibrium non-existence, as discussed above, is a possible outcome.

Theorem 6.1 can now be extended to problems with any number of players.

Theorem 6.2 (*equilibrium existence and neutrality generalized*). (i) The equilibrium of a policy game between any *N* players exists (in target space) if the intersection of their controllable target sets is empty; or if the variables contained in the set are associated with the same quantitative target value for all the players that control them. (ii) Player *i*'s policy is neutral for all his targets contained in the union set of the other players' controllable target sets.

[9] Note that the possibility – for a leader who does not satisfy the Tinbergen controllability conditions – to control his sub-system by exploiting his first mover advantage is a different issue.

[10] The instrument cost version of this theorem is examined in the next section.

6.3 The issue of instrument costs

So far we have not taken account of any instrument costs in the players' loss functions. However, as shown in Chapter 2, the costs of using an instrument can easily be included by adding an auxiliary target variable into Equation (6.1), and an equality constraint between it and the instrument in question into Equation (6.2). Hence the introduction of instrument costs implies that the dimensions of matrices Q_i become $(q(i) + m(i)) \times (q(i) + m(i))$. This will affect the results of the game and the existence of a policy equilibrium.

To illustrate, it is useful to recall that Dasgupta and Maskin (1986) showed that a sufficient condition for the Nash equilibrium to exist is that the space of strategies of each player should be convex and compact. If the players' controls are unbounded, the Nash equilibrium may not exist.

However, in static LQ games, the introduction of quadratic instrument costs for each player would automatically make them bounded and ensure the existence of an equilibrium. But then the number of instruments would always be less than the number of target values. The system would no longer be controllable by any player and the corresponding policy equilibrium will exist. In the case of two players, if only one has quadratic instrument costs, the equilibrium will exist and the other player will dictate the outcomes when/if he is able to control the economy.

It is worth noticing that, in an LQ context, our theorem is more general than the Dasgupta–Maskin result since a policy game with instrument costs is just one special case of our theorem. Introducing instrument costs into a loss function can be done only when there is an underlying justification in terms of the outcomes, since it changes the properties of the game. Introducing such costs simply to guarantee the existence of an equilibrium is not in itself sufficient justification.

6.4 A generalization: non-satiated preferences and Q-controllability

Now we consider the general setup with LQ preferences, described in Section 2.7.2. We suppose that each player minimizes

$$L_i = \tfrac{1}{2}(y_i - \bar{y}_i)' Q_i (y_i - \bar{y}_i) + y_i' r_i + \tilde{y}_i' l_i \quad \forall i \in N, \tag{6.8}$$

where N – with a little abuse of notation – indicates both the set and the number of players; $y_i \in R^{q(i)}$ is a vector of target variables that enter Equation (6.8) in a quadratic manner; $\bar{y}_i \in R^{q(i)}$ is a vector of target values; $\tilde{y}_i \in R^{l(i)}$ is a vector of target variables that enter only linearly; Q_i is a positive diagonal matrix; and $r_i \in R^{q(i)}$ and $l_i \in R^{l(i)}$ are appropriate vectors with $t(i) = q(i) + l(i)$ indicating the total number of target variables of interest to player i.

Recall, from Section 2.7.3, that preferences (6.8) are unbounded when $l(i) \neq 0$, i.e., the first best of (6.8) implies infinite values for any of the variables that enter the loss function only linearly. Moreover, if $r_i \neq 0$, the first best of (6.8) is no longer the vector of target values, i.e., $\bar{y}_i$.[11]

As in Section 6.2.1, we can extract y_i and $\tilde{y}_i$ from Equation (6.2) to obtain the relevant sub-system for player i:

$$\begin{bmatrix} y_i \\ \tilde{y}_i \end{bmatrix} = \begin{bmatrix} C_i \\ \tilde{C}_i \end{bmatrix} u_i + \sum_{j \in N/i} \begin{bmatrix} E_{ij} \\ \tilde{E}_{ij} \end{bmatrix} u_j + f_i . \tag{6.9}$$

where $C_i \in R^{q(i)\times m(i)}$, $\tilde{C}_i \in R^{l(i)\times m(i)}$, $E_{ij} \in R^{q(i)\times m(j)}$, $\tilde{E}_{ij} \in R^{l(i)\times m(j)}$, and $f_i \in R^{t(i)}$ are appropriately defined matrices and vectors.

Now we can introduce a refined definition of controllability, discussed in Chapter 2, but one that still lies within the Tinbergen–Theil framework (see Section 2.7.2).

Definition 6.1 (*Q-controllability*). Player i can *Q-control* system (6.3) if the number of its instruments equals the number of its quadratic targets: $m(i) = q(i)$. If policymaker i can Q-control his system, $y_i \in R^{q(i)}$ is his controllable set.

As before, the Nash equilibrium can be decomposed into a set of N individual Tinbergen–Theil problems (minimizing Equation (6.8) subject to (6.9) for each of the N players), to produce the set of optimal reaction functions for this type of problem. With reference to this decoupled representation, we can state the following theorem.

Theorem 6.3 (*existence with N players and LQ losses*). The Nash equilibrium of the policy game just described does not exist if (a) for

[11] As an example, let us assume that the policymaker's preferences are $U = -L = y - \pi^2$ (where y is real output and π is inflation); it is easy to verify that the first best implies zero inflation (i.e., the policymaker's target value) and an infinite level of real output. If instead preferences are $U = \alpha y - (y - y_P)^2 - \pi^2$, for $\alpha = 0$ the first best is given by the target values: y_P for output and zero for inflation; but for $\alpha \neq 0$, the first best is given by $y_P - \alpha/2$ and zero, respectively.

at least one player: $l_i \neq 0$ and $t(i) = m(i)$; or (b) the intersection of players' controllable sets is not empty.

Proof. The optimization problem of each player implies the following n first-order conditions:

$$\frac{\partial L_i}{\partial u_i} = C_i'Q_iC_iu_i + C_i'Q_i\sum_{j\in N/i} E_{ij}u_j + C_i'(r_i + l_i - Q_i\bar{y}_i + Q_if_i) \tag{6.10}$$
$$= 0 \quad \forall i \in N.$$

Now, and without loss of generality, let us consider the case of player 1 and assume that $m(1) = t(1) > q(1)$ and that a solution (u_1^*, u_j^*) exists – where u_j^* represents the controls of all the players other than player 1 If (u_1^*, u_j^*) is the solution, given u_j^*, u_1^* must satisfy the first-order condition (6.10) for player 1. But no finite value of u_1 could do that since $C'_1Q_1C_1$ is singular and cannot be inverted if $m(1) = t(1) > q(1)$.[12]

Next, let us consider the second part of the theorem focusing on the first two players. Assume for the moment that they share all their variables and can Q-control their sub-systems. Assume also that a solution (u_1^*, u_2^*, u_1^*) exists. Then, given u_j^*, (u_1^*, u_2^*) must satisfy the system of first-order conditions of the first two players: i.e.,

$$\begin{bmatrix} C_1'Q_1C_1 & C_1'Q_1E_{12} \\ C_2'Q_2E_{21} & C_2'Q_2C_2 \end{bmatrix}\begin{bmatrix} u_1 \\ u_2 \end{bmatrix} =$$
$$\begin{bmatrix} C_1'Q_1 \sum_{j\in N/\{1,2\}} E_{1j}u_j^* + C_1'(r_1 + l_1 - Q_1\bar{y}_1 + Q_1f_1) \\ C_2'Q_2 \sum_{j\in N/\{1,2\}} E_{2j}u_j^* + C_2'(r_2 + l_2 - Q_2\bar{y}_2 + Q_2f_2) \end{bmatrix}. \tag{6.11}$$

However, the first matrix of (6.11) cannot be inverted since, according to our assumptions (all target variables shared and Q-controllability), $C_1 = E_{21}$ and $C_2 = E_{12}$ which makes the matrix on the left of (6.11) singular. Hence no (u_1^*, u_2^*) can satisfy (6.11). In other words, (u_1^*, u_2^*, u_j^*) cannot be a solution.

[12] To see this, write $Q_1 = T_1T'_1$ where $T_1 = [\sqrt{Q_1} : \varnothing] \in R^{q(1)\times t(1)}$. Then T_1 may be obtained in two steps: first by considering a $q(1) \times q(1)$ matrix with the square roots of each element Q_1 and then by adding $l(i)$ columns of zeros. Thus $\det(C'_1Q_1C_1) = \det(C'_1T_1)\det(T'_1C_1)$ equals zero since it is easy to verify that all the elements of the last $l(i)$ columns of C'_1T_1 are zeros.

Finally, consider the case where the first two players do not share all their target values. This case can be solved by considering each player's problem as an independent one:

(a) Minimize the LQ loss considering only second-order shared target variables with respect to an arbitrary set of instruments equal in number to the number of target variables.
(b) Minimize LQ loss considering non-shared plus all the linear (first-order) target variables with respect to the remaining instruments.

Now the impossibility of a solution emerges for the first-order condition of the problems in (a).[13]

Thus, to summarize, if at least two players can Q-control their sub-systems and share at least one target variable (implying that the players' controllable set is not empty), the Nash equilibrium does not exist – as claimed. ■

Next, once the Nash equilibrium is decomposed into a set of N independent Tinbergen–Theil problems, provided that an equilibrium exists, player i's policy is ineffective with respect to the targets shared with the players who can perfectly Q-control their sub-systems. A straightforward condition for policy ineffectiveness can therefore be defined as follows:

Theorem 6.4 (*ineffectiveness with N players and LQ losses*). Assuming that a Nash equilibrium exists, player i's policy is neutral with respect to all the target variables contained in the union of all other players' controllable sets.

Proof. First-order conditions written in terms of quasi-reaction functions are

$$\frac{\partial L_i}{\partial u_i} = C_i' Q_i \left(y_i - \bar{y}_i \right) + C_i' r_i + \tilde{C}_i' l_i = 0 \quad \forall i \in N. \tag{6.12}$$

Equation (6.12) represents the optimal value of the target variables that would minimize player i's criterion, given the policy decisions of the others. Thus, by definition, all first-order conditions in (6.12) have to be mutually verified to ensure the Nash equilibrium. Formally, Equation (6.12) maps the vector of target variables into that of the

[13] Notice that, given controllability by one player, this result holds independently of the assignment of the instruments to (a) and (b).

desired target values. If player i can Q-control his sub-system, then condition (6.12) becomes

$$y_i = \bar{y}_i - Q_i^{-1} r_i - \left(C_i' Q_i\right)^{-1} \tilde{C}_i' l_i. \tag{6.13}$$

If the equilibrium exists and player i can Q-control its sub-system, the Nash equilibrium will satisfy Equation (6.13) and no other player will be able to affect the value of any of the variables in y_i, being those in the controllable set of player i. ■

It is worth noticing that the case of LQ preferences is different from that of purely quadratic preferences, and that Q-controllability has different implications when Stackelberg games are considered. In fact, when first-order terms are present in the losses (i.e., $l(i) \neq 0$), Q-controllability never implies the achievement of the player's first best (recall that, in this case, losses are unbounded). Q-controllability will only lead to the best outcome that can be obtained independently from the actions of the other players.

In the Nash equilibrium, this implies that the player who Q-controls the system will fully exploit the power of his Q-controllability as he takes the actions of the rivals as given by assumption. By contrast, in a Stackelberg game (if the player considered is the leader) the actions of his rivals depend on his choice. Since he does not achieve his first best, he could always improve his position by using his first-mover advantage. In other words, the leader, even if he Q-controls his sub-system, takes account of the preferences of the follower, choosing an outcome on his reaction function preferred to the Nash equilibrium. Thus, his choices vary according to the preferences of the other player: non-neutrality of the follower's policies will ensue.

Hence, when linear costs are considered, Q-controllability implies neutrality of non-controlling players only if the player concerned is the follower or plays simultaneously with respect to the other players. By contrast, if $l(i) = 0$, LQ preferences can be exactly analyzed as quadratic deviations with the only difference that *optima optimorum* (i.e., first best positions) no longer correspond to the target values.

We illustrate this point by an example. Consider an economy where the central bank and the government interact to affect inflation (π) and real output (y). Their preferences are defined as follows.

$$U_B = -L_B = -\frac{1}{2}(\pi - \pi_B)^2 + \alpha y, \tag{6.14}$$

$$U_G = -L_G = -\frac{1}{2}(\pi - \pi_G)^2 - \frac{1}{2}(y - y_G)^2, \qquad (6.15)$$

where subscripts identify the central bank (B) and the government(G). The central bank preferences are clearly unbounded unless either $\alpha =$ 0, or π and y are not linearly independent.

We assume that each policymaker manages one instrument (m for the monetary authority and f for the fiscal one). Hence, the central bank Q-controls its relevant sub-system. The relation between instruments and targets is modeled by two equations:

$$\pi = m + f, \qquad (6.16)$$

$$y = \pi - \pi^e - bf, \qquad (6.17)$$

where π^e are inflation expectations, which are assumed as given (hence, monetary policy has real effects). In Equations (6.16) and (6.17), both instruments are inflationary, and thus positively affect real output via inflation surprises, whereas the direct effect of fiscal policy on output is negative. Equations (6.16) and (6.17) are used just as an example; the monetary policy transmission mechanism is rather standard, fiscal policy is model specific, but a discussion of its effect is beyond our scope.[14]

Deriving (6.14) and (6.15) with respect to m and f, taking (6.16) and (6.17) into account, leads to the following quasi-reaction functions:

$$\frac{\partial U_B}{\partial m} = -(\pi - \pi_B)\frac{\partial \pi}{\partial m} + \alpha\frac{\partial y}{\partial m} = -(\pi - \pi_B) + \alpha = 0, \qquad (6.18)$$

$$\begin{aligned}\frac{\partial U_G}{\partial f} &= -(\pi - \pi_G)\frac{\partial \pi}{\partial f} - (y - y_G)\frac{\partial y}{\partial f} \\ &= -(\pi - \pi_G) - (1 - b)(y - y_G) = 0.\end{aligned} \qquad (6.19)$$

By solving (6.18) and (6.19), the outcomes of the Nash equilibrium are found. As shown in Chapter 5, the Stackelberg equilibrium instead is

[14] For a discussion of the transmission mechanism of fiscal policy in this kind of context, see Alesina and Tabellini (1987), Acocella and Ciccarone (1997), Beetsma and Bovenberg (1998), Beetsma and Uhlig (1999), Dixit and Lambertini (2003a), Hughes Hallett and Viegi (2003), Demertzis, Hughes Hallett and Viegi (2004), Ciccarone, Marchetti and Di Bartolomeo (2007).

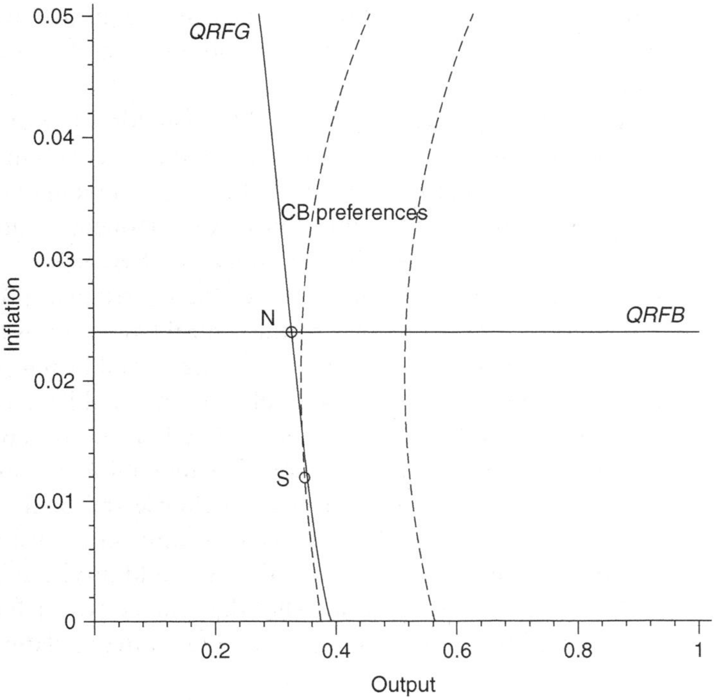

Figure 6.1 A monetary and fiscal policy game

found by maximizing (6.14) constrained by (6.19) if the central bank is the game leader, or (6.15) constrained by (6.18) if the government is the leader.

The game equilibria in outcome space are illustrated in Figure 6.1.[15] Point N represents the Nash equilibrium and point S represents the equilibrium where the central bank is the leader while the government is the follower. In Figure 6.1 we also represent the quasi-reaction functions (6.18) and (6.19), and the central bank's preferences.

It is easy to notice that government policy is neutral with respect to inflation when policymakers act simultaneously. The central bank's quasi-reaction function (*QRFB*) is in fact a line parallel to the output axis (implying a constant inflation rate, even if different from the

[15] Figure 6.1 is built by assuming that the inflation target is 2% for both policymakers; the government aims to obtain an output equal to 1/3; α is 0.004 and b is 1/2. Inflation is 2.4% and 1.2% in Nash and Stackelberg equilibrium, respectively; real output is instead 0.325 and 0.349.

central bank's target value); it follows that any change in the government's preferences (indicated by *QRFG*) has no effect on the equilibrium inflation.

By contrast, monetary leadership tells a different story. The central bank's problem consists now in choosing a point on the government's quasi-reaction function that maximizes its utility. N is no longer optimal since, by exploiting its commitment power, the monetary authorities can reach S which ensures a higher utility. A different system of *QRFG*, deriving from different parameters of the government preferences, would imply a different choice by the central bank. This is then no longer neutral, even if it was neutral in the Nash equilibrium.

It is worth noticing that the above result does not hold for fiscal leadership. In such a case, the leader's problem is still to choose a point on the opponent's quasi-reaction function that maximizes its utility, but the best choice for the government is to choose the point (not reported in the figure) along *QRFB* where its output target value is achieved, as the government understands that it would not be able to affect inflation. The government leadership then implies the achievement of its preferred output but fiscal policy cannot affect inflation as in the Nash case.

The above results are not surprising; in fact, they could have been uncovered by our theorems before the model was solved. In particular, we know that the central bank is able to Q-control its relevant sub-system; therefore, π enters its controllable set. The government's controllable set is instead empty as it aims to achieve two quadratic targets by using one instrument. It follows that, in the Nash equilibrium and under fiscal leadership, the government's policy cannot affect inflation; whereas if the central bank is the game leader, it can do so.

The above results hold implicitly assuming that all parameters are different from zero; different cases can emerge removing this assumption. For instance, if $\alpha = 0$, monetary authorities control π, and neutrality characterizes all equilibria. The following examples will help to clarify how our approach is used in practice.

6.5 Implications for model building and applications

The fundamental propositions derived in the previous sections are essential for model building, as they state the conditions for the consistency of the optimal strategies of all the players (and thus the existence of the equilibrium of the game) as well as describing the effectiveness of the policy instruments. Using the same standard models as presented in Chapter 5, we now show how their properties (equilibrium existence, policy invariance) can be derived from the theory of economic policy in a strategic setting without solving the policy game explicitly.[16] For instance, we have shown how monetary policy non-neutrality may be introduced by considering three different, apparently unrelated, assumptions about unions' inflation aversion, open economies and monopolistic competition in labor markets. Now we will put them under a common roof. The advantage of taking our approach is that it is no longer necessary to solve the underlying game to derive its policy implications or its consistency.

6.5.1 *The debate on monetary policy neutrality revisited*

In the Barro-Gordon model, the government and the private sector seek to maximize the following preferences:

$$G=-\frac{a_1}{2}(n-n_G)^2-\frac{a_2}{2}(p-p_G)^2, \tag{6.20}$$

$$P=-\frac{1}{2}(n-n_P)^2, \tag{6.21}$$

subject to the following constraint:

$$n=(p-p^e)+n_P. \tag{6.22}$$

As shown in Section 5.4, the Nash solution to this model is

$$n=n_P, \tag{6.23}$$

$$p=p_G+\frac{a_1}{a_2}(n_G-n_P). \tag{6.24}$$

The model is characterized by monetary policy neutrality[17] and an inflationary bias. If $a_2 = 0$, the equilibrium does not exist (see Section 5.4).

[16] Simple procedures for computing controllable sets and policy effectiveness are indicated in Acocella, Di Bartolomeo and Hughes Hallett (2006, 2007).

[17] As in the examples of Chapter 5, by monetary policy neutrality we mean with respect to the real variables (employment, unemployment or real output).

Let us begin by considering the general case where a_1 and a_2 are nonzero and finite: the government has two independent target variables and one instrument. Hence, (6.22) is not controllable by the government and its controllable target set is empty, $\Theta_G = \varnothing$. By contrast, the private sector has one target variable and one control variable. Hence the economy in (6.22) is controllable by the private sector: its controllable target set is $\Theta_P = \{n\}$. A solution exists, since $\Theta_G \cap \Theta_P = \varnothing$, and government policy is ultimately neutral with respect to employment, since the private sector controls it, i.e., $\Theta_P = \{n\}$. As a result, the equilibrium employment will be equal to n_P, which is also the private sector's *optimum optimorum*.

The above result is standard and rather simple to obtain. However, it is presented here with a more direct proof and a far more obvious explanation; and, more important, with a more obvious interpretation of why it arises. Finally, as previously noted, we have investigated the implications and the consistency of model (6.20)–(6.22) without solving it (Equations (6.23) and (6.24) are only reported to show the validity of our investigation based on controllable sets). This is ultimately the benefit of our approach. More complex examples below support our claim.

Now consider two variations of this classical model.

1. Suppose instead that $\alpha_1 = 0$. Then we have $\Theta_G = \{p\}$, $\Theta_P = \{n\}$, and $\Theta_G \cap \Theta_P = \varnothing$. In that case a new solution exists in which the government is neutral (ineffective) with respect to employment and the private sector is neutral with respect to price level: see (6.23)–(6.24). Both players control their systems but they do not share any target variable.
2. By contrast, if $\alpha_2 = 0$ the same system is controllable for both players. Thus $\Theta_G \cap \Theta_P = \{n\}$ is non-empty and two possibilities arise: either the two players share the same target values (i.e., $n_G = n_P$), in which case a simple solution does exist,[18] or they aim to reach different target *values* and a solution does not exist.

The debate on monetary policy neutrality can be better understood by considering an economy in which strategic interactions are explicitly modeled. We now assume that the government manages aggregate

[18] In this case multiple (infinite) solutions emerge. Each implies $n = n_G = n_P$, but a different level of prices.

demand by setting the quantity of money m (instrument variable), instead of the price level (target variable). The demand side of the economy is then described by

$$n = m - p. \tag{6.25}$$

At the same time, the private sector sets the nominal wage, w, as instrument rather than price expectations, which determines the economy's supply side:

$$n = p - w. \tag{6.26}$$

According to Gylfason and Lindbeck (1994), and as shown in Chapter 5, the union or private sector preference function can then be generalized to

$$P = -\frac{b_1}{2}(w - p - \omega_P)^2 - \frac{b_2}{2}(n - n_P)^2 - \frac{b_3}{2}(p - p_P)^2 \tag{6.27}$$

which clearly contains Equation (6.21) as a special case.

In the above expression, however, the real wage target is not independent of the employment target (see Equation (6.26)).[19] Thus our theorems are not immediately applicable. By using (6.26), after some tedious algebra, the union/private sector preferences can be rewritten in terms of independent targets only, as follows:

$$P = -\frac{\tilde{b}_1}{2}n^2 + \tilde{b}_2 n - \frac{b_3}{2}(p - p_P)^2 + K. \tag{6.28}$$

In fact, simple manipulations give

$$\begin{aligned} P &= -\frac{b_1}{2}(-n - \omega_P)^2 - \frac{b_2}{2}(n - n_P)^2 - \frac{b_3}{2}(p - p_P)^2 \\ &= -\frac{b_1}{2}(n^2 - 2n\omega_P + \omega_P^2) - \frac{b_2}{2}(n^2 - 2nn_P + n_P^2)^2 - \frac{b_3}{2}(p - p_P)^2 \\ &= -\frac{b_1 + b_2}{2}n^2 + (b_1\omega_P + b_2 n_P)n - \frac{b_3}{2}(p - p_P)^2 + \frac{b_1\omega_P^2 + b_2 n_P^2}{2}, \end{aligned} \tag{6.29}$$

19 Now the private sector is no longer able to achieve its desired target values as they are not feasible. The private sector needs to trade off the real wage against employment. The first best corresponds to the inflation target value and the employment/real wage obtained by minimizing (6.27) with respect to (6.26), as discussed in the example of Section 2.7.3.

from which (6.28) follows. The meanings of $\tilde{b}_1$, $\tilde{b}_2$ and K in (6.28) are straightforward from Equation (6.29).

As a result, the union/private sector problem is to maximize (6.28) subject to Equations (6.25)–(6.26). Note that (6.28) is an LQ preference, but it is bounded as it does not contain terms that are first-order only.[20] Therefore, the previous theorem fully applies to both Nash and discretionary equilibria.

The government's problem meanwhile is to maximize (6.20) subject to Equations (6.25)–(6.26).

Under those conditions, if a_1 and a_2 are finite and nonzero, (6.25)–(6.26) are not controllable by the government and the set Θ_G is empty. Thus, the Nash equilibrium will exist, as the intersection of the controllable sets is also empty.

The properties of the equilibrium will be derived by analyzing the private sector preferences.

1. If the trade union is indifferent to inflation ($b_3 = 0$), it has one instrument for only one target. The union can therefore control the system and get its *optimum optimorum*, since the number of its instruments equals the number of its targets. According to Theorem 6.3, this implies that, if the equilibrium exists, the government is neutral (ineffective) with respect to employment.
2. If, by contrast, the private sector is inflation averse (i.e., $b_3 \neq 0$), the union retains two independent targets and one instrument. In that case, an equilibrium solution exists and neither policy will be neutral.

The richer model presented in Section 5.4.3 can emphasize the value of our approach even better. For this example, we assume that the government and the private sector preferences are, respectively,

$$G = -\frac{\beta}{2}p^2 - \frac{1}{2}(n - n_G)^2, \tag{6.30}$$

$$P = \alpha_1 (w - cpi) - \frac{\alpha_2}{2}(w - cpi - \omega_P)^2 - \frac{1}{2}(n - n_P)^2 - \frac{\vartheta}{2}p^2, \tag{6.31}$$

and the consumer price index is

$$cpi = (1 - h)p + hp^* \quad h > 0. \tag{6.32}$$

[20] It is easy to verify that this case cannot occur for any value of parameters.

As a representation of the supply side, we still use Equation (6.26). Now we consider the following simple logarithmic demand in place of Equation (6.25):

$$n = m - p - (\mu - 1)(p - e - p^*), \tag{6.33}$$

where e and p^* are the exogenously given nominal exchange rate and the foreign price level, respectively, and $(\mu - 1)$ is the real exchange rate elasticity of output. For the sake of brevity, and without loss of generality, we assume e and p^* equal zero.

As before, the policymaker sets the nominal money supply and the union sets the nominal wage to govern aggregate demand and supply.

The solution of the model was derived in Section 5.4.3, where both Nash and Stackelberg discretionary equilibria were considered. Let us analyze these solutions in Tinbergen–Theil terms.

First of all, similarly to the case of Equation (6.28), by using the *cpi* definition (6.32) to obtain a relation between the independent target variables, we rewrite Equation (6.31) as

$$\begin{aligned} P = &-\frac{1}{2}\begin{pmatrix} n \\ p \end{pmatrix}' \begin{bmatrix} 1+\alpha_2 & -\alpha_2 h \\ -\alpha_2 h & \vartheta + \alpha_2 h^2 \end{bmatrix} \begin{pmatrix} n \\ p \end{pmatrix} \\ &+ \begin{pmatrix} n \\ p \end{pmatrix}' \begin{pmatrix} n_p - \alpha_1 - \alpha_2 \omega_P \\ \alpha_2 h \omega_P + \alpha_1 h \end{pmatrix} - \frac{1}{2}\left(\alpha_2 \omega_P^2 + n_P^2\right), \end{aligned} \tag{6.34}$$

which clearly has an LQ structure. We could therefore apply Theorem 6.3 and Q-controllability to determine controllable sets.

Preferences (6.34) may be bounded or not according to the values of parameters. In detail, if no parameter is assumed to be zero, Equation (6.31) is always a second-order expression in all variables. Preferences are then bounded, and Q-controllability and controllability are equivalent concepts. As a result, using Theorem 6.1 or Theorem 6.3 makes no difference to what is contained in the controllable sets.

By contrast, since employment (n) always enters at least in a quadratic manner in (6.34), because $1 + \alpha_2$ cannot be zero, unbounded preferences emerge when inflation (p) enters in a linear way only. This occurs, if $\alpha_2 = 0$ and $\vartheta = 0$; i.e., the union takes account of the real wage only linearly and is not inflation averse. Under these circumstances, Theorem 6.3 must be used. In what follows we consider the two cases of $\alpha_1 = 0$ and $\alpha_1 > 0$ separately.

When $\alpha_1 = 0$, it is easy to verify the following statements for both the Nash and all Stackelberg equilibria.

1. If α_2, ϑ, β are zero, $\Theta_P = \{n\}$ and $\Theta_G = \{n\}$. It follows that $\Theta_P \cap \Theta_G = \{n\}$ is non-empty and a solution does not exist. If, however, α_2 and/or $\vartheta \neq 0$, $\Theta_P = \varnothing$, $\Theta_P \cap \Theta_G = \varnothing$, a solution exists and monetary policy is not neutral with respect to employment.
2. If α_2, ϑ are zero and $\beta \neq 0$, $\Theta_P = \{n\}$ and $\Theta_G = \{\varnothing\}$. It follows that $\Theta_P \cap \Theta_G = \varnothing$ and thus a solution now exists. Moreover, as $\Theta_P = \{n\}$, monetary policy neutrality holds. In fact, in such a case, $n = n_P$ always holds. If, however, α_2 and/or $\vartheta \neq 0$, $\Theta_P = \varnothing$, $\Theta_P \cap \Theta_G = \varnothing$, a solution exists and monetary policy is not neutral with respect to employment.
3. If α_2, ϑ are zero and $\beta = +\infty$, $\Theta_P = \{n\}$ and $\Theta_G = \{p\}$. It follows that $\Theta_P \cap \Theta_G = \varnothing$ and a solution exists. In this case, monetary policy neutrality holds and wage policy cannot affect (is neutral with respect to) the price level. However, in this case the preferences of the union contain some first-order terms and the result will not generally apply to the case of a discretionary regime.
4. The Nash equilibrium always implies $n = n_P$ and $p = 0$. If, however, α_2 and/or $\vartheta \neq 0$, $\Theta_P = \varnothing$, $\Theta_P \cap \Theta_G = \varnothing$, a solution exists and the price level depends on the preferences of both players.

When $\alpha_1 > 0$, and if α_2 or ϑ are different from zero, Q-controllability and controllability are equivalent concepts and there is nothing to add to what we illustrated about neutrality and equilibrium existence in the above discussion – which still holds true. If, however, $\alpha_2 = 0$ and $\vartheta = 0$, things change and we must apply Theorem 6.3.

1. If α_2 and ϑ are both zero, and $\beta \neq 0$, then the Nash equilibrium (as well as the Ramsey solution) exist and monetary policy is neutral with respect to employment. In fact, $\Theta_P = \{n\}$ and $\Theta_G = \varnothing$, and $n = n_P - (1 + h/\mu)\alpha_1$.
2. By contrast, if α_2 and ϑ are both zero and $\beta \neq 0$ in the Stackelberg equilibrium with the private sector acting as a leader (a discretionary regime) monetary policy is not neutral, i.e., $n = n_P - (1 + h/\beta)\alpha_1$.

Table 6.1 *Properties of the model*

	Preferences			Controllable sets		
	Private sector	Government	Solution[a]	Θ_P	Θ_G	Model properties
1.	$\alpha_1 \geq 0$, α_2 or $\vartheta \neq 0$	$\beta = (0, +\infty)$	N, R, D	$\varnothing$	$\varnothing$	Employment and inflation depend on the preferences of both players
2.	$\alpha_1 \geq 0$, α_2 or $\vartheta \neq 0$	$\beta = 0$	N, R, D	$\varnothing$	n	Private sector does not affect n (determined by the central bank's preferences)
3.	$\alpha_1 \geq 0$, α_2 or $\vartheta \neq 0$	$\beta = +\infty$	N, R, D	$\varnothing$	n	As above
4.	$\alpha_1 = 0$, $\alpha_2 = \vartheta = 0$	$\beta = 0$	N, R, D	n	n	Equilibrium does not exist
5.	$\alpha_1 = 0$, $\alpha_2 = \vartheta = 0$	$\beta = +\infty$	N, R, D	n	p	Monetary policy neutrality, inflation set by the central bank
6.	$\alpha_1 > 0$, $\alpha_2 = \vartheta = 0$	$\beta \neq 0$	N, R	n	$\varnothing$	Monetary policy neutrality
7.	$\alpha_1 > 0$, $\alpha_2 = \vartheta = 0$	$\beta \neq 0$	D	$\varnothing$	n	Private sector does not affect n (determined by the central bank's preferences)

[a] N = Nash; R = Ramsey (commitment); D = discretionary (Stackelberg, private sector leadership).

These results are summarized in Table 6.1, which presents a full classification of the model properties under different assumptions about parameters.

It is important to note that, although neutrality does not hold in the discretionary case, the losses of the union in this solution are lower than those in the Nash regime where neutrality holds. The rationale of this result lies in the fact that neutrality does not necessarily imply the achievement of the best possible outcomes when LQ preferences are considered.

6.5.2 *N-player coordination and externalities: wage bargaining and policy*

Here we return to the model in Section 5.9. The central bank and each of the N unions seek to maximize the following quadratic objective functions:

$$B = -\frac{\beta}{2}p^2 - \frac{1}{2}u^2, \tag{6.35}$$

$$U_i = b_1(w_i - p) - \frac{1}{2}u_i^2 \quad i \in \{1, 2, \ldots N\}. \tag{6.36}$$

Taking account of the constraints, described in Section 5.4.4, the union's preferences can be rewritten as

$$U_i = -\frac{1}{2}u_i^2 - \frac{\alpha b_i}{\eta}u + \frac{b_1[\alpha + \eta(1-\alpha)]}{\eta}u_i, \tag{6.37}$$

where all the arguments (target variables u_i and u) are independent and our approach can be applied. The reduced form model representing the economy is

$$\begin{pmatrix} p \\ u \\ u_i \end{pmatrix} = \begin{pmatrix} 1-\alpha & \sigma\alpha & (1-\sigma)\alpha \\ 1 & -\sigma & (\sigma-1) \\ -1 & \frac{\eta-\alpha\sigma(\eta-1)}{\alpha+\eta(1-\alpha)} & -\frac{\alpha(1-\sigma)(\eta-1)}{\alpha+\eta(1-\alpha)} \end{pmatrix} \begin{pmatrix} m \\ w_i \\ w_{-i} \end{pmatrix}, \tag{6.38}$$

where w_{-i} is the average wage of the unions different from union i. Notice that the three target variables are independent in this example.

The solution to this policy game was provided in Section 5.4.4, but its properties could have been derived even without solving it by proceeding with the theorems in Section 6.4.

In the general case of finite and positive parameters, union i has one instrument (w_i) and two independent targets (u_i and u). It therefore cannot control its relevant sub-system (6.38). However, as the union's preferences include a second-order (u_i) and a first-order (u) term, it is able to Q-control it.

It follows that in the Ramsey (commitment) and Nash regimes, if an equilibrium exists, monetary policy neutrality will hold. By contrast, under discretion, the union will exploit its first-mover advantage to obtain a better outcome by taking account of the government's preferences. As a result, monetary policy will affect the equilibrium unemployment rate. In fact, under discretion the unemployment rate varies with the policymakers' preferences: that is, it falls with the conservatism (inflation aversion) at the central bank.

Focusing on the central bank's problem, the sub-system formed by the first two rows of Equation (6.38) can be controllable by monetary authorities in only two circumstances, namely, when

1. $\beta = 0$ (then $\Theta_G = \{n\}$).
2. $\beta = +\infty$(then $\Theta_G = \{p\}$).

In all other cases, $\Theta_G = \varnothing$.

The first case, a central bank with no intention of controlling inflation, is hardly likely. But the second case, $\beta = +\infty$, a central bank that is concerned only with inflation and therefore highly conservative, is entirely plausible.

In other words, to get controllability, we have to have an *extreme* central bank in term of preferences. In all other cases, the policy outcomes are going to be a compromise (a flexible target outcome) mediated by the unions' behavior; with the inevitable consequence that wage bargaining may weaken (if not undermine) the anti-inflation policies of the bank. This is a situation clearly recognized by the European Central Bank (ECB) (see Issing, 1999), and it shows why the ECB elected to pursue an inflation target in the early years of the euro, to the exclusion of almost every other objective.

Returning now to the representative union's preference function, (6.37), we can see that each trade union has one instrument and two targets; but, as said, of different order. The unions' Q-controllable set is thus not empty (it contains u_i), and differs from that of the policymaker provided that b_1 is finite and nonzero. As a result, if β and b_1 are different from zero, neutrality cannot emerge when the union is a policy leader, since $[\alpha + \eta(1 - \alpha)]/\eta \neq 0$ for all possible parameter values in the problem. However, it could emerge in the case of a Nash equilibrium, since the union controllable set contains u_i. It is worth noticing that if $\eta \to +\infty$ (perfect competition), Equation (6.37) will become $U_i = -\frac{1}{2}u_i^2 + b_1(1-\alpha)u_i$. Now standard neutrality results apply since $u_i = u$ and $\Theta_P = \{u_i\}$ for all types of policy games (possible orders of moves). In that case the union's controllable outcome is $u_i = b_1(1 - \alpha)$, rather than zero.

It follows that, in this class of models, the rationale of monetary policy non-neutrality lies in the interaction among non-atomistic multiple unions. Once again, this feature of the model can be derived ex ante, before solving it.

6.5.3 Public conflicts and economic stabilization

Let us now consider a different kind of conflict; that arising between the fiscal and monetary authorities as described in Section 5.4.5, where both the government and the central bank aim to stabilize output and inflation around their desired targets after a shock. They both maximize quadratic preferences constrained by an aggregate demand equation and by an inflation adjustment equation. Their instruments (one for each player) affect the economy via a linear reduced form. Hence, both players face two non-controllable problems, and both monetary and fiscal policies are effective (Theorem 6.1: part (ii)). However, an equilibrium exists since the intersection of their controllable sets is empty (Theorem 6.1: part (i)). Moreover, it is easy to verify that, if the central bank cares about inflation only, fiscal policy becomes neutral with respect to price stability since inflation is in the central bank's controllable set (Theorem 6.1: part (ii)). But, if both players only care about the same targets, the equilibrium does not exist, unless they share the same target values (Theorem 6.1: part (i)).

6.6 Conclusions and a look ahead

This chapter has applied the tools developed by Tinbergen and Theil in their theory of economic policy to static LQ policy games. We have shown that these tools can be useful for dealing with policy neutrality and existence problems in a context, policy games, that is not subject to the Lucas critique. In particular, our approach leads to two fundamental propositions on policy neutrality and equilibrium existence. These propositions are obtained by restating controllability to take account of the intrinsically strategic nature of policy games, where players share some targets, but usually aim at different values for them. Once this is done, neutrality and equilibrium existence merely become an instrument/target counting problem in the traditional Tinbergen sense.

Our first proposition, in fact, states that, if a player controls some target variables, other players' policies are neutral with respect to these variables if an equilibrium exists. Our second proposition shows that, when at least two players control their relevant sub-systems, no Nash or Stackelberg equilibrium exists if they aim to obtain different target values for some common variables, or if there are infinite equilibria in instrument space when their target values coincide. These two propositions can easily be translated into simple counting rules for checking policy game properties. This is of the utmost importance when building models to express conflicts among agents. Introducing the case of instrument costs in terms of our theory has also proved useful for providing reasons why an equilibrium should always exist.

The next two chapters will generalize our fundamental propositions while remaining in a static context. Specifically, Chapter 7 extends our concept of controllability from the case of a single player to the system as a whole. This will allow us to assert conditions under which an equilibrium exists and is unique in terms of the total number of targets and instruments in the system. In a similar fashion, Chapter 8 deals with controllability by groups and the existence of implicit coalitions between players who have non-conflicting targets. This chapter also generalizes the concept of controllability with the more powerful idea of "decisiveness," which applies the idea of controllability to "implicit" coalitions. Chapter 9 closes our static analysis by looking at the equilibrium selection problem when multiple equilibria arise. Part IV will then generalize all our propositions to dynamic games.

7 From individual players to system controllability

Summary. This chapter complements some previous results involving equilibrium multiplicity and existence. In particular, by focusing on system controllability instead of controllability by single players, we find conditions for the multiplicity and existence of the Nash equilibrium that differ from those required by the previous chapter. The usefulness of our results is then demonstrated by examples in the field of international monetary arrangements and trade agreements. This chapter also derives the principles that need to underlie problems of model building. We then extend this discussion further by drawing out some implications of these results for institutional design purposes, and extensions for the case where the use of policy instruments is costly.

7.1 Introduction

The possibility of interactions between policymakers has raised many issues. One strand of literature concerns problems of coordination and comparisons between the outcomes of decentralized and centralized solutions.[1] Only occasionally have these issues been dealt with in terms of controllability of the system and the existence of an equilibrium. However, the essence of this problem is already well-known in the economic literature, at least since Mundell (1968) raised the "n-th country problem." In a world of n countries, there are $n-1$ independent external balances, trade balances or exchange rates as possible targets; but n possible independent policy instruments, such as interest rates, which could in theory be set by the n policymakers. As a result, if each policymaker made independent use of his instrument, a

[1] Starting from the pioneering studies of Mundell (1962) or Cooper (1969), through the policy coordination work of Hughes Hallett (1986b), to more recent works such as Corsetti and Pesenti (2001), Benigno (2002), Pappa (2004), and Plasmans, Engwerda, van Aarle, Di Bartolomeo and Michalak (2006).

conflict would arise among the n countries and no equilibrium would exist because of the adding up constraint that must hold between the n external balances or n exchange rates.[2]

In Chapter 6, we illustrated the existence condition by first decoupling the policy game in a set of single-player problems, and then applying the Tinbergen and Theil tools to each of them. Our analysis there was performed in outcome space only and issues of multiplicity of equilibria either in this space or in instrument space were not investigated. By contrast, we now focus on the entire system to derive general conditions for equilibrium existence and multiplicity, in terms of the controllability of the whole system.

Specifically, we show that a decentralized equilibrium is characterized by multiple equilibria in instrument space when the total number of independent instruments, summing across players, is greater than the total number of their (independent) targets when taken together. Surprisingly perhaps, the availability of instruments more numerous than the targets, which is a virtue in a centralized or "social planner" solution as it confers some degrees of freedom, becomes a problem in a decentralized environment as coordination on an equilibrium is difficult.

Equilibrium existence is shown to be unlikely in games with conflicts over the target values. Instead, in common interest games, i.e., in games where the players share common target values, at least one equilibrium exists that is also Pareto optimal. However, the excess of instruments may cause a problem of coordination on how to set the instrument values to achieve it. We show that the players can be given an incentive to choose exactly the values of the instruments leading to that Pareto optimal equilibrium. This is done by introducing some "virtual" instrument costs.

The chapter is organized as follows. In the next section, we set up the general policy game framework and derive our main propositions. In Section 7.3, we present the implications of our results by discussing them in instrument and target spaces. Section 7.4 explores the effects of introducing instrument costs into the loss functions. Section 7.5

[2] Robert Mundell was well aware that the existence of a redundancy issue depends on the set of assumptions about targets and instruments as well as on the working of the economic system (see Mundell, 1962; 1968). This was even more evident in von Neumann Whitman (1969).

illustrates our main results with some examples in the area of international economics, investigating in particular the nature and design of international monetary and trade agreements. We finish with a section on the specific implications for model building and some general lessons to be learned from the chapter.

7.2 The basic argument: multiple vs. non-existent equilibria

We focus on a simple LQ game, where players aim to maximize preferences defined on the same target variables (but potentially different target values). We refer to games of this type as games with *fully shared preferences*.

We consider a game among N players (we denote by N both the set of players and its cardinality), who aim to maximize quadratic preferences defined on K possible target variables. Formally, player i minimizes

$$L_i = \frac{1}{2}(y - \bar{y}_i)' Q_i (y - \bar{y}_i), \tag{7.1}$$

where Q_i and $\bar{y}_i$ are preference parameters with the usual interpretations; Q_i is of full rank as we assumed fully shared preferences. If they share the same bliss point (desired target value), then $\bar{y}_i = \bar{y}$ for all i. We refer to this case as a *common interest game*.

The variables are related by the following reduced form system:

$$y = Bu + v = \sum_{i \in N} B_i u_i + v, \tag{7.2}$$

where u is the vector of players' instruments u_i; each u_i is the vector of the $m(i)$ independent instruments controlled by player i; B is the matrix of policy multipliers.

From now on, we only consider Tinbergen systems; we assume that the total number of independent instruments available to the players is not smaller than the number of independent targets, i.e., $\sum_{i \in N} m(i) \geq K$.[3] As we know, this means that the whole system is always controllable in a parametric context. Formally, it implies that B has full row rank.

We can then state the following theorem.

[3] This assumption will be relaxed in the next chapter.

Theorem 7.1 (*instruments, targets and multiple equilibria*). If the total number of instruments exceeds the total number of independent targets, Nash equilibria are multiple in instrument space, if they exist.

Proof. The proof is rather trivial. Assume that a Nash equilibrium u^* exists and indicate the corresponding outcome by y^*, which is $y^* = Bu^* + v$. Since (7.2) is a Tinbergen system with $\Sigma_{i\in N}\, m(i) > K$, each outcome, including y^*, can be achieved by an infinite combination of instruments. All the (infinite) combinations supporting y^* are then also Nash equilibria. ■

Comment 7.1. In the proof we did not use the assumption of fully defined preferences (i.e., Q_i is full rank); thus the theorem applies also to a broader set of cases.

Comment 7.2. The theorem shows that if the number of instruments exceeds that of the targets, there are multiple Nash equilibria in instrument space. However, it does not necessarily imply that there are multiple equilibria in target space.

The following theorem deals with the existence problem in outcome space for the special case of common interest games.

Theorem 7.2 (*existence of Nash equilibrium in outcome space*). In a common interest game with a Tinbergen system, at least one Nash equilibrium exists.

Proof. As we know from the previous chapters, each player's first-order condition can be written in target space as follows:

$$B_i'Q_i\left(y-\bar{y}_i\right)=0 \quad \forall i \in N. \tag{7.3}$$

Putting all the first-order conditions together, we obtain the following equation system:

$$\begin{pmatrix} B_1'Q_1 \\ B_2'Q_2 \\ \cdots \\ B_N'Q_N \end{pmatrix} y = \begin{pmatrix} B_1'Q_1\bar{y}_1 \\ B_2'Q_2\bar{y}_2 \\ \cdots \\ B_N'Q_N\bar{y}_N \end{pmatrix} \quad \text{or } Zy=\bar{z}, \tag{7.4}$$

where Z is a rectangular $\Sigma_{i\in N}\, m(i) > K$ matrix. Equation (7.4) represents a necessary condition for the existence of one or more (infinite) Nash equilibria. If $\bar{y}_i = \bar{y}$ for all $i \in N$, $\bar{y}$ is a solution of system (7.4), as $\bar{z}$ can be rewritten as $Z\bar{y}$. Moreover, by the full rank assumption on B, there always exists at least a vector of instruments $\bar{u}$ such that $\bar{y} = B\bar{u} + v$. ∎

Comment 7.3. The conditions of Theorem 7.2 ensure that $y = \bar{y}$ is a Nash equilibrium in outcome space. But, counter-intuitively, these are not sufficient to guarantee that this equilibrium is unique in the space of outcomes. Although the outcome $\bar{y}$ is "privileged" by being the unanimous best choice for all players, there might be cases in which other vectors of targets satisfy the system (7.4) as well. A possible example arises when the quasi-reaction functions of all players are coincident: at each of these infinite points, no player has any incentive to deviate.

Comment 7.4. Theorem 7.2 guarantees the existence of at least one equilibrium in outcome space; each of them is supported by multiple equilibria in instrument space if the total number of instruments is larger than the number of targets (as stated by Theorem 7.1).

From the above theorems, we can easily derive the following corollaries.

Corollary 7.1. If at least one player satisfies controllability, Nash equilibria (if they exist) are multiple in instrument space and unique in outcome space.

Corollary 7.2. In a common interest game, if at least one player satisfies controllability, there exist multiple equilibria in instrument space and a unique one in outcome space.

These corollaries relate our results to those illustrated in the previous chapter where we analyzed the existence of a solution in terms of controllability by single players. In particular, Corollary 7.1 tells us that controllability by one player implies that the only outcome satisfying the first-order conditions (7.4) is its first best; moreover, the presence of an excessive number of instruments leads to either non-existence or multiple equilibria in instrument space. Conversely, Corollary 7.2 tells us that controllability by at least one player, combined with fully shared target values, leads to a unique Nash equilibrium in outcome space (while multiplicity in instrument space is implied by Theorem 7.1).

Theorem 7.3 (*existence and the "(n+1)-th player"*). Assume that a game between N players endowed with K independent instruments has a unique Nash equilibrium (in outcome space y^*) and consider a variation of this game where an additional player (endowed with some instruments) is introduced. Then in a game among $N + 1$ players, an equilibrium exists if and only if $B'_{N+1}Q_{N+1}(y^* - \bar{y}_{N+1}) = 0$. Moreover, if the equilibrium exists, it is unique in outcome space (it is y^*), but multiple in instrument space.

Proof. In the game between N players, their quasi-reaction functions determine a unique outcome y^* by assumption. This corresponds to the Nash equilibrium. The introduction of an additional player does not change these quasi-reaction functions; thus, these must also hold in the game between $N + 1$ players. It follows the quasi-reaction function of player $N + 1$ must also be compatible with y^*, $B'_{N+1}Q_{N+1}(y^* - \bar{y}_{N+1}) = 0$. Existence in instrument space then follows by the fact that the system is a Tinbergen one; multiplicity is a consequence of Theorem 7.1. ■

Comment 7.5. Some specific comments may better explain the scope of this theorem.

1. Insofar as we consider N players endowed with a total number of instruments equal to the number of their targets, the equilibrium of the game between N players assumed in the theorem is also unique in instrument space.
2. However, our results are more general. In fact, it is easy to verify that if a game between N players in a Tinbergen system has a unique Nash equilibrium in outcome space, y^*. Then, in the game between $N + 1$ players, an equilibrium exists if and only if the compatibility condition of Theorem 7.3 holds.
3. By induction, moreover, our argument can easily be extended to any number of additional players. To guarantee existence of the equilibrium, all of them must satisfy the compatibility condition.

Comment 7.6. The theorem equally applies to the case where additional instruments for an existing player are introduced, instead of those of an additional player.

Comment 7.7. The compatibility condition, $B_j'Q_j(y^* - \bar{y}_j) = 0$, is a sort of knife-edge condition; it is satisfied only by chance. It requires that the preferences of the additional player j are such that he has no incentive to deviate from the y^* value determined by the game among the other players.

Summarizing, in contrast to the results presented in the previous chapters, here conditions for existence and uniqueness are defined in terms of the total number of instruments and targets of all the players, rather than in terms of controllability by one or more players.

7.3 The importance of institutions

If there are too many instruments available in the game, a problem of coordination arises. In this case, there are some degrees of freedom, and it might become impossible for each player to make conjectures about the policy of the opponents.[4] The inability to forecast the strategy selected by the other players is likely to lead to a series of randomized policy interventions, which would destroy the policymakers' ability to coordinate on a Nash equilibrium.

A case of particular interest arises when common interest games are considered. If all players have the same target values, one Nash equilibrium in the space of outcomes is clearly represented by $y_i = \bar{y}$, since no player has any incentive to deviate from his first best. However, even in this case, a unique equilibrium in instrument space will not exist and instrument values remain somehow "indeterminate."

By contrast, the over-determination of an economic system in LQ games has no consequences for the centralized solution. In fact, a social planner can always select one of the infinite solutions arising when the economic system (7.2) is over-determined. They are simply obtained by fixing the values of the instruments in excess of the targets: arbitrary values of a group of $\sum_{i \in N} m(i) - K$ instruments, which are linear combinations of the others, may be taken to make up the excess set.

7.4 Equilibrium multiplicity and instrument costs

A way to solve the problem of multiple equilibria is to introduce instrument costs. As noted in Section 2.7.4, to account for the costs of using an instrument, we can simply introduce an additional target variable into the preferences of each player and an equality constraint between it and the instrument in question into the model. But, the introduction of instrument costs implies that the dimensions of the matrices replacing B_i in (7.3) become $(K + m(i)) \times m(i)$. Then the number of instruments would always be less than that of the targets, and Theorem 7.1 never applies.[5]

[4] Here we implicitly interpret the Nash equilibrium as the result of each player making REs about the policy of its opponents. See Sections 4.5 and 5.3.

[5] As well as Corollaries 7.1 and 7.2.

From this point of view, Theorem 7.1 is a useful complement in that it displays the features of the game when that game is not affected by instrument costs. That instrument costs can alter the results may appear to be an ad hoc assumption designed to confer different – and perhaps more appealing – features on the game. As a result, introducing instrument costs may be seen as an ad hoc way in which the features of the game can be changed. Given this possibility, their inclusion should be treated as a legitimate way to ensure equilibrium existence *only* if there is a genuine (theoretical) justification for them.

A case of particular interest is that of the common interest game. Here the introduction of negligible instrument costs may act as an equilibrium selection device. Assuming that the total number of instruments is greater than the number of targets, a way to coordinate players' instrument choices on the desired equilibrium is to consider one of the infinite equilibria in instrument space and impose a negligible (quadratic) cost on deviations from it for all players. As a result, a unique equilibrium in the space of instruments supporting the desired outcome is obtained. Note that the cost of using instruments in the Nash equilibrium is zero.

Indeed, in common interest games, we do not need to assume that all players have instrument costs: it suffices to add to them the "superfluous" players to ensure a unique equilibrium. The number of "superfluous" players is equal at least to the difference between instruments and targets. This number could be even larger if the game with instrument costs has multiple equilibria in outcome space. However, as we will show in the next chapter, multiple equilibria in outcome space arise only under some very specific circumstances.

In the case described above, the introduction of extra costs for the players in excess of the number of instruments really acts as an equilibrium selection device, by selecting one of the multiple equilibria existing in instrument space. If the equilibrium is unique in outcome space, instrument costs clearly coordinate players toward the desired target. Moreover, if there are multiple equilibria in that space, introducing costs can coordinate players on the Pareto efficient one. Furthermore, the imposition of a cost is fictitious. In fact, in this case, *any arbitrary deviation cost* imposed implies that the players will not actually bear that cost, since they would prefer to do nothing. In that way they would obtain their first best solution.

7.5 Global public goods and the international monetary system

Our theorems have many practical applications throughout the literature on policy games. In this section, we emphasize how coordination and non-existence problems may emerge in decentralized regimes by studying a simple policy game between N countries in the context of the international monetary system. For the sake of brevity, we indicate both the set of countries and its cardinality by N.

7.5.1 Global trade imbalances

Consider the case where each country tries to stabilize its balance of payments, but is also concerned to preserve the stability of the international monetary system. The latter is then the shared target of the N countries, which plays the role of a global public good.[6] Formally, we can write the preferences for country i among the first $N - 1$ countries as

$$U_i = -\frac{\beta_i}{2} b_i^2 - \frac{1}{2} s \quad i \in N \setminus j, \tag{7.5}$$

and, for the N-th country j,

$$U_j = -\frac{\beta_j}{2} (b_j - \bar{b}_j)^2 - \frac{1}{2} s, \tag{7.6}$$

where b_i is the balance of payments and s is an index of the international monetary system's stability or sustainability. More precisely, the latter can be defined as

$$s = \sum_{i \in N} b_i^2. \tag{7.7}$$

Each player controls an instrument, indicated by m (it might be an exchange rate, an interest rate or domestic expenditures), and the model in reduced form can then be expressed as

$$b_i = \alpha_i m_i + \sum_{i \in N \setminus i} \delta_i m_j \quad i \in N, \tag{7.8}$$

[6] On the possibility of considering shared targets as true public goods, see Acocella and Di Bartolomeo (2010, 2011).

where α_i measures the effectiveness of country i's instrument and δ_j measures the spillover effects from actions taken in other countries.

An additional constraint is represented by Walras' law (the adding up constraint):

$$\sum_{i\in N} b_i = 0. \tag{7.9}$$

The model can be rewritten in an LQ form that allows us to apply our results. From (7.9), we obtain

$$b_j = -\sum_{i\in N\setminus j} b_i. \tag{7.10}$$

The stability index therefore becomes

$$s = \sum_{i\in N\setminus j} b_i^2 + b_j^2 = \sum_{i\in N\setminus j} b_i^2 + \left(\sum_{i\in N\setminus j} b_i\right)^2. \tag{7.11}$$

By using Equations (7.10) and (7.11), the individual country utilities can be rewritten as

$$U_i = -\frac{1+\beta_i}{2} b_i^2 - \frac{1}{2}\sum_{z\in N\setminus j,i} b_z^2 - \frac{1}{2}\left(\sum_{i\in N\setminus j} b_i\right)^2 \quad i \in N\setminus j \tag{7.12}$$

for all countries in N, not including country j; and

$$U_j = -\frac{1}{2}\sum_{i\in N\setminus j} b_i^2 - \frac{\beta_j + 1}{2}\left(\sum_{i\in N\setminus j} b_i\right)^2 + \beta_j \bar{b}_j \sum_{i\in N\setminus j} b_i - \frac{\beta_j}{2}\bar{b}_j^2 \tag{7.13}$$

for country j.

The Nash equilibrium can now be found by maximizing Equations (7.12) and (7.13) under the constraint

$$b_i = \alpha_i m_i + \sum_{j\in N\setminus i} \delta_j m_j \quad i \in N\setminus j. \tag{7.14}$$

The model (7.12)–(7.14) is a policy game between N players endowed with N instruments, with fully shared preferences directed at $N-1$ independent target variables. Moreover, the game is a common interest game if and only if $\bar{b}_j = 0$.

In order to understand the model properties, we do not need to solve the game explicitly. We can note the following points.

1. As the overall number of independent targets is $N - 1$ and each of the N players can use an instrument, we know, from Theorem 7.1, that if an equilibrium exists there are multiple equilibria in instrument space.
2. If $\bar{b}_j \neq 0$, the equilibrium in outcome space is, however, unlikely to exist. To show this we assume that one unique equilibrium in outcome space exists in the game with $N - 1$ players for $i \in N \setminus j$, who play a common interest game; if player j is added to this game, in order to preserve this equilibrium, the knife-edge condition described in Theorem 7.3 must be satisfied, which is highly unlikely.
3. Instead, in a common interest game, there always exists at least one Nash equilibrium in outcome space, i.e., $b_i = 0$ for all $i \in N$ as stated by Theorem 7.2, supported by multiple equilibria in instrument space (see Comment 7.4).[7]

In a common interest game, moreover, $b_i = 0$ for all $i \in N$ can be achieved as the unique Nash equilibrium of the game, under very general circumstances, by adding an instrument cost to at least one player as discussed in the previous section.[8] The same thing can be achieved by assuming that one country exits the game by setting its instrument in advance.

By way of contrast, consider the more general game with $\bar{b}_j \neq 0$. Suppose that one country exits the game by setting its instrument in advance, i.e., country z fixes $m_z = \bar{m}$. A solution in the space of instruments always exists, but with a potentially different distribution of the outcomes across countries.[9]

[7] In principle, it is possible to have multiple equilibria in outcome space, but under very specific assumptions. These cases will be studied in the next chapters.

[8] Thus, there is a way to overcome the impasse resulting from the excess of instruments, e.g., some players are forbidden to, or induced not to use their instruments as a result of political, historical (path-dependent) reasons, or some additional (possible common) targets are introduced (see, e.g., Acocella and Di Bartolomeo, 2011).

[9] The statement holds if we assume that there are no multiple equilibria in outcome space. As said in Section 7.4, this is unlikely to be the case unless some specific conditions hold. The point will be discussed in detail in the next chapter.

So, even in a model where the differences between countries are at a minimum (or even where there is no conflict at all), we can see that there is a need either for an international institution to coordinate the countries' policies, or for a country-leader or hegemon *à la* Kindleberger (1973) – a leader acting to impose such a solution by picking arbitrary values for his instrument, and thereby performing the role of an anchor for the expectations of other countries.

Both solutions highlight the need for international coordination in this case. However, the nature of this coordination is very specific. It is not necessarily a problem of coordination arising from the existence of externalities of conflicting targets, as is usually the case in policy games.[10]

The problem is also related to the formation of expectations by rational players. It is easy to understand the point by considering the Nash equilibrium as the outcome of a self-fulfilling process of REs.[11]

Even if there are no differences between countries, if they play simultaneously but non-cooperatively they will not be able to predict the behavior of the other players (because there is no equilibrium in their game) and the RE equilibrium will no longer exist because their private interventions (and the final outcomes) become randomized.[12]

7.5.2 *Negotiated tariff reductions*

Now consider the case where N countries can meet to negotiate a series of tariff reductions under World Trade Organization (WTO) auspices, as in the Doha and earlier rounds of world tariff reductions. In this case there will be a target reduction value for the average tariff level after the negotiations: from its existing level to say $N^{-1}\Sigma_{i\in N}b_i = \tilde{b}$. We can define national deviations from the desired average tariff rate to be $\tilde{b}_i = b_i - \bar{b}$, for each $i \in N$. The adding up constraint now becomes

$$\sum_{i\in N}\tilde{b}_i = 0 \tag{7.15}$$

[10] Setting $\delta_j = 0$ in (7.8) and (7.14) changes nothing and our results still hold.

[11] As discussed in Section 5.3.

[12] A similar problem, with less dramatic consequences for the existence of the Nash equilibrium, emerges in Dixit and Lambertini (2003b).

in place of (7.9); and the desire to keep the system as a whole in place without undue strains, as evidenced by the WTO's dispute resolution procedure which all participants have signed up to, will be represented by

$$s = \sum_{i \in N} \tilde{b}_i^2 \tag{7.16}$$

plus the presence of this definition in each country's objective function (7.5).

Our results go through in this example as before. There are more instruments (national tariffs) than there are free and independent targets. Multiple decentralized equilibria in instrument space follow by Theorem 7.1; and at least one equilibrium in outcome space in case of a common interest game (i.e., all countries have a target value of $\tilde{b}$ equal to zero or want to set their tariff rate at the average level, which is a rather unlikely case) as a consequence of Theorem 7.2. In the case when target values differ, no equilibrium in outcome space is the likely result. A decentralized equilibrium therefore is unlikely to exist and a multiplicity of equilibria in instrument space might arise unless some specific circumstances are verified. And an equilibrium outcome *without* randomized behavior and tariff wars is only possible with either a hegemon (a leader-country acting as a social planner) or cooperation, in the form of a common institution with agreed rules for resolving disputes when either $\tilde{b}_i > 0$ gets too large (protection) or when $\tilde{b}_i < 0$ gets too negative (dumping). Otherwise, there will be no equilibrium, and policy instability or periodic trade wars will result.

History bears the above result out. Trade policies were stable in the 1950s and 1960s under US hegemony, and arguably progressive in the 1980s with the USA and European Union (EU) as social planners. However, they had fallen into chaos in the 1930s in the absence of such conditions, and threatened to do so again in the 1970s until the need for explicit coordination was accepted by the G7 policymakers at the time of the Bonn summit in 1978. The possibility that the same would happen again in the 1990s and 2000s, when the EU and then China emerged as possible rivals to the USA, led to the creation of the WTO as a mutual coordination and dispute resolution device.

7.5.3 Exchange rate targeting and stabilization regimes

Exchange rate targeting mechanisms also fit straight into our framework. A bilateral peg implies

$$e_i = e_j^{-1} \text{ for any two countries } i,\ j, \text{ and } N = 2, \tag{7.17}$$

where e_i is the nominal exchange rate of country i in terms of country j's currency. That supplies the adding up constraint which can be substituted straight into (7.5) with a sufficiently large value of β to represent the degree of commitment being given to the fixed parity values underlying (7.17). The monetary stability index s, defined in terms of the exchange rates, can also be incorporated if exchange rate stability in an absolute sense is thought to be important.

Similarly, multilateral exchange rate mechanisms, such as the European Monetary System (EMS), may also be included in our framework. In this case, the adding up constraint is

$$w_1 DM/\$ + w_2 FF/\$ + \cdots - Ecu/\$ = 0, \tag{7.18}$$

where w_i are the country weights; and *DM/\$*, *FF/\$* and so on represent the component exchange rates expressed against the dollar as an outside currency and *Ecu* stands for European Currency Unit, the indicator of divergence devised for the EMS. This is just an alternative version of (7.17) with a larger number of countries, N.

In each of the above cases, our results go through as before. They demonstrate that an exchange rate regime also requires a hegemon, or some explicit coordinating mechanism, in order to allow the players to coordinate on an equilibrium. Otherwise, one can expect erratic policies and periods of financial instability. Again, history bears this result out. The Bretton Woods system had the IMF as a coordinating institution, and US trade deficits (or more accurately, open access to the US markets) created US hegemony. The EMS had the European Commission (actually the monetary policy committee) as social planner in its initial phases; but later that role fell to the Bundesbank. The euro now has the European Central Bank as coordinating institution. But at other times there has been little tendency for exchange rates to find equilibrium values, and evident periods of financial stress appear as a consequence.

7.5.4 Prevention of contagious diseases

Now we consider a different kind of example. We move to a simple two-country public good model for the prevention of contagious diseases. Each country, indexed by *i*, has a preference over a local public good, the level of prevention of local contagious diseases, g_i, and a global public good, G – prevention of such diseases at a world level.

Formally, country *i* maximizes a preference function that depends on the quadratic deviations from some target values, $\bar{g}_i$ and G_i, of the levels of both its local public good and the global public good:

$$U_i = -\frac{1}{2}\left[b_i(g_i - \bar{g}_i)^2 + (G - G_i)^2\right] \quad i = \{1,2\}. \tag{7.19}$$

Let us assume that the level of the local public good in each country is the result of a linear *technology*, which derives from the decisions by consumers and producers both in the country in question and abroad, depending on policy instruments. In formal terms:

$$g_i = \alpha_i r_i + \beta_i s_1 + \delta_i p_2. \tag{7.20}$$

The equation representing the technology is indeed a reduced form of a more complex structural model. Country 1 (say, India before its accession to the WTO) mainly produces subsidized generic drugs, but can consume both these and licensed specialties. Country 2 (say, the USA) mainly produces specialties, but can consume both these and the subsidized generic drugs produced abroad.[13] Then, in both countries, the level of the local public good, e.g., the prevention of a disease like HIV or bird flu, depends on the following.

1. The level of local public expenditure for information dissemination, medical training, and so on (r_i).
2. The level of subsidies granted to country 1's firms in order to produce generic drugs (s_1).
3. The regime of patent protection enacted in country 2. The level of protection achieved might be measured by the number of years

[13] This is really a special kind of technology, but not unrealistic, since it is the result of decisions by consumers and producers both in the country in question and abroad. As noted in the text, the equation representing the technology is indeed a reduced form of a more complex structural model.

of patent protection (p_2), which influences the cost of the drugs imported.

The provision technology of the global public good is additive, i.e.,

$$G = \sum_{i=1}^{2} g_i. \tag{7.21}$$

Each country has two independent instruments available to reach its two targets. Globally there are thus four instruments to determine two independent target variables, as the global public good can always be expressed as a linear combination of the two local levels of prevention (for example, Equation (7.21)).

We can now distinguish two cases according to whether a conflict of interest between the two countries exists or not. In the situation where the target values G_i differ, a conflict arises between the two countries and an equilibrium is unlikely to exist. The conflict can only be settled by some kind of coordination exercise, or through some institutional solution different from simple decentralization.

By contrast, if there is no conflict (the values of common targets are equal for both countries), multiple solutions arise, but all support the same outcomes. Thus, even in the absence of a conflict, some kind of an institutional device – such as communication of the intentions of the different players about the levels of the instruments they would like to set and an explicit or implicit agreement on their implementation – must take place to eliminate the indeterminacy in the equilibrium. In a similar way, one can easily see that, if one of the two instruments, say s_1, is not used by country 1, there is an equilibrium in the space of outcomes, which is unique, as this country does not control its system whereas country 2 does. However, in the whole system there are 2 + 1 instruments for 2 independent targets. Thus there are infinite combinations of policies supporting the unique equilibrium outcome. This raises an issue of coordination on how to arrange to converge on this outcome with the most favorable or cheapest use of the instruments.

Finally, a unique equilibrium exists only if each policymaker has one instrument and two targets. The equilibrium will not be efficient unless there is no conflict between the two policymakers, i.e., they share the same value for the common target in terms of global public good and this target is the sum of the targets in terms of the two local public goods.

7.6 Lessons from this chapter

This chapter offers a new perspective from which to study some properties of non-cooperative games among several policymakers. In particular, we concentrate on the Nash equilibrium in multi-player LQ games with fully shared preferences, which is a very common situation in studying the international (economic) interactions between national policymakers.

Abstracting from controllability by one or more players, but focusing on controllability of the (decentralized) system as a whole, we find that a sufficient condition for the multiplicity of Nash equilibria in instrument space to arise is that the total number of instruments available to all players combined exceeds the total number of targets of all the players. Moreover, we have also shown that, in such a case, existence of an equilibrium is highly unlikely when target values differ among the players.

In the above context, common interest games are of particular interest (i.e., all players share the same target values). Although in these games (at least) one equilibrium always exists, indeterminacy about which instrument values to choose in order to implement that solution might impede the ability to coordinate. Introduction of a controlling player reduces the extent of these difficulties by making, under some general circumstances, the equilibrium unique in the space of outcomes, but cannot completely solve the difficulty of players to coordinate on a specific strategy among the infinite available. Instrument coordination can be achieved instead by imposing instrument costs. In fact, in order to induce the players to choose the Pareto optimal equilibrium in outcome space (that which corresponds to the common target value), instrument costs can play a role as a device that can be used to avoid a problematic source of multiple equilibria, even if those costs are actually virtual (i.e., zero) in equilibrium.

Our results are again relevant for model building. However, their most important implications lie in the existence of a fundamental asymmetry in institutional design. If an economic system is over-determined, it can be solved by some "social planner." A decentralized solution, by contrast, is problematic. Hence, the advantages of centralization are lost due to an oversupply of instruments, while decentralization leads to indeterminacy and a destabilization (if not collapse) of the system as players randomize their policies in response.

A possible solution is that of a player acting as a hegemon, who sets the excess of instruments over targets at suitably chosen but arbitrary values before the other players choose their instruments. Alternatively, coordination can be achieved by introducing some instrument costs or implementing a cooperative solution. However, all these solutions imply the existence of some kind of "public" institution that indicates the hegemon, imposes instrument costs, or guarantees compliance with the cooperative solution. Our propositions are then relevant in many areas of economics: for example, the international monetary system, trade policy, global public goods, natural resource games, all of which have the features of the general game analyzed here.

Results obtained in this chapter complement those stated in Section 6.2. While those results were based on cases in which policymakers individually satisfy Tinbergen's controllability conditions, this chapter considers the case in which the system as a whole may be (over-)controllable in Tinbergen's terms. The derived sufficient conditions for the existence and multiplicity of the Nash equilibria are thus additional and highlight the complexity of this issue. Chapter 8 will generalize these results by proposing a unifying general framework.

8 *Conflicts and coordination among groups*

WITH PAOLO GIOVANNI PIACQUADIO

Summary. This chapter concludes our derivation of theorems for existence, policy invariance and multiple equilibria in a static framework. We move from a situation of conflict among all the players to a situation where there is absence of a conflict among some players, with a residual opposition among groups of them. We introduce first the concept of implicit coalition, and find that when more than one such coalition controls conflicting targets no equilibrium exists. And that implies, if only one coalition controls the economic system, policy invariance. Then, we discuss how an implicit coordination can also emerge if some players' policies are not in opposition, even if they do not necessarily share the same target values. In such a case, the concept of Tinbergen controllability should be substituted by that of decisiveness, which implies a degree of *control* of some variables by a player or a group of them – but not necessarily the achievement of all desired targets. With reference to this idea of implicit coordination, we provide necessary and sufficient conditions for the existence (and multiplicity) of Nash equilibria; and for policy neutrality and Pareto efficiency.

8.1 Introduction

This chapter concludes our derivation of theorems for existence, policy invariance and multiple equilibria in a static framework. In Chapter 6 we derived existence theorems by taking account of the Tinbergen–Theil concept of controllability from the perspective of a single player. In Chapter 7, by contrast, we analyzed conditions for policy invariance and Nash equilibrium existence by using the same concept of controllability, but applying it to the entire economic system under some restrictive conditions. Now we mix the two approaches together to derive a general framework that encapsulates both, and to allow for the possibility that "coalitions" may emerge from within the system as a whole.

After showing that a situation of no conflict can arise where two agents aim to obtain the same desired targets, we fully consider the possibility of a convergence of interests between different players, i.e., the formation of "implicit" coalitions among the players that share the same target values of the common target variables. Thus we move from a situation of conflict among all players, such as that assumed in the previous chapters, to a situation where there is absence of a conflict among some players, but a residual opposition or rivalry among certain groups of them. In a nutshell, we will find that, similarly to previous chapters, the existence of a conflict implies an opposition among the (implicit) coalitions that will lead to the non-existence of an equilibrium if more than one coalition controls conflicting targets. By contrast, if only one coalition controls (in the same sense) the economic system, we end up with policy invariance.

In addition, the concept of implicit coalitions may be generalized. In fact, an implicit coordination can emerge even without players sharing the same target values. In such a case, the concept of Tinbergen controllability should be substituted by a new tool, that of decisiveness, which implies a degree of *control* of some variables by a group of players; but not necessarily the achievement of any desired targets.

Once implicit coordination and its properties are introduced, we can fully describe LQ policy games and their properties. We can in fact provide necessary and sufficient conditions for existence (and multiplicity) of Nash equilibria, and for policy neutrality, and explore the relationship between Nash equilibria and Pareto efficiency.

The rest of the chapter is structured as follows. In Section 8.2 we illustrate the idea of implicit coordination in a $2 \times 2 \times 2$ (2 agents, 2 instruments, 2 target variables) policy game and derive, in that context, all the necessary and sufficient conditions for equilibrium existence and uniqueness. Thereafter we investigate some specific issues – different targeting policies, common interest games (i.e., policy symbiosis), partial effectiveness of instruments – to fully characterize this framework, being the framework used most frequently in policy games. In Section 8.3 we introduce more than two players and admit the possibility of implicit coalition of a sub-set of the N players, studying its consequences for existence and multiplicity of equilibria, as well as for neutrality. Section 8.4 provides an example of implicit coalitions by considering a game between the government, the central bank and an all-encompassing trade union. In Section 8.5, we generalize the model presented in Chapters 6 and 7, providing theorems for existence and multiplicity of equilibria, and policy neutrality, with reference to an $N \times M \times K$ model (N agents, M instruments, K target variables). The crucial idea of decisiveness upon which these theorems are founded is then illustrated by an example in Section 8.6. A final section concludes.

8.2 Two-player interactions and implicit coordination

8.2.1 The 2 × 2 × 2 policy game

We consider a simple LQ policy game between two players with two instruments (one for each of them) constrained by a simple economy described by two variables (targets): a 2 × 2 × 2 framework. The game is static, simultaneous, and non-cooperative. Thus its equilibrium is described by a Nash solution.

Each player i sets an instrument, u_i, to minimize the loss functions, which we can present in the simple following way:

$$L_i = \frac{1}{2}\left[(x-\bar{x}_i)^2 + \beta_i (y-\bar{y}_i)^2\right] \qquad i = \{1,2\}, \tag{8.1}$$

defined over the deviations of two target variables (x,y) from some desired values $(\bar{x}_i, \bar{y}_i)$; β_i are the given weight (relative priority) parameters.

From the above equation, we can define the marginal rate of substitution (MRS) between the targets as

$$MRS^i_{xy} = -\frac{dy}{dx} = \frac{\partial L_i / \partial(x-\bar{x}_i)}{\partial L_i / \partial(y-\bar{y}_i)} = \frac{1}{\beta_i}\frac{x-\bar{x}_i}{y-\bar{y}_i} \qquad i = \{1,2\}. \tag{8.2}$$

This rate represents the slope of the indifference curve.[1] Notice that, if $x \to \bar{x}_i$ for $y \neq \bar{y}_i$, $MRS^i_{xy} = 0$ and, if $y \to \bar{y}_i$ for $x \neq \bar{x}_i$, $MRS^i_{xy} \to \pm\infty$. In a similar manner, we can define elasticities of substitution among the deviations:

$$\eta^i_{xy} = \frac{\partial L_i / \partial(x-\bar{x}_i)}{\partial L_i / \partial(y-\bar{y}_i)} \frac{y-\bar{y}_i}{x-\bar{x}_i} = \frac{1}{\beta_i} \qquad i = \{1,2\}. \tag{8.3}$$

[1] As usual, it measures the compensation in terms of the target variable y, for an infinitesimal variation of x, which makes agent i indifferent between accepting the change or not.

The relationships between instruments and targets are summarized by a system of linear equations that describes the economy:

$$\begin{bmatrix} x \\ y \end{bmatrix} = \begin{bmatrix} a_{11} & a_{12} \\ a_{21} & a_{22} \end{bmatrix} \begin{bmatrix} u_1 \\ u_2 \end{bmatrix} + \begin{bmatrix} c_x \\ c_y \end{bmatrix}, \tag{8.4}$$

where a_{ij} are parameters, c_x and c_y are constants.

We can rewrite (8.4) in a more compact matrix form as

$$z = Au + c. \tag{8.5}$$

We assume that A is a full rank matrix. In fact, for the moment we will assume that all the elements a_{ij} are nonzero; we will introduce the case of lower rank and *sparse* (some a_{ij} elements are zero) matrices later (see Section 10.4.2).

It is worth reminding the reader that the full rank of A means that the system (8.5) is controllable in the Tinbergen sense; i.e., any given 2×1 vector $\bar{z}$ can be achieved. That is, given $\bar{z}$, a unique vector $u^* = A^{-1}(\bar{z} - c)$ exists such that $z = \bar{z}$.

From system (8.4), we can define a "marginal rate of transformation" (MRT) between the target variables with respect to the instrument of agent i. Formally, these marginal rates are

$$MRT_{xy}^{i} = -\frac{dy}{dx} = \frac{\partial y / \partial u_i}{\partial x / \partial u_i} = \frac{a_{2i}}{a_{1i}} \qquad i = \{1,2\}. \tag{8.6}$$

The MRT measures the impact on y of a marginal change in x induced by agent i. Implicitly, it shows how player i's instrument affects the target variables: if the signs of a_{2i} and a_{1i} are different, to increase the value of a target variable one needs to reduce the value of the other. Otherwise, the two variables move together. Because of the linearity of the system (8.4), MRTs are constant. Moreover, of necessity they will be different between the two players because we have assumed A to be of full rank.

As shown in Chapter 6, the Nash equilibrium is a vector u of players' instruments derived from minimization of (8.1) subject to (8.4) for both players. The first-order conditions for the two agents can be described as follows:

$$a_{1i}\left(x - \bar{x}_i\right) + \beta_i a_{2i}\left(y - \bar{y}_i\right) = 0 \qquad i = \{1,2\}, \tag{8.7}$$

where Equations (8.7) are quasi-reaction functions (see Section 5.2.3).[2] Optimization of this system clearly implies that both players set their MRS equal to their MRT.[3]

We will assume that the players are both active in the game in order to avoid degenerate cases due to the non-existence of the first-order conditions for any player. This requires that $(a_{1i}, a_{2i}\beta_i)' \neq (0,0)'$ for $i = \{1,2\}$. A solution to the first-order conditions in (8.7) is then assured. Notice that, if the βs are finite and different from zero, this is simply implied by the full rank assumption on matrix A.

In a compact form, the equation system (8.7) can be written as

$$Zz - \bar{z} = 0, \tag{8.8}$$

where $z = (x - \bar{x}_i, y - \bar{y}_i)$, $i = \{1,2\}$ and

$$Z = \begin{bmatrix} a_{11} & \beta_1 a_{21} \\ a_{12} & \beta_2 a_{22} \end{bmatrix}, \qquad \bar{z} = \begin{bmatrix} a_{11}\bar{x}_1 + \beta_1 a_{21}\bar{y}_1 \\ a_{12}\bar{x}_2 + \beta_2 a_{22}\bar{y}_2 \end{bmatrix}$$

contain nonzero coefficients.

8.2.2 *Existence, uniqueness and multiple equilibria*

We can state the following theorem.

Theorem 8.1 (*uniqueness*). In the $2 \times 2 \times 2$ policy game, a unique Nash equilibrium exists if and only if $MRT^1_{xy} / MRT^2_{xy} \neq \eta^1_{xy} / \eta^2_{xy}$.

Proof. Matrix Z is square and is of full rank if and only if $\frac{a_{21} / a_{11}}{a_{22} / a_{12}} \neq \frac{\beta_2}{\beta_1}$, i.e., $\frac{MRT^1_{xy}}{MRT^2_{xy}} \neq \frac{\eta^1_{xy}}{\eta^2_{xy}}$. Then there is a unique vector of target variables that satisfies the optimality conditions for both players: $z^* = Z^{-1}\bar{z}$. The unique Nash equilibrium follows from the full rank assumption on A and is given by $u^* = A^{-1}(Z^{-1}\bar{z} - c)$. ■

2 In our example, since all the outcomes can be achieved by an appropriate combination of instruments (recall that the system as a whole is controllable in Tinbergen's terms), if a Nash equilibrium exists in the space of quasi-reaction functions, there exists also a couple of instrument values supporting it. In other words, there exists a solution in the space of reaction functions. We will investigate the problem further in the more general model presented in Section 8.4.

3 Each player aims at equating the ratio of the deviations of outcomes from his target values (expressed in the same terms, i.e., by using β_i as a weight) to his constant MRT $(-a_{2i}/a_{1i})$.

Less formally, condition $MRT^1_{xy}/\eta^1_{xy} \neq MRT^2_{xy}/\eta^2_{xy}$ simply implies that the reaction functions of the two players are not parallel. Hence they can have an intersection only in one point, which is the Nash equilibrium.

Corollary 8.1. This unique Nash equilibrium is generally not Pareto efficient. In fact, the equilibrium is obtained from $MRT^i_{xy} = MRS^i_{xy}$, $i = \{1,2\}$; see Equation (8.7). But the MRTs are constant and different between the two players (recall, A has full rank). Thus $MRS^1_{xy} \neq MRS^2_{xy}$, $i = \{1,2\}$. However, Pareto optimality requires $MRS^1_{xy} = MRS^2_{xy}$. Thus Nash non-cooperative equilibria will not, in general, be efficient.

All the same, it is possible that an equilibrium exists where an agent reaches his desired bliss point. This situation would occur when the first best of an agent is, by chance, on the quasi-reaction function of the other (and would then be the Nash equilibrium of the game).[4] In that case, the equilibrium would be efficient.

Call α the common ratio between the MRT and the elasticity for the two players and consider the case:

$$\frac{MRT^1_{xy}}{\eta^1_{xy}} = \frac{MRT^2_{xy}}{\eta^2_{xy}} = \alpha. \tag{8.9}$$

A unique equilibrium no longer exists since $MRT^1_{xy}/MRT^2_{xy} \neq \eta^1_{xy}/\eta^2_{xy}$ does not hold, and multiple equilibria may emerge. Formally we have Theorem 8.2:

Theorem 8.2 (*multiple equilibria*). In the 2 × 2 × 2 policy game, multiple Nash equilibria exist if and only if $(\bar{x}_1 - \bar{x}_2) = \alpha(\bar{y}_1 - \bar{y}_2)$: the differences in the agents' desired values are proportional to one another.

Proof. If $(\bar{x}_1 - \bar{x}_2) = \alpha(\bar{y}_1 - \bar{y}_2)$, each desired allocation of an agent satisfies the first-order condition of the other. The quasi-reaction functions of the two agents are thus the same and all points lying on them are potential Nash equilibria. By the full rank assumption of A, every z on the quasi-reaction function has a corresponding strategy vector u, implying that infinite Nash equilibria arise. More formally, a candidate

[4] Formally, this requires that $a_{12}\bar{x}_1 + a_{22}\beta_2\bar{y}_1 = a_{12}\bar{x}_2 + a_{22}\beta_2\bar{y}_2$ or that $a_{11}\bar{x}_2 + a_{21}\beta_1\bar{y}_2 = a_{11}\bar{x}_1 + a_{21}\beta_1\bar{y}_1$.

outcome for a Nash equilibrium must satisfy both quasi-reaction functions. If they have the same slope (i.e., r[Z] = 1), the only case of existence arises when the quasi-reaction functions are coincident. We rewrite the first-order conditions as follows:

$$x - \bar{x}_i = \beta_i \frac{a_{2i}}{a_{1i}} \left(\bar{y}_i - y \right) \quad i = \{1,2\}. \tag{8.10}$$

Subtracting the equations in (8.10), one from the other, and using $\beta_1 a_{21} / a_{11} = \beta_2 a_{22} / a_{12} = -\alpha$, we obtain

$$\bar{x}_1 - \bar{x}_2 = \alpha \left(\bar{y}_1 - \bar{y}_2 \right), \tag{8.11}$$

as required by the condition stated in the theorem. ■

These equilibria are efficient if and only if the equilibrium outcome z^* happens to be the first best outcome of one of the players, that is, $z^* = (\bar{x}_1, \bar{y}_1)'$ or $z^* = (\bar{x}_2, \bar{y}_2)'$. But that could happen only by chance.

In summary, by the two theorems we have a complete taxonomy of existence and multiplicity in the canonical 2 × 2 × 2 game (i.e., when A is of full rank and has no zeros, and the βs are strictly positive and finite).

1. If $\frac{MRT^1_{xy}}{\eta^1_{xy}} \neq \frac{MRT^2_{xy}}{\eta^2_{xy}}$, a unique Nash equilibrium exists.
2. If $\frac{MRT^1_{xy}}{\eta^1_{xv}} = \frac{MRT^2_{xy}}{\eta^2_{xv}} = \alpha$, *either* there are multiple equilibria (where, for some value of α, $(\bar{x}_1 - \bar{y}_2) = \alpha(\bar{y}_1 - \bar{y}_2)$ holds); *or* no equilibrium exists.

In the next sub-sections, we consider some useful special cases that depart from the canonical model that we have analyzed so far. In Chapter 9 we will investigate the general 2 × 2 × 2 game with multiple equilibria.

8.2.3 *Equilibrium properties of targeting policies*

We can now investigate the properties of a Nash equilibrium with reference to a framework where, for one or both players, the elasticities of substitution among target deviations are zero or infinite, $\beta_i \to 0$ or $\beta_i \to \infty$ by (8.3). This can be thought of as equivalent to targeting player i's policies on one objective only.

Formally, agent i is interested in one target only if

1. $\beta_i \rightarrow 0$, the relative importance of the deviation of y from the preferred target $\bar{y}_i$ in his loss function shrinks to zero and we can say that player i is only interested in variable x.
2. $\beta_i \rightarrow \infty$, the player is interested only in the deviations of target variable y.

In this context, we can consider three cases:

1. One player is interested in only one target variable (while the other is interested in both).
2. Both players are interested in only one, but different variables.
3. Both players are interested in only one and the same variable.

These cases are very common in the economic literature and exemplify some of the most important applications[5] of the new theory of economic policy insofar as the existence or other features of an equilibrium are concerned.

Consider the first case (one player is interested in both targets, and the other player is interested in only one). If the coefficients of the instruments are different from zero for both agents, there will always be a Nash equilibrium. It will be Pareto efficient if the agents share the target values for the variable in common. It will be not efficient otherwise.

In the second case the agents are interested in singular but different variables, i.e., $\beta_1 = 0$ and $\beta_2 = \infty$; or, conversely, $\beta_1 = \infty$ and $\beta_2 = 0$. This time they are not in conflict. Moreover, each agent controls his relevant sub-system and is able to get his first best allocation for any given strategy of the other player, as in the previous case. The first-order conditions are compatible since there is no conflict and the unique Nash equilibrium is Pareto efficient since it ensures the first best for each player.

Finally, if both agents are interested in the same variable,[6] $\dfrac{MRT^1_{xy}}{\eta^1_{xy}} = \dfrac{MRT^2_{xy}}{\eta^2_{xy}} = \alpha$ holds (with α either zero or infinite) and

[5] One of the most common examples is that of inflation targeting, where the central bank is interested only in inflation. For further examples, see Chapters 5 and 6.

[6] That is, either $\beta_1 = \beta_2 = 0$, or $\beta_1 = \beta_2 = \infty$.

Theorem 8.2 applies. Then no equilibrium exists, unless the players share the same desired value. In that case, $\bar{x}_1 - \bar{x}_2 = \alpha\,(\bar{y}_1 - \bar{y}_2) = 0$ or $\frac{\bar{x}_1 - \bar{x}_2}{\alpha} = \bar{y}_1 - \bar{y}_2 = 0$, and an infinite number of equilibria exist.

8.2.4 Symbiosis and implicit coordination

Another specific case of interest is that of symbiosis, which arises when the two agents share the same desired values for all the target variables, as in common interest games analyzed in the previous chapter. In our context (of two players with two targets each), symbiosis occurs for $\bar{x}_1 = \bar{x}_2 = \bar{x}$ and $\bar{y}_1 = \bar{y}_2 = \bar{y}$. It implies that there is no "conflict" between the players.[7] Other cases of "symbiosis" will be dealt with in the next section.

By assuming symbiosis, a trivial solution in terms of outcomes emerges, i.e., $z = \bar{z}$ where $\bar{z} = [\bar{x}, \bar{y}]'$, which is the same efficient solution that can be obtained if there were only one player, or a social planner, setting both instruments. Formally, the system of first-order conditions is now

$$Zz - \bar{z} = 0. \tag{8.12}$$

If Z is of full rank, only one Nash equilibrium exists (Theorem 8.1). The two players will choose their own best policy; and, in doing so, they implicitly coordinate to achieve their first best. In fact, the first-order conditions they must satisfy are the same as those of a single player endowed with the same two instruments; and as instruments are linearly independent (A is of full rank) those conditions now ensure a single-valued correspondence between the vector of target variables and that of the instruments.

By contrast, if Z is not of full rank, multiple equilibria arise (see Theorem 8.2) as the first-order conditions are linearly dependent; the quasi-reaction functions are the same for the two agents. A coordination failure *à la* Cooper and John (1988) will then emerge since the equilibria are related to different and "rankable" outcomes.[8]

[7] Examples of policy games with symbiosis are Dixit and Lambertini (2003b), Di Bartolomeo, Giuli and Manzo (2009) and Acocella, Di Bartolomeo and Piacquadio (2009).

[8] In the next chapter, we will show how announcements can be used as an equilibrium selection device in this framework, to ensure that a well-defined outcome emerges.

8.2.5 *Partial effectiveness of instruments*

Now we consider cases where agents can only partially influence the outcome of the economic system; that is, are able to influence only some of the variables. This partial ineffectiveness of instruments can be viewed as an exogenous policy neutrality of an agent and is completely different from the endogenous policy neutrality of Chapters 2, 5 and 6. As exogenous neutrality arises when A contains at least one zero, MRTs become infinite (or zero).[9] We also consider a further case of partial ineffectiveness in which the two agents can only affect the outcomes in the same way; i.e., the instruments are not independent across players. In this case, not all $z \in R^2$ can be reached as the matrix A is not of full rank. In other words, the economic system is no longer globally controllable in Tinbergen terms.

Under a partial effectiveness of instruments, four possible cases can arise.

1. Both agents are able to influence only one and the same variable,[10] and are by assumption interested in that variable. In this case, it is obvious that each agent controls only the target variable he is interested in and, as a consequence, the Nash equilibrium can exist if and only if both agents share the same target value for that variable. Again, however, a problem of coordination arises. There are, in fact, an infinite number of combinations of their instruments, which support the achievement of the common desired targets.
2. Each agent influences only one, but a different variable.[11] As we have assumed that both players are active, they should be interested in at least the variable for which their instrument is effective. The quasi-reaction function of each player only depends on one target variable; it follows that the optimal policy of each player is to set the instrument to achieve the *optimum optimorum* for that variable, for any given value of the instrument of the other. Therefore, a unique Nash equilibrium always arises. This

[9] It is worth noticing that it would not make sense to consider the case in which one agent has no influence on any variable, leading to an indeterminate MRT. However, this case is ruled out by our assumption that all the players are active in the game.

[10] That is, $a_{11} = a_{12} = 0$ (or, symmetrically, $a_{21} = a_{22} = 0$).

[11] Formally, $a_{12} = a_{21} = 0$ (symmetrically, $a_{11} = a_{22} = 0$); the reverse of the previous case.

equilibrium is Pareto efficient if and only if one agent is interested in only one variable; or if, by chance, the first best of one agent lies on the quasi-reaction function of the other.

3. One agent influences both target variables, but the other only one. In this case, as above, the latter always achieves the target value for the variable he is able to affect. Thus, no equilibrium exists if the former agent is uniquely interested in the same target variable (as he controls his relevant sub-system) and does not share the same target value. By contrast, if they share the same target value for the common variable, an equilibrium always exists and is unique and Pareto efficient. The same occurs in the case of symbiosis.
4. Both agents influence both variables, but with linearly dependent instruments. The whole system is not controllable in Tinbergen terms. Thus, even if there were a z^* value for which the quasi-reaction functions intersect, there would be no guarantee that there is at least one vector of instruments u^* supporting it. Only if $r[A|z^*] = 1$, could z^* be achieved. But even then multiple Nash equilibria would arise as, in this case, infinite combinations of instrument values support z^*. This is because the reaction functions are coincident.

8.3 Implicit coalitions

8.3.1 The model

In the two-player case, implicit coordination may emerge as the result of a decentralized setting without conflict between the two players. In a multiple-agents context more general situations can be considered; for instance, implicit coordination among a sub-set of players or among a sub-set of target variables. This section explores the former; the next one will generalize our approach to the latter case.

In order to introduce multiple players, as in Chapter 7, we consider an economy where N agents interact strategically. We assume that each agent is endowed with only one instrument; implying there are N instruments in total. This assumption is not restrictive. The case of an agent who is endowed with more than one instrument can be simply introduced by assuming more agents minimizing the same criterion.

This economy is described by generalizing (8.4) to the following linear system:

$$Ay = Bu + c = \sum_{i=1}^{N} B_i u_i + c, \tag{8.13}$$

where y is a vector of K target variables; $u' = (u_1, \ldots, u_N)$ is the vector of the N instruments; and A, B_i are appropriate matrices of parameters ($A^{-1}B_i$ is the vector of policy multipliers for u_i). We assume that targets and instruments are both linearly independent, i.e., A and B_i are of full rank and column rank respectively. We also assume that the total number of instruments is not greater than the total number of target variables (i.e., $N \leq K$).[12]

Each agent i aims at minimizing a quadratic criterion defined in terms of deviations from a desired target vector ($\bar{y}_i$):[13]

$$L_i = (y - \bar{y}_i)' Q_i (y - \bar{y}_i), \tag{8.14}$$

where Q_i is a positive semi-definite diagonal matrix, which represents the weights that the agent places on deviations from the desired targets. Differently from the previous chapters,[14] we do not require that Q_i be of full rank as one agent may not be interested in one or more of the target variables. The agent i's first best is obtained for $y = \bar{y}_i$; as a consequence $L_i = 0$.

The weight that player i places on deviations from his targets is indicated by vector q_i, the i-th diagonal element of Q_i. Thus $q_i(k)$ is the weight placed by player i on the deviation of $y(k)$ from his k-th target value. Similarly, $y(k)$ and $\bar{y}_i(k)$ are the k-th target variable and the k-th desired target value for player i.

We also assume that the instrument set by agent i is effective on his target variables. Formally this requires $(A^{-1}B_i)' \; Q \neq 0$, for all i.

[12] This assumption is introduced to rule out cases that would lead to infinite Nash equilibria in instrument space, as discussed in the previous chapter.

[13] For the sake of brevity, without loss of generality, the criterion is assumed to be strictly quadratic. However, as shown in Section 6.5, this can be easily generalized to LQ losses.

[14] It is worth noticing that the representation of the policy game here is alternative, but equivalent to that proposed in the previous chapters. In fact, we usually assumed that Q_i were full rank by referring to sub-systems of (8.13), i.e. extracting y_i, instead of considering the whole system describing y. See Chapter 5.

The assumption simply implies that each player is active in the game; otherwise, his reaction function would not exist.

8.3.2 Coalition controllability

Before analyzing the issues of existence, multiple equilibria and policy invariance, we need to introduce some preliminary concepts.

Definition 8.1 (*implicit coalition*). An implicit coalition, $C(Y)$, associated with a given set of values for some (or all) target variables, Y, is the set of agents for whom Y contains their first best.

Given the $\bar{y}_i$ for $i = 1, \ldots, N$, there is a finite set of sets of values for target variables that define and distinguish a particular coalition. We denote this set by Ω and indicate a generic element of it by Y_Z, i.e., $Y_Z \in \Omega$ for all Z. Each Y_Z can contain from 1 to K elements. Since we have assumed that some agents may be interested only in certain sub-sets of target variables, we can have implicit coalitions formed by agents each with a different number of target variables.[15] Moreover, notice that implicit coalitions can also be formed by only one agent.

We must stress that our concept of implicit coalition does not imply any kind of cooperative solution. In particular, the concept is different from that arising from a coalition Nash equilibrium or those associated with other endogenous coalition models. In a coalition Nash equilibrium, agents usually play a two-stage game. In the first stage, they negotiate the formation of coalitions and, if successful, sign a binding agreement to play the second stage as a coalition against other players or coalitions.[16] By contrast, when we consider the idea of implicit coalitions, each agent always acts non-cooperatively and coalitions just emerge naturally from the absence of conflict among their members. No commitment mechanism is needed.

[15] For instance, $Y_1 = \{5, 7\} \in \Omega$ is a set that contains the first best of players i and j if they aim to minimize $L_i = q_i(2)(y_2 - 5)^2$ and $L_j = q_j(2)(y_2 - 5)^2 + q_j(3)\, y_3 - 7)^2$. In this case they are both members of the implicit coalition $C(Y_1)$.

[16] Different equilibrium concepts can be defined according to the way players form expectations about the behavior of other players: see, among others, Chwe (1994), Yi (1997), Ray and Vohra (1999); Carraro (2003) for a survey. For applications in LQ contexts, see, e.g., Kohler (2002), van Aarle, Di Bartolomeo, Engwerda and Plasmans (2002, 2004).

Now, we can formally define a conflict of interest between two coalitions: from now on we assume that the coalitions considered do not overlap, i.e., no player belongs to two coalitions.

Definition 8.2 (*conflict of interest between coalitions*). We say that two coalitions $C(Y_1)$ and $C(Y_2)$ have a conflict of interests if there exists at least one desired target value k such that $\bar{y}_i(k) \neq \bar{y}_j(k)$ with $q_i(k) \neq 0$, $q_j(k) \neq 0$ for $i \in C(Y_1)$ and $j \in C(Y_2)$.

Less formally, a conflict of interest between two coalitions means that Y_1 and Y_2 contain at least one different target value for the same variable which is of interest to both of them.

It is useful to extract from the matrix of policy multipliers, $A^{-1}B$, only those multipliers which are relevant to the members of coalition $C(Y_Z)$. We thus define matrix $M(Y_Z)$ as the matrix obtained from $A^{-1}B$ by selecting only the rows corresponding to the target variables included in Y_Z and only the columns corresponding to the instruments of the coalition players. The order of matrix $M(Y_Z)$ is given by the dimension of Y_Z and the cardinality of the coalition $C(Y_Z)$. We also define a matrix of members' weights for the coalition $C(Y_Z)$ as a matrix where each row j is the vector of weights q_j for the j-th member of $C(Y_Z)$. From this matrix we extract the matrix $Q(Y_Z)$ by deleting the columns corresponding to the target variables not included in Y_Z. The order of matrix $Q(Y_Z)$ is given by the cardinality of $C(Y_Z)$ and the dimension of Y_Z.

Finally, we define the notion of coalition controllability.

Definition 8.3 (*coalition controllability*). A coalition is said to possess coalition controllability if the strategies of coalition members always imply that they reach their first best outcomes for any given strategy of the other players.

Coalition controllability implies that a combination of instruments of the coalition members (coalition policy) exists such that, for any given set of values for the instruments chosen by non-coalition members, the coalition members always achieve their first best outcomes. Coalition controllability is assured by the conditions stated in the following theorem.

Theorem 8.3 (*coalition controllability*). A coalition $C(Y_Z)$ satisfies coalition controllability if (1) $M(Y_Z)$ is of full column rank; and (2) $M(Y_Z)' \cdot Q(Y_Z)$ is of full column rank, where "$\cdot$" denotes the *Hadamard product*, i.e., the element-by-element product.

Proof. Given the policies of non-coalition members, if condition (1) is satisfied the coalition Y_Z faces a sub-system of the economy that is controllable in the Tinbergen sense, by a unique decision maker. A policy assuring that $y_Z - \bar{y}_Z = 0$ thus exists, where $y_Z - \bar{y}_Z$ are the deviations from the target values included in Y_Z. However, coalition members play in a non-cooperative manner: i.e., each member sets one instrument separately. It is then not obvious that they can implement this policy. Their first-order conditions are $(A^{-1}B_i)'Q_i(y - \bar{y}_i) = 0$ for all $i \in C(Y_Z)$, which can be written in compact form as $[M(Y_Z)' \cdot Q(Y_Z)](y_Z - \bar{y}_Z) = 0$. This system has a unique solution $y_Z = \bar{y}_Z$, if the matrix $[M(Y_Z)' \cdot Q(Y_Z)]$ is left-invertible. This will be the case if condition (2) is satisfied. ∎

Coalition controllability clearly generalizes the traditional Tinbergen–Theil conditions to the case of multiple players, and augments the traditional results with an implementation requirement. Condition (1) in fact simply means that the coalition has a number of independent instruments greater than or equal to its independent targets (existence in the space of targets), while condition (2) means that the agents can independently implement a jointly determined Tinbergen policy (existence in the space of instruments).

8.3.3 Existence, policy invariance and multiple equilibria

The concept of coalition controllability can be used to derive necessary conditions for Nash equilibrium existence.

Theorem 8.4 (*non-existence and implicit coalitions*). A Nash equilibrium does not exist if there is a conflict of interest between two controlling coalitions.

Proof. Assume that an equilibrium exists and there are two controlling coalitions, $C(Y_1)$ and $C(Y_2)$, with conflicting interests. Taking as given the equilibrium values for the agents who do not belong to the coalitions, coalition controllability, by definition, implies that the equilibrium satisfies $y(k) = \bar{y}_i(k)$ for any k such that $q_i(k) \neq 0$ for all members of the two coalitions. However, the definition of a conflict of interest also implies that there are at least two agents, j and h, for whom: $\bar{y}_j(k) \neq \bar{y}_h(k)$ with $q_j(k) \neq 0$, $q_h(k) \neq 0$ and $j \in C(Y_1)$, $h \in C(Y_2)$. Hence, no equilibrium can exist. ∎

The nature of the conditions implied by the theorem must be clear. It shows sufficient conditions for non-existence, and thus necessary conditions for the existence of a Nash equilibrium. These conditions extend the case of non-existence to situations where some agents who have conflicting target values do not control them individually, but can do so through the coalitions they belong to. As for existence, these conditions are more stringent than those stated by Theorems 6.1 and 6.3. This is because, for an equilibrium to exist, one needs to rule out the existence of a conflict not only between individual players but also between coalitions.

We can use the discussion above to derive some sufficient conditions for policy invariance as defined in Chapter 6. By using an argument similar to those already largely introduced in the book, from Theorem 8.4, the following corollary can be stated.

Corollary 8.2 (*policy neutrality and implicit coalitions*). Provided that a Nash equilibrium exists, a controlling coalition $C(Y_Z)$ implies that the policies of all the players not belonging to $C(Y_Z)$ are neutral with respect to the target variables in Y_Z.

In other words, if an equilibrium exists, policy invariance now emerges when there is at least one controlling coalition, $C(Y_Z)$, that does not include all players. In this case, all the variables defined in Y_Z are set by the coalition and changes in the preference parameters of the non-coalition members cannot affect them. Hence non-coalition policies are neutral with respect to the target variables defined in Y_Z. If this is not the case, i.e., if players outside the coalition were able to influence the same targets, a contradiction would arise with the assumption that these are controlled by the coalition.

The concept of coalition controllability can also be used to derive interesting properties about uniqueness of the equilibrium, and indeed sufficient conditions for multiple equilibria.

Theorem 8.5 (*multiple equilibria and implicit coalitions*). In a game where at least one equilibrium exists, multiple equilibria will arise if the cardinality of a controlling coalition $C(Y_Z)$ is greater than the dimension of Y_Z.

Proof. The proof is trivial. Assume that an equilibrium exists. If the cardinality of $C(Y_Z)$ is greater than the dimension of Y_Z, there are other infinite combinations of the policies of coalition members supporting their first best outcomes, given the policy of non-coalition members. All these combinations will also be Nash equilibria. ∎

Generalizing the results derived in Chapter 7, multiple equilibria therefore always emerge when there is "too large" a controlling coalition: i.e., a controlling coalition with more members (that is, instruments under our assumptions) than targets. This means that, even if no player has more instruments than targets, the controlling coalition faces an over-determined problem; and, since its members play in a non-cooperative manner, they have the problem of coordinating their action toward one of the first best equilibria.[17] This result complements those obtained in the previous chapter, where we considered games with more instruments than targets.

The case of excess instruments is thus cumbersome for establishing a Nash equilibrium, not only in the case of independent players, but also when the possibility of (implicit) coalitions is assumed. This problem is more likely to be relevant if N is large. However, it would find a natural resolution in the focal point approach,[18] or with a centralization of policymaking. Alternative solutions can be related to the idea of correlated equilibria (Aumann, 1974).

8.4 An example: a three-player game

To discuss the issue of implicit coalitions we clearly need to leave the $2 \times 2 \times 2$ world. However, to keep things simple we consider just a small variation, i.e., a $3 \times 3 \times 3$ example. As we aim to illustrate the application of our theorems, we keep the economic relations as simple as possible, perhaps paying some cost in terms of realism.

We assume that three policymakers – a trade union (U) and fiscal (F) and monetary (M) authorities – interact, potentially aiming to influence the values of real output (y), real wage (ω), and inflation (π). For the sake of simplicity, we restrict our attention to the pure quadratic preferences case. Policymakers' preferences are as follows:

$$L_i = \tfrac{1}{2}a_i\left(y-\bar{y}_i\right)^2 + \tfrac{1}{2}b_i\left(\pi-\bar{\pi}_i\right)^2 + \tfrac{1}{2}c_i\left(\omega-\bar{\omega}_i\right)^2 \quad i \in \{U,F,M\}, \tag{8.15}$$

where subscript i identifies the policymaker and bar-variables their targets; a, b and c are the weights associated with deviations of target variables from the bliss points.

[17] The same problem arises in the battle of the sexes, when both players only care about being together.

[18] Demertzis and Viegi (2008).

These target variables are related by the following economic system:

$$y = \alpha\pi + f - \delta s, \tag{8.16}$$

$$\pi = m + \gamma f, \tag{8.17}$$

$$\omega = -\chi y + s, \tag{8.18}$$

where f, m and s are the policymakers' instruments. The fiscal stimulus is captured by f; money growth, m, has real effects due to the existence of some nominal rigidities; finally, the all-encompassing union affects the economy by its activity s (e.g., by increasing strikes it is able to obtain higher real wages at the cost of a lower real output). All parameters of the model (α, γ, χ, δ) are assumed to be strictly positive and less than 1.

The system (8.16)–(8.18) can then be written in reduced form as

$$\begin{bmatrix} y \\ \pi \\ \omega \end{bmatrix} = \begin{bmatrix} \alpha\gamma+1 & \alpha & -\delta \\ \gamma & 1 & 0 \\ -\chi(\alpha\gamma+1) & -\alpha\chi & 1+\delta\chi \end{bmatrix} \begin{bmatrix} f \\ m \\ s \end{bmatrix}. \tag{8.19}$$

In order to illustrate our results, we consider some simple cases from the above model where policymakers are not interested in all target variables.

Example 1. Policy invariance

Consider the case where the central bank and the government are not interested in the real wage ($c_G = c_M = 0$), whereas the union is interested in all the variables. The former assumption is usual in policy games. However, the union's preferences for inflation (and output) may depend on its political attitude with respect to the government,[19] or the fact that unions often also represent retired workers who earn transfers that are not indexed to price changes.[20]

[19] See, for example in LQ contexts, Detken and Gartner (1992), Di Bartolomeo (2002, 2007), Acocella, Di Bartolomeo and Tirelli (2009), Acocella, Di Bartolomeo and Pauwels (2010), Acocella and Di Bartolomeo (2012); for a survey, see Gartner (2000).

[20] See Cukierman (2004) for a discussion.

Notice that in this setting no player has enough instruments to control his relevant sub-system (each is endowed with only one instrument and aims to influence at least two target variables). Thus the results (derived from the assumption of controllability) presented in Chapter 6 are not applicable.

Assume that $\bar{y}_G = \bar{y}_B = \bar{y} \neq \bar{y}_U$ and $\bar{\pi}_G = \bar{\pi}_B = 0$. An implicit coalition now arises between the fiscal and monetary authorities and allows them to unequivocally determine y and π independently of the actions of the union (as they together have two instruments for two targets).[21] Moreover, their optimal strategies are to achieve their compatible targets (which are indeed the same) for any policy of the union. It follows that, as there is a unique way to react to each possible policy of the union in order to reach $y = \bar{y}$ and $\pi = 0$, they set their policy in a "cooperative" way even if they cannot communicate between themselves or sign binding agreements. This is the essence of implicit coalitions.

As a result, the union will not be able to affect both inflation and output, which are instead equal to the coalition's *common* target value in the Nash equilibrium. Although the union's strategy about strikes is unable to affect the output gap and the inflation, its attempt to do so implies a sub-optimal equilibrium value for the real wage. Under realistic assumptions about parameters (e.g., its desire to obtain a larger output gap compared to the coalition's optimum) this will lead to lower real wages. It is worth noticing that the same result occurs in other, more general cases since we do not require that the members of the coalition have the same target values, as in common interest games; only that these values are compatible.[22] For instance, assuming $\bar{y}_G = \bar{y}_B$ and $b_G = 0$ (the government is not interested in inflation) leads to the same result for any desired inflation target of the central bank. In this case, an implicit controlling coalition between the fiscal and monetary authorities for y and π in fact always exists.

Example 2. Non-existence

Assume now that no player is interested in the real wage (parameters c_i are all zero) and, in addition, the union is not interested in inflation

[21] It is easy to check that their relevant sub-matrix is full rank (unless $\phi = 0$, which cannot occur under our assumptions) due to the instrument–target independence.

[22] In the next section we will further extend this neutrality result to the case where compatibility does not hold, by introducing the concept of decisiveness.

($b_U = 0$). It follows that the union controls the real output (one instrument for one target) and the other policymakers do not. Thus apparently an equilibrium exists and monetary and fiscal policy neutrality holds.

However, this is not necessarily true. By assuming that $\bar{y}_G = \bar{y}_B = \bar{y} \neq \bar{y}_U$ and $\bar{\pi}_G = \bar{\pi}_B = 0$, an implicit coalition between the fiscal and monetary authorities affecting y and π also exists. Following Theorem 8.4, the Nash equilibrium will not exist as two controlling coalitions have a conflict of interest (the union forms a degenerate controlling coalition). It is straightforward to observe that the same occurs for any central bank's inflation target if $\bar{y}_G = \bar{y}_B = \bar{y} \neq \bar{y}_U$ and $b_G = 0$.

Example 3. Multiplicity

Finally we reconsider the previous example and relax the hypothesis of different output target values between policy authorities and the union by assuming $\bar{y}_U = \bar{y}$, instead. Now, a coalition among the three players controls compatible targets in terms of π and y, but there are infinite combinations of their instruments that lead to $y = \bar{y}$ and $\pi = 0$.[23] As a result, multiple equilibria arise according to Theorem 8.5. As discussed in Chapter 7, a way to solve this impasse is to assume that one of the players faces an instrument cost or, alternatively, that he exits the game. Perhaps more surprisingly, the same result can be obtained by assuming that one player is interested in the real wage with an arbitrary target value ($\bar{\omega}$). Then the implicit coalition unambiguosly determines the only Nash equilibrium of the game ($y = \bar{y}$, $\pi = 0$, $\omega = \bar{\omega}$) in either outcome and instrument spaces.

8.5 Group interactions and issues of coordination

8.5.1 *The N × M × K policy game*

In this section, we consider the most general case by introducing a generalization of coalition controllability, namely *decisiveness*, to a model where N agents, setting M instruments, interact to control an economy where K endogenous variables are present.

The model of the economy is again (8.13) and (8.14), i.e.,

$$Ay = Bu + c = \sum_{i=1}^{N} B_i u_i + c, \tag{8.20}$$

[23] Indeed, there are multiple equilibria, in the space of instruments but not in the space of the outcomes.

$$L_i = (y - \bar{y}_i)' Q_i (y - \bar{y}_i). \tag{8.21}$$

Again, without loss of generality, we assume that each agent is endowed with only one instrument, so there are $M = N$ agents; the total number of instruments is not greater than the total number of target variables; each player is active in the game.

8.5.2 *Existence, uniqueness and multiple equilibria*

The system of quasi-reaction functions, the N first-order conditions in outcome space, is

$$Zy - \bar{z} = 0, \quad \text{where } Z = \begin{bmatrix} (A^{-1}B_1)' Q_1 \\ \vdots \\ (A^{-1}B_i)' Q_i \\ \vdots \\ (A^{-1}B_N)' Q_N \end{bmatrix}, \ \bar{z} = \begin{bmatrix} (A^{-1}B_1)' Q_1 \bar{y}_1 \\ \vdots \\ (A^{-1}B_i)' Q_i \bar{y}_i \\ \vdots \\ (A^{-1}B_N)' Q_N \bar{y}_N \end{bmatrix}. \tag{8.22}$$

Lemma 8.1. The system of quasi-reaction functions (8.22) has a solution if and only if $\mathrm{r}[Z] = \mathrm{r}[Z|\bar{z}]$.

Proof. The proof is obvious. ■

Notice that the existence of a target vector y^* that solves (8.22) is not necessarily a Nash equilibrium outcome: there might not be a vector of strategies to support it.

Theorem 8.6 (*existence in the generalized game*). A solution y^* of the system of quasi-reaction functions (8.22) is the outcome of a Nash equilibrium if and only if $\mathrm{r}[(A^{-1}B)'] = \mathrm{r}[(A^{-1}B)'|y^*]$.

Proof. The proof is trivial. ■

Comment 8.1. Lemma 8.1 assures that there exists a vector of values for the target variables that is on the quasi-reaction functions of all the agents, which in turn implies that no agent has an incentive to change his instrument and deviate. The theorem, by contrast, guarantees the feasibility of that outcome; i.e., that there exists a strategy u^* which the players may use to support that outcome. It follows that if u^* is a Nash equilibrium of the game, no agent has an incentive to deviate: so u^* should support a vector of targets for which the first-order conditions are verified for all agents.

Corollary 8.3. The Nash equilibrium is unique if and only if $ZA^{-1}B$ is full rank.

Proof. The conditions to be satisfied for a Nash equilibrium are $Zy - \bar{z} = 0$ and $y = A^{-1}Bu$. By substituting the latter into the former, we can see that uniqueness will arise if the matrix $ZA^{-1}B$ is invertible and, since it is square, of full rank. ■

8.5.3 Policy invariance and decisiveness

In order to derive the conditions for neutrality we consider a sub-group χ of agents. Given this sub-group, we can rearrange the system (8.20) as

$$\begin{bmatrix} A_{y_\chi y_\chi} & A_{y_\chi y_{\bar{\chi}}} \\ A_{y_{\bar{\chi}} y_\chi} & A_{y_{\bar{\chi}} y_{\bar{\chi}}} \end{bmatrix} \begin{bmatrix} y_\chi \\ y_{\bar{\chi}} \end{bmatrix} = \begin{bmatrix} B_{y_\chi u_\chi} & B_{y_\chi u_{\bar{\chi}}} \\ B_{y_{\bar{\chi}} u_\chi} & B_{y_{\bar{\chi}} u_{\bar{\chi}}} \end{bmatrix} \begin{bmatrix} u_\chi \\ u_{\bar{\chi}} \end{bmatrix}, \tag{8.23}$$

where u_χ is the vector of the instruments of the agents of group χ, while $u_{\bar{\chi}}$ is the vector of the instruments of the other agents; y_χ is the vector of all the target variables, $y_\chi(k)$, for which there is at least one agent, i, of group χ for whom $(A^{-1}B_i)'(k)q_i(k) \neq 0$. In other words, we select the vector of targets y_χ of group χ to include all (and only) the targets for which some agent in χ is both interested and ex ante effective; $y_{\bar{\chi}}$ are the other target variables.

From (8.23), we can extract the relationship between y_χ and u_χ, i.e.,

$$A_{y_\chi y_\chi} y_\chi = B_{y_\chi u_\chi} u_\chi + c, \tag{8.24}$$

where $c = B_{y_\chi u_{\bar{\chi}}} u_{\bar{\chi}} - A_{y_\chi y_{\bar{\chi}}} y_{\bar{\chi}}$.

Now we can introduce the following definitions.

Definition 8.4 (*χ-game*). We define the χ-game as the non-cooperative simultaneous game among agents of a sub-group χ of the players, where, for all the target variables $y_\chi(k)$, it holds that $[A^{-1}B_i]'(k)q_i(k) \neq 0$ for at least one agent $i \in \chi$. The policies of all the agents not belonging to χ, $u_{\bar{\chi}}$, are instead considered as an arbitrary constant (i.e., c is given in (8.24)).

Since we assumed that every agent is active in the game, i.e., $(A^{-1}B_i)' \, Q_i \neq 0$, all agents in χ are active in the χ-game as well as a consequence of the way we selected the targets. In particular, $\left(A_{y_\chi y_\chi}^{-1} B_{y_\chi u_\chi}\right)' Q_i \neq 0$ holds for all $i \in \chi$.

Definition 8.5 (χ-*group decisiveness*). If an equilibrium of the χ-game exists and the outcomes associated to this equilibrium are independent of variations of c, then the χ group is decisive with respect to the target variables x_χ.

Theorem 8.7 (χ-*group decisiveness*). The χ group is decisive with respect to the target variables y_χ if and only if Lemma 8.1 holds for the χ-game and the matrix $A_{x_\chi x_\chi}^{-1} B_{x_\chi u_\chi}$ is invertible or left-invertible.

Proof. Lemma 8.1 assures us that an outcome from which agents have no incentive to deviate exists. Conditions on $A_{y_\chi y_\chi}^{-1} B_{y_\chi u_\chi}$ assure us that, if such an outcome exists, it is feasible and independent of c. Note that, as matrix $A_{x_\chi x_\chi}^{-1} B_{x_\chi u_\chi}$ is of full rank or left-invertible, the system of reaction functions is either determinate or over-determined. ■

Two corollaries follow.

Corollary 8.4. When an equilibrium for the entire game exists, if the χ group is decisive with respect to the target variables y_χ, then the policies of agents that do not belong to that group are neutral with respect to y_χ.

Corollary 8.5. If there are at least two non-overlapping groups that are decisive with respect to a non-empty intersection of target variables, then the equilibrium either does not exist or is multiple. The latter is the only case if there is no *implicit* conflict between groups, i.e., the outcomes associated with the χ-games are compatible.

Corollary 8.4 shows that the selection of the targets of the χ-game implies that the first-order conditions of the agents of group χ for the χ-game are the same as for the original game. Assume that an equilibrium of the entire game exists; as the agents in χ are decisive, the χ-game will be fully determined for whichever outcome vector y_χ satisfies Lemma 8.1. Since the first-order conditions are invariant, any strategy change by the other agents (not belonging to χ) will have no effect on the vector of targets x_χ. This results in a policy-neutral outcome.

Corollary 8.5 shows that, if two groups χ and χ' have overlapping targets ($y_\chi \cap y_{\chi'} \neq 0$), the equilibrium either does not exist or is multiple. In particular, since both groups are decisive, each of them has a set of outcomes that satisfies first-order conditions (by Lemma 8.1) and that can be achieved independently of the choices of the other agents. Therefore, if these sets of targets have an empty intersection, an equilibrium exists but it is not unique since the system is over-determined (it is at least determined for each group of agents). Conversely, if the intersection is non-empty, no equilibrium exists.

Corollaries 8.4 and 8.5 extend the results on coalition controllability derived in the previous section. Implicit coalition controllability is in fact a particular case of group decisiveness. It arises when the targets of interest to the members of the group coincide. The results in this section are more general, since controllability is not required for decisiveness. Decisiveness does not need symbiosis among the group members because conflict is then possible and controllability may not be achieved. Decisiveness only requires that the conflict among them is completely interior to the group and therefore independent of the policies of non-members.

8.6 A further example: the three-player game revisited

It is useful to go back to the 3 × 3 × 3 example presented above to show the additional insight brought by the idea of decisiveness.

Even if the government and the central bank do not share any value for the targets, the simple fact that they are interested only in the output gap and inflation may be sufficient to rule out any effect on these variables by the union.

Providing that their relevant sub-system is Tinbergenian, the government and the central bank are in fact decisive with respect to output and inflation. Interestingly, for any policy of the union, the strategic interaction between the government and the central bank leads to the same Nash equilibrium in outcome space, which is in general sub-optimal with respect to any cooperative solution between the three. This means that the union is not able to interfere with the strategic interaction between the other players, even if these players do not agree on any compatible outcome.

We can illustrate the result by a numerical example. Reconsider the model (8.19) under the following parameterization:

$$\begin{bmatrix} y \\ \pi \\ \omega \end{bmatrix} = \begin{bmatrix} 1 & \frac{1}{2} & -\frac{1}{2} \\ \frac{1}{2} & 1 & -\frac{1}{4} \\ -\frac{1}{3} & -\frac{1}{6} & \frac{11}{12} \end{bmatrix} \begin{bmatrix} f \\ m \\ s \end{bmatrix}, \tag{8.25}$$

and assume the players aim to minimize

$$L_B = \tfrac{1}{2}(y-0.8)^2 + \tfrac{3}{2}(\pi)^2, \tag{8.26}$$

$$L_G = \tfrac{1}{2}(y-1)^2 + \tfrac{1}{2}(\pi-2)^2, \tag{8.27}$$

$$L_U = \tfrac{1}{2}a_U\left(y-\bar{y}_U\right)^2 + \tfrac{1}{2}b_U\left(\pi-\bar{\pi}_U\right)^2 + \tfrac{1}{2}c_U\left(\omega-\bar{\omega}_U\right)^2. \tag{8.28}$$

Consider the game between the central bank and the government only (i.e., take s as given in (8.25)). The policymaker's constraint then becomes

$$\begin{bmatrix} y \\ \pi \end{bmatrix} = \frac{1}{2}\begin{bmatrix} 2 & 1 \\ 1 & 2 \end{bmatrix}\begin{bmatrix} f \\ m \end{bmatrix} - \frac{1}{4}\begin{bmatrix} 2 \\ 1 \end{bmatrix} s. \tag{8.29}$$

The system (8.29) is clearly controllable in the Tinbergen sense. A social planner would be able to achieve any vector of target values for y and π by appropriately using the controls f and m. However, here the instruments are set in a decentralized manner. There is no social planner, but two independent institutions aiming at different target values.

By minimizing (8.26) with respect to m constrained by (8.29) and (8.27) with respect to f constrained, again, by (8.29), we obtain the optimal policies of the central bank and the government, given the action of the union, i.e., s. We do not need to solve these problems to note that these policies in the outcome space do not depend on s as it enters linearly in the problem. As a consequence, by solving the system of the optimal policies, we find the optimal values for y and π:

$$\begin{bmatrix} y \\ \pi \end{bmatrix} = \begin{bmatrix} 2.11 \\ 0.22 \end{bmatrix}, \tag{8.30}$$

which are independent of s.

Now reconsider the entire game; how does the above result affect it? Clearly in a destructive way – at least for the union. In fact, as in the Nash equilibrium, each agent computes its optimal policy taking as given the actions of the other. The outcome (8.30) should also characterize the full game. Perhaps surprisingly, it implies that the union's policies are neutral with respect to inflation and real output, even if no player and no coalition controls the game. All players in fact have only one instrument but aim at influencing at least two target variables, and do not share any target value.

If instead the union is interested only in output,[24] the Nash equilibrium does not exist. The presence of two decisive groups (the union is a degenerate decisive group) with non-compatible targets, i.e., the ones that each decisive group would achieve, would impede existence.

Another illustrative case is obtained by assuming that players aim to minimize the following preferences:

$$L_B = \tfrac{1}{2}a_B\left(y-\bar{y}_B\right)^2 + \tfrac{1}{2}b_B\left(\pi-\bar{\pi}_B\right)^2 + \tfrac{1}{2}c_B\left(\omega-\bar{\omega}_B\right)^2, \qquad (8.31)$$

$$L_G = \tfrac{1}{2}a_G\left(y-\bar{y}_G\right)^2 + \tfrac{1}{2}c_G\left(\omega-\bar{\omega}_G\right)^2, \qquad (8.32)$$

$$L_U = \tfrac{1}{2}a_U\left(y-\bar{y}_U\right)^2 + \tfrac{1}{2}c_U\left(\omega-\bar{\omega}_U\right)^2. \qquad (8.33)$$

One might think that decisiveness on the part of the union and government could prevent the central bank from affecting real variables. And this is the case in this example, as the reader can easily check (rewrite the relevant sub-system for decisiveness). But, if the relevant sub-system had been

$$\begin{bmatrix} y \\ \omega \end{bmatrix} = \frac{1}{6}\begin{bmatrix} 6 & 3 \\ -2 & -1 \end{bmatrix}\begin{bmatrix} f \\ s \end{bmatrix} + \frac{1}{9}\begin{bmatrix} 6 \\ -2 \end{bmatrix} m, \qquad (8.34)$$

it would be to check that it is not controllable in the Tinbergen sense (the rank of the multiplier matrix is 1). In this case, the union and the government would not be decisive for real output and wages. Once again, the relevance of the tools developed by Tinbergen and others is revealed.

8.7 Conclusions

In this and the previous chapter, we have provided an analysis of the LQ policy game framework looking at the system as a whole or for groups of players. In this context, different situations may emerge depending on the number of variables of interest, the existence of a

[24] As well as when it is only interested in inflation.

conflict, "symbiosis" or group decisiveness among the agents and the effectiveness of the instruments.

In Chapter 7, by considering the system as a whole – under some general conditions – we showed that when the total number of instruments of the individual players with different target values exceeds the total number of their targets, multiple equilibria exist, in the case of conflicting target values. We added that an equilibrium is unlikely to exist in the case when the total number of instruments is higher than that of targets and the target values of the players differ.

In this chapter we have been able to prove that a Nash equilibrium does not exist if there is a conflict between at least two implicit coalitions or groups of players each of which, respectively, controls its sub-system or is decisive with respect to their targets. By contrast (but making use of the same concepts), we again prove that there are multiple equilibria when a controlling coalition has more instruments available than targets or, with respect to groups, if there are two decisive groups which share the same target values. In this chapter we also restate our previous result of neutrality in terms of implicit coalitions and group decisiveness: neutrality of agents not belonging to a controlling coalition or a group that is decisive with respect to some targets in fact holds if an equilibrium of the game exists.

Our results are essential to fully understand policy games and for model building, as they state the conditions for the consistency of the optimal strategies of all the players (and thus the existence of an equilibrium to the game) as well as the effectiveness of policy instruments. In addition, they are relevant for institution building, as they can help us to show the conditions under which a decentralized equilibrium may fail to exist or to be Pareto efficient.

9 *Announcements as a coordination mechanism*

WITH PAOLO GIOVANNI PIACQUADIO

Summary. This chapter studies the relation between communication and coordination failures. We have already shown how multiple (Nash) equilibria are likely to characterize policy interactions. If this is the case, policymakers may not be able to form consistent expectations of other players' strategies and coordination failures may arise. We introduce a complete information announcement model with an outside option (based on exogenous beliefs) to study whether the nonbinding announcement of a policy (cheap talk) can resolve or mitigate the coordination issue. Our results show that the outside option may force the sender to announce a second best outcome to keep the message "credible" and achieve coordination. A comparison with policy commitment (binding messages, which are a fortiori credible) highlights the appeal of considering weaker promises that are consistent with real-world announcements about future strategy choices.

9.1 Introduction

In the previous chapters, we have seen that cases of multiple equilibria can emerge in policy games and have derived the formal conditions under which this occurs. In such a case, the Nash equilibrium concept is too broad to tell us how policymakers interact and what the outcome of the game would be. Consequently the issue arises, how to select one equilibrium? This chapter examines that issue.[1] We use non-binding announcements (cheap talk) as a device for coordinating the policymakers onto a solution. Along the way, we consider the "credibility" of those announcements and their consistency across players and reaction functions.

[1] Most of the concepts used in this chapter draw from Acocella, Di Bartolomeo, and Piacquadio (2009).

The problem of multiple Nash equilibria has often been discussed in the literature. For instance, David Kreps considers multiple equilibria, and how to choose between them, to be one of the paramount problems in game theory. Many sorts of games have, in fact, multiple equilibria "and the theory is often of no help in sorting out whether any one is the solution and, if one is, which one is" (Kreps, 1990).

In some games with multiple equilibria, players know what to do. This knowledge comes from directly relevant past experience and from a sense of how individuals act generally. However, formal mathematical game theory still has much to say about where these expectations come from; how and why they persist; or when and why we might expect them to arise (Kreps, 1990). The problem of equilibrium selection, in particular, is closely related to various kinds of coordination failures (see, e.g., Cooper and John, 1988).

The natural solution to coordination failures is based on the idea of focal points (Schelling, 1960)[2].That idea, however, is not always appealing – in particular, when there is a conflict of interest among the agents. More interesting are the solutions that prevent the emergence of coordination problems by considering small two-stage variations of the standard coordination game that are based on pre-play communication or the introduction of outside options.

Common sense tells us that agents make use of communication to avoid coordination failures. Think, for example, of a situation in which two cars reach a bridge with two lanes from two opposite directions. There are two Nash equilibria in pure strategies (both drivers take their left lane, both take their right lane) and one in mixed strategies. Adding the option for one player to make an announcement does not alter the set of possible Nash equilibria; but it is easy to think that if one driver can make an announcement they will not crash.

In a complete information context,[3] Farrell (1988) assumes that before playing the coordination game there is a pre-play stage in which agents can send non-binding messages (announcements). Then he defines *self-committing* announcements as those that satisfy two

[2] Some refinements of the Nash equilibrium have also been proposed. The most relevant probably is that of Harsanyi and Selten (1988), which is based on the concept of risk dominance.

[3] In addition, cheap talk has also been applied to incomplete information games. See the seminal paper of Crawford and Sobel (1982); or, among others, Gibbons (1992), Chen, Katik and Sobel (2008), and references therein.

conditions: (a) it is optimal for the sender to keep the promise and (b) the sender expects the receiver to believe the announcement. Farrell argues that, under many circumstances, *self-committing* announcements will resolve the issue of equilibrium selection by acting as a coordination device.[4] However, Farrell's solution may no longer be able to resolve coordination failures if announcements are permitted in both directions. Meanwhile, cheap talk models have been extensively used to study coordination problems in a complete information context (Farrell, 1987, 1995; Rabin, 1994; Farrell and Rabin, 1996; Cooper, 1999, 1995; Baliga and Morris, 2002).[5]

Kohlberg and Mertens (1986) consider another variation based on a forward induction argument. A player has the option of obtaining a sure outcome instead of playing a coordination game. In the first stage the agent has to decide whether or not to play the coordination game; if he decides to play, the coordination phase will be the second stage of the game; if not, the game ends. In this context, by rejecting an outside option that is better than the Nash equilibrium, the agent signals (or "announces") his action and reduces coordination failure.

In this chapter, we consider a general LQ coordination game and introduce a pre-play stage that takes account of both cheap talk and outside options. In particular, we assume that an agent can make an announcement in the first stage of the game that other agents can take into account or not as they wish. If they do not coordinate on the announcement equilibrium, they expect the payoff given by the outside option. Therefore, the sender has to take account of this possibility in determining his *self-committing* announcements. We then extend our results to the case of "announcement wars" in which pre-play allows multiple announcements by both players.

Finally, we investigate the traditional time inconsistency issue by clarifying the relationship between credible and non-credible promises. Costless announcements and the traditional commitment solution

[4] Farrell's solution has been criticized by Aumann (1990). However, evolutionary models and experimental evidence support Farrell's view (see Kim and Sobel, 1995; and Charness, 2000).

[5] Experimental studies also show that cheap talk or well thought out announcements can help agents coordinate their actions to mutual advantage, theoretical predictions notwithstanding. See Cooper, De Jong, Forsythe and Ross (1989, 1990, 1992), van Huyck, Battalio and Beil (1990, 1991), Crawford (1998), Charness (2000), Blume and Ortmann (2007) and the survey in Camerer (2003).

are compared as alternative techniques for creating credible policy commitments.

The LQ structure of the game allows us to derive closed form solutions and to describe the entire taxonomy of it, including necessary and sufficient conditions to observe and solve coordination failures.

The chapter is structured as follows. Section 9.2 illustrates the coordination failure game and shows, in particular, the necessary and sufficient conditions for multiple equilibria to arise. Section 9.3 describes the rationale of our contention by considering a one-sided announcement two-stage game. Section 9.4 discusses the difference between announcement equilibrium and commitment. Section 9.5 applies the idea of announcement equilibria to a monetary–fiscal policy coordination problem in order to illustrate the essence and importance of our announcements mechanism in practice. Section 9.6 extends our result to announcement wars, where sequential non-binding messages can be sent. Section 9.7 provides a further example, drawn from an industrial organization problem where two firms face multiple equilibria in choosing their R&D and advertising strategies. Section 9.8 concludes.

9.2 A simple coordination game

We consider a static LQ game between two players with complete information. Each player, k, sets an instrument, u_k, to minimize the following loss functions:

$$L_k(z) = \frac{1}{2}\left[(x - \bar{x}_k)^2 + \beta_k (y - \bar{y}_k)^2\right] \qquad k = \{1,2\}, \tag{9.1}$$

defined over the deviations of two target variables, x and y, from their desired values $\bar{x}_k$ and $\bar{y}_k$. In vector notation $z = (x,y)'$, $\bar{z}_k = (\bar{x}_k, \bar{y}_k)'$; and $\beta_k \in (0, +\infty)$ are given preference weights or relative priority parameters.

The relationships between targets and instruments are summarized by a system of linear equations that describes the economy:

$$\begin{bmatrix} x \\ y \end{bmatrix} = \begin{bmatrix} a_{11} & a_{12} \\ a_{21} & a_{22} \end{bmatrix} \begin{bmatrix} u_1 \\ u_2 \end{bmatrix} + \begin{bmatrix} c_x \\ c_y \end{bmatrix}, \tag{9.2}$$

where a_{ji} are the (policy) multipliers of the instruments u_1 and u_2, and c_x and c_y are constants. In compact form, Equation (9.2) can be rewritten as $z = Au + c$.

We assume that the instruments of the players are linearly independent.[6] Thus

$$r[A] = r\begin{bmatrix} a_{11} & a_{12} \\ a_{21} & a_{22} \end{bmatrix} = 2. \tag{9.3}$$

The Nash equilibrium is a vector $u^* = (u_1^*, u_2^*)$ if $u_1^* \in \arg\min L_i\ (u_i^*, u_{-t}^*)$ for $k = 1,2$. As we know from Chapter 8, necessary and sufficient conditions to obtain multiple Nash equilibria in this linear setting are given by:

$$\text{(a) } r\begin{bmatrix} a_{11} & \beta_1 a_{21} \\ a_{12} & \beta_2 a_{22} \end{bmatrix} = 1 \text{ and (b) } \begin{pmatrix} a_{11} \\ a_{21}\beta_1 \end{pmatrix}(\overline{z}_2 - \overline{z}_1) = 0 \tag{9.4}$$

or, more concisely, $r\begin{bmatrix} a_{11} & \beta_1 a_{21} & a_{11}\overline{x}_1 + \beta_1 a_{21}\overline{y}_1 \\ a_{12} & \beta_2 a_{22} & a_{12}\overline{x}_2 + \beta_2 a_{22}\overline{y}_2 \end{bmatrix} = 1$.

The conditions in Equation (9.4) can easily be derived from the usual first-order conditions by introducing the associated quasi-reaction functions (see Section 5.2.3). These reaction functions are given by the following pair of equations:

$$a_{1k}(x - \overline{x}_k) + \beta_k a_{2k}(y - \overline{y}_k) = 0 \qquad k = \{1,2\}. \tag{9.5}$$

Clearly one can derive the conventional reaction functions from quasi-reaction functions, and vice versa, by using (9.2).

Part (a) of (9.4) implies that the quasi-reaction functions (and the reaction functions) of the two agents have the same slopes; and part (b) that they are overlapping (i.e., the first best outcomes for player 2 lies along the quasi-reaction function of player 1, and vice versa for player 2).[7]

Thus, all outcomes satisfying

$$\begin{pmatrix} a_{11} \\ a_{21}\beta_1 \end{pmatrix}(z - \overline{z}_1) = 0 \tag{9.6}$$

[6] If this assumption does not hold, there may be multiple Nash equilibria that support the same outcome as discussed in Chapter 7; and as a result, the same payoffs for the agents. In that case, the problem faced by each agent is to anticipate the strategy played by the other player correctly, in order to get to one of these Nash equilibria.

[7] If only part (a) holds, there will be no equilibrium, as stated in Theorem 6.1. Multiple equilibria arise if part (b) also holds (see Section 8.2.2).

are the outcomes of a Nash equilibrium.[8] Moreover, if $\bar{z}_1 \neq \bar{z}_2$, the set of all Nash equilibria can be expressed as

$$z^N = \lambda\bar{z}_1 + (1-\lambda)\bar{z}_2 \quad \text{with } \lambda \in \mathrm{R}. \tag{9.7}$$

Finally, among this set of Nash equilibria, we can identify the efficient sub-set: that is, the equilibria not Pareto dominated by any other Nash equilibrium. This sub-set is given by all the (linear) convex combinations of the first best outcomes of the players: i.e., all the equilibria identified by $\lambda \in [0,1]$. We denote this sub-set by Θ. By contrast, Nash equilibria outside that range represent coordination failures in the sense of Cooper and John (1988). Of course, if $\bar{z}_1 = \bar{z}_2$, then all Nash equilibria that lead to different outcomes are Pareto inefficient (when the betas are finite and different from zero and players are interested in both targets).

All these cases of multiple equilibria, however, need some kind of story of how a particular equilibrium may finally be selected. This we can provide by showing that sequences of appropriately designed announcements can lead players to coordinate their actions around one set of outcomes.

9.3 One-sided announcement games

We allow players to make an announcement in the underlying game described in the previous section (where condition (9.4) holds). At the beginning of the period, a player, say i (j is the other player), makes a public announcement about his policy. Thereafter, without any binding commitment, the two players simultaneously set their instruments. Since the announcement is not binding, the players can take it into account or not as they prefer. If they do not take account of that announcement, the outside option is obtained.[9]

Following Farrell (1988), we assume that credible non-binding announcements exist.[10] If a credible announcement is made, it will not be ignored by the receiver and will be used to coordinate the

[8] The condition can be expressed equivalently in terms of $\bar{z}_2$.

[9] As we note below, the outside option is naturally defined as the expected outcome of the underlying Nash game.

[10] It is worth noticing that, as the announcement is cheap talk, it will not restrict the set of the Nash equilibria of the underlying game (babbling equilibrium).

agents' actions. This means that agents will act according to that announcement. Credibility of non-binding announcements is based on *self-committing* messages and on an additional constraint, induced by the introduction of the outside option, which ensures that the coordination phase is implemented.

We use announcements about an outcome (z_i^A), instead of the policy itself, by assuming that the sender *forecasts* the optimal policy of the receiver. If this is the case, announcing a policy, u_i^A, is exactly equivalent to announcing the outcome of the game corresponding to that policy and the other agent's optimal reaction to that policy. The outcome then is $z_i^A = (x_i^A, y_i^A) = A(u_i^A, r_j(u_i^A))' + c$ where $r_j(u_i^A)$ is the reaction function of agent j to the policy announcement by agent i.[11]

Definition 9.1 (*announcements*). An announcement, z_i^A, is a vector of outcomes of the underlying game. Its supporting strategies are a unique pair (u_i^S, u_j^S) such that $z_i^A = A(u_i^S, u_j^S)' + c$, where $u_j^S = r_j(u_i^A)$.

We assume that agents can communicate by a common language. Since an announcement can be seen as a non-binding commitment about the agent's own supporting strategy, we assume that the agent receiving the announcement interprets it correctly. He also correctly links the announced outcome to the supporting strategies.

If an agent decides to ignore the announcement, the outcome of the underlying game is driven by an exogenously given probability distribution $g(z)$, which generates a loss $\tilde{L}_k = \int L_k(z)g(z)dz$, for $k = \{1,2\}$, defining both the sender's and the receiver's outside option. Without entering into a discussion about its possible derivation, we point out that this outcome distribution could have had its origin in a mixed strategy equilibrium; as well as in the players' beliefs, which may ultimately be derived from institutional or historical experiences. However, a detailed analysis of the form of this probability distribution is beyond the scope of this chapter.

We define the set of credible announcements (Ψ) as the set of announcements for which the following axioms hold.

As in Farrell (1988), in fact, we are restricting the outcomes by changing the concept of equilibrium of the game.

[11] In our model, announcements about policies or outcomes can be used interchangeably. However, we prefer to use announcements about outcomes, since our focus is on policy games. We have in mind announcements of the kind implied by inflation targets.

Axiom 9.1 (*self-commitment*). The supporting strategies (u_i^S, u_j^S) associated with an announcement z_i^A are self-committing if $L_i(u_i^S, u_j^S) \leq L_i(u_i, u_j^S)\ \forall u_i$.

Axiom 9.2 (*acceptability*). An announcement is acceptable if $L_k(z_i^A) \leq \tilde{L}_k$, $k = \{1,2\}$.

Axiom 9.1 satisfies Farrell's requirements (it is worth noting here that $u_j^S = r_j(u_i^S)$ by definition). Axiom 9.2 requires that the outside option is not preferred to the announced outcome. Therefore, there is no incentive for the agents to deviate. As a result, if a credible message is announced in the first stage of the game, it will be implemented at the second stage by both agents (Farrell, 1988). The equilibrium of the game can then be obtained by backward induction and the optimal announcement can be found as the solution to a Stackelberg problem (Baliga and Morris, 2002).

The conditions for the existence of a non-empty set of credible announcements are identified by the following lemma.

Lemma 9.1. There is at least one outcome on the quasi-reaction functions, Equations (9.5), which Pareto dominates the expected outcome (or outside option) associated with $g(z)$ if and only if the following condition holds: $\alpha_1^{-1/2}\sqrt{\tilde{L}_1} + \alpha_2^{-1/2}\sqrt{\tilde{L}_2} \geq |\bar{x}_1 - \bar{x}_2|$, where $\alpha_1 = 1 + a_{11}^2/\,\beta_1 a_{21}^2$ and $\alpha_2 = 1 + a_{12}^2/\,\beta_2 a_{22}^2$.

Proof. Agent k will prefer the outcome z^* on the quasi-reaction function (9.5) to the outside option if $L_k(z) = \alpha_k(x - \bar{x}_k)^2 \leq \tilde{L}_k$ for $k = \{1,2\}$, where $\alpha_k = 1 + a_{1k}^2/\,\beta_k a_{2k}^2$. We can rewrite this condition as $|x - \bar{x}_k| \leq \alpha_k^{-1/2}\sqrt{\tilde{L}_k}$, which must hold for both agents. Lemma 9.1 now follows. ■

It is worth noting that, to be credible, an announcement must lie on the quasi-reaction functions of both players (in order to avoid incentives to deviate), and that both players must prefer it to the outside option. Moreover, as the expected losses associated with the outside option increase, the more likely is this condition to be satisfied. In particular, since agents are risk averse (due to the quadratic form of the payoffs), their risk premium is an increasing function of the variance of $g(z)$. In addition, the condition above is always satisfied if there is no conflict between the agents (i.e., if $\bar{x}_1 = \bar{x}_2$). Finally, if we restrict the set of possible random outcomes to the set of Nash equilibria, as Cooper and John (1988) do, then $g(z)$ will be defined with a positive probability only for those outcomes that satisfy Equations (9.5) – with the result that the condition specified in Lemma 9.1 is always met. The intuition behind this is not trivial: one has to notice that the expected outcome, $z^e = \int zg(z)dz$, fulfills (9.5) – which means that it is always preferred to the outside option since players are risk averse.

Now we can define the announcement equilibrium in a one-sided announcement game.

Definition 9.2 (*announcement equilibrium*). An announcement equilibrium of the one-sided game is an announcement $\tilde{z}_i^A$ such that $L_i(\tilde{z}_i^A) \leq L_i(z_i^A)$ for every $z_i^A \in \Psi$.

Clearly, given our assumptions, if an announcement equilibrium exists at all, it will completely describe the outcome and actions of the agents in the game. Then the outcome of the game is the one announced by player i, which corresponds to his most favorable outcome from among all the credible announcements.

Theorem 9.1 (*announcement equilibrium uniqueness*). If there is at least one outcome on the quasi-reaction functions that Pareto dominates the outside option, then the one-sided announcement game has a unique announcement equilibrium.

Proof. As explained in Section 9.3, if an announcement is credible it will be implemented in the second stage of the game. Since the instruments are linearly independent, if there is a unique optimal announcement, the Nash equilibrium of the game will also be unique. Thus, to prove the theorem, we need only show that an optimal announcement for player i exists and is unique. We do this in three steps:

Step 1. If the set of credible announcements (Ψ) is non-empty, it contains at least one outcome of the set Θ defined in Section 9.2.[12] Formally, $\Omega = \Theta \cap \Psi \neq \varnothing$. Moreover, Ω is a compact set.

Let us assume, without loss of generality, that $\bar{x}_i < \bar{x}_j$. This implies that the conditions of Lemma 9.1 are satisfied (and thus Ψ *is non-empty*) if and only if

$$\bar{x}_i + \sqrt{\frac{1}{\alpha_i}\tilde{L}_i} \leq \bar{x}_j - \sqrt{\frac{1}{\alpha_j}\tilde{L}_j}. \tag{9.8}$$

[12] It is the set of all the linear convex combinations of the first best outcomes of the players, identified by $\lambda \in [0,1]$.

Using Equation (9.7), we can rewrite (9.8) as a linear convex combination of the agents' first best outcomes:

$$\lambda_i \bar{x}_i + (1-\lambda_i)\bar{x}_j \le \lambda_j \bar{x}_i + (1-\lambda_j)\bar{x}_j, \tag{9.9}$$

where (λ_i, λ_j) satisfy $\sqrt{\frac{1}{\alpha_i}\tilde{L}_i} = \lambda_i \bar{x}_i + (1-\lambda_i)\bar{x}_j$ and $\bar{x}_j + \sqrt{\frac{1}{\alpha_j}\tilde{L}_j} = \lambda_j \bar{x}_i + (1-\lambda_j)\bar{x}_j$.

Equation (9.9) holds if and only if $\lambda_j \ge \lambda_i$. Moreover, $\lambda_i \le 1$ and $\lambda_j \ge 0$ since $\bar{x}_i + \sqrt{\frac{1}{\alpha_i}\tilde{L}_i} \ge \bar{x}_i$ and $\bar{x}_j - \sqrt{\frac{1}{\alpha_j}\tilde{L}_j} \le \bar{x}_j$. There then exists a $\lambda^* \in [0,1]$ such that $\lambda_j \ge \lambda^* \ge \lambda_i$. The sub-set Ω is therefore non-empty. It is, moreover, compact, since it is the intersection of two compact sets.

Step 2. Agent i announces the outcome z^*, which is his most favorable outcome in the sub-set Ω.

Agent i minimizes a continuous function on a compact set (Ψ). This guarantees the existence of at least one optimal announcement. Now assume agent i selects his most favorable outcome that does not belong to the sub-set Ω. There are then two cases in which a credible announcement could be Pareto dominated:

(a) If $z' = \lambda' \bar{z}_i + (1-\lambda')\bar{z}_j$ for $\lambda' < 0$. Since z' belongs to the credible announcement set, $\bar{z}_i$ is also credible. Therefore, agent i will never announce z' since it does not minimize his loss among the credible announcement set. This leads to a contradiction.
(b) If $z'' = \lambda'' \bar{z}_i + (1-\lambda'')\bar{z}_j$ for some $\lambda'' > 1$, then by a similar argument it can be shown that $\bar{z}_j$ belongs to the credible announcement set that agent i would strictly prefer to z''. Again, we find a contradiction. Hence, step 2 follows.

Step 3. The announced outcome is unique.

Assume that the announced outcome is not unique. Then outcomes z' and z'' exist, such that $z' \neq z''$ and $L_i(z') = L_i(z'')$, that minimize player i's loss function. Now define $z''' = \lambda z' + (1-\lambda)z''$ with $\lambda \in (0,1)$. Then z''' is (a) credible, since the credible set is convex; and (b) such that $L_i(z''') < L_i(z') = L_i(z'')$, since the loss is strictly concave. Thus the announced outcome is unique. ■

As the announcement equilibrium is always unique, and always a Nash equilibrium, it acts as an equilibrium selection device. The idea is simply that player i can use his "announcement power" to eliminate the random outcomes generated by the probability density function $g(z)$ to obtain his most favored of all the credible outcomes. However, if there is no outcome on the quasi-reaction functions that Pareto dominates the outside option, no credible announcement can be made and the outside option is the expected outcome. The announcement therefore succeeds in solving the equilibrium selection dilemma because it is a way to signal a common strategy that will lead to an outcome which is better than the random outcomes for both players.[13]

Finally, notice, from Lemma 9.1, that announcements as an equilibrium selection device are more likely to be observed when there is a large degree of uncertainty, little disagreement between agents about the targets, and higher expected losses when players do not coordinate their actions.

Our theorem has two important corollaries.[14]

Corollary 9.1. No coordination failure can arise in our game if there is at least one outcome on the quasi-reaction functions that Pareto dominates the outside option.

It is worth noticing that an outcome on the quasi-reaction functions that Pareto dominates the outside option is not necessarily Pareto efficient. The above corollary simply derives from the fact that credibility requires that player i announces a Nash equilibrium. Since he will choose the best among those available, that announcement cannot be Pareto dominated by other Nash equilibria. More generally, the selection device generated by these announcements gives us an explicit method for agents to coordinate on non-dominated Nash outcomes, and also to avoid the uncoordinated responses that follow from the impossibility of being able to forecast the rival's strategy to which they need to react.

Corollary 9.2. Player i will announce his first best $\tilde{z}_i^A = \overline{z}_i$ if and only if $\overline{z}_i$ satisfies player j's participation constraint, i.e., $L_j(\overline{z}_i) \leq \tilde{L}_j$.

In other words, agent i can announce his first best only under certain circumstances. If the necessary circumstances do not obtain, he

13 When the outside option defines a (non-dominated) outcome with probability 1, the model recovers the prediction of Schelling's (1960) focal point idea.

14 The proofs of these two corollaries follow directly from the proof of Theorem 9.1.

can promise only second best outcomes. The participation constraint is the key element that distinguishes the announcement solution from commitment – as we show next.

9.4 Announcements and commitment

Agents or policymakers routinely promise future actions. These promises can be considered policy commitments or cheap talk announcements depending on whether they are supported by commitment technologies or not. Although in the real world it is often difficult to distinguish between announcements and commitments, they are in fact quite different, leading to different outcomes. However, both may be used as equilibrium selection devices, as both transform the committed/announced outcome into a type of focal point.

By using promises based on commitment, one always obtains a better outcome than by making announcements. However, these promises must be supported by an appropriate commitment technology, and that technology is not always available.[15] In the absence of such a technology, player *i* must resort to making an announcement.

If we look at an announcement as a substitute for a commitment for which the appropriate commitment technology is not available, we can understand why, in some cases, players do not always promise their first best option. Our results therefore give a rationale for the otherwise puzzling evidence of policymakers making promises leading to outcomes that are sub-optimal from their own point of view – such as positive inflation targeting or incomplete reform strategies.

In summary, our results can be illustrated by the simple diagram in Figure 9.1.[16] In Figure 9.1, points $\bar{z}_i$ and $\bar{z}_j$ represent the first best outcomes for the two players. Thus, assuming condition (9.4) holds, the straight line $\bar{z}_i\bar{z}_j$ represents the two overlapping quasi-reaction functions.

[15] If this is not the case, the policy to which the player has committed may be time inconsistent and the promised outcomes never reached.

[16] This diagram has been obtained by assuming $a_{11} = a_{12} = a_{21} = 1$ and $a_{22} = -2$. The first best of player *j* is (−3, 3), and that of player *i* is (1, 1). We assume that $g(z)$ associates a ½ probability to (−3, 3) and ½ to (−3, 2). It is easy to verify that these values satisfy the sufficient and necessary conditions for multiple equilibria and describe our results without loss of generality.

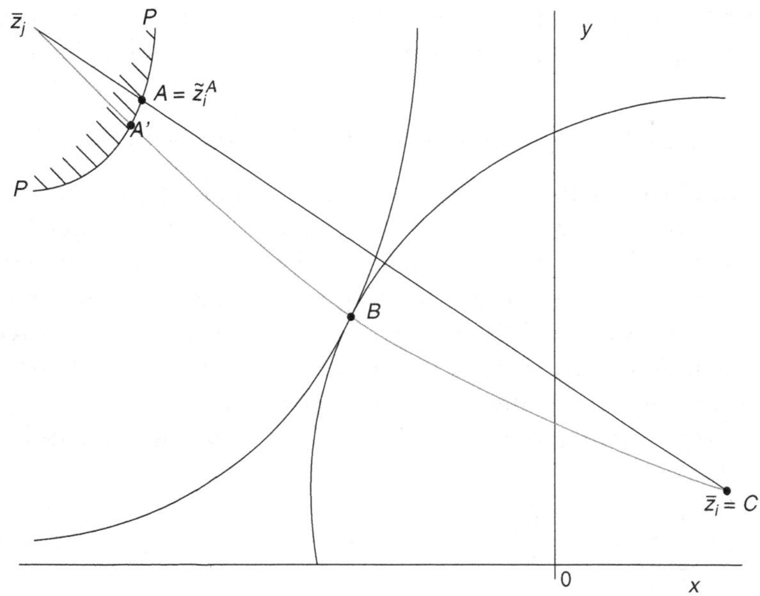

Figure 9.1 Announcement equilibrium vs. commitment

If player i is endowed with a commitment technology, he will choose his best option along the reaction function of j. Hence, the commitment solution is represented by point C, his first best outcome.

By contrast, if player i cannot use a commitment technology, yet credible announcements are available, he will announce the best outcome available given the participation constraint of j. This constraint is represented by the north-west region of the PP line, which is the iso-loss curve corresponding to $\tilde{L}_j$. The announcement solution is therefore described by point A. Player i would then announce his first best (point C) if and only if the participation constraint was not binding along the line $\bar{z}_i \bar{z}_j$.

The figure also illustrates the locus of Pareto efficient outcomes, i.e., the contract curve (the curve passing through B). Different from commitment, the announcement solution is always Pareto inefficient when the participation constraint of j is binding: point A' clearly Pareto dominates point A since it is possible to improve the satisfaction of player i while keeping that of j constant. However, player i cannot announce A' because it is not a credible proposition since it is not on either of the reaction functions.

Commitment and announcement equilibrium are then closely related concepts, but reflect different kinds of institutions or assumptions.

9.5 An application: inflation and fiscal announcements

We consider a stylized underlying game between the government (G) and the central bank (B) that is characterized by multiple equilibria. We assume that the central bank sets the interest rate (i) and the government sets the average tax rate (t), as measured by the ratio of fiscal revenues to potential GDP, and that these policymakers have different preferences for internal and external stabilization (i.e., different priorities for maintaining internal and external balance).

Formally, government (G) and central bank (B) losses are defined as follows:

$$L_k = \frac{1}{2}(b - b_k)^2 + \frac{1}{2}\beta_k(\pi - \pi_k)^2 \quad k = \{G, B\}, \tag{9.10}$$

where b represents the balance of payments (external stability), measured as the surplus or deficit as a proportion of potential output, and π is the inflation rate (internal stability). For the sake of simplicity, we assume that the economy is characterized by a Phillips curve. Hence, different targets for inflation imply different opinions about how to solve the trade-off between unemployment and inflation. We assume that the central bank aims to fully stabilize the balance of payments and that its inflation target is 2% (i.e., $b_B = 0$ and $\pi_B = 2\%$). As for fiscal targets, we assume that the government aims to reach a more inflationary equilibrium and a large surplus for electoral reasons and/or for the benefit of political lobbies. For the sake of being concrete, we assume that its inflation target is 4% and the surplus target is 6% (i.e., $b_G = 6\%$ and $\pi_G = 4\%$). We also assume $\beta_B = 3$ and $\beta_G = 2$: the bank is far more conservative with respect to achieving low inflation than the government.

That said, monetary policy sets the interest rate and fiscal policy sets taxation. The effects of these policies are controversial (especially regarding the fiscal one), but this debate is not of interest in the present example. Thus, in Mundell fashion, we simply assume that monetary and fiscal policies are strategic complements:[17] an increase in the

[17] See Dixit and Lambertini (2003a) for an analysis of the different possible interactions between central banks and governments. Different assumptions

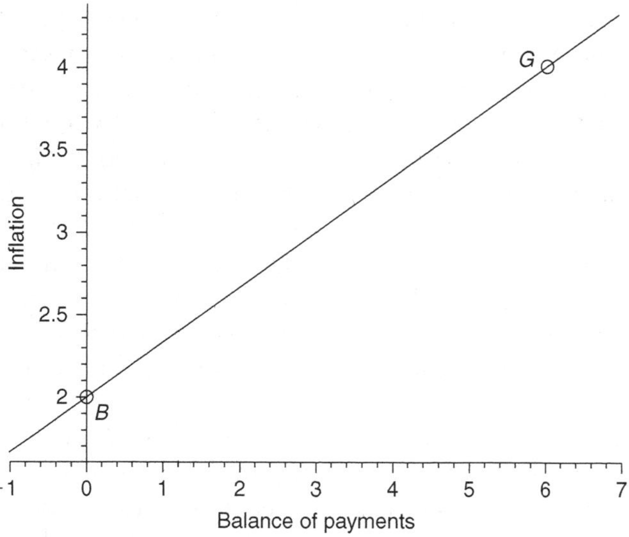

Figure 9.2 Multiple Nash equilibria

interest rate lowers inflation and improves the surplus (reduces the deficit) in the balance of payments (i.e., the income effect outweighs the relative price or exchange rate effect). The same occurs when taxes are raised. The reduced form of the model is assumed to be

$$\begin{bmatrix} b \\ \pi \end{bmatrix} = \begin{bmatrix} 2 & 1 \\ -2 & -3/2 \end{bmatrix} \begin{bmatrix} i \\ t \end{bmatrix} + \begin{bmatrix} -22 \\ 35 \end{bmatrix}. \tag{9.11}$$

The multiplier matrix of (9.4) is full rank; instruments are thus independent. But it is easy to verify by (9.4) that (9.10) and (9.11) imply multiple equilibria. In fact, both quasi-reactions function are given by

$$\pi = \frac{1}{3}b + 2, \tag{9.12}$$

which means they are coincident. Nash equilibria are represented in Figure 9.2, where Equation (9.12) is drawn. The first best positions of the two players are *B* and *G*. All equilibria can be clearly identified by a real number as in (9.7). Those between *B* and *G* are the only Pareto efficient equilibria.

about the impact of fiscal and monetary policy do not affect the qualitative results of our example.

Next we assume that, before the game begins, one player decides to make a non-binding declaration and computes an announcement equilibrium. Expected outcomes of the underlying game as an effect of this announcement are common knowledge. We set them equal to $E(\pi) = 3\%$ and $E(b) = 3\%$ with variance equal to σ^2 for both.[18] The expected losses for the central bank and the government are then $E(L_B) = 6 + 2\sigma^2$ and $E(L_G) = 5.5 + 1.5\sigma^2$, respectively.

As there is a perfect equivalence between credible announcements in terms of outcomes and instruments,[19] we illustrate our example by considering an inflation announcement made by the central bank and a taxation announcement for the government, as is often observed in the real world.

The game is illustrated by Figure 9.3, where we draw the expected outcome of the underlying game (E) and the expected losses corresponding to different levels of σ^2 – specifically, 10, 5 and 2. Clearly, losses relative to the central bank are centered on B, and those relative to the government on G, and iso-losses farther from the center correspond to higher variances.[20]

Each player would like to announce his first best (as in the Stackelberg solution), but for the announcement to be credible it must be at least as good for the other player as the outside option. For instance, if $\sigma^2 = 2$, the outside options are the iso-losses drawn closer to E. If the central bank is chosen (by nature) to make an announcement, it cannot announce a policy implying point B, as there the government is worse-off than in *AB02* (a point on the iso-loss corresponding to the loss when the government expects E and believes $\sigma^2 = 2$). Therefore, the optimal announcement for the central bank is to announce exactly *AB02*. As uncertainty increases, the optimal announcement of the central bank will move closer to the

18 Assuming different variances, as we do in the next example, does not affect our results

19 Recall that a credible announcement implies that the instruments/outcomes announced are on the (quasi-) reaction functions. Moreover, for the same reason, announcing one outcome (or instrument) is sufficient (for example, if the central bank were to announce its inflation rate) since only one balance of payments outcome exists on its quasi-reaction function that corresponds to that announcement.

20 It is worth noticing that iso-losses do not intersect point E as this is an expected value and uncertainty is not additive (so certainty equivalence cannot be claimed).

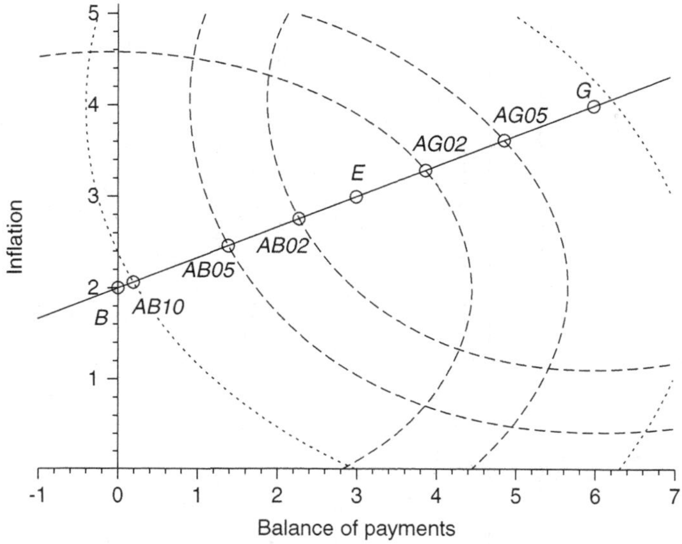

Figure 9.3 Announcement equilibria

Stackelberg solution *B*, as a consequence of the fact that the government's "resistance" vanishes as its expected loss increases.

Similarly the government, if chosen, announces *AG02* or *AG05* if $\sigma^2 = 2$ or $\sigma^2 = 5$ respectively. However, if the uncertainty is large enough, the central bank's outside option constraint is no longer binding and the government can announce the policy corresponding to its first best *G*. This occurs when $\sigma^2 = 10$.

Table 9.1 summarizes our results, reporting all announcement equilibrium outcomes.

If the variance about the expected outcomes is 2, the central bank will announce an interest rate equal to 4.16% (or an inflation rate of 2.76%). As the variance increases, the central bank will reduce its announcement by 162 basis points when $\sigma^2 = 5$, and by 378 basis points when $\sigma^2 = 10$, and so on. The higher the uncertainty, the more favorable is the equilibrium that the central bank can reach by using its announcements. This occurs since uncertainty increases the expected losses of the government in the underlying game. A symmetric result is obtained when nature selects the government for making the first announcement.

Table 9.1 *Monetary and fiscal announcements (all values in %)*

	First announcement made by:									
	Central bank (announces inflation)					Government (announces taxation)				
	Announcement	Equilibrium				Announcement	Equilibrium			
Variance		b	π	t	i		b	π	t	i
10	0.38	0.21	2.07	42.88	0.38	12.00	6.00	4.00	12.00	11.00
5	2.54	1.38	2.46	36.60	2.54	17.87	4.90	3.63	17.87	8.98
2	4.16	2.27	2.76	31.89	4.16	23.34	3.87	3.29	23.34	7.10

9.6 Two-sided announcement games: a war of announcements

9.6.1 *The time preference model*

Following Rubinstein (1982), we now model a process of alternating announcements that takes place between the two players over time. At the beginning of the game, at time 0, one player (e.g., player i) announces an outcome $[z_i^A(0)]$. The other player, j, observes the announcement and either declares that he is ready to play; or waits a period before making his own announcement $[z_j^A(1)]$. If player j declares that he is ready without any binding commitment being made, the two players simultaneously set their instruments. If, on the other hand, player j decides to wait and then make an announcement, player i can either declare that he is ready to play at that stage or wait one more period before making a new announcement about his own policy.

We assume that agents are, to some degree, time impatient: that is, the later the underlying game is played, the higher will the loss of a given outcome be. The loss functions can then be rewritten as

$$L_k(z,t) = \gamma_k^t L_k(z) = \gamma_k^t \frac{1}{2}\left[(x-\bar{x}_k)^2 + \beta_k(y-\bar{y}_k)^2\right] \quad k \in \{1,2\}, \qquad (9.13)$$

where $\gamma_k > 1$ are the agents' loss "capitalization" rates, or patience factors, equal to the inverse of the discount factor. These patience factors are not necessarily equal among the players.[21]

The set of credible announcements is the same as that described by Lemma 9.1 because outcomes outside the quasi-reaction functions are associated with incentives to deviate, and because any announcements made need to Pareto dominate the outside option.[22]

However, we still need to redefine the announcement equilibrium for a two-sided announcement game.

Definition 9.3 (*announcement equilibrium with multiple cheap talk*). An announcement equilibrium of the two-sided game is a sub-game

[21] Patience factors can also be interpreted as factors that discount the risk of breakdown in the bargaining process (see Osborne and Rubinstein, 1990).

[22] Discount factors do not affect this set because the comparison between announced outcomes and the random solution always refers to the same period.

perfect Nash equilibrium of the first stage of the game constrained to the credible announcement set.

Again, the game is solved by backward induction. The second stage of the game constrains the agents to bargain only over the set of credible announcements. If an announcement equilibrium exists, it will completely describe the outcome of the entire game.

We can now state the following theorem and corollary.

Theorem 9.2 (*announcement equilibrium uniqueness with two-sided cheap talk*). If there is at least one credible announcement to be made, the two-sided announcement game has a unique announcement equilibrium. The outcome of this game will be that announced by player i at time zero, but it will never be his most favorable outcome among the credible announcements unless there is only one single credible announcement.

Proof. We have already explained the following results. From proof of Theorem 9.1 policymakers will never announce an outcome that does not belong to the sub-set Ω. Since each of these announcements is uniquely defined by $\lambda \in [\underline{\lambda},\overline{\lambda}]$ according to Equation (9.7), we identify them by the corresponding λ. This is legitimate because the sub-set Ω contains outcomes satisfying (9.7) that can be expressed and ordered by $U_k(\lambda,t) = \gamma_k^t [\hat{L}_k - L_k(\lambda)]$; see also below, in terms of λ.

Let us define the pair $\hat{L}_i = L_i(\underline{\lambda})$ and $\hat{L}_j = L_j(\overline{\lambda})$ as the instantaneous losses associated with the agents' worst outcomes. Then, preferences (9.8) can be rewritten as utility functions defined on the set Ω:

$$U_k(\lambda,t) = \gamma_k^t\left[\hat{L}_k - L_k(\lambda)\right] \quad k = \{1,2\}. \tag{9.14}$$

These utility functions satisfy the following five properties: (a) they imply a conflict between the two players (when λ increases, the utility of player i rises while that for player j falls); (b) agents' utilities are strictly decreasing in t, except for their worst outcome; (c) agents' utilities for their worst outcome is zero, independently of time; (d) utilities are time stationary; (e) utilities are continuous. These conditions guarantee that we can apply Rubinstein's (1982) theorem. Thus, a unique sub-game perfect Nash equilibrium exists for the two-sided announcement game. ■

Again the announcement equilibrium is unique and is one of the Nash equilibria. We can therefore conclude that announcements act as an equilibrium selection device.

Corollary 9.3. The outcome associated with the above announcement equilibrium is given by the values z_i^A and z_j^A that solve the following system of two equations:

$$\begin{cases} U_i(z_j^A,0) = \gamma_i U_i(z_i^A,0) + (1-\gamma_i)\hat{U}_i \\ U_j(z_i^A,0) = \gamma_j U_j(z_j^A,0) + (1-\gamma_j)\hat{U}_j \end{cases} \tag{9.15}$$

where $\hat{U}_i$ and $\hat{U}_j$ are the players' utilities defined above relative to their worst credible announcement.

In informal terms, the Rubinstein equilibrium requires each player to be indifferent between either accepting an offer, or waiting to make his own proposal (expecting it to be accepted). Thus, we need to define an acceptance constraint as the condition that makes player j indifferent between accepting player i's proposal at time 0, $z_i^A(0)$, or getting his own announcement accepted next period.

The acceptance constraint can formally be written as $U_j(z_i^A,0) \geq U_j(z_j^A,1)$. However, in order to assume that $z_j^A(1)$ could be accepted in due course, this inequality requires a similar condition to be imposed on player i, who also needs to be indifferent between accepting player j's pwroposal at time 1 and making another proposal at time 2. Thus we also require $U_i(z_j^A,1) \geq U_i(z_i^A,2)$ to hold, and so on for $z_i^A(2)$. As a result, we obtain an infinite set of conditions. These can be reduced to a pair of equations because of their stationarity. Operationally, the equilibrium conditions that then define sub-game perfect Nash equilibrium offers z_i^A and z_j^A are those satisfying

$$\begin{cases} U_j\left(z_i^A,0\right) = U_j\left(z_j^A,1\right) \\ U_i\left(z_j^A,0\right) = U_i\left(z_i^A,1\right). \end{cases} \tag{9.16}$$

Since $U_k(z_k^A, s+1) = \gamma_k U_k(z_k^A, s)$ for $k = 1{,}2$ and any s, conditions (9.16) can be expressed as

$$\begin{cases} U_j\left(z_i^A,0\right) = \gamma_j U_j\left(z_j^A,0\right) \\ U_i\left(z_j^A,0\right) = \gamma_i U_i\left(z_i^A,0\right) \end{cases}, \tag{9.17}$$

Since we can set $z_i^A = \lambda_i^A \overline{z}_i + (1-\lambda_i^A)\overline{z}_j$, and $z_j^A = \lambda_j^A \overline{z}_i + (1-\lambda_j^A)\overline{z}_j$, Equation (9.17) can easily be rewritten as

$$\begin{cases} U_j\left(z_i^A,0\right) = \gamma_j U_j(\lambda_j^A \overline{z}_i + \left(1-\lambda_j^A\right)\overline{z}_j,0) \\ U_i\left(z_j^A,0\right) = \gamma_i U_i\left(\lambda_i^A \overline{z}_i + \left(1-\lambda_i^A\right)\overline{z}_j,0\right) \end{cases}. \tag{9.18}$$

By applying Equations (9.14), we can substitute the utility functions with the correspondent instantaneous loss functions and obtain the conditions of Corollary 9.3:

$$\begin{cases} L_j\left(z_i^A,0\right)=\gamma_j L_j\left(z_j^A,0\right)+\left(1-\gamma_j\right)\hat{L}_j \\ L_i\left(z_j^A,0\right)=\gamma_i L_i\left(z_i^A,0\right)+\left(1-\gamma_i\right)\hat{L}_i \end{cases}. \tag{9.19}$$

Allowing agents to play a war of announcements in order to select the Nash equilibrium gives us a richer tool for equilibrium selection, and one which again solves the problem of coordination failure. The difference from a one-sided announcement is that the announcing agent now has to take into account the fact that the other player might refuse the current announcement and make his own offer instead.

Theorem 9.2 guarantees the existence of a unique announcement equilibrium in the two-sided announcement game under exactly the same conditions as the one-sided announcements in Theorem 9.1. The same conclusions can therefore be drawn about the likelihood of agents announcing their policies and using announcements to solve coordination problems.

In contrast to the one-sided announcement game, however, players will never announce their most favorable outcomes among those that are credible (unless there is only one credible announcement to be made). This result may seem surprising and needs some explanation. In this section, player i has to propose an outcome that is not only better for j than the outside option, as required by Theorem 9.1, *but also* one at least as good as the outcome that player j could have obtained by waiting and then having his own announcement accepted.

9.6.2 *Limit cases*

In the previous sub-section, we have assumed that agents are impatient. Relaxing this assumption is interesting because different outcomes can then arise.

If player i is patient ($\gamma_i = 1$) and j is not, the game of two-sided announcements leads to the same solution as the one-sided game: player i will announce his most favorable outcome among the credible announcements. However, the opposite case where only j is patient is surprising: from among the credible announcements, player i will in fact choose the most favorable outcome for the other agent. In other words, player i will offer player j's most favorable outcome from among those that j would be prepared to accept. Hence, if player j can wait forever, player i can only offer j the outcome that is the best available for j from among those that are credible.

Finally, when both players are patient, the equilibrium outcome of the game cannot be determined unless $\bar{z}_i = \bar{z}_j$. However, as in Osborne and Rubinstein (1990), we can study this type of game as a limiting case of the original game where the length of the interval between the announcement on offer and the following one tends to zero. The bargaining process then becomes frictionless in the sense that the cost, to a player, of waiting to see his own offer accepted shrinks to zero and patience factors tend to one. More formally, we rewrite patience factors of agent k as $\gamma_k^t = \chi^{\alpha_k \Delta t}$, where $\chi > 1$ is a common factor and $\alpha_k > 0$ is the intrinsic time preference of player k, and consider the case when the time interval tends to zero, $\Delta t \to 0$.[23]

We can now prove the following theorem.

Theorem 9.3 (*multiple-announcement equilibrium and Nash bargaining solution*). For $\Delta t \to 0$, the announcement equilibrium with multiple announcements is equivalent to the Nash bargaining solution constrained by the set of credible announcements, i.e., $\min_{z \in \Omega} \left(\hat{L}_i - L_i(z)\right)^{\varphi} \left(\hat{L}_j - L_j(z)\right)^{1-\varphi}$ with $\varphi = \alpha_j / \alpha_i + \alpha_j$.

Proof. From the proof of Theorem 9.2, we know that the conditions that characterize the equilibrium in the announcement war state that both agents will be indifferent between accepting the other agent's offer or waiting one period to see their own offer accepted; i.e., in the equilibrium, the pair z_i^A and z_j^A must satisfy

$$\begin{cases} U_i\left(z_j^A, 0\right) = \chi^{\alpha_i \Delta t} U_i\left(z_i^A, 0\right) \\ U_j\left(z_i^A, 0\right) = \chi^{\alpha_j \Delta t} U_j\left(z_j^A, 0\right) \end{cases}. \tag{9.20}$$

By taking the limit for $\Delta t \to 0$ of (9.20), it follows that $z_i^A - z_j^A \to 0$.

Take the logarithm of the equations in (9.20), and multiply the first by ϕ and the second by $1 - \phi$:

[23] This formulation is a very common one. Alternatively, different patience factors could be based on different aversions to the probability of a breakdown in the bargaining process.

$$\begin{cases} \varphi \ln U_i\left(z_j^A,0\right) = \varphi\left[\alpha_i \Delta t \ln \chi + \ln U_i\left(z_i^A,0\right)\right] \\ (1-\varphi)\ln U_j\left(z_i^A,0\right) = (1-\varphi)\left[\alpha_j \Delta t \ln \chi + \ln U_j\left(z_j^A,0\right)\right]. \end{cases} \tag{9.21}$$

Subtracting the first from the second and rearranging gives

$$\begin{aligned} &\varphi\left[\ln U_i\left(z_i^A,0\right) - \ln U_i\left(z_j^A,0\right)\right] \\ &\quad + (1-\varphi)\left[\ln U_j\left(z_i^A,0\right) - \ln U_j\left(z_j^A,0\right)\right] = 0. \end{aligned} \tag{9.22}$$

Now divide by the difference between the two announcements:

$$\begin{aligned} &\varphi \frac{\ln U_i\left(z_i^A,0\right) - \ln U_i\left(z_j^A,0\right)}{z_i^A - z_j^A} \\ &\quad + (1-\varphi)\frac{\ln U_j\left(z_i^A,0\right) - \ln U_j\left(z_j^A,0\right)}{z_i^A - z_j^A} = 0. \end{aligned} \tag{9.23}$$

Taking the limit of (9.23) as $z_i^A - z_j^A \to 0$ yields

$$\varphi \frac{U_i'\left(z^*,0\right)}{U_i\left(z^*,0\right)} + (1-\varphi)\frac{U_j'\left(z^*,0\right)}{U_j\left(z^*,0\right)} = 0, \tag{9.24}$$

which corresponds to the first-order conditions of the Nash bargaining problem described in Theorem 9.3.

Therefore, since uniqueness and optimality are guaranteed by the strict convexity of the problem, when $\Delta t \to 0$ both z_i^A and z_j^A converge to the Nash bargaining solution:

$$\begin{aligned} x^* &= \arg\max U_i\left(z,0\right)^{\varphi} U_j\left(z,0\right)^{1-\varphi} \\ &= \arg\max\left[\hat{L}_i - L_i\left(z,0\right)\right]^{\varphi}\left[\hat{L}_j - L_j\left(z,0\right)\right]^{1-\varphi} \end{aligned} \tag{9.25}$$

as claimed. ■

Theorem 9.3 may seem counterintuitive. The selected outcome is not Pareto efficient, even if it is equivalent to a Nash bargaining solution. This apparently puzzling result can be explained by the fact that the agents bargain over outcomes which have to be consistent with the announcements; that is to say, the agents have to constrain themselves to be in the credible announcement set. The Nash bargaining solution, therefore, achieves inferior allocations in this case. The announcement is in fact Pareto efficient only among the Nash equilibria.

As shown, an announcement equilibrium could be considered as the result of a bargaining on Nash equilibria. However, its nature is different. If a bargaining technology is available, there will be no reason why the cooperative agreement should be restricted to inferior outcomes such as those corresponding to Nash equilibria.

These results are in line with Binmore (1987), who establishes a connection between the bargaining games of alternating offers and the cooperative Nash solution obtained in a more general framework. In particular, he shows that the value of the unique subgame-perfect equilibrium in a non-cooperative bargaining game of alternating offers converges to the unique Nash bargaining solution to the corresponding bargaining problem.

9.7 Advertising, R&D and firms' competition

Next, we consider a simple game between two firms that have to decide the amount they are prepared to spend on advertising. The game lasts two periods. One firm, chosen by nature, can make an announcement about its expenditure for the advertising campaign. More specifically, each firm has to decide, in the first period, the amount in its exogenously fixed budget that it wishes to allocate to increasing or decreasing its advertising expenditure. The rest is used for R&D in order to influence the results in the second period.

R&D can affect the relative quality of the product and thus the market share, whereas advertising affects the (relative) perceived quality. A higher amount for advertising *ceteris paribus* increases current market share, and reduces that for the rival firm; but it reduces future market shares as it corresponds to lower investment in R&D (but increases that of the rival firm). The fixed budgets of the two firms are common knowledge. Thus announcing a budget for advertising is equivalent to announcing a budget for R&D; moreover, credible announcements about the market share target are also equivalent.

Formally each firm aims to maximize its market share, $q_k(s)$, at both stages. In other words, it aims to minimize the deviation of market share, $q_k(s)$, from 100% in both periods:

$$L_k(t) = \delta_k^{\Delta t} \sum_{s=1}^{2} \delta_k^{s-1} \left(q_k(s) - 1\right)^2 \quad k = \{1,2\}, \tag{9.26}$$

where $\Delta_1 = 1.1$ and $\Delta_2 = 1.15$ are the capitalization factors of the firms. Note that, Δt being the time interval between one announcement and another, the firms discount later agreements by a factor of Δ_k.

We define $m(s)$ to be the market share of firm 1 at stage s, $q_1(s)$; it follows that $q_2(s) = 1 - m(s)$ and we can write the economic system as

$$\begin{bmatrix} m(1) \\ m(2) \end{bmatrix} = \begin{bmatrix} 1.1 & -1 \\ -1.32 & 1.2 \end{bmatrix} \begin{bmatrix} p_1 \\ p_2 \end{bmatrix} + \begin{bmatrix} 0.5 \\ 0.5 \end{bmatrix}. \tag{9.27}$$

Clearly firm 1's advertising spending (p_1) *ceteris paribus* increases the current market share, and reduces that of firm 2. But it reduces future market shares (and increases that of the rival firm) because firm 1's investment in R&D will be lower.

By using the condition at (9.4), it is now easy to verify that this game admits multiple equilibria. Assume that the expected outcome of the underlying game is characterized by an equal division of the market, $E_0(m(s)) = 0.5$, with $\text{var}(m(1)) = 0.1$ and $\text{var}(m(2)) = 0.2$, so uncertainty increases with time (without loss of generality, we can assume that the expected market share in the two stages are not correlated).

The equilibrium now depends on the length of the interval between one announcement and another. Figure 9.4 describes the relationship between the market share announced and Δt.

The larger the interval, the higher the cost of a counter announcement. Thus, larger intervals give an advantage to the first mover. Indeed, the game converges to the unilateral announcement case when Δt becomes very large. Note that the market share announced will be the same for both stages.[24]

9.8 Lessons from this chapter

Multiple equilibria usually lead to coordination failures. In such cases, the concept of Nash equilibrium does not allow us to predict the behavior of agents. As the optimal reaction of each player depends on the expected equilibrium strategy played by the other agents, multiple

[24] In fact, if firm 1 announces high advertising expenditures, firm 2 (if it believes the announcement) will respond by increasing its expenditure. In the second stage, both will then invest less in R&D and their market shares will remain unchanged.

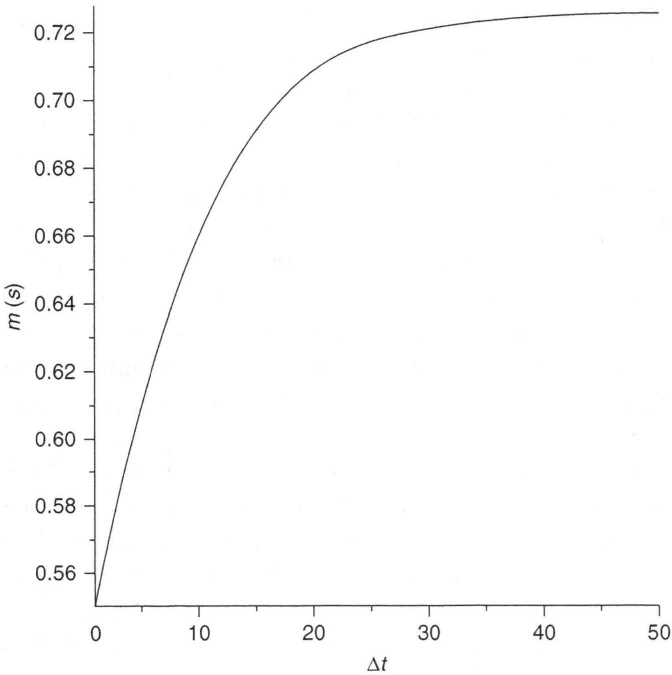

Figure 9.4 Market shares and Δt

equilibria do not help us to determine how to set the policy instruments. A standard solution to the multiple equilibrium problems in the policy games literature has been to use commitment as an equilibrium selection device. This would be very favorable to the committing agent, but needs an additional external enforcing mechanism to make the commitment credible.

This chapter illustrates an alternative mechanism. We consider cheap talk promises (non-binding announcements) with the expected outcomes of the underlying game without announcements as the natural outside option. We find that a one-sided announcement is a "weak" promise in comparison to commitment. It is less favorable for the agent that makes the promise, but crucially does not need any external credibility support in order to be implemented. Announcements therefore allow the players to convert a desirable outcome into a focal point upon which to coordinate, and thereby reduce (but not in general eliminate) inefficiencies even if the players are in conflict. In this way, they solve two very annoying problems of games with multiple equilibria: (a) how to arrange convergence to a Nash equilibrium, and (b) how to solve coordination problems.

By allowing for cheap talk announcements by both agents and adapting an easy-to-handle and well-known framework of bargaining theory, we have been able to derive additional insights into the outcomes without affecting the properties of the game. Indeed, in contrast to the case of commitment where having two committing agents would bring no equilibrium (for example, when there are two Stackelberg leaders), using sequential announcements from both sides we will always have a unique equilibrium. In the limiting case of a frictionless bargaining process (no transaction costs), this corresponds to implementing the Nash bargaining solution with appropriate weights representing bargaining powers.

The introduction of an outside option strongly affects the results: this is a common knowledge expectation about the payoff of the game when communication is not possible or unsuccessful. Specifically, the existence of an outside option restricts the set of credible announcements and forces the sender to announce a second best outcome. Multiple announcements strengthen this result further because the sender has to take account of the possibility that the receiver can dismiss the proposal and announce a new one. Finally, we have shown that announcements, as an equilibrium selection device, are more likely to be observed when there is a large degree of uncertainty and high expected losses in the absence of coordination.

PART IV

The new theory of economic policy: dynamics

10 *Controllability in a strategic dynamic setting*

Summary. This chapter generalizes the results developed for static policy games to a dynamic setting, but without forward-looking expectations other than those generated within the game itself. We show that the new theory of economic policy can be usefully adapted and applied in a dynamic strategic context, described here by linear difference games. Specifically, we consider the importance of having target independence vs. instrument independence. Extensions of our static controllability theorems are straightforward for open loop Nash equilibria in finite horizon difference games since they can be rewritten as the equilibria of a static game. More interesting are the feedback and closed loop Nash strategies. For those cases we also establish conditions for equilibria to exist compared with when policies are ineffective or equilibria fail to exist. In this context, we illustrate how easily small variations in target values, or the model, can create the opportunity, or take away the opportunity, for policymakers to reach their policy goals. We also illustrate the usefulness of our results in a simple example borrowed from the theory of monetary policy. Finally, we consider a class of policy games where players aim to achieve a certain level of satisfaction at a given instant of time, or aim to achieve a certain set of targets in the shortest period of time, by using the concept of dynamic controllability.

10.1 Introduction

In previous chapters we have provided general conditions for policy ineffectiveness and equilibrium existence in static LQ games of the kind used in the Tinbergen–Theil theory of economic policy; and we have shown how this can be used to define general properties for policy games.

This chapter now extends the same idea of controllability to difference games;[1] and in that context we consider the importance of target independence, as opposed to instrument independence, which has been a point of particular controversy in monetary policy design.

After a brief description of dynamic policy interactions, we first show a trivial extension of our earlier results. Assuming that players behave according to open loop strategies, we show how finite policy games can be written as a static game. As a result, all results presented in the previous chapters can be applied to investigate the properties of such games. Next, we consider the more complex case of the Feedback Nash equilibrium for LQ difference games, deriving conditions for policy ineffectiveness and the equilibrium existence for that case. We again show the usefulness of our results by describing how easily policy effectiveness, or indeed the existence of a policy equilibrium, can appear and disappear with small variations in the expectations process, or underlying policy rules, using a standard model of monetary theory. We also illustrate how certain variations in the problem can introduce or take away the opportunity for policymakers to operate with differing target values for their policy goals. To do this, we make use of some properties of sparse matrices, since nearly all economic models display sparseness in practice.

Finally, we consider a class of policy games where players aim to achieve a certain level of satisfaction at a given instant of time or aim to achieve a certain vector of targets in the shortest period of time. We apply to this kind of game the most natural concept of controllability – dynamic controllability instead of static. This leads to some further generalizations of our approach.

The rest of the chapter is organized as follows. Section 10.2 defines basic concepts and introduces a formal framework to describe LQ difference games. We give two different representations of the policy problem: the canonical and the decoupled, where each individual player's problem is isolated as in Chapter 6. Section 10.3 discusses the application of the new theory of economic policy to the open loop policy games with a finite horizon. As we shall see, the application is immediate as these games can be written in a static form. Section 10.4

[1] Recent developments extend this approach by introducing the concept of decisiveness (discussed in Chapter 8) in coalition games. This analysis is still a work in progress and will not be discussed here. For further details, see, e.g., Piacquadio (2011).

re-examines static controllability in this context by introducing feedback strategies, and identifies the situations in which the associated policies can become ineffective. We derive two specific theorems: a sufficient condition for policy ineffectiveness, and a necessary condition for equilibrium existence in the traditional Tinbergen fashion. This section also provides a relaxation of these theorems for the case of sparse economic systems and, to illustrate our results, an example borrowed from the theory of monetary policy. Section 10.6 then discusses the implications of dynamic controllability for both equilibrium existence and policy invariance in dynamic systems where each agent aims to obtain his own vector of target values. In the last section, Section 10.7, we draw some preliminary conclusions about a full extension of our approach to dynamic policy problems.

10.2 The general framework

10.2.1 The economy and preferences: canonical representation

In this chapter, we consider the policy problem where N players try to minimize their individual quadratic objective functions. The game is played for T periods, where T may be arbitrarily large. Each player controls a different set of inputs to a single system, which is described by the following difference equation:

$$y_t = Ay_{t-1} + \sum_{i \in N} B_i u_t^i + v_t \quad \text{given } y_0, \tag{10.1}$$

where N, with a little abuse of notation, is also the set of the players; $y \in \mathrm{R}^S$ is the vector of the states of the system; $u^i \in \mathrm{R}^{m(i)}$ is the control or instrument variable vector that player i can manipulate; and $A \in \mathrm{R}^{S \times S}$ and $B_i \in \mathrm{R}^{S \times m(i)}$ are matrices describing the system parameters that (for simplicity) are assumed to be constant. We assume that B_i are full rank matrices. Finally, v_t is a vector of exogenous shocks or other influences on y_t, which has a known mean but comes from an unspecified probability distribution.

The criterion that player $i \in N$ intends to minimize is

$$L_i = E\sum_{t=1}^{T} (y_t - \bar{y}_t^i)' \, Q_{i,t} \, (y_t - \bar{y}_t^i), \tag{10.2}$$

where $Q_{i,t} \in R^{S\times S}$ is a symmetric positive semi-definite matrix of weights assigned to player *i's* targets, $\bar{y}_t^i$, in each period t. $Q_{i,t}$ is of order S; but has rank $q(i) \leq S$ depending on how many variables in y_t eventually turn out to be among player *i*'s ultimate targets and therefore have a preference ordering defined upon them. All elements in y_t are in fact potential targets, even if player i may choose not to pursue $S - q(i)$ of those targets.[2] We define $\bar{y}_t^i$ to be player *i*'s ideal values (different perhaps from the ideal values of another player). We also assume that $q(i) \geq m(i)$. The interpretation of $q(i) \geq m(i)$ is straightforward: the total number of independent instruments is given by $\Sigma_{i\in N} m(i) = M$ (recall that we have assumed B_i to be of full rank).

Regarding the preferences in (10.2), three points need to be underlined:

1. Equation (10.2) implies that preferences are time varying. But for the sake of brevity, we will often assume that they are not, i.e., $Q_{i,t} = Q_i$ and $\bar{y}_t^i = \bar{y}^i$.
2. In order to avoid trivial cases, we assume that there are at least two players who share at least one target variable. We also say that a potential conflict of interest between them arises if, for the targets held in common, $\bar{y}_t^i \neq \bar{y}_t^j$ for all $i \in N \neq j \in N$ in at least one element and in at least one period.[3]
3. The representation (10.2) is rather general. However, we do not include the instrument variables in the loss function (10.2). Nevertheless, to take account of the costs of using an instrument, we could simply introduce an additional target variable into Equation (10.2), and an equality constraint between it and the instrument in Equation (10.1), as we did in Section 6.3. That would allow us to keep instruments and targets strictly separate. It is worth noticing that in this case a player facing instrument costs never satisfies the Golden Rule since matrix B_i will necessarily become rectangular.

[2] This would imply that there are $S - q(i)$ zero rows/columns in $Q_{i,t}$.

[3] It is worth noticing that, even if the policymakers all share the same desired targets, inefficient non-cooperative equilibria may emerge when the agents cannot achieve their targets by implicit coordination (see Section 8.2.4) due to the conflicts between the different weights assigned to them by the different policymakers. A simple illustration appears in Dixit and Lambertini (2003b).

The above representation implies that each player will minimize (10.2) subject to (10.1) and that player's information set.[4] We discuss this case in Section 10.2.3. However, as in Section 6.2.2, in order to better illustrate how to use the Tinbergen–Theil tools in a strategic context, it is useful to represent the policy problem in a decoupled manner, by separating out the single-player problems individually. In the next section we present this decoupled representation.

10.2.2 *An alternative decoupled representation*

A more useful representation of the economy and preferences can be obtained by isolating (decoupling) each player's problem from those of the other players. This can be done by rewriting criterion (10.2) as

$$L_i = E\sum_{t=1}^{T}\left(y_t^i - \bar{y}_t^i\right)' Q_{i,t}\left(y_t^i - \bar{y}_t^i\right) \quad i \in N, \tag{10.3}$$

where $y^i \in R^{q(i)}$ is the vector of target variables extracted from system (10.1) that agent i aims to achieve. Therefore, $\bar{y}^i \in R^{q(i)}$ is player i's vector of desired target values, and Q_i is now a full rank matrix of assigned weights. Of course, if Q_i is of rank S, player i is interested in all the variables of system (10.1) and thus $y_t^i = y_t$.

By using the above loss functions, the relevant sub-system of (10.1) for player i can be written as

$$y_t^i = A_i y_{t-1}^i + \sum_{j\in N} B_{ij} u_t^j + v_t \quad \text{given } y_0, \tag{10.4}$$

where $A_i \in R^{q(i)\times q(i)}$ and $B_{ij} \in R^{q(i)\times m(i)}$ are the appropriate sub-matrices extracted from A and B_i. We assume that B_{ij} is of full column rank and $q(i) \geq m(i)$.

Now the policy problem for each player becomes: minimize (10.3) subject to (10.4) according to rules defined by the information set assumed. Of course, the observations made in the previous sections regarding time-varying preferences, potential conflict of interest, and instrument variables hold in the decoupled framework as well.

[4] The information set defines the information that each player has when their decisions have to be taken.

It is worth noticing that if all players are interested in all target variables (i.e., $q(i) = S$ for all $i \in N$), there is no difference between the decoupled and the canonical representation of the policy problem.

10.2.3 Dynamic control rules and concepts of equilibrium

This description of our general framework is closed by introducing a solution (or equilibrium) concept, both in the case when we use the canonical form and when we use a decoupled representation. Each solution concept defines the information necessary for the players to possess when they adopt their decision rules.

At this stage, we will restrict our attention to two information structures. By using the definitions of open loop and feedback strategies given in Section 3.9.1, the losses incurred by each player can be described by the optimal strategies played. We can informally define the two best-known solution concepts.[5]

Definition 10.1 (*open loop Nash equilibrium*). An open loop Nash equilibrium is an N-tuple of *open loop strategies* $u_t^* = (u_t^{1*}, \ldots, u_t^{i*}, \ldots, u_t^{N*})$ such that, for every possible initial condition, we have $L_i(u_t^*) \leq L_i(u_t^{1*}, \ldots, u_t^i, \ldots, u_t^{N*})$ for all $i \in N$ and for $t = 1,\ldots,T$.

Definition 10.2 (*Feedback Nash equilibrium*). A Feedback Nash equilibrium is an N-tuple of *feedback strategies* $u_t^* = (u_t^{1*}, \ldots, u_t^{i*}, \ldots, u_t^{N*})$ such that, for every possible initial condition, $L_i(u_t^*) \leq L_i(u_t^{1*}, \ldots, u_t^i, \ldots, u_t^{N*})$ for all $i \in N$ and for $t = 1,\ldots,T$.

Clearly, as follows from Chapter 3, these definitions are based on different assumptions about the information sets used by the players. Specifically, the open loop solution is a sequence of decisions for each time period, each of which depends on the initial state. The open loop Nash equilibrium is derived from the presumption that at the beginning of the game each player can make binding commitments about the actions he will undertake over the entire planning period. That is, each player designs his optimal policy based on his own loss function at the beginning of the period and sticks to that policy sequence

[5] More complex information structures can be also considered, e.g., by taking account of the anticipation effects as in the Stackelberg games described in Chapter 6. See Holly and Hughes Hallett (1989) and Petit (1990) for more details.

throughout the entire period. Hence, as explained in Chapter 3, open loop strategies are not usually time consistent. Feedback strategies provide instead a strongly time consistent (i.e., sub-game perfect) equilibrium. Sub-game perfectness requires that, for every possible sub-game, u^* will remain the equilibrium and optimum value for that sub-game. In practice, a feedback strategy means that a contingent rule (dependent on the system's state vector at time t) is provided for each player, and that the rules themselves can be obtained from the backward recursions of dynamic programming (Holly and Hughes Hallett, 1989). That in turn requires the constrained optimization problem faced by each player at each t to be recursively additively separable with respect to each $t,\ldots,T$. This is necessary for the Markov property to hold. That property, in turn, guarantees that the Bellman principle of optimality will hold (Bellman, 1957). As we shall see, the recursive nature of the problem is upset if there are anticipations effects from REs or actions expected from other players in the future.

10.3 Open loop Nash solutions

In the open loop Nash context by definition each agent sets his optimal rule, u_t^{i*}, at the beginning of the game, taking as given the rules used by the other agents: u_t^{j*} for $j \in N / i$. This allows us to express his optimization problem as a static one.

An open loop dynamic problem of this kind can be reduced to a static one. We can show that by using a simple example where $T = 2$. In this case, by using the decoupled representation of the policy problem, the criterion (10.3) that each agent must minimize, given the initial condition y_0, can be expressed as follows:[6]

$$L_i = \left(y_1^i - \bar{y}^i\right)' Q_i \left(y_1^i - \bar{y}^i\right) + \left(y_2^i - \bar{y}^i\right)' Q_i \left(y_2^i - \bar{y}^i\right) \;\forall\; i \in N. \tag{10.5}$$

Note that, for the sake of brevity, we ignore stochastic disturbance and expectations, as certainty equivalence can always be advocated (see Chapter 3).

[6] Here we assume that the dimensions of the target and the instrument vectors and the vector of the desired targets are time invariant. However, results can easily be generalized to the case where these assumptions do not hold.

The constraint (10.4) in turn becomes $y_1^i = A_i y_0^i + \sum_{j\in N} B_{ij} u_1^j$ in the first period; and $y_2^i = A_i A_i y_0^i + A_i \sum_{j\in N} B_{ij} u_1^j + \sum_{j\in N} B_{ij} u_2^j$ in the second period.

The optimization problem can then be put into matrix form as follows:

$$\min L_i = \left(\begin{bmatrix} y_1^i \\ y_2^i \end{bmatrix} - \begin{bmatrix} \bar{y}^i \\ \bar{y}^i \end{bmatrix} \right)' \begin{bmatrix} Q_i & 0 \\ 0 & Q_i \end{bmatrix} \left(\begin{bmatrix} y_1^i \\ y_2^i \end{bmatrix} - \begin{bmatrix} \bar{y}^i \\ \bar{y}^i \end{bmatrix} \right), \text{ s.t.} \tag{10.6}$$

$$\begin{bmatrix} y_1^i \\ y_2^i \end{bmatrix} = B_{ii} \begin{bmatrix} I & 0 \\ A_i & I \end{bmatrix} \begin{bmatrix} u_1^i \\ u_1^i \end{bmatrix} + \begin{bmatrix} A_i y_0^i + \sum_{j\in N\setminus i} B_{ij} u_1^j \\ A_i A_i y_0^i + A_i \sum_{j\in N\setminus i} B_{ij} u_1^j + \sum_{j\in N\setminus i} B_{ij} u_2^j \end{bmatrix}, \text{ or}$$

$$\begin{bmatrix} y_1^i \\ y_2^i \end{bmatrix} = B_{ii} \begin{bmatrix} I & 0 \\ A_i & I \end{bmatrix} \begin{bmatrix} u_1^i \\ u_2^i \end{bmatrix} + \sum_{j\in N\setminus i} \left(\begin{bmatrix} B_{ij} & 0 \\ A_i B_{ij} & B_{ij} \end{bmatrix} \begin{bmatrix} u_1^j \\ u_2^j \end{bmatrix} \right) + A_i \begin{bmatrix} y_0^i \\ A_i y_0^i \end{bmatrix}. \tag{10.7}$$

Equations (10.6) and (10.7) now describe a *static* problem, in which the dimension of the target vector $[y_1^i \, y_2^i]'$ is $2q(i)$; that of instruments $[u_1^i \, u_2^i]'$ is $2m(i)$; and the independence of instruments is ensured by the full rank of $B_{ii} \begin{bmatrix} I & 0 \\ A_i & I \end{bmatrix} \in \mathrm{R}^{2q(i)\times 2m(i)}$. Static controllability for problems (10.6) and (10.7) clearly requires $2q(i) = 2m(i)$.

Although, in our example, controllability requires the total number of instruments to be equal to the total number of targets, it is worth noticing that the above transformation of the dynamic policy problem from a dynamic setting into a static framework is not a mere transposition into a static policy problem. The transformation into a static setting allows us to use the tools developed in Part III, but the nature of the problem remains dynamic. In general, we cannot reduce the solution to a simple counting rule neglecting the role played by dynamics. We could do so in the example presented above, but this was a special case because we assumed that m and q do not vary during the policy interval and also that there are no lags in the effects of policy instruments. A simple example will clarify the point.

Let us reconsider our previous example but assume now time-varying availability, and effectiveness, of the instruments. We have to rewrite the constraints faced by policymaker i in the first and second periods as

$$\begin{cases} y_1^i = A_i y_0^i + \sum_{j \in N} B_{ij,1} u_1^j \\ y_2^i = A_i A_i y_0^i + A_i \sum_{j \in N} B_{ij,1} u_1^j + \sum_{j \in N} B_{ij,2} u_2^j \end{cases}, \tag{10.8}$$

where $B_{ij,1}$ and $B_{ij,2}$ are static policy multipliers at times one and two respectively. Notice that (10.9) below, derived from (10.8), is different from (10.7) since the former contains time-varying matrices of static policy multipliers.

The reduction of the dynamic policy problem to a static context requires solving (10.6) subject to (10.8), which can be rewritten in a compact form as

$$\begin{bmatrix} y_1^i \\ y_2^i \end{bmatrix} = \begin{bmatrix} B_{ii,1} & 0 \\ B_{ii,1} A_i & B_{ii,2} \end{bmatrix} \begin{bmatrix} u_1^i \\ u_2^i \end{bmatrix} + \sum_{j \in N \setminus i} \left(\begin{bmatrix} B_{ij,1} & 0 \\ A_i B_{ij,1} & B_{ij,2} \end{bmatrix} \begin{bmatrix} u_1^j \\ u_2^j \end{bmatrix} \right) + A_i \begin{bmatrix} y_0^i \\ A_i y_0^i \end{bmatrix}. \tag{10.9}$$

We need to consider two different cases here.

First, we assume that policymaker i has too many instruments at the wrong time, i.e., $B_{ii,1} = 0$ but $u_2^i \in \mathrm{R}^{2q(i)}$. Although the total number of instruments managed by player i in the two periods is the same as his total number of targets, it is easy to verify that the transformation of the dynamic problem into a static one, (10.9), does not support controllability, since in this case

$$\begin{bmatrix} B_{ii,1} & 0 \\ B_{ii,1} A_i & B_{ii,2} \end{bmatrix} = \begin{bmatrix} 0 & 0 \\ 0 & B_{ii,2} \end{bmatrix}. \tag{10.10}$$

It follows that (10.10) cannot be inverted.[7] Note that now, different from (10.6) and (10.7), policymaker i does not satisfy the Golden Rule in each period of time, but only in the transformed problem as a whole. This does not allow him to control the system in both periods, but only in period 2 (similar to dynamic controllability). Controllability, when there are time-varying lists of instruments or targets, is therefore going to depend entirely on whether the matrix of policy multipliers is nonsingular.

Second, we consider the reverse case. An example is trivial: suppose $B_{ij,2} = 0$ and $u_1^i \in \mathrm{R}^{2q(i)}$ in (10.9). It follows that

[7] Note that (10.10) is not left-invertible as it does not have full column rank.

$$\begin{bmatrix} B_{ii,1} & 0 \\ B_{ii,1}A_i & B_{ii,2} \end{bmatrix} = \begin{bmatrix} B_{ii,1} & 0 \\ B_{ii,1}A_i & 0 \end{bmatrix}, \tag{10.11}$$

where $\begin{bmatrix} B_{ii,1} \\ B_{ii,1}A_i \end{bmatrix} \in \mathrm{R}^{2q(i)\times 2q(i)}$. If this matrix is invertible, controllability is assured, even if the Golden Rule is not satisfied in both periods.[8]

Going beyond this example, various cases can be conceived where controllability is satisfied neither in each single period nor in the aggregate, but controllability of (10.6) and (10.9) emerges.[9] If the Golden Rule is instead satisfied in each single period, controllability of the whole system (10.9) always holds. *Static controllability* in each period thus always implies *multi-period static controllability*, but the reverse may not be true. The reason is simple and is related to the dynamic nature of the policy problem, which therefore also affects its static representation. The transposition of the dynamic policy problem in a static setting takes account of both static and dynamic multipliers, since the effects of instruments are no longer purely static, as was the case in Part III.

In other words, expanding static controllability to a multi-period context, i.e., counting the number of instruments available in each period and the number of targets, is something weaker than requiring static controllability to hold in each period. They are equivalent only if the lists of targets and instruments are time invariant. When the lists of targets and/or instruments are time varying instead, the dynamic multipliers must be taken into account. We could have the conditions for multi-period static controllability satisfied without having those for static controllability satisfied in the same dynamic system. Imagine, for example, that the policymaker has two targets over a two-period model (four targets); in the first period he has three instruments, in the second one. The policymaker can statically control the system only in period 1, but multi-period controllability is assured, as any four-target vector can be achieved in the two periods.

[8] The matrix (10.11) is left-invertible.

[9] More complex cases can be built by considering the indirect effects of the instrument through the economic dynamics, longer policy intervals, and time-varying objectives, but this is beyond the scope of this book.

More generally, assuming an open loop information structure, the dynamic policy problem can be transformed into a static problem by a simple change of variables, i.e.,[10]

$$\min_{\tilde{u}^i} L_i = \left(\tilde{y}^i - \bar{\tilde{y}}^i\right)' \tilde{Q}_i \left(\tilde{y}^i - \bar{\tilde{y}}^i\right) \quad \forall \ i \in N, \tag{10.12}$$

$$\text{s.t. } \tilde{y}_1^i = \tilde{B}_i \tilde{u}^i + \sum_{j \in N \setminus i} \tilde{B}_{ij} \tilde{u}^j + \tilde{A}_i \quad \text{given } \tilde{y}_0, \tag{10.13}$$

where $\tilde{y}^i = \left[y_1^i, y_2^i, ..., y_T^i\right]'$, $\bar{\tilde{y}}^i = \left[\bar{y}_1^i, ..., \bar{y}_T^i\right]' \in R^{q(i)T}$, $\tilde{u}^i = \left[u_1^i, u_2^i, ..., u_T^i\right]' \in R^{m(i)T}$; and the other symbols indicate appropriately defined matrices.[11]

Clearly, Equations (10.12) and (10.13) imply that all the results derived in Part III for the generalized static game can be applied to the dynamic open loop policy game described by Equations (10.3) and (10.4). For instance, all the theorems about equilibrium existence, implicit coalitions, policy neutrality and Pareto optimality established in Part III also hold here.

10.4 The Golden Rule and its properties in Feedback Nash equilibrium

10.4.1 *The basic argument*

In a dynamic setting, the properties of controllability (or the Golden Rule of economic policy), policy ineffectiveness, and the existence of a Feedback Nash equilibrium, are related to one another through the following two theorems.

Theorem 10.1 (*ineffectiveness in Feedback Nash equilibrium*). In a LQ difference game where an equilibrium exists, if one player satisfies the Golden Rule then all other players' policies are ineffective for all the target variables shared with that player.

[10] For the sake of brevity we apply this generalization to the time-invariant system. The extension to the time-varying case is trivial.

[11] The vector of target values, $\bar{\tilde{y}}^i$, is time invariant here, meaning that the target values (as well as the list of target variables) are the same in every period. This is a common situation. The inflation target is usually set at, say, 2% every period; the output gap at zero, etc. But in this context, it would make no difference to allow those values to change over time.

Proof. We again consider a decoupled representation of the policy problem (10.3)–(10.4), i.e.,

$$L_i = E_0 \sum_{t=1}^{T} (y_t^i - \bar{y}_t^i)' Q_{i,t} (y_t^i - \bar{y}_t^i) \quad i \in N, \tag{10.14}$$

$$y_{t+1}^i = A_i y_t^i + \sum_{j \in N} B_{ij} u_t^j \quad \text{given } y_0, \tag{10.15}$$

where we use an assumption about the timing which is slightly different from that in (10.4). Current instruments affect endogenous variables only from the next period. Instrument values are therefore given at time zero.

We assume value functions that are quadratic,[12] $V_i(y^i) = (y_t^i - \bar{y}_t^i)' P_i (y_t^i - \bar{y}_t^i)$, where P_i are negative definite symmetric matrices so that there are no redundant targets. By using the transition law to eliminate the next period's state, the N Bellman equations become

$$\begin{aligned}(y^i - \bar{y}^i)' P_i (y^i - \bar{y}^i) = \min_{u^i} \Big\{ & (y^i - \bar{y}^i)' Q_i (y^i - \bar{y}^i) \\ & + \Big(A_i y^i + \sum_{j \in N} B_{ij} u^j - \bar{y}^i \Big)' P_i \Big(A_i y^i + \sum_{j \in N} B_{ij} u^j - \bar{y}^i \Big) \Big\}.\end{aligned} \tag{10.16}$$

For the sake of simplicity, time indexes are omitted. But a Feedback Nash equilibrium must satisfy the following first-order conditions:

$$(B_{ii}' P_i B_{ii}) u^i = -B_{ii}' P_i \Big((A_i y^i - \bar{y}^i) + \sum_{j \in N \setminus i} B_{ij} u^j \Big) \quad i \in N. \tag{10.17}$$

Those conditions then yield the optimal policy rule:

$$u^i = -(B_{ii}' P_i B_{ii})^{-1} B_{ii}' P_i \{ A_i y^i - \bar{y}^i + \sum_{j \in N \setminus i} B_{ij} u^j \} \quad i \in N. \tag{10.18}$$

[12] Since we know that the value function must be at least convex for a solution to exist (see, e.g., Başar and Olsder, 1995; Sargent, 1987; Dockner, Jorgensen, Van Long and Sorger, 2000). See Engwerda (2000a, 2000b) for a more advanced exposition of this point.

To prove Theorem 10.1, we can focus (without loss of generality) on player 1. If player 1 satisfies the *Golden Rule*, then $m(1) = q(1)$ and $B_{11} \in R^{q(1)\times q(1)}$ is square and non-singular. Equation (10.18) then becomes

$$u^1 = -B_{11}^{-1}\left(A_1 y^1 - \bar{y}^1\right) - B_{11}^{-1}\sum_{j=2}^{N} B_{1j}u^j. \tag{10.19}$$

By using (10.19) in (10.15) we obtain

$$\begin{aligned} y_{t+1}^1 = A_1 y_t^1 + B_{11}u_t^1 + \sum_{j=2}^{N} B_{1j}u_t^j \equiv A_1 y_t^1 - \left(A_1 y_t^1 - \bar{y}^1\right) \\ - \sum_{j=2}^{N} B_{1j}u_t^j + \sum_{j=2}^{N} B_{1j}u_t^j. \end{aligned} \tag{10.20}$$

It follows that

$$y_t^1 = \bar{y}^1 \quad \forall \;\; t \in [1, +\infty]. \tag{10.21}$$

Thus, if a Feedback Nash equilibrium exists, the value of the target vector y^1 depends only on the goals of player 1 because, in that case, condition (10.19) will hold for all periods $t \in [1, +\infty]$. This completes the proof of Theorem 10.1. ∎

Theorem 10.2 (*non-existence in Feedback Nash equilibrium*). The Feedback Nash equilibrium of the policy game described does not exist if two or more players satisfy the Golden Rule and aim to achieve different target values for at least one shared target variable.

Proof. With no loss of generality, let us assume that in addition to player 1, also player 2, who shares some common target variables with player 1, satisfies the Golden Rule. In order to prove Theorem 10.2 we must show that the equilibrium does not exist when players 1 and 2 aim to achieve different target values. Then if a solution exists, it will be characterized by a set of optimal policy vectors $u^* = (u^{1*}, u^{2*}, \ldots, u^{N*})$. Given $(u^{3*},\ldots,u^{N*})$, u^{1*} and u^{2*} must satisfy the following system (obtained from (10.17)):

$$\begin{bmatrix} B_{11}'P_1B_{11} & B_{22}'P_2B_{12} \\ B_{11}'P_1B_{21} & B_{22}'P_2B_{22} \end{bmatrix} \begin{bmatrix} u^1 \\ u^2 \end{bmatrix} = -\begin{bmatrix} B_{11}'P_1 & 0 \\ 0 & B_{22}'P_2 \end{bmatrix} \begin{bmatrix} A_1\left(y^1 - \bar{y}^1\right) + \sum_{j\in N\backslash 1,2} B_{1j}u^{j*} \\ A_2\left(y^2 - \bar{y}^2\right) + \sum_{j\in N\backslash 1,2} B_{2j}u^{j*} \end{bmatrix}. \tag{10.22}$$

Notice that the partitioned matrix on the left hand side of Equation (10.22) is not necessarily square (a solution only requires that it is left-invertible). However, if both players satisfy their Golden Rule, then all the sub-matrices of the partitioned matrix and this matrix itself are square.

Assume, for simplicity, that players 1 and 2 share all the target variables:[13] that is, $y^1 = y^2 = y^S$. In this case, we have $A_1 = A_2$ and $B_{ii} = B_{ij}$ for $i, j \in \{1,2\}$. The partitioned matrix on the left hand side of Equation (10.22) now has a zero determinant (as $B_{11} = B_{21}$ and $B_{12} = B_{22}$) and cannot be inverted. Thus, Equation (10.22) cannot hold unless ($\bar{y}^1 = \bar{y}^2 = y^S$) and a pair such as $u^{1*} = u^{2*}$ satisfying (10.22) cannot exist. As a consequence, u^* cannot be the solution as claimed at the start. The case $\bar{y}^1 = \bar{y}^2 = y^S$ is trivial as, by implicit coordination,[14] it is equivalent to a problem of a single policymaker who aims to control a system that is over-determined. Multiple solutions in instrument space would then support $\bar{y}^1 = \bar{y}^2 = y^S$. ■

Comment 10.1. The proof of Theorem 10.2 can easily be generalized to the case where two players satisfy the Golden Rule but are not interested in all the same target variables (but only in a sub-set of them, say); i.e., their problems are only partially overlapping. Unlike the case above, this implies that we do not have $A_1 = A_2$ and $B_{ii} = B_{ij}$ for $i, j \in \{1,2\}$, and the partitioned matrix in the left hand side of Equation (10.22) may be invertible. However, now player 1 has $q(1)$ targets and $m(1) = q(1)$ instruments, and player 2 has $q(2)$ targets and $m(2) = q(2)$ instruments (recall that both satisfy the Golden Rule). Among the respective targets, they share s targets. Again by implicit coordination, we can think of the problem of player 1 as achieving the non-shared $q(1) - s$ targets by use of $q(1) - s$ arbitrarily chosen instruments among the $q(1)$ available (see Theorem 10.1) and then letting his *fictitious brother* (player 1b) achieve the s targets by use of the remaining s instruments (according again to Theorem 10.1). Similarly, player 2 can delegate her *fictitious sister* (player 2b) to achieve the s shared targets by using s arbitrary instruments. Then players 1b and 2b share the same s target variables and the above proof can be applied to the sub-system derived from their optimal policies. If they also share

[13] It is worth noticing that this assumption is less general than the theorem requires. Below we discuss a generalization of this proof.

[14] See Section 8.2.4.

target values for the target variables held in common, multiple solutions will emerge. If they disagree on at least one target value, then no solution can exist.

The above argument can be illustrated by considering target space instead of instrument space. If the first two players both satisfy the Golden Rule, it is easy to show that the first-order conditions for the two players cannot both be satisfied unless they both share the target values (see Theorem 10.1).

Comment 10.2. Theorem 10.1 gives a sufficient condition for policy effectiveness. It is worth noticing that, in a game where all players are interested in all the same target variables, the theorem does not assure the existence of any equilibrium, as the economic system is over-determined. In such a case, $q(j) = M$, where j is the controlling player, and thus $M > \Sigma_{i \in N} q(i)$ – if there are any strategic interactions. Moreover, even if we do not assume that all the players are interested in all the same target variables, the system may be over-determined when the number of instruments of non-controlling players is large with respect to the number of non-shared targets.[15] In all these cases, no equilibrium exists.

Comment 10.3. In a game where all the players are interested in all the same target variables, Theorem 10.2 gives instead a necessary condition for an equilibrium to exist because it states a sufficient condition for the opposite. However, that may not be sufficient for existence.[16] Note also that, in this case, if Theorem 10.1 is satisfied, then Theorem 10.2 is not (and vice versa).

Comment 10.4. The importance of these results for economic policy is highlighted by Theorem 10.2. This theorem says that if two independent policy authorities – say fiscal policymakers and the central bank – decide to pursue different inflation targets, then the Nash equilibrium may not exist. If it does not, the economy will not be able to reach a stable equilibrium position even when both sets of policymakers try to optimize their policies. Moreover, the conditions for this are not

[15] It is easy to check this when $N = 2$: assuming that player 1 satisfies the conditions for controllability. The system is over-determined if $m(2)$ is larger than the number of his non-shared target variables.

[16] Equilibrium existence is a rather complex matter in this context. For example, in a dynamic system stability is also required: see Engwerda (2000a, 2000b).

particularly stringent. In fact, except for certain sparse economies to be discussed below, target independence may actually be unhelpful – not because fiscal and monetary policies cannot be coordinated properly, but because the underlying equilibrium cannot be reached if both policymakers try to optimize their policy choices simultaneously and independently.

10.4.2 The sparse economic system problem

We now relax Theorems 10.1 and 10.2 in a way that is important for many economic models. Most economic models display sparseness. That is, when written in structural form, they typically relate each endogenous variable to just one or two other endogenous variables; and to a small number of lagged endogenous variables, control variables, or predetermined variables. In such cases, the structural model from which (10.15) is derived could be written as

$$y_{t+1} = Cy_{t+1} + Dy_t + \sum_{i \in N} F_i u_t^i \quad \text{given } y_0, \tag{10.23}$$

where C, D and F_i are sparse matrices (predominantly zero matrices, with just a few nonzero elements). For simplicity, we will assume (in this sub-section only) that all the players share all their target variables. As discussed in the previous sub-section, this assumption is easily relaxed.

By using (10.23), the coefficient matrices in (10.15),

$$y_{t+1} = Ay_t + \sum_{i \in N} B_i u_t^i + v_t,$$

are

$$A = (I - C)^{-1}D \qquad \text{and} \qquad B_i = (I - C)^{-1}F_i, \tag{10.24}$$

where $(I - C)^{-1}$ exists by virtue of the normalization in (10.23) irrespective of the definitions of C, D and F_i. But A and B_i are now no longer of full rank. However, we can pre-multiply (10.23) by a permutation matrix T_p, the term $T_p^{-1}T_p$ should be inserted in all the terms of the right hand side of (10.23). This allows us to separate those target variables that are affected *directly* by dynamic adjustments over time, from those that are not. We get the reordered system:

$$\tilde{y}_{t+1} = \tilde{A}\tilde{y}_t + \sum_{i \in N} \tilde{B}_i u_t^i, \tag{10.25}$$

where $\tilde{y}_t = T_p y_t$, $\tilde{A} = (I - T_p C T'_p)^{-1} T_p D T'_p$ and $\tilde{B}_i = (I - T_p C T'_p)^{-1} T_p F_i T_p'$. This now implies $\tilde{A} = \begin{bmatrix} A_{11} & 0 \\ A_{21} & 0 \end{bmatrix}$, where A_{11} is a square full rank matrix of order ℓ and $A_{21} \in \mathrm{R}^{(M-\ell)\times\ell}$, where ℓ is the number of target variables in the system that are *directly* subject to dynamic adjustments (i.e., the rank of C). Hence, $M - \ell$ target variables are not directly subject to dynamic adjustments. They appear in the second sub-vector of $\tilde{y}_t$.

We can now rework Theorem 10.2; we get the following.

Theorem 10.3 (*ineffectiveness and equilibrium existence in sparse economies*). If the targets of one (and only one) player that are directly subject to dynamic adjustments also satisfy the Golden Rule, then the policies of all other players will be ineffective with respect to their dynamic targets. Conversely, no Feedback Nash equilibrium exists in this policy game if two or more players satisfy the Golden Rule for their dynamic targets – unless they happen to share target values for those variables. Nonetheless, the Nash equilibrium may still exist if the Golden Rule is satisfied and the target values for non-dynamic targets differ across players. And the policies of the other players will still be effective for those targets even if one (or some) player satisfies the Golden Rule.

Proof. Recall that, until now, if players 1 and 2 satisfy the Golden Rule, their reaction functions imply $A(\bar{y}^1 - \bar{y}^2) = 0$. In a sparse economic system, the equivalent condition is $\tilde{A}(\bar{y}_1 - \bar{y}_2) = 0$ (note that $\tilde{B}_1^{-1}$ still exists if it is square and the Golden Rule applies to player 1). We now write $\bar{y}^{11}$ as the first ℓ elements of $\bar{y}^1$ (corresponding to the first ℓ elements, and hence dynamic targets, in $\tilde{y}$); and $\bar{y}^{21}$ as the remaining $M - \ell$ elements of $\bar{y}^1$. Similarly, we define $\bar{y}^{12}$ and $\bar{y}^{22}$ to be the corresponding sub-vectors of $\bar{y}^2$. These partitions conform to the partitioning in $\tilde{A}$. Our theorem now follows from the fact that both $A_{11}(\bar{y}^{11} - \bar{y}^{12}) = 0$ and $A_{21}(\bar{y}^{11} - \bar{y}^{12}) = 0$. Hence $\bar{y}^{11} = \bar{y}^{12}$ (because A_{11} and A_{21} differ in dimension and A_{11} is of full rank) will be needed to satisfy the replacement for $A(\bar{y}^1 - \bar{y}^2) = 0$ in this case: namely, $\tilde{A}(\bar{y}^1 - \bar{y}^2) = 0$. However, $\bar{y}^{21} - \bar{y}^{22} \neq 0$ is consistent with $\tilde{A}(\bar{y}^1 - \bar{y}^2) = 0$. That completes our proof. ■

10.5 An example from monetary policy

We now turn to a simple example to illustrate the usefulness of these results in practice. Consider an economy that can be described by the following well-known model:

$$y_t = \rho y_{t-1} + \alpha(\pi_t - \pi_t^e) - \beta(i_t - \pi_t^e) + \varepsilon_t, \tag{10.26}$$

$$i_t = c_0 + c_1(\pi_t - \pi^*) + c_2 y_t, \tag{10.27}$$

$$\pi_t^e - \pi_{t-1}^e = d(\pi_{t-1} - \pi_{t-1}^e) \quad \text{with } d \in (0,1). \tag{10.28}$$

Equation (10.26) is an elaboration of the standard model that has been part of the theory of monetary policy since Barro and Gordon introduced it in 1983. It consists of a short run Phillips curve with persistence ($\rho \neq 0$), set within a standard Lucas supply function (long run Phillips curve), and elaborated to include the effects of interest rate changes on output. It could therefore be interpreted *either* as a dynamic open economy Phillips curve *or* as a New Keynesian IS curve with dynamics. In either context, y_t is the deviation of output from its natural rate (the output gap); π_t is the rate of inflation, and π_t^e the rate of inflation expected by the private sector for period t; i_t is the nominal rate of interest ($i_t - \pi_t^e$ is the corresponding real rate of interest); and ε_t is a supply shock with mean zero and constant variance.

The policy instrument or control variable in this example is i_t. Equation (10.27) is a Taylor rule: c_0 is a constant term, reflecting control errors and/or the equilibrium rate of interest; π^* is the target inflation rate, and determinacy (the Taylor principle) suggests $c_1 > 1$. Finally, (10.28) says that expectations are formed by the adaptive principle (we expand on that assumption later); and all parameters, in all three equations, are defined to be positive. This model has lags in all three endogenous variables: y_t, π_t and π_t^e

To obtain the reduced form of (10.26)–(10.28), corresponding to (10.1), we renormalize (10.27) on π_t. This then yields the model's structural form, corresponding to (10.23):

$$\begin{bmatrix} 1 & -\alpha & \alpha-\beta \\ c_2 c_1^{-1} & 1 & 0 \\ 0 & 0 & 1 \end{bmatrix} \begin{pmatrix} y_t \\ \pi_t \\ \pi_t^e \end{pmatrix} = \begin{bmatrix} \rho & 0 & 0 \\ 0 & 0 & 0 \\ 0 & d & 1-d \end{bmatrix} \begin{pmatrix} y_{t-1} \\ \pi_{t-1} \\ \pi_{t-1}^e \end{pmatrix} + \begin{pmatrix} -\beta \\ c_1^{-1} \\ 0 \end{pmatrix} i_t + \begin{pmatrix} \varepsilon_t \\ \pi^* - c_0 c_1^{-1} \\ 0 \end{pmatrix}. \tag{10.29}$$

From here we can determine the value of A in the reduced form of this model by using (10.24). We obtain

$$A = \Delta^{-1} \begin{bmatrix} \rho & -d(\alpha-\beta) & -(1-d)(\alpha-\beta) \\ -\rho c_2 c_1^{-1} & d(\alpha-\beta)c_2 c_1^{-1} & (1-d)(\alpha-\beta)c_2 c_1^{-1} \\ 0 & d\left(1+c_2 c_1^{-1}\alpha\right) & \left(1+c_2 c_1^{-1}\alpha\right)\left(1-d\right) \end{bmatrix}, \tag{10.30}$$

where $\Delta = 1 + \alpha c_2 c_1^{-1}$. The determinant of the Jacobian matrix derived from system (10.29) is nonzero so long as $\alpha c_2 + c_1 \neq 0$, a condition that always holds. But (10.30) cannot be reorganized to deliver zeros in the right hand column, which is the condition that allows one target to be decoupled. Hence, if there are multiple policymakers in this model, they would have to set identical target values for the output gap, the inflation rate, and the inflation expectations they intend the markets to have, if there is going to be any equilibrium for the policy game *and* if those targets are to be controllable. Moreover, there could be competing policymakers, with the central bank using nominal interest rates to control inflation, but another authority (the government) setting the long term inflation target π^*; or where the fiscal policymakers try to moderate the effects of monetary policy by means of tax breaks or certain budgetary policies; or where monetary policymakers try to influence inflation expectations by setting intermediate targets, or by talking the exchange rate up or down.[17] These are all situations that are common enough in practice. The Bank of England is an example of the first case; the United States, and Italy in the Euro, are examples of the second; and Turkey, China and certain other countries with emerging inflation problems are examples of the third.

Next, we consider a variant. Suppose that, because of data revisions, policymakers recognize that it is difficult to measure the current output gap accurately, and prefer to use a more reliable past measure y_{t-1} as an indicator in Equation (10.27) instead. Suppose also that private agents, perhaps for similar reasons, find that imperfect expectations introduce too much noise and volatility into the system; and find it cheaper to extrapolate past values as expectations instead. That implies $\pi_t^e = d\pi_{t-1}$. The model, as set up now, has no lags in π_t^e. Solving through (10.23) and (10.24), we now find

[17] This would require an extra "constant" term in (10.28) and, hence, the third equation of (10.29).

$$\tilde{A} = \begin{bmatrix} \rho - \alpha c_2 c_1^{-1} & -d(\alpha - \beta) & 0 \\ -c_2 c_1^{-1} & 0 & 0 \\ 0 & d & 0 \end{bmatrix}. \tag{10.31}$$

This setup allows our policymakers to disagree on the intermediate inflation targets they announce to the markets (π_t^e), but still have controllable targets and a reachable Nash equilibrium. This happens because, in this model, there is a delay before some of the target variables are affected by the policy instruments. That means the policymakers can set policies to reach some agreed targets first, allowing differences to persist elsewhere, and then use those policies again to reach the other target values later.

A stronger version of the same result is obtained if the contemporaneous output gap is restored to the Taylor rule (10.27) but expectations are *rational*. That means (10.28) is replaced by

$$\pi_t^e = \pi_t - v_t, \tag{10.32}$$

where v_t is a random expectations error with mean zero. This is the form of the model that most theorists would favor. It implies that we now have no lags in either π_t or π_t^e. As a consequence,

$$\tilde{A} = \Delta^{-1}\Gamma^{-1} \begin{bmatrix} 1 & 0 & 0 \\ -c_2 c_1^{-1} & 0 & 0 \\ -c_2 c_1^{-1} & 0 & 0 \end{bmatrix}, \tag{10.33}$$

where $\Gamma = (\Delta + c_2 c_1^{-1}(\alpha - \beta))\rho^{-1}$. In this third model, policymakers can have different target values for both π_t and π_t^e and still reach a Nash equilibrium outcome for their target variables.

Thus, different policymakers (in government and the central bank) could once again have target independence (and hence different inflation targets) and still expect to reach an equilibrium position. Nevertheless, that outcome could prove to be a dream if expectations are not rational (because it is too expensive to gather all the necessary information to compute those expectations accurately), or if it is difficult to measure the current output gap reliably. In such cases they will not be able to reach their idealized equilibrium – nor, indeed, any other solution that allows both of them to optimize their policies.

The cases we have dealt with here are of devolved decision making within a single economy, where the government and the central bank are concerned with output, employment and inflation for that economy, and have a variety of different fiscal and monetary instruments at their disposal to reach their preferred target values. Other situations could be devised to extend our analysis to other agents (such as unions) within that economy; or to a multi-country setting, where some targets (for example, exchange rates, bilateral trade balances, or inflation if in a currency union) are held in common, but other targets are not, just as we did in Chapter 7.

10.6 Dynamic controllability in a strategic context

In this section we are going to derive the minimum time needed to reach targets. In Section 3.7 we assumed that the policymaker could aim to achieve a certain target vector at time S. The concept used was dynamic controllability. Dynamic controllability is obtained for any t equal to or larger than that which solves the following optimization problem:

$$\min_S L_S = \left(y_S^i - \bar{y}^i\right)' Q_i \left(y_S^i - \bar{y}^i\right) \qquad \text{s.t. Equation}(10.4). \qquad (10.34)$$

A trivial case arises if $m = q$, as then $S = 1$ provides the solution. The policymaker always satisfies static as well as dynamic controllability. By contrast, if $m < q$, the policymaker should exploit the dynamic multipliers to obtain the desired targets and this requires $S > 1$. The shortest time needed to reach his desired targets depends on how many targets and instruments the policymaker has. For instance, if only one instrument is available to him, he can expect to reach one target value in period one; two after two periods and so on; i.e., dynamic controllability requires at least $S = q$ periods. In general, if the policymaker has m instruments, dynamic controllability requires at least $S = q/m$ periods. For a formal proof of this, see Preston and Pagan (1982).

By applying the above result to a multiple-player context it emerges that if two (or more) players aim to solve a problem of the kind (10.34), where $q(1)/m(1) = S$ and $q(2)/m(2) = S$, both would be able to achieve their targets and no equilibrium would exist. By contrast, if $q(i)/m(i) \geq S$ for all i, the existence of an equilibrium of problem (10.34) with multiple players is ensured. In other cases, the conditions for equilibrium existence will be more complex, but we do not analyze them here.

The second case of interest is where player i aims to reach certain target values in the shortest possible time. Assuming dynamic controllability, what can be achieved now depends on how many target values player i attempts to reach. Again, if a player has only one instrument available, he can expect to reach one target value in period one; two after two periods; ...; and all targets after a number of periods equal to the integer value of $q(i)/m(i)$, if $q(i) > m(i)$. In the absence of static controllability, this is as far as he can go in minimizing the time taken to reach various targets.

If dynamic controllability applies in period S, player i can achieve his target values $\bar{y}_i$ exactly, in expectation, in period S at least. That means, applying certainty equivalence, that player i can achieve a value of $E(L_S) = 0$ in his loss function and maximum expected utility in period $t = S$. But the same result does not hold if there are instrument costs since both static and dynamic controllability no longer apply. Nor does this result say anything about the costs along the way. In general we should expect $E(L_t) \neq 0$, for all $t = 1,\ldots,S - 1$ and $m(i)\ S \leq Tq(i)$. To analyze the utility costs in either of those two cases requires a full specification of the preferences in the loss functions $E(L_t)$ for each t.

There is one exception to the assertion that, when the system is only dynamically controllable, the policymaker must wait in order to achieve his target values. Chapter 12 will show that, in an economy with forward-looking REs of future outcomes, dynamic controllability may be available from period one if announcements of future policy actions are used alongside the actual (current or past) policy interventions. If that is the case, and in the absence of instrument costs, then the costs along the way will fall away: $E(L_t) = 0$ for all $t = 1,\ldots,T$.

10.7 Lessons from this chapter

This chapter generalizes the results developed for static policy games to a dynamic setting. We find that the Tinbergen–Theil theory of economic policy can also be usefully applied to a strategic context of difference games.

Specifically, we extend our static controllability theorems to policy games based on open loop strategies and finite time, and to policy games based on Feedback Nash equilibria. Extensions of the new theory of economic policy are straightforward as far as finite horizon difference games characterized by open loop Nash equilibria are concerned, as they can be rewritten as a static game. Similarly, we show how, assuming Feedback Nash equilibrium, if one player satisfies the Golden Rule, either all the other players' policies are ineffective with respect to dynamic target variables shared with that player; or no equilibrium exists without exact agreement on all the (dynamic) target values. We illustrated the usefulness of our results with reference to a model incorporating a Taylor rule, a description of expectations formation, and a relation that can be interpreted as either a dynamic open economy Phillips curve or a dynamic New Keynesian IS curve. Small variations in the model specification can allow, or take away, policy effectiveness – which grants the policymakers the latitude to disagree on none, one, or several of the exact target values. Likewise, our general results show how easily target independence, in a world where institutional and policy independence are considered important, can prove to be counterproductive when policymakers try to optimize their choices. Finally, we show how the existence and policy invariance properties of a game where policymakers simply aim to achieve a given desired objective at a certain time in a dynamic context can be usefully explored by using a dynamic controllability criterion instead of a static one.

Our results lead us to note one obvious area for generalization. In this chapter we have introduced contemporaneous and adaptive expectations based on the argument that backward-looking models fit the data better than forward-looking models (Galì and Gertler, 1999). But that may conflict with actual practice. For example, central banks react to inflation forecasts, and the private sector are more likely to be forward-looking in their wage bargains or asset holdings. It is crucial to check if our concepts continue to apply in such cases. We will introduce REs of the private sector in the following two chapters.

11 Dynamic policy games with rational expectations

Summary. Lucas (1976) argued that a traditional Tinbergen-type decision model would be inconsistent with the assumption of rationality since private sector behavior, which, in that model, does not anticipate the policymakers' actions, cannot be said to be rational. We therefore need to investigate what happens to controllability, equilibrium existence and policy stability in our framework once private sector rationality is restored by introducing REs. This chapter derives conditions under which a number of theorems stated by the new theory of economic policy extend to a RE context, allowing us to refine our existing results for policy neutrality and the existence of Nash equilibria with multiple policymakers in that context. The importance of this aspect of the theory of economic policy is that it settles an old issue (policy controllability) in the only setting (policy games) in which it can be placed to overcome the Lucas critique.

11.1 Introduction

We know from Chapter 4 that REs have been used as an element of the Lucas (1976) criticism of the Tinbergen–Theil approach. In Section 5.3 we saw that their introduction means, heuristically, that we need to take account of strategic interactions (or policy anticipation) in some form. For example, we showed that models in which a single policymaker faces RE constraints when choosing optimal policies are in fact implicitly solving a policy game where the private sector (or another agent) is acting as Stackelberg leader.

It is natural, therefore, to extend the analysis of Chapter 10, where we showed how to apply our approach to dynamic policy games, to the case where a single strategic policymaker (or more than one) acts in a dynamic environment with the private sector modeled as having REs. It is assumed that the private sector can anticipate the policymakers' actions without suffering systematic errors. In such a context, we are interested in exploring if, and how, the presence of REs affects our controllability-based approach, and/or the relationship between controllability and credibility (which is clearly founded on the RE concept). This chapter investigates the former problem, while the latter will be examined in the following chapter.

Put differently, our problem can be summarized as follows. Lucas (1976) showed that traditional Tinbergen-type decision models would be inconsistent with the assumption of rationality since private sector behavior (in that model) does not anticipate the policymakers' actions and therefore cannot be said to be rational. We therefore need to investigate what happens to controllability, equilibrium existence and policy stability in our policy optimization exercises once the private sector rationality is restored by introducing REs.

To highlight a typical problem that arises in this context, we can look to the classic Blanchard and Kahn (1980) analysis that establishes conditions for the existence and stability of an equilibrium solution to RE models assuming "given behavior or given decision rules" on the part of the private sector.[1] In reality, private sector behavior will vary as a function of the authorities' policy choices. In that case, it is not clear if the existence of equilibrium and controllability will still remain when private expectations and private behavior are allowed to shift with the policy choices as they should.[2] What we need instead is

[1] To be more precise, compared to the standard solutions in the literature (such as Blanchard and Kahn, 1980), the matrix equation at the center of our analysis, Equation (11.5) below, has endogenous variables chosen (if indirectly) by the policy authorities. The Blanchard–Kahn paper does not. Hence the difference is that the Blanchard–Kahn paper analyzes the solution and stability of linear RE systems *given* the behavior of the economy. Our analysis considers the possible solutions and their stability when the policy authority is capable of influencing the behavior of the system *and* private expectations (albeit restricted by (11.5)). Our discussion of state and dynamic controllability [Section 3.7.2 of Chapter 3] then applies.

[2] In a New Keynesian model, Evans and Honkapohja (2003, 2006) show that standard optimal policies may be unstable if agents follow a learning process. In that case, standard optimal policies would not satisfy the Blanchard and Kahn (1980) conditions and a policy rule properly designed to ensure stability needs to take account of private sector expectations explicitly. That is, it should be an expectation-based rule – as is standard practice in the literature on monetary policy. By assuming learning, Evans and Honkapohja (2003) consider a kind of interaction and then apply Blanchard and Kahn's (1980) technique. But their agents are atomistic and can only form expectations of the future passively. By contrast, we are interested in strategic interactions between a small number of agents or policymakers who interact consciously and actively – and

an analysis that allows policymakers to actively manage expectations for the express purpose of shifting the expectations path to a path consistent with the outcomes they want. If they can do that, private behavior will be exactly consistent with what private agents and policymakers expect the outcomes to be. No one will be required to make any expectations errors for the policies to work.

The rest of the chapter is divided into five sections. The next section describes a general framework for taking account of strategic interactions in a dynamic context with REs. In Section 11.3 we derive the conditions for controllability in a dynamic system with REs and a single policymaker. From there we derive the results we need on policy neutrality and policy effectiveness. Section 11.4 then uses the tools of the new theory of economic policy to characterize the conditions for the existence of equilibrium outcomes or policy invariance when there are several players. In Section 11.5 we apply our theorems to a simple New Keynesian model to determine the existence and features of the equilibrium without the need to compute any explicit solutions. Section 11.6 concludes with a discussion of the sources of time inconsistency and the Lucas critique. This provides a bridge to the following chapter where the relationship between controllability, credibility, REs and the limits to time-inconsistent behavior will be investigated more closely.

11.2 Policy games with forward-looking variables

We reconsider the strategic game between N policymakers presented in a canonical form in Chapter 10 to take account of past and expected future values of the state variables. In practice, these expectations are made by the private sector and may act as a constraint on the policymakers' choices. Each player, $i \in N$,[3] has a set of $m(i)$ independent policy instruments u_t^i, and a preference function defined on a sub-set of $q(i)$ linearly independent target variables drawn from the set of all S possible target variables in the game y_t. We assume that $m(i) \leq q(i)$ for

can stabilise the economy in the process – in order to steer the economy in a strategic manner. We therefore focus on Feedback Nash equilibrium outcomes.

[3] As in the previous chapters, policymakers are grouped, with a little abuse of notation, in the set N.

all players and that $m(i)$ and $q(i)$ are constant through time. The game is played for T periods, where T may be arbitrarily large.

Formally, the dynamics of the economy is now represented by a linear difference equation with expectations and multiple policymakers:

$$y_t = Ay_{t-1} + \sum_{i \in N} B_i u_t^i + Cy_{t+1|t} + v_t \quad \text{for } t = 1 \ldots T, \tag{11.1}$$

given values for y_0 and y_{T+1}, where $y_{t+1|t} = E[y_{t+1}|\Omega_t]$ denotes the mathematical expectation of y_{t+1} conditional on Ω_t (the common information set available to all at t) and u_t^i is the vector of control variables in the hands of player i. The matrices A, C and B_i are constant and of order S, S and $S \times m(i)$, respectively, and have at least some elements that are nonzero. Recall that $\Sigma_{i \in N} m(i) = M$. In this representation, y_0 is a known initial condition, and y_{T+1} is some known, assumed or expected terminal condition that is part of the information set Ω_t. Note that the u_t^i values are not part of Ω_t since they are determined within the game. Finally v_t is a vector of exogenous shocks or other influences on y_t, which has a known mean but comes from an unspecified probability distribution. Notice also that, if player i satisfies the Golden Rule and has only $q(i)$ targets, $m(i)$ is equal to $q(i)$ and B_i (after deleting the rows corresponding to the non-targets in y_t) is a square, invertible matrix because the instruments are assumed to be linearly independent.

The preference or cost function that player i aims to minimize is (10.3), i.e.:

$$L^i = E \sum_{t=1}^{T} \left(y_t^i - \bar{y}_t^i \right)' Q_{i,t} \left(y_t^i - \bar{y}_t^i \right) \quad i \in N, \tag{11.2}$$

where $\bar{y}_t^i$ is a vector of known target values and $Q_{i.t}$ is a symmetric positive semi-definite matrix of weights assigned to player i's targets in each period.

The description of the policy problem is completed by introducing the definitions for the players' information sets, which have been already described in Section 10.2.3. The policy problem of each policymaker is thus the minimization of (11.2) subject to (11.1), y_0, y_{T+1}, and his information set. When it exists, the game equilibrium will result in a set of policy rules (not necessarily unique) of the form:

$$\Pi = \left(u^{1*}, u^{2*}, \ldots, u^{N*} \right) \tag{11.3}$$

supporting an equilibrium path $y^* = \{y_t\}_{t=1}^{T}$ for the endogenous variables, given (11.1) and y_0 and y_{T+1}.

11.3 Controllability under REs: the single-player case

11.3.1 The model in final form

Without loss of generality, we can write the generic linear RE model (11.1) in its reduced form for a single player, as follows:[4]

$$y_t = Ay_{t-1} + Bu_t + Cy_{t+1|t} + v_t \quad \text{for} \quad t = 1,\ldots,T. \tag{11.4}$$

Because there is only one player, we can omit the index i in Equation (11.4) in this section. Thus, $y \in R^S$ and $u \in R^M$; note also that the policymaker is interested in controlling S variables.

This model can now be solved from the perspective of any particular period, say $t = 1$, by putting it into its final form conditional on the information set available in that period:

$$\begin{pmatrix} y_{1|1} \\ \vdots \\ \vdots \\ \vdots \\ y_{T|1} \end{pmatrix} = \begin{bmatrix} I & -C & 0 & \cdots & 0 \\ -A & I & & \ddots & \vdots \\ 0 & \ddots & \ddots & & 0 \\ \vdots & \ddots & \ddots & \ddots & -C \\ 0 & \cdots & 0 & -A & I \end{bmatrix}^{-1} \left\{ \begin{bmatrix} B & 0 & \cdots & 0 \\ 0 & \ddots & & \vdots \\ \vdots & & \ddots & 0 \\ 0 & \cdots & 0 & B \end{bmatrix} \begin{pmatrix} u_{1|1} \\ \cdot \\ \cdot \\ \cdot \\ u_{T|1} \end{pmatrix} + \begin{pmatrix} v_{1|1} \\ \cdot \\ \cdot \\ \cdot \\ v_{T|1} \end{pmatrix} + \begin{pmatrix} Ay_0 \\ 0 \\ \cdot \\ \cdot \\ 0 \end{pmatrix} + \begin{pmatrix} 0 \\ \cdot \\ \cdot \\ 0 \\ Cy_{T+1|1} \end{pmatrix} \right\}. \tag{11.5}$$

In this representation, y_0 is a known initial condition for $t = 1$; and $y_{T+1|1}$ is a known, assumed or expected, terminal condition – most probably one that describes the economic system's long run equilibrium state.[5] Although (11.4) has been solved from the point of view of Ω_1, it must be understood that it could have been derived for each

[4] The generalization of Equation (11.1), and hence (11.4), to include any number of leads and lags is set out in Appendix 11A.

[5] There is no indeterminacy problem here. The reason is that the dynamic conditions that guarantee the existence of a solution are automatically satisfied: a solution to our model exists, given any particular information set, if the

Ω_t, $t = 1,\ldots,T$, in turn (where $y_{j|t} = E_t(y_j)$ if $j \geq t$, but $y_{j|t} = y_j$ if $j < t$; and similarly for u and v).

The equation to which (11.5) is the solution makes it clear that *neither* policymakers, *nor* the private sector, are required to make expectation errors for the policies to work. In fact Equation (11.8) below shows just the opposite; that those expectations are exactly consistent with what the private sector/policymakers expect the outcomes to be. It remains only to determine if it is possible to shift expectations in such a way that the economy's final outcomes reach certain target values at certain points of time.

It is easy to show that this final form solution always exists since the inverse matrix in (11.5) is well defined provided the matrix product AC does not contain a unit root. To see this, define the Toeplitz matrix in (11.5) to be

$$T_T = \begin{bmatrix} I & -C & 0 & . & 0 \\ -A & I & & . & . \\ 0 & & . & & 0 \\ . & . & & . & -C \\ 0 & . & 0 & -A & I \end{bmatrix}. \tag{11.6}$$

This matrix is of order ST. Using the partitioning by time, the determinant of T_T is given by

$$|T_{T-1}| \cdot \left| I_n - (-C, 0.....0) T_{T-1}^{-1} (-A', 0.....0)' \right|. \tag{11.7}$$

However, $|T_{T-1}| = |T_{T-2}| \left| I_n - (-C, 0.....0) T_{T-2}^{-1} (-A', 0.....0)' \right|$, and so on. Hence we can write

inverse in (11.5) exists – which we show to be the case. But given such an inverse, Hughes Hallett and Fisher (1988) show that the saddle point property (that the system has the correct number of stable and unstable eigenvalues to ensure a solution in the sense of Blanchard and Khan (1980)) is automatically satisfied. One implication is that it no longer matters what the value of the terminal condition is or, if none is specified, if the policy horizon is far enough away (if $T \to \infty$). In other cases, if the inverse in (11.5) does exist and T is finite, indeterminacy may follow if $y_{T+1|1}$ cannot be specified.

$$|T_i| = |T_{i-1}|\left|I_n - (-C:O)T_{i-1}^{-1}(-A':0)'\right|$$
$$= |T_{i-1}||T_{i-2}|\ldots|T_3||I_n - CA| \neq 0 \quad \text{for } i = 2,\ldots,T.$$

These equalities follow from the partitioning in T_{i-j}^{-1} and repeated applications of the Woodbury formula for the inverse of a matrix sum; and the inequality from the absence of a unit root in AC. But $|T_1| = |I_n|$. Hence the inverse always exists by induction, subject to this no unit root condition.

Given that the inverse discussed above always exists, we can now write the final form model in the following way:

$$\begin{pmatrix} y_{1|1} \\ \cdot \\ \cdot \\ \cdot \\ y_{T|1} \end{pmatrix} = \begin{bmatrix} R_{11} & \cdot & \cdot & \cdot & R_{1T} \\ \cdot & \cdot & & & \cdot \\ \cdot & & \cdot & & \cdot \\ \cdot & & & \cdot & \cdot \\ R_{T1} & \cdot & \cdot & \cdot & R_{TT} \end{bmatrix} \begin{pmatrix} u_{1|1} \\ \cdot \\ \cdot \\ \cdot \\ u_{T|1} \end{pmatrix} + \begin{pmatrix} b_{1|1} \\ \cdot \\ \cdot \\ \cdot \\ b_{T|1} \end{pmatrix}, \tag{11.8}$$

or $y = Ru+b$,

where $R = T_T^{-1}(I \otimes B)$, $b = T_T^{-1}\left\{E(v\,|\,\Omega_1) + (A':0)'\,y_0 + (0:C')y_{T+1|1}\right\}$,

and $\otimes$ denotes the Kronecker product. In this representation of the model, each $R_{t,j} = \partial y_{t|1} / \partial u_{j|1}$ is an $S \times M$ matrix of policy multipliers for $t, j = 1,\ldots,T$. But notice that $R_{t,j} \neq 0$ even if $t < j$. Hence Equation (11.8) implies that $R_{t,j}$ is a matrix of conventional policy multipliers between $y_{t|1}$ and $u_{j|1}$, with a delay of $t - j$ between implementation and realization if $t \geq j$ (i.e., causality runs forward). Likewise, $R_{t,j}$ represents a matrix of anticipatory effects on $y_{t|1}$ of an announced or anticipated policy change, $u_{j|1}$, at some point in the future if $t < j$.[6]

[6] A conventional *backward-looking* model will have $R_{t,j} = 0$ for all $t < j$, *and* constant multipliers $R_{t,j} = R_{t-j}$ for $t - j = 0,\ldots,T - 1$, if the model at (11.5) is linear. Neither of these things is true in (11.8). This makes our problem of static controllability in a multi-period setting entirely different from that arising in a myopic environment. In Chapter 12 we will build on existence of announcement or anticipatory effects.

11.3.2 Multi-period static controllability

Static or Tinbergen controllability defines the set of conditions that must hold if an arbitrary set of target values can be achieved for the endogenous variables y_t in each period – at least in expectation given that the original model is stochastic. Define those target values to be $\bar{y}_{t|1}$, where the bar denotes desired values from the perspective of period 1; and $\bar{y}$ to be the corresponding stacked vector of those desired values across all time periods.

Static controllability, meaning the ability to reach desired values for the targets in each period, evidently requires the matrix R in (11.8) to possess an inverse:[7]

$$u = R^{-1}(\bar{y} - b), \tag{11.9}$$

where y, u and b are all understood to be expectations conditioned on the current information set Ω_t, including the terminal condition, as specified in (11.8). Hence:

Theorem 11.1 (*static controllability under REs*). Under REs, static controllability by a single player, as in a conventional backward-looking model, requires as many independent policy instruments as there are target variables in each time period.

Proof. From (11.8), $R = T_T^{-1}B_T$ where $B_T = I_T \otimes B$. Hence $R_T^{-1} = (T_T^{-1}B_T)^{-1} = B_T^{-1}T_T$ exists if and only if $B_T^{-1} = I_T \otimes B^{-1}$ exists, since we already know that T_T^{-1} always exists. But the instrument coefficient matrix, B, can only possess an inverse if $S = M$ *and* if it has full rank: i.e., has rows and columns that are linearly independent. But those are exactly the same conditions as would provide period-by-period static controllability in a conventional static model ($A = 0$, $C = 0$), or in a backward-looking dynamic model ($C = 0$, but $A \neq 0$).■

Corollary 11.1. Theorem 11.1 assumes that the same number of targets and instruments are to be used in each time period since the matrix inverse of R_T is of order $ST \times MT$. If that is not the case, then we need $S = M$ and linear independence in each period if static controllability is to hold across the whole policy interval since $I \otimes B^{-1}$ now becomes

[7] Note that we have assumed that the number of instruments and targets does not vary over time.

$B_T^{-1} = diag\{B_t^{-1}\}$. The sufficient condition, in terms of linear independence within each B_t, cannot be inferred from R in this case.

Comment 11.1. Theorem 11.1 implies there is no change to the static controllability conditions when there are rational or forward-looking expectations. As always $S = M$, the conventional Tinbergen static controllability theorem, is a *necessary* condition for static controllability in this case. The sufficient condition is linear independence in the impact of the instruments on the targets (together with $S = M$).

Comment 11.2. In the event that we have surplus instruments, $M > S$, then we may transfer $M - S$ of them from $u_{t|1}$, times their coefficients from B, to the corresponding element of $v_{t|1}$ in Equation (11.5) before proceeding with Theorem 11.1 on the reduced system.

Comment 11.3. In contrast to the time inconsistency literature, the conditions that provide multi-period static controllability in a conventional model go through unchanged in a model with rational (forward-looking) expectations. Theorem 11.1 therefore shows that there is a range of circumstances in which the Lucas critique need not apply (since the policymakers can achieve the ideal values $\bar{y}$ whatever the private sector does, government policymakers can have no interest in changing their decisions). Hence time inconsistency issues do not arise in this case. This conclusion will be revisited and discussed in much greater detail in Chapter 12.

Of course, the introduction of REs may very well still imply time inconsistency for policymaking in other contexts; in particular when the static controllability condition is not satisfied, as will happen in the standard example of stabilization policies under an expectations-augmented Phillips curve. To see this, notice that the traditional vertical Phillips curve model would not be controllable in the long run, i.e., as $T \to \infty$, when contemporaneous inflation expectations are associated with lagged actual values. This is because T_T^{-1} would be a lower triangular companion matrix, whose lower border elements do not die away as $T \to \infty$ since $A = I$ and $C = 0$. It also happens if the expectations are in fact genuinely contemporaneous because T_T will be singular having $I - C$ on the diagonal where $C = I$. Or if the inflation expectations are defined for the next period because T_T^{-1} is an upper triangular companion matrix, whose upper border elements do not vanish as $T \rightarrow \infty$ since $A = 0$ and $C = I$. (The third case is the classic textbook formulation.)

In the first and third cases, the solution to the model is undefined in the long run because the roots of the system lie on the unit circle (because the natural dynamics contain a unit root in the first case, $A = I$; and through the expectations effects in the third, $C = I$). In those two cases, the model fails the no unit root test for their respective specifications. But the model may still be controllable for finite horizons (small values of T, the short run Phillips curve case) where we are no longer concerned with infinite band Toeplitz matrices.[8] In the second case, the model has no finite solution because there is a contemporaneous unit root; the expectations cancel out current developments in the outcomes exactly.

11.4 Equilibria and policy neutrality with multiple players

Given the above framework, we can now reintroduce the possibility of multiple policymakers whose decisions may interact. Two new theorems can be derived, which relate to the existence of the Feedback Nash equilibrium and the effectiveness of the players' policies in an economy with REs.[9] We consider the Nash equilibrium because we are concerned with sequences of period-by-period decisions. At period t, we do not exploit (nor do we need to exploit) the Markov property for targets y_{t+j} since under controllability, both static and multi-period, the commitment solution coincides with the discretionary solution.

[8] For proofs of these propositions, see Hughes Hallett and Fisher (1988). We might also argue a loss of controllability because we have two targets (output, inflation) and one instrument (interest rates). For that case we need dynamic controllability, but these models fail the unit root test before we get there.

[9] We must be clear on the meaning of a policy game in an economy where there are REs. From Chapters 4 and 5, a policy game already implies a representation of the REs held by the players. When, in addition, the rest of the economy is represented as having REs, we are in effect introducing a strategic interaction not only between players (in an explicit manner), but also between these players and the rest of the economy (in an implicit manner).

Theorem 11.2 (*non-existence of Feedback Nash equilibrium with REs*). No Feedback Nash equilibrium exists for the policy game described if at least two players having at least one target variable in common satisfy the Golden Rule (unless they share the same target values, in which case a Nash equilibrium is possible).

Proof. Assume that an equilibrium described by (11.3) to the policy game exists. By focusing on player i, we can rewrite Equation (11.1) as

$$y_t = Ay_{t-1} + B_i u_t^i + Cy_{t+1|t} + K_{it} \quad \text{for } t = 1,\dots,T, \tag{11.10}$$

where $K_{it} = \sum_{j\in N|i} B_j u_t^j + v_t$ captures the effect of other players' decisions, and external events, on each target variable. Equation (11.10) can now be put into its final form conditional on the common information set available in the initial period, Ω_1, as follows (the version of (11.5) faced by player i):

$$\begin{pmatrix} y_{1|1} \\ \vdots \\ \vdots \\ \vdots \\ y_{T|1} \end{pmatrix} = \begin{bmatrix} I & -C & 0 & . & 0 \\ -A & I & & . & . \\ 0 & & . & & 0 \\ . & . & & . & -C \\ 0 & . & 0 & -A & I \end{bmatrix}^{-1} \left\{ \begin{bmatrix} B_i & 0 & . & . & 0 \\ 0 & . & & & . \\ . & & . & & . \\ . & & & . & 0 \\ 0 & . & . & 0 & B_i \end{bmatrix} \begin{pmatrix} u_{1|1}^i \\ . \\ . \\ . \\ u_{T|1}^i \end{pmatrix} + \begin{pmatrix} K_{i1|1} \\ . \\ . \\ . \\ K_{iT|1} \end{pmatrix} + \begin{pmatrix} Ay_0 \\ 0 \\ . \\ . \\ 0 \end{pmatrix} + \begin{pmatrix} 0 \\ . \\ . \\ 0 \\ Cy_{T+1|1} \end{pmatrix} \right\}. \tag{11.11}$$

As before, this final form solution exists if AC does not contain a unit root. So Theorem 11.2 gives a necessary condition for the existence of a policy equilibrium since it states a sufficient condition for non-existence, given that the inverse in (11.11) is well defined. To see that, note that the Toeplitz matrix is exactly the same as that in (11.7). Note also that the information set contains a well-defined terminal condition, as before.

Given that the inverse of T_T exists, we rewrite (11.11) as

$$\begin{pmatrix} y_{1|1} \\ \cdot \\ \cdot \\ \cdot \\ y_{T|1} \end{pmatrix} = \begin{bmatrix} R_{i11} & . & . & . & R_{i1T} \\ \cdot & \cdot & & & \cdot \\ \cdot & & \cdot & & \cdot \\ \cdot & & & \cdot & \cdot \\ R_{iT1} & . & . & . & R_{iTT} \end{bmatrix} \begin{pmatrix} u^i_{1|1} \\ \cdot \\ \cdot \\ \cdot \\ u^i_{T|1} \end{pmatrix} + \begin{pmatrix} b_{i1|1} \\ \cdot \\ \cdot \\ \cdot \\ b_{iT|1} \end{pmatrix}, \quad \text{or } y = R_i u^i + b_i, \tag{11.12}$$

where $R_i = T_T^{-1}B_{iT}$, $b_i = T_T^{-1}\left\{E(K_i \mid \Omega_1) + (A' : 0)' y_0 + (0 : C')y_{T+1|1}\right\}$, and $B_{iT} = I \otimes B_i$. If player i satisfies the Golden Rule, the instrument coefficient matrix, B_i, can be inverted. If B_i can be inverted, B_{iT} can also be inverted. Hence, if player i satisfies the Golden Rule, then R_i can be inverted too, $R_i^{-1} = B_{iT}^{-1}T_T$, and we have

$$u^i = R_i^{-1}(\bar{y}^i - b_i) \quad \text{where} \quad \bar{y}^i = \left[\bar{y}_1^{i\prime} : \bar{y}_2^{i\prime} : \ldots : \bar{y}_T^{i\prime}\right]', \tag{11.13}$$

which implies

$$y = \bar{y}^i. \tag{11.14}$$

From Equation (11.14) it clearly follows that

$$y_{t|1} = \bar{y}_t^i \quad \text{for } t = 1, \ldots, T. \tag{11.15}$$

Now assume that player k also satisfies the Golden Rule. It then follows that

$$y_{t|1} = \bar{y}_t^k \quad \text{for } t = 1, \ldots, T. \tag{11.16}$$

However, the realized values of the target variables implied by Equations (11.15) and (11.16) cannot be mutually satisfied, at least in period 1, unless $\bar{y}_t^i = \bar{y}_t^k$; and, therefore, no equilibrium can exist. ■

Theorem 11.2 defines a necessary condition for the existence of a policy equilibrium. But it is not *sufficient* to demonstrate the existence of such an equilibrium. However, as a corollary to Theorem 11.2, we can state the following theorem.

Theorem 11.3 (*policy ineffectiveness in Feedback Nash equilibrium with REs*). If one, and only one, player satisfies the Golden Rule, all the other players' policies are ineffective with respect to the targets shared with the first player.

Proof. Obvious from Theorem 12.2, since (11.15), (11.16) would otherwise follow, where $\bar{y}_t^i \neq \bar{y}_t^k$ in at least one element.■

Comment 11.4. Theorem 11.3 gives a sufficient condition for policy ineffectiveness, but it does not assure the existence of an equilibrium, which might still fail to occur. Put differently, Theorem 11.2 gives a necessary condition for an equilibrium to exist because it states a sufficient condition for the opposite. However, if Theorem 11.3 is satisfied, then Theorem 11.2 is not (and vice versa).

Comment 11.5. In the Nash equilibrium, the optimal policy of each player is such as to minimize his preference function given the equilibrium policies of all the other players. In the open loop solution, this is required in the initial period; whereas in the feedback case, the condition must be satisfied in all periods.

11.5 Examples: Controllability with REs and multiple policymakers

11.5.1 A simple New Keynesian model with policy interactions

To illustrate the usefulness of our results we take a simple model with fiscal and monetary interactions, and examine the conditions under which the equilibrium may exist and the conditions where it cannot exist. For the sake of transparency, we work in two stages: first we analyze the case in which there are forward-looking expectations but no inertia, and then the case where there are backward-looking dynamics as well. We do this to expose all the elements in the optimal policy reaction functions. These elements can be seen explicitly in Equations (11.22) and (11.23) below for the first case, but the corresponding reaction functions for the second case are too complicated to give the same insight. That makes our case. It is easier to check non-existence using our targets-instruments approach than it is to compute the equilibrium itself. Note in particular, that our tests rule out equilibria that do not exist (necessary conditions). Of the remainder which may exist, it is easy to check that they do exist. In fact, in Equation (11.19) below the sub-matrices of R_T are such that R_T is itself nonsingular (a sufficient condition).

As an example, consider a simple economy with a New Keynesian structure:

$$\pi_t = (1-\lambda)\beta E_t\pi_{t+1} + \lambda\pi_{t-1} + \kappa x_t + \phi f_t + v_t, \tag{11.17}$$

$$x_t = E_t x_{t+1} - \sigma(i_t - E_t\pi_{t+1}) + \chi f_t + \varepsilon_t, \tag{11.18}$$

where ε_t and v_t are white noise; π_t is the inflation rate; x_t is the output gap relative to a non-market clearing trend or relative to the natural rate of output arising from monopolistic competition in the goods markets (Blanchard and Kiyotaki, 1987), or from tax distortions elsewhere in the economy (Alesina and Tabellini, 1987). Finally, f_t is some fiscal policy instrument, and i_t is the nominal interest rate. We assume a large value of T, so that the dynamic effects of any external shocks will have been absorbed long before the policy exercise is complete.

This model has the following reduced form:

$$\begin{bmatrix}\pi_t\\ x_t\end{bmatrix} = \begin{bmatrix}1 & -\kappa\\ 0 & 1\end{bmatrix}^{-1} \cdot \left\{\begin{bmatrix}(1-\lambda)\beta & 0\\ \sigma & 1\end{bmatrix} E_t\begin{bmatrix}\pi_{t+1}\\ x_{t+1}\end{bmatrix} + \begin{bmatrix}\lambda & 0\\ 0 & 0\end{bmatrix}\begin{bmatrix}\pi_{t-1}\\ x_{t-1}\end{bmatrix} + \begin{bmatrix}\phi\\ \chi\end{bmatrix} f_t - \sigma\begin{bmatrix}0\\ 1\end{bmatrix} i_t + \begin{bmatrix}v_t\\ \varepsilon_t\end{bmatrix}\right\}. \tag{11.19}$$

The monetary authority's (central bank) loss function is

$$B = E_t \sum_{t=1}^{T} \beta^t \frac{1}{2}\left[\alpha_B x_t^2 + \eta_B \pi_t^2\right]. \tag{11.20}$$

The fiscal authority's (government) loss function is

$$G = E_t \sum_{t=1}^{T} \beta^t \frac{1}{2}\left[\alpha_G (x_t - k)^2 + \eta_G \pi_t^2\right]. \tag{11.21}$$

Obviously the monetary authority controls i_t, whereas f_t is the government's control variable. This model is simple to solve explicitly for the equilibrium outcomes when that equilibrium exists. To ensure tractability, however, we consider first the case without inflation inertia (i.e., with purely forward-looking behavior): $\lambda = 0$.

In the discretionary equilibrium, the optimal fiscal policy is given by

$$\begin{aligned} f_t = &-\frac{(\alpha\chi + \kappa\eta_G(\kappa\chi + \phi))\varepsilon_t}{\alpha_G\chi^2 + \eta_G(\kappa\chi + \phi)^2} - \frac{(\alpha_G\chi\sigma + \eta_G(\kappa\chi + \phi)(\kappa\sigma + \beta))E(\pi_{t+1})}{\alpha_G\chi^2 + \eta_G(\kappa\chi + \phi)^2} \\ &- \frac{(\alpha_G\chi + \kappa\eta_G(\kappa\chi + \phi))Ex_{t+1}}{\alpha_G\chi^2 + \eta_G(\kappa\chi + \phi)^2} \\ &+ \frac{\sigma(\alpha_G\chi + \kappa\eta_G(\kappa\chi + \phi))i_t}{\alpha_G\chi^2 + \eta_G(\kappa\chi + \phi)^2} + \frac{\alpha_G\chi\kappa}{\alpha_G\chi^2 + \eta_G(\kappa\chi + \phi)^2} \end{aligned} \tag{11.22}$$

and the optimal monetary policy is

$$\begin{aligned} i_t = &\frac{\varepsilon_t}{\sigma} + \frac{(\eta_B\kappa\beta + \alpha_B\sigma + \eta_B\kappa^2\sigma)E(\pi_{t+1})}{\sigma(\alpha_B + \eta_B\kappa^2)} \\ &+ \frac{(\alpha_B\chi + \eta_B\kappa^2\chi + \eta_B\kappa\phi)f_t}{\sigma(\alpha_B + \eta_B\kappa^2)} + \frac{Ex_{t+1}}{\sigma}. \end{aligned} \tag{11.23}$$

By imposing the RE constraint, we can obtain the Nash equilibrium outcomes as

$$i_t = \frac{\varepsilon_t}{\sigma} + \frac{\alpha_G\chi(\chi\eta_B\kappa^2 + \alpha_B(-\beta\chi + \sigma\phi + \chi))k}{(\alpha_B\eta_G(\kappa\chi + \phi) - \alpha_G\chi\eta_B\kappa)\phi\sigma}, \tag{11.24}$$

$$f_t = \frac{(-\beta\alpha_B + \alpha_B + \eta_B\kappa^2)\alpha_G\chi k}{\phi(\alpha_B\eta_G(\kappa\chi + \phi) - \alpha_G\chi\eta_B\kappa)}, \tag{11.25}$$

$$x_t = -\frac{\kappa\eta_B\alpha_G\chi k}{-\alpha_G\chi\eta_B\kappa + \alpha_B\eta_G(\kappa\chi + \phi)}, \tag{11.26}$$

$$\pi_t = \frac{\alpha_B\alpha_G\chi k}{-\alpha_G\chi\eta_B\kappa + \alpha_B\eta_G(\kappa\chi + \phi)}, \tag{11.27}$$

which are already fairly complicated expressions to analyze. In fact, without computing limits for particular values of the parameters, or for combinations of zero restrictions on the α and η parameters, it is not immediately obvious from (11.24)–(11.27) when a policy equilibrium and equilibrium outcomes do or do not exist; nor when one player might find that he has no influence over that part of the solution of particular concern to him. On the other hand, it is extremely easy to ascertain the existence of policy equilibrium and/or policy neutrality by simply using our theorems. For the sake of conciseness we do not perform this task here, but move directly to apply our theorems to the more complex case in which there are both REs *and* inertia.

11.5.2 A more general but more complicated case

We reconsider the same model as in the previous sub-section, but now allow inflation inertia ($\lambda \neq 0$) and more general preferences:

$$B_t = E_t \sum_{t=1}^{T} \beta^t \frac{1}{2}\left[\alpha_B \left(x_t - x_B\right)^2 + \eta_B \left(\pi_t - \pi_B\right)^2\right], \tag{11.28}$$

$$G_t = E_t \sum_{t=1}^{T} \beta^t \frac{1}{2}\left[\alpha_G \left(x_t - x_G\right)^2 + \eta_G \left(\pi_t - \pi_G\right)^2\right], \tag{11.29}$$

$$\pi_t = (1-\lambda)\beta E_t \pi_{t+1} + \lambda \pi_{t-1} + \kappa x_t + \phi f_t + v_t, \tag{11.30}$$

$$x_t = E_t x_{t+1} - \sigma\left(i_t - E_t \pi_{t+1}\right) + \chi f_t + \varepsilon_t, \tag{11.31}$$

where ε_t and v_t are demand shocks from a stochastic process with a known distribution.

Note that we have two linearly independent target variables here (inflation and output) with, by assumption, two mutually inconsistent sets of target values across the players: $x_B \neq x_G$ and $\pi_B \neq \pi_G$. And this time, there is no need to impose the inertia restriction: $\lambda = 0$.

As before, the model's reduced form solution (11.19) demonstrates the linear independence of the instruments (sufficiency). Thus, *and without the need to compute an explicit solution*, the model's policy equilibria can be summarized as follows by using our theorems and

Table 11.1 *A complete taxonomy*

Game	Real output gap	Inflation rate
1. $\alpha_B, \eta_B, \alpha_G, \eta_G \neq 0$	Both players affect output	Both players affect inflation
2. $\alpha_B = 0$	Both players affect output	$\pi = \pi_B$
3. $\eta_B = 0$	$x = x_B$	Both players affect inflation
4. $\alpha_G = 0$	Both players affect output	$\pi = \pi_G$
5. $\eta_G = 0$	$x = x_G$	Both players affect inflation
6. $\alpha_B = 0$ and $\alpha_G = 0$		The equilibrium does not exist
7. $\eta_B = 0$ and $\eta_G = 0$		The equilibrium does not exist
8. $\alpha_B = 0$ and $\eta_G = 0$	$x = x_G$	$\pi = \pi_B$
9. $\eta_B = 0$ and $\alpha_G = 0$	$x = x_B$	$\pi = \pi_G$

target-instrument counting rules. Table 11.1 provides a complete taxonomy of all possible cases. The complete taxonomy is included only to show that in every conceivable instance (or even in cases that some might consider "pathological," like cases 6 and 9) our theorems can help in providing information as to the existence and nature of the equilibrium.

The value of our results is that they allow us to determine instantly (a) when an equilibrium does not exist; and (b) who will find that their policies have become ineffective, when it does exist.

In support of Table 11.1, it is important to note that some of the cases identified are unlikely to be encountered in practice. But many of them are cases that the literature deals with on a daily basis – including those where an equilibrium does not exist, or where one player finds his policies to be ineffective and therefore subject to time inconsistency effects by others. Case 1, "no overall control", is surely the most general specification. But the literature on independent and conservative central banks fits into case 2: the central bank targets low inflation exclusively. Cases 3 and 4, with the reverse assignments, appear unlikely.

Cases 6 and 7, where equilibrium outcomes do not exist, are perhaps the most interesting. In case 6 both policy authorities agree that inflation is the overriding problem, albeit with differing target values and/or priorities (Europe in the 1980s; the USA in the 1970s; South America post-1950; Germany in the 1920s). Likewise, case 7 is that where both agree that recession/depression is the main problem (Japan in its lost decade of the 1990s; the USA and Europe in the 1930s, in 2001, and since 2007).

The last two cases then define policy assignments that "decouple" the policy problem into two separate components. Case 8 has monetary policy assigned to inflation control, and fiscal policy to output stabilization – a textbook paradigm widely used by policymakers. For example, the euro area is predicated on national governments being concerned only with output stabilization since, by statute, they can have no influence on the common monetary policy,[10] while the ECB is designed to focus on inflation control to the virtual exclusion of output stabilization. Finally, case 9 has the reverse assignment (sometimes discussed in the context of exchange rate targeting).

We can also give a simple heuristic interpretation of our results. In case 1, we have two players who simultaneously trade off inflation and output because neither can control the model. For each of them, we can say that the attempt to control output has an implicit cost in terms of inflation and each imposes an externality on the other policymaker that affects his utility. This makes their implicit "instrument sets" bounded and guarantees that the Nash equilibrium exists. By contrast, if policymakers do not trade off, they have no implicit costs; the instruments are then unbounded and equilibrium may fail to exist. In fact an equilibrium fails to exist even if they are interested in the same target variable but do not share the target values (cases 6 and 7).[11] If also the same target values were shared, an infinite set of equilibria (in the space of instruments) would arise.

[10] However, being unable to influence inflation directly (they have no instrument assigned to that target) does not mean that government actions do not affect inflation, or that they do not need to account for inflation when setting fiscal policy. In fact they do affect inflation, and take it into account, as a result of the spillovers from the actions induced in their opponent: see the second term in Equation (11.22).

[11] Recall that a bounded instrument set is a sufficient, not a necessary, condition for existence (Dasgupta and Maskin, 1986). Section 6.3 discussed the controllability implications of introducing instrument costs.

11.5.3 *The role of instrument costs: a further extension*

Adding instrument costs produces the following economic model:

$$B_t = E_t \sum_{t=1}^{T} \beta^t \frac{1}{2}\left[\alpha_B (x_t - x_B)^2 + \eta_B (\pi_t - \pi_B)^2 + \theta_B s_t^2\right], \tag{11.32}$$

$$G_t = E_t \sum_{t=1}^{T} \beta^t \frac{1}{2}\left[\alpha_G (x_t - x_G)^2 + \eta_G (\pi_t - \pi_G)^2 + \theta_G b_t^2\right], \tag{11.33}$$

$$\pi_t = (1-\lambda)\beta E_t \pi_{t+1} + \lambda \pi_{t-1} + \kappa x_t + \phi f_t + v_t, \tag{11.34}$$

$$x_t = E_t x_{t+1} - \sigma(i_t - E_t \pi_{t+1}) + \chi f_t + \varepsilon_t, \tag{11.35}$$

$$s_t = i_t, \tag{11.36}$$

$$b_t = f_t. \tag{11.37}$$

This time an equilibrium *always* exists, because no player can control the system, unless we have one of the two cases in which the policy problem separates into two parts: ($\alpha_G = 0$, $\eta_B = 0$) and ($\alpha_B = 0$, $\eta_G = 0$). But even in those two cases, where both players care only about their own controls, and both fully control their own sub-systems, the equilibrium will again exist since there are no shared target variables between them. But it is not an equilibrium in which the players can get exactly what they want. Arguably, this is the most likely situation in practice. Policymakers seldom like to use their instruments too vigorously if they can avoid it.

11.6 Lessons from this chapter

This chapter has generalized our approach to the case where REs of future behavior are included in the model, and it has extended the result to sufficient conditions for policy neutrality and to necessary conditions for the existence of the Nash equilibrium in the case of dynamic games (multiple policymakers) where the players also face RE constraints and forward-looking variables. We have shown that if one player controls an economic system given some exogenous expectations, then that player is also able to control it when expectations are endogenously formed by an RE mechanism. As a consequence, all theorems stated by the new theory of economic policy also extend to the RE context since they are founded on the controllability exercised by that player. Rational private expectations will recognize that and adjust.

In a strategic context, the sufficient conditions for policy neutrality and the necessary conditions for equilibrium existence are also related to the relationship between the number of independent instruments and targets associated with each player. This applies to both exogenous and endogenous expectations. Thus if neutrality emerges under exogenous expectations, it also occurs when the model contains REs.

To avoid confusion it is helpful to stress that, in a model where a player cannot control the underlying economic system with exogenous expectations, the inclusion of REs may imply the emergence of policy neutrality, as it changes the underlying policy coefficients. The most prominent example of this effect is the Barro–Gordon case. This is not inconsistent with our findings. In fact, the new theory of economic policy states sufficient, not necessary, conditions for policy neutrality.

Using a simple New Keynesian framework, we have also illustrated how to explore a model's policy characteristics without having to solve for the underlying equilibria explicitly: that is, how to determine the existence of a Nash equilibrium, the conditions under which no equilibrium exists, and who gets to dominate in those equilibria (or who will find their policies to have become ineffective) – all without having to compute and evaluate those equilibria explicitly.

The importance of this theory of economic policy therefore lies first in the fact that it settles an old issue (policy controllability) in the only setting (policy games) in which it can be consistently placed to overcome the Lucas critique. Second, it does so by returning to the propositions of the Tinbergen–Theil theory. Third, and most important, its two fundamental propositions appear to be essential for model building, since they state conditions for the mutual consistency of optimal strategies by all players, and thus for the existence of an equilibrium to the game. This is the key result because it underwrites the effectiveness of our usual policy instruments.

Lastly, we have related our results, somewhat indirectly, to the existence of RE equilibria as determined by the well-known counting rule of explosive roots assuring system stability. This shows that our methods could be used just as well to assess the possibility and stability of policy equilibria in models where the private sector follows some learning process – as recently popularized in the work of Evans and Honkapohja (2003) and Eusepi and Preston (2010) – or where the existence of an equilibrium may be related to the E-stability property. To put that idea on a firmer footing, we turn in the next chapter to the question of dynamic controllability, as opposed to multi-period static controllability in a dynamic framework.

Appendix 11A. A generalization to multiple leads and lags

Consider a general linear RE model, with p lags and g leads (expectations) terms. This can be converted to a first-order model, such as in (11.1), as follows. The (p, g) model is of the form

$$y_t = A(\mathrm{L})y_t + \sum_{i\in N} B_i u_t^i + C(\mathrm{L}^{-1})y_{t+1/t} + v_t \qquad t = 1,\ldots,T, \tag{11A.1}$$

where $A(\mathrm{L}) = A_0 + A_1\mathrm{L} + A_2\mathrm{L}^2 + \cdots + A_p\mathrm{L}^p$ and $C(\mathrm{L}^{-1}) = C_0 + C_1\mathrm{L}^{-1} + \cdots + C_g\mathrm{L}^{-g}$, with $A_0 = 0$ and $C_0 = 0$, are both polynomials in the lag operator $\mathrm{L}y_t = y_{t-1}$. In such models, we can always rewrite (11A.1) by stacking the variables as follows:

$$\begin{aligned}\begin{pmatrix} y_{t+g-1} \\ \cdot \\ y_t \\ \cdot \\ y_{t-p+1} \end{pmatrix} &= \begin{bmatrix} 0 & \cdot & \cdot & \cdot & 0 \\ \cdot & 0 & \cdot & \cdot & 0 \\ 0 & A_1 & \cdot & \cdot & A_p \\ \cdot & I & \cdot & \cdot & 0 \\ 0 & \cdot & 0 & I & 0 \end{bmatrix} \begin{pmatrix} y_{t+g-2} \\ \cdot \\ y_{t-1} \\ \cdot \\ y_{t-p} \end{pmatrix} \\ &+ \begin{bmatrix} 0 & I & 0 & \cdot & 0 \\ \cdot & \cdot & \cdot & I & 0 \\ C_g & \cdot & \cdot & C_1 & 0 \\ 0 & \cdot & \cdot & \cdot & 0 \\ 0 & \cdot & \cdot & \cdot & 0 \end{bmatrix} \begin{pmatrix} y_{t+g|t} \\ \cdot \\ y_{t+1|t} \\ \cdot \\ y_{t-p+2|t} \end{pmatrix} + \sum_{i\in N} B_i u_t^i + v_t,\end{aligned} \tag{11A.2}$$

or, in obvious notation,

$$\tilde{y}_t = \tilde{A}\tilde{y}_{t-1} + \sum_{i \in N} B_i u_t^i + \tilde{C}\tilde{y}_{t+1|t} + v_t, \tag{11A.3}$$

which has exactly the same form as the model at (11.1) of the main text. Equation (11.1) and those that follow do not imply any loss in generality.

12 *Credibility, dynamic controllability and rational expectations*

Summary. Economic theory does not have a general model of how announcements of future policies affect economic performance, or of how such announcements can be used to manage expectations. In this chapter we show that the dynamic controllability conditions continue to hold under REs or forward-looking behavior. In fact we find that, when those conditions are satisfied, the presence of REs may even enhance our power to control an economy over time using policy announcements. Good communication will therefore be essential. These results are crucial because they show that underlying policy equilibria will still generally exist, even if some traditional policy exercises have been special cases that lead to invariance or time inconsistency. We establish limits to time-inconsistent behavior – chiefly where policymakers are impatient and lack sufficient policy instruments. This chapter therefore provides a theoretical underpinning for the recent literature on anchoring expectations in order to make monetary policy effective enough to achieve or maintain low inflation.

12.1 Introduction

Policymakers routinely use announcements as policy instruments to influence future expectations and, through them, future results. Announcements and signaling effects in fact imply that the announcement of a change in policy will typically affect agents' behavior, even before the change is actually made. Rational policymakers should therefore internalize announcement effects and use the signals strategically. The economic policy literature, however, does not have a formal model of whether, and under what conditions, policy announcements can be used to systematically affect economic performance. The conventional wisdom, starting with the Lucas critique, has been that policy announcements are likely to prove ineffective or inconsistent with private expectations. That in turn is inconsistent with the very evident attempts by governments and central banks to manage expectations. In that case, is it reasonable that they should try?

Although announcements are often used strategically by policymakers in many areas,[1] the work of Barro (1974), Sargent and Wallace (1975) and Lucas (1976) has led many economists to regard policy announcements and commitments to achieve certain policy targets with suspicion in a world with forward-looking expectations. Time inconsistency and REs are said to imply that such commitments cannot be considered credible and would inevitably lead to Pareto inferior outcomes. If that were true, policy announcements could have no effect. However, the credibility problem can be solved in a repeated game context (Kreps and Wilson, 1982; Milgrom and Roberts, 1982). In that context, there would be no need for the private sector to adjust their expectations of the outcomes as a result of the government's interventions. As for reputation, the policymaker can always mimic a *forthright type* who honors his policy announcements. In this context, the final few periods of the game apart, policy signals are always credible. Applications have been made to a vast array of problems with credibility aspects to them.[2]

In this chapter we approach the credibility problem from a fresh perspective, by considering REs within the traditional Tinbergen framework and by showing that under certain circumstances the usual dichotomy between REs, on the one hand, and the ineffectiveness or time inconsistency of policy actions on the other, may not arise. Specifically, we show that, if expectations are rational, policy invariance and time inconsistency emerge *only* in a special case of a short run Tinbergen flexible targets problem. In a more general framework – that is, in an unconstrained optimization (free from any externally imposed preferences or particular optimization techniques) and where policymakers can be said to control the economic system either statically or dynamically – REs will not only present

[1] See Persson and Tabellini (1990) for a general survey; and Blinder, Ehrmann, Fratzscher, de Haan and Jansen (2008), Woodford (2005), or Rudebusch and Williams (2008) for examples in central banking. Instances in the financial markets will be found in Balduzzi, Elton and Green (2001), Andersen, Bollerslev, Diebold and Vega (2003), Fair (2003) and Faust, Rogers, Wang and Wright (2007).

[2] See, among others, Barro and Gordon (1983), Backus and Driffill (1984, 1985). For detailed surveys and discussions, see Persson and Tabellini (1990, 2000).

the policymakers with no problem of how to set their policies consistently but may actually add to the scope of their policy instruments, in effect giving them additional sources of policy power. Further, given sufficient time, the opportunities for time-inconsistent behavior shrink to zero, unless policymakers have no control over their targets at all. Our contribution is therefore to bridge the gap between actual practice and what traditional policy models tell us; and to determine the conditions under which announcements can be successfully used in support of a particular set of policies or policy strategy.

In order to achieve our aim, we have to solve a problem with complex dynamics and identify the limits to time-inconsistent behavior. Controllability under REs requires the solution to a nonlinear problem in the dynamics of expectations formation plus the existence of sufficient policy impacts. However, this solution boils down to a no unit root test (an econometric problem) and a rank condition (an existence test). In reality, since the model is likely to be a linearization based on nonlinear behavior in the markets, the expectations the policymakers need to announce, or that the private agents need to check for consistency with those announcements, must now be extended to account for any systematic effects of the unavoidable linearization errors that arise in the expectations dynamics.

The chapter is organized as follows. Section 12.2 presents the general baseline dynamic framework. Section 12.3 extends this set-up for nonlinear models and shows how to deal with approximation errors in the expectations dynamics. Section 12.4 derives conditions for static and dynamic controllability in this model and demonstrates that dynamic controllability can be enhanced or extended by REs. Section 12.5 completes that analysis with the RE version of Wonham's stabilizability theorem. Section 12.6 is rather dense. It first underlines the importance of the results of the previous sections by showing that, unless policymakers are both impatient and have very few policy instruments at their disposal, time-inconsistent behavior would be of limited interest – even outside a world of repeated games. Then it takes these ideas one step further by emphasizing the importance of policy communication when (economic) stabilization is the key issue. In addition, it provides a simple illustration of the value of our results using a New Keynesian model of the economy. Finally, a second example is introduced in order to stress the importance of good communication in monetary policy design. Section 12.7 concludes with the implications for policy design.

12.2 The economic model with a single policymaker

In this chapter we focus on the perspective of a single policymaker only. Without loss of generality, we again write the generic linear RE model in reduced form, as Equation (11.4), which is reproduced below for convenience:

$$y_t = Ay_{t-1} + Bu_t + Cy_{t+1|t} + v_t \quad \text{for } t = 1,\ldots,T. \tag{12.1}$$

Recall that $y \in R^S$ and $u \in R^M$.

This model can now be solved from the perspective of any particular period, say $t = 1$, by putting it into its final form conditional on the information set available that period, giving the same result as in (11.5):

$$\begin{pmatrix} y_{1/1} \\ : \\ : \\ : \\ y_{T|1} \end{pmatrix} = \begin{bmatrix} I & -C & 0 & . & 0 \\ -A & I & & . & . \\ 0 & & . & & 0 \\ . & . & & . & -C \\ 0 & . & 0 & -A & I \end{bmatrix}^{-1} . \tag{12.2}$$

$$\left\{ \begin{bmatrix} B & 0 & . & . & 0 \\ 0 & . & & & . \\ . & & . & & . \\ . & & & . & 0 \\ 0 & . & . & 0 & B \end{bmatrix} \begin{pmatrix} u_{1|1} \\ . \\ . \\ . \\ u_{T|1} \end{pmatrix} + \begin{pmatrix} v_{1|1} \\ . \\ . \\ . \\ v_{T|1} \end{pmatrix} + \begin{pmatrix} Ay_0 \\ 0 \\ . \\ . \\ 0 \end{pmatrix} + \begin{pmatrix} 0 \\ . \\ . \\ 0 \\ Cy_{T+1|1} \end{pmatrix} \right\}.$$

As in Chapter 11, the equation to which (12.2) is the solution makes it clear that neither the policymakers nor the private sector are required to move off their expected paths (or make expectation errors) for the policies to work. In fact, Equation (12.2) and Equation (12.3) below show just the opposite: that those expectations are exactly consistent with what private agents and policymakers *expect* the policy outcomes will be. The only question is whether policies, or announcements of policies, can be found that would shift the expectations path itself by the required amount.

The task of this chapter is to derive the conditions under which this can be done. That means we aim to determine when it is possible to shift expectations in such a way that the economy's final outcomes can be expected to reach certain target values at specified points of time, *and* when it is not possible.[3]

Finally, since (as shown in Chapter 11) the inverse in Equation (12.2) exists given that AC satisfies the no unit root condition, we can now rewrite the model in final form as follows:

$$y = Ru + b, \tag{12.3}$$

where the matrices and vectors are defined in (11.8).

12.3 Nonlinearities and the expectations dynamics

It is very common to find that a linear model such as (12.1) is the result of linearizing some more complicated nonlinear system. In fact, it is almost certain that this will be the case, if the underlying markets or economy contain any nonlinear behavior, because REs are not well, or even uniquely, defined in nonlinear models. This is because

$$\begin{aligned} E(y_t) &= E\{f(y_{t-1}, y_{t+1}, u_t, v_t)\} \\ &\neq f(y_{t-1}, E(y_{t+1}), E(u_t), E(v_t)), \end{aligned} \tag{12.4}$$

which means that the difference $[y_t - f(E(y_t) \mid E(u_t), E(v_t))]$ is not a pure random variable with mean zero. Since it is neither possible to generate a closed form analytic solution, nor practical to generate a numerical solution by alternating the steps of a contraction mapping (with no guarantee of convergence) with the numerical integrations needed to evaluate the expectations, the only practical way out is to create a linearization on a first-order certainty equivalence basis. But that means that the economic behavior being modeled will be subject to linearization and certainty equivalence errors, especially in the expectations process, even if there are only small shocks or small policy changes (or announcements of small policy changes). Both policymakers and private agents need to take these errors into account when

[3] We can operate with (12.2) without loss of generality. The extension of (12.2) to any number of leads and lags was detailed in Appendix 11A. It is also easy to show that this final form solution generally exists since the inverse matrix in (12.2) is always well defined, as long as the matrix product AC satisfies the no unit root condition: see Chapter 11.

computing their policies or checking that the announced outcomes of those policies coincide with their private expectations.[4]

In our case, the expectations are highly nonlinear in the parameters of the dynamic adjustment process, although they are linear in the remaining elements of (12.2) and in variations in $u_{t|j}$ (or in variations of C, but not both together). One can, in fact, evaluate the impact of these nonlinearities from the Toeplitz matrix in (12.2):

$$\frac{\partial y_{\bullet|1}}{\partial p_{ij}} = -T_T^{-1} \frac{\partial T_T}{\partial p_{ij}} T_T^{-1} \{[diagC]u_{\bullet|1} + \text{terms in } (y_0, y_{T+1|1}, v_{\bullet|1})\}, \quad (12.5)$$

where $y_{\bullet|1}$, $u_{\bullet|1}$, $v_{\bullet|1}$ are the stacked vectors y, u and v from (12.2) conditioned on Ω_1; and p_{ij} represents the (i,j)-th element from the matrix pair $[A,B]$, for $i = 1,\ldots,ST$ and $j = 1,\ldots,(S + M)T$. We can therefore rewrite (12.5) as

$$\frac{\partial y_{\bullet|1}}{\partial p_{ij}} = -T_T^{-1} \frac{\partial T_T}{\partial p_{ij}} y_{\bullet|1}, \quad (12.6)$$

which is highly nonlinear in the elements of A and B, i.e., in the parameters that control the dynamics of the expectations process and hence of the expected outcomes. Notice also that $\partial T_T / \partial p_{ij}$ is a matrix with -1 in the (i,j)-th position, but zeros elsewhere. Using (12.6), policymakers and private agents can correct their expected outcomes, or conduct their expectation checks, for the linearization errors that may have been a necessary part of generating a closed form solution to their particular problem. Equally, and more importantly, this development shows that the principle of controllability which follows will, in general, *not* be affected by linearization errors.

12.4 Dynamic controllability with forward-looking behavior

12.4.1 Dynamic controllability

As we know from the previous chapter, an economy (model) is said to be dynamically controllable if a sequence of instrument values $u_1,\ldots,u_t$

[4] The importance of taking these linearization errors explicitly into account is emphasized by the distinction, and numerical differences between the risky and stochastic paths studied in Juilliard (2011).

can be found that will reach any arbitrary values, $\bar{y}_t$, for the target variables in period t (at least in expectation) given an arbitrary starting point y_0. In this case we are not concerned with the period-by-period controllability of the target variables between periods 1 and $t - 1$. Starting from period 1, dynamic controllability therefore requires a sequence of intended instrument values, $u_{1|1},\ldots,u_{T|1}$ say, that guarantee that $\bar{y}_{t|1}$ is reached in period $t = T$. This is possible only if the sequence of policy multipliers and anticipatory effects in the t-th row block of (12.3), i.e., $[R_{t,1}\ldots\ldots R_{t,T}]$, is of full rank, given an arbitrary initial state y_0 and a specified terminal condition $y_{T+1|1}$. That is, $r[R_{t,1} \ldots R_{t,T}] = S$.

Theorem 12.1 (*sufficient condition for dynamic controllability with REs*). The economy represented by (12.1) is dynamically controllable over the sub-interval $(1, t)$, when $T \geq S$ and where $t < T$, if $r[R_{t,1} \ldots R_{t,S}] = S$.[5]

Proof. $\bar{y}_{t|1} = (R_{t,1}\ldots R_{t,T})u + b_{t|1}$ is reachable over $(1, t)$, using a Moore–Penrose generalized left-inverse in $u = (R_{t,1}\ldots R_{t,T})^{+}[\bar{y}_{t|1} - b_{t|1}]$, if $r[R_{t,1}\ldots R_{t,T}] = S$. But if $T \geq S$, then $r[R_{t,1}\ldots R_{t,T}] = r[R_{t,1}\ldots R_{t,S}] = S$, which provides the result.∎

Comment 12.1. Theorem 12.1 is an important generalization over the conventional case of dynamic controllability in backward-looking models. If $S > t$, which is entirely possible for small values of t, dynamic controllability will be available through the reactions of $y_{t|1}$ to the implemented policy choices $u_{1|1}\ldots u_{t|1}$; and through the anticipatory effects of announced or anticipated policy interventions that still lie in the future, $u_{t+1|1}\ldots u_{T|1}$. In other words, a policymaker can use policy announcements, in addition to actual interventions, to guide the course of the economy. In a conventional model that would not be possible since $R_{t,j} = 0$ for all $j > t$. In effect, the policymaker now has a greater number of policy "instruments" at his disposal than he would have had in an economy without anticipations.

Corollary 12.1. Hence all $y_{t|1}$ values, including the first period's targets $y_{1|1}$, are now dynamically controllable if the rank condition in Theorem

[5] This theorem provides a sufficient condition for dynamic controllability. The corresponding necessary condition involves a smaller sub-set of $R_{t,j}$ having full rank depending on how many policy instruments are available. Theorem 12.2 below provides the result for the general case when $M \geq 1$.

12.1 holds. This represents a significant extension over the conventional case where period $t = S$ is the earliest date at which we can guarantee controllability if there is a single policy instrument; or $t = S/2$ if there are two instruments, and so on. By contrast, $y_{1|1}$ is controllable here from the first period onward, even if there are insufficient instruments $M < S$, provided that $T \geq S$ and Theorem 12.1 both hold.

In effect, we have a result potentially far more powerful than static controllability. The astute policymaker will therefore realize that good communication lies at the heart of the policy problem if he wants to reach his policy targets in the early periods or at lower cost; a fact which has attracted considerable interest in the central banking literature (Woodford, 2005; Blinder, Ehrmann, Fratzscher, de Haan and Jansen, 2008; Rudebusch and Williams, 2008). The opportunity to increase their policy power has not escaped policymakers in practice. Compared with earlier times, policy announcements, and careful explanations of why the policy changes are necessary, are now routinely made when there are shifts in the policy stance and/or changes in the policy outlook.

Comment 12.2. Evidently dynamic controllability may also be possible with a reduced instrument set, compared with static controllability. There are two parts to this reduction: (a) the ability to use one or more instruments repeatedly rather than a group of several instruments used once and in parallel; and (b) the ability to augment, or even replace, parts of an existing instrument set with announcements of future policy changes.

Comment 12.3. There is also a distinction to be made in that the $u_{1|1} \ldots u_{t|1}$ values will be implemented decisions when it comes to the controllability of $y_{t|1}$; but the remaining $u_{t+1|1} \ldots u_{T|1}$, being announcements, may never actually be carried out. However, because they lie in the future from the perspective of $y_{t|1}$, any subsequent time inconsistency plays no role in the controllability of $y_{t|1}$ as long as they are genuinely held expectations at that point. We return to this discussion about the potential for time inconsistency in more detail in Section 12.6.

Comment 12.4. It is important to see why time inconsistency will not appear. Controllability at period t means that, barring unforeseen shocks, the policymaker will be able to reach his desired values for y_t in expectation.

Hence, $y_{t|t} = y_{t|1} = \bar{y}_t$ are fixed or at least known quantities. But $y_{1|t} = y_{1|1}$ is fixed by history and $u_{1|t} = u_{1|1}$ likewise. It is then easy to see that, if nothing else changes, $u_{t|t} = u_{t|1}$. The policymaker is of course free to set $u_{t|t} \neq u_{t|1}$. But he would never do so, because $\bar{y}_t$ is a first best value that he can reach given no information changes or unforeseen shocks. Policymakers have no incentive, still less strategic advantage or strategic interest in choosing to make themselves worse off than they need to be. Hence, to assert time inconsistency is to claim that rational policymakers would deliberately choose to make themselves worse off: a contradiction.

Summarizing this discussion, we now have the following.

Theorem 12.2 (*necessary condition for dynamic controllability with REs*). Forward-looking expectations or REs enhance the power to control an economy over time in that (a) policy announcements, made at $t = 1$, may be used to supplement and extend the impact of conventional policy instruments; and (b) controllability is now available, with a reduced instrument set, from a much earlier date; and, in particular, from $t = 1$ if $\mathrm{r}[R_{1,1}\ldots R_{1,S}] = S$.

Proof. See Corollary 12.1 and Comments 12.1 and 12.2.■

12.4.2 *A further generalization*

If only a sub-set of the variables in each vector y_t are genuine targets of policy (say, s of them), then we may delete the $S - s$ rows from each y_t, and from the blocks of policy multipliers $[R_{t,1}\ldots R_{t,T}]$ that correspond to the non-target variables, before moving on to evaluate our controllability conditions.

The *static controllability condition* will now be $s \leq M$, and the condensed R matrix just constructed must have rank sT. But it is no longer possible to characterize the associated sufficient condition in terms of the elements of B or T_T. Nevertheless, it will be easier to control this sub-set of policy targets than it is to control the whole economy.

For *dynamic controllability*, we can follow the same logic to apply Theorem 12.1 to the condensed system. We then get, as a sufficient condition, $\mathrm{r}[R_{t,1}\ldots\ldots R_{t,S}] = S$ for controllability over the interval $[1, t]$ – implying dynamic controllability from the first period as before. Once again, it is easier to control the sub-set of target variables than to control the entire economy by period t.

12.5 Stabilizability under REs

12.5.1 A theoretical analysis

We can apply the reasoning underlying Theorems 12.1 and 12.2 to show that any economy can also be stabilized to an arbitrary degree under rational, forward-looking expectations if it is dynamically controllable in the sense of Theorem 12.1. An arbitrary degree of stabilization means that policy rules can be found to make the economy follow an arbitrarily stable path, based on an arbitrary set of eigenvalues, such that it returns to the original path following a shock. Theorem 12.3 gives the RE analogue of the standard stabilizability theorem for backward-looking, or physical, systems that we encountered in Chapter 3.[6]

Theorem 12.3 (*stabilizability and REs*). For any economy represented by (12.1), with arbitrary matrices A, B and C, we can find a series of forward-looking policy rules, $u_{t|1} = \sum_{j=1}^{T} K_{tj} y_{j-1|1} + k_{t|1}$, say,[7] such that the controlled economy is stabilizable up to an arbitrary set of eigenvalues, if the economy is controllable in the sense of Theorem 12.1.

Proof. Equation (12.1), with arbitrary coefficient matrices A, B and C, can be reduced to its final form (12.2). Substituting the policy rule $u_{t|1} = \sum_{j=1}^{T} K_{tj} y_{j-1|1} + k_{t|1}$ for each $t = 1,\ldots,T$ shows that the controlled economy will behave as, similarly to (12.3),

$$\begin{pmatrix} y_{1|1} \\ \cdot \\ \cdot \\ \cdot \\ y_{T|1} \end{pmatrix} = \begin{bmatrix} R_{11} & \cdot & \cdot & \cdot & R_{1T} \\ \cdot & \cdot & & & \cdot \\ \cdot & & \cdot & & \cdot \\ \cdot & & & \cdot & \cdot \\ R_{T1} & \cdot & \cdot & \cdot & R_{TT} \end{bmatrix} \begin{bmatrix} K_{1,1} & K_{1,2} & \cdot & \cdot & K_{1,T} \\ K_{2,1} & \cdot & & & \cdot \\ \cdot & & \cdot & & \cdot \\ \cdot & & & \cdot & K_{T-1,T} \\ K_{T,1} & \cdot & \cdot & K_{T,T-1} & K_{T,T} \end{bmatrix} \cdot \begin{pmatrix} y_0 \\ y_{1|1} \\ \cdot \\ \cdot \\ y_{T-1|1} \end{pmatrix} + \begin{pmatrix} c_{1|1} \\ \cdot \\ \cdot \\ \cdot \\ c_{T|1} \end{pmatrix}, \tag{12.7}$$

[6] See Wonham (1974) and the discussion in Section 3.9.

[7] Note that this control rule for use in period $t < T$, employs actions and anticipates actions up to the end of the policy period T.

where $y_{0|1} = y_0$ and $c_{t|1} = b_{t|1} + T_T^{-1}Bk_{t|1}$ ($b_{t|1}$ is defined in (11.8)). Rewriting (12.7) in obvious notation, we now have

$$\tilde{y}_t = RK\tilde{y}_{t-1} + c, \tag{12.8}$$

where $\tilde{y}_t$ is the stacked vector on the left of (12.7).

For an economy to be stabilizable at t, it must possess the property that it would return to the initially expected path, whatever the initial conditions and shocks experienced up to that point, given that no further shocks or changes in expectations emerge (Wonham, 1974). This property will exist if the iteration matrix, RK, has its roots inside the unit circle. But we can go further. Any particular $y_{t|1}$ will follow an arbitrarily stable path if we can pick $K_{t1}.....K_{tT}$ to generate an arbitrary set of eigenvalues for that matrix for each t. Suppose we want to choose an iteration matrix $D = Z\Lambda Z^{-1}$, where Λ is a diagonal matrix of the chosen eigenvalues and Z is a matrix of the corresponding eigenvectors. Then, as long as $T > S$ and the matrix R has full rank ST (i.e., $M \geq S$, so that static controllability applies), we can calculate the required K from $K = R^{-1}Z\Lambda Z^{-1}$. But if $M < S$ and dynamic controllability applies (as in the theorem), then we can use a generalized left-inverse instead: $K = R^{+}Z\Lambda Z^{-1}$, with $R^{+} = (R'R)^{-1}R'$ as one obvious example. This generalized inverse always exists, given dynamic controllability, since $R'R$ has full rank with $\mathrm{r}[R] = MT$ by Sylvester's inequality. To see this, recall $R = T_T^{-1}(I \otimes B)$ where T_T^{-1} is a square $ST \times ST$ matrix of full rank and $(I \otimes B)$ is a block diagonal matrix with rank MT. Hence, by Sylvester's inequality, $\mathrm{r}[R] \geq ST + MT - ST = MT$. But if $M < S$, then $\mathrm{r}[I \otimes B]$ cannot be greater than MT by definition. Hence $\mathrm{r}[R] = MT$, which means that $(R'R)^{-1}$ exists and this value of R^{+} is always available. ■

Comment 12.5. Note that policy rules described in Theorem 12.3 are indeed both forward- and backward-looking in that they react *both* to expected future developments (including the effects of applying these rules in the future) *and* to feedback from past outcomes ("failures" in the usual sense) – in exactly the same way as the private agents in the economy are assumed to do.

Comment 12.6. Policies implying stabilizability are obviously not unique, even if the choice of Λ is unique. We could have used policies further in the past, or policy announcements about the future from the second and third terms in Equation (12.8), to derive Theorem 12.3 (given $T \geq S$). In any case, the generalized inverse is not unique.

Comment 12.7. Nevertheless, we can infer that an RE model that is dynamically controllable at $t = 1$ (as in Theorem 12.2) is also stabilizable from $t = 1$. Theorem 12.3 therefore generalizes on Wonham's original theorem where stabilizability is achieved for the first time only in period S.

Comment 12.8. Notice that it is *not* possible, in general, to dispense with the feed-forward, feedback nature of the policy rule here for the obvious reason that it has to control (or compensate for) both the feed-forward and the feedback behavior of the private agents in the model. However it would be possible to apply a block diagonalization to the matrix K just obtained in Theorem 12.3, and transform the policy instruments to match, in order to remove any dependence on past or expected future outcomes. A block diagonalization exists since $R^{+}D$ is square. However, in general the transformation will involve a Jordan canonical form and the off-diagonal elements may still cross time intervals. To implement such a rule, given the instruments we actually have, we would therefore have to reverse that transformation and recreate some kind of feed-forward, feedback rule.

Comment 12.9. The key lesson is therefore that, in models with forward-looking behavior, the closed loop (as opposed to just feedback) characteristics of our policy rules become of special importance. Closed loop means reacting to changes in expectations of future events as they appear, in addition to past outcomes as they deviate from plan. In backward-looking models, future events are represented by future exogenous variables. In such models, those variables do not influence current behavior (although economic performance might improve if they did). As a result, the distinction between closed loop and feedback rules is traditionally ignored as being unimportant numerically. But given forward-looking markets where current behavior and outcomes are directly dependent on expectations of the future, and where expectations of the future depend on the current outcomes, the distinction can be large (see Hughes Hallett, Di Bartolomeo and Acocella, 2012).

12.5.2 An illustration: stabilizability with and without forward-looking policies

We now construct some simple examples of this stabilizability result to illustrate the importance of using forward-looking policies when facing forward-looking behavior by the private sector. The examples are constructed to explain a paper by Cochrane (2011) which claims that the Taylor rule in a New Keynesian model will produce results that are typically unstable. The claim is correct, but not for the reason Cochrane supposes. The reason is, no rational policymaker would ever attempt to use a backward-looking policy rule to manage forward-looking behavior in the private sector.

For the purposes of illustration, consider a one-equation RE model with dynamics:

$$y_t = ay_{t-1} + by^e_{t+1} + cx_t + \varepsilon_t \quad \text{with } y^e_{t+1} = E_t(y_{t+1}). \tag{12.9}$$

Such a model can be derived from a conventional New Keynesian model of the type used by Mishkin (2002), say, to assess the effectiveness of Taylor rules for controlling inflation and stabilizing the output gap. That is, we can start from

$$\pi_t = (1-\lambda)\beta E_t\pi_{t+1} + \lambda\pi_{t-1} + \kappa z_t + \phi f_t + v_t, \tag{12.10}$$

$$z_t = \varsigma E_{t-1}z_t - \sigma(i_t - E_t\pi_{t+1}) + \chi f_t + \eta_t, \tag{12.11}$$

where (12.10) is an aggregate supply equation with dynamics, π_t is the rate of inflation, z_t the output gap; f_t is the stance of fiscal policy, i_t is the interest rate (monetary policy instrument); and v_t and η_t are random shocks.[8] Equation (12.11) is therefore a forward-looking IS curve. Eliminating z_t between (12.10) and (12.11) now yields

$$\pi_t = (1-\lambda)\beta E_t\pi_{t+1} + \lambda\pi_{t-1} - \kappa\sigma(i_t - E_t\pi_{t+1}) + \varepsilon_t, \tag{12.12}$$

where $\varepsilon_t = \kappa E_{t-1}z_t + (\kappa\chi + \phi)f_t + \kappa\eta_t + v_t$ represents a composite term of "shocks" exogenous to both monetary policy and the economy. This definition of ε_t involves a natural approximation in that $E_{t-1}z_t$ should, strictly speaking, be an endogenous (rational) expectation of the output gap. So classifying it as part of the composite error term is to recognize the reality that the private sector either does not have full REs for the output gap, or cannot measure them properly; or that the private sector is no

[8] Many New Keynesian models specify marginal costs, mc_t, as the push factor in inflation, in place of f_t. In this case (12.12) would have $\kappa\chi f_t + \phi mc_t$ in ε_t in place of the $(\kappa\chi + \phi)f_t$ term. This alternative specification would make no difference to the problem at hand therefore.

more able to separate cyclical from structural changes in the trend of output on time than the policymakers; the typical delay needed for the data to do that accurately is four years. Agents therefore usually use a simple forecasting or extrapolation device for $E_{t-1}z_t$ instead. Given that, we can recast (12.12) as a particular case of (12.9) where $b = (1 - \lambda)\beta + \kappa\sigma$; $a = \lambda$; $c = -\kappa\sigma$. Then, x_t is the policy instrument (interest rate); y_t is the policy target (inflation), and ε_t is the composite error term above.

Stabilization in expectation, consistent with our controllability analysis elsewhere in this book, can now be investigated using Theorem 12.3. Consider two alternative decision rules for controlling (12.9) in a more general setting:

(a) with no forward-looking elements,

$$x_t = k_1 y_{t-1} + k_2; \text{ and} \tag{12.13}$$

(b) with a forward-looking element,

$$x_t = k y_{t-1} + d y_{t+1}^e + k_2 \text{ say.} \tag{12.14}$$

We can substitute (12.13) and (12.14) into (12.9) to see the behavior of the economy under control in each case: respectively,

$$y_t = (a + ck_1) y_{t-1} + y_{t+1}^e + \varepsilon_t^*; \text{ and} \tag{12.15}$$

$$y_t = (a + ck) y_{t-1} + (b + cd) y_{t+1}^e + \varepsilon_t^*, \tag{12.16}$$

where $\varepsilon_t^* = \varepsilon_t + k_2$. Renormalizing (12.15) and (12.16) on the lead term, taking expectations conditional on the current information in period t, and dropping the superscript e for simplicity, leaves us with two alternatives to be stabilized:

$$y_{t+1} = b^{-1} y_t + b^{-1}(a + ck_1) y_{t-1} + b^{-1}\varepsilon_t^*, \text{or} \tag{12.17}$$

$$y_{t-1} = (b + cd)^{-1} y_t + (b + cd)^{-1}(a + ck_1) y_{t-1} + (b + cd)^{-1} \varepsilon_t^*. \tag{12.18}$$

It is already obvious that (12.17) presents us with only one opportunity, via k_1, to choose the coefficients and hence the roots of the economy under control. Yet there are two roots. In fact, it will not be possible to stabilize this economy with a simple feedback rule at all unless $b > 1$, let alone do so to an arbitrary pair of eigenvalues.

Equation (12.18), by contrast, gives us the opportunity to choose two coefficients, and hence both characteristic roots in the economy under control, given our freedom to choose both k and d. Hence, this system is stabilizable; that is stabilizable up to an arbitrary set of eigenvalues as in Theorem 12.3.

We can demonstrate these two claims as follows. The roots of Equation (12.17) are

$$\lambda_{1,2} = \frac{1}{2} b^{-1} \left\{ 1 \pm \left[1 + 4b\left(a + ck_1\right) \right]^{\frac{1}{2}} \right\}. \tag{12.19}$$

We can therefore only choose to have real roots (by choosing $k_1 > -(1 + 4ab)/4ac$, if $b,c > 0$ for example); or to have the product of the roots less than 1 (by setting $k_1 < (b - a)/c$ in (12.17), under the same conditions). But we cannot choose the size of the roots individually. In fact to minimize the larger of the two, the best we can do is set $k_1 = -a/c$. That will give us $\lambda_{1,2} = \{0, b^{-1}\}$, which means that we can stabilize the system with a simple feedback rule *only* if the system is stable already, i.e., if and only if $b > 1$. Otherwise we can never do so.

Notice that $b > 1$ is half of the usual saddle point property for stability under REs. In other words, a backward-looking feedback rule can *only* stabilize the backward-looking part of our model. Notice too that stabilizability is, in this case, determined by the coefficients of the model – not by the policy rule. So Cochrane (2011) is right to say that a forward-looking New Keynesian model *may* not be stabilized by a Taylor rule. More precisely, the correct inference is: a New Keynesian economy can be stabilized by a Taylor rule, but only when that model is already stable. So if instability follows, the fault lies not with the rule but with the model. Taylor rules do not, in themselves, destabilize the economy.

By contrast, if we use a forward-looking rule like (12.14), the controlled economy will behave as in (12.18). The roots of this system are

$$\lambda_{1,2} = \frac{1}{2}\left(b + cd\right)^{-1} \left\{ 1 \pm \left[1 + 4\left(b + cd\right)\left(a + ck\right) \right]^{\frac{1}{2}} \right\}, \tag{12.20}$$

which can be made arbitrarily close to zero – for example, by choosing $d = -b/c + \omega$ where $\omega > 1$, and $k = -a/c$. This implies roots of $\lambda_{1,2} = \frac{1}{2}\left(\omega^{-1} \pm \omega^{-1}\right) = \left\{0, \omega^{-1}\right\}$ in (12.20) which both lie within the unit circle. Stability is therefore assured in *all* possible circumstances. Indeed these roots are arbitrarily small (occupy an arbitrarily small interval) if ω is made large enough. In this case, an arbitrary degree of stability can be conferred on any model, including those that are unstable to start with. Moreover, the stabilization is done by the policy rule, not the model. The key difference is that, in this case, the forward-looking component in the rule, d, supplies the roots of the *stabilized* economy.

An analogy will help fix the point. If you face forward-looking behavior in the model or economy, but choose a backward-looking rule to deal with it, it is equivalent to having constructed a clear windscreen in your car (model) so that the passengers (agents) can see forward and anticipate what happens, and then reversing the seats and steering wheel so that the driver (policy rule) can only look out backward.

12.6 Applications

12.6.1 Expectations, announcements and the limits to time inconsistency

We summarize the results from Chapters 11 and 12 by comparing them with those of the traditional Tinbergen–Theil theory of economic policy. We can then discuss whether, and under what conditions, we will need an explicit announcement-based commitment mechanism to ensure the consistency and optimality of policies – that is, in order to be able to rule out the incentive for time-inconsistent behavior by policymakers.

For the purposes of comparison, the main differences between our ability to control an economy when forward-looking expectations are present, or when policymakers seek to influence future outcomes by making announcements about future policies, compared with the traditional Tinbergen–Theil theory of economic policy, are as follows:

1. The static controllability property is not affected, either in one single period or across a policy interval as a whole.
2. Dynamic controllability generalizes that result to include the possibility that a given number of targets can be controlled by a smaller number of instruments than in the Tinbergen–Theil case. As before, any number of targets can be controlled (ultimately by only one

instrument) if the policy horizon, T, is long enough. But we can also say that any number of policy targets can be controlled from the first period if the policy horizon is long enough.

3. In addition, there is an extension to generalize Wonham's stabilizability theorem from backward-looking physical systems to the ability to stabilize an economy in the presence of forward-looking expectations.

Chapter 11 and this chapter have also made a number of contributions that refine our understanding of where time-inconsistent behavior by policymakers may become a problem; and of where we need a commitment mechanism to ensure the consistency and optimality of the outcomes, and where we do not.

It is always important to examine the conditions that permit effective signaling and a proper commitment to future policy intentions. But it is equally important to recognize that there is a whole class of problems for which they are neither necessary, nor relevant – although clear communication is still required (to show that the necessary policy changes are justified and will, in the policymakers' own interest, be made). And it will typically be a *large class*, given that we can get full controllability, even in models with just one instrument and many targets, if $T \geq S$ is large enough.

Thus, time-inconsistent behavior is an exception, not the general rule. It will appear only with insufficient instruments, and when governments are both impatient and make announcements about the future that either are not believed or are not believable, or are thought to be ineffective.

Likewise, our results also explain when commitment technologies are needed and when they are not needed. So long as the no unit root condition and the rank condition in Theorem 11.1 are satisfied, the private sector knows that policymakers have controllability and can reach their desired target values (whatever they are) in all cases. There is no point in expecting anything else. The system is fully tied down by Theorem 11.1, and its solution from the perspective of any particular period can be seen by putting the system into final form conditional on the information set available in that period (Section 11.2). But if the controllability conditions are not satisfied, or if private expectations are capable of offsetting the policymaker's actions, then expectations are not tied down and commitment is necessary. But these are also the cases where the underlying policy equilibrium either does not exist or is undefined. Time inconsistency will easily appear in those cases.

12.6.2 Stabilization policies and communication: a simple example

Suppose policymakers aim to stabilize the economy around a certain equilibrium[9] within a given time interval after a given shock, or when facing a sequence of stochastic disturbances. This type of policy problem may seem unusual from the point of view of the recent models in the macroeconomic literature, where the emphasis is usually placed on intertemporal welfare maximization. However, it is probably closer to the actual management procedures of central bankers and governments.

As a specific example, consider a generalization of the well-known New Keynesian economic model. It generalizes on the standard model in that it includes both a hybrid Phillips curve (Fuhrer and Moore, 1995) and fiscal policy (Dixit and Lambertini, 2003a, 2003b; Lambertini, 2006). But it can be reduced to the standard model by restricting three particular parameter values to zero. Formally, our economy is described by the following two-equation structure taken from Section 11.5:

$$\pi_t = (1-\lambda)\beta E_t \pi_{t+1} + \lambda \pi_{t-1} + \kappa x_t + \phi f_t + v_t, \tag{12.21}$$

$$x_t = E_t x_t - \sigma (i_t - E_t \pi_{t+1}) + \chi f_t + \varepsilon_t, \tag{12.22}$$

where ε_t and v_t are white noise, and where $x_t = y_t - \bar{y}_t$ is the output gap relative to the flexible-price equilibrium; π_t is the inflation rate; i_t is the nominal interest rate; f_t is a fiscal variable. It is worth noting that fiscal policy can be introduced in different ways with different implications depending on the signs and sizes of ϕ and χ. However, an extensive debate about the effects and appropriate modeling of fiscal policy is beyond our remit here.[10] Finally, λ is a measure of the degree

[9] For example, the steady state of a DSGE New Keynesian model (zero inflation, natural rate of output).

[10] For instance, in Equation (12.21) f_t might represent the impact of fiscal policy (say payroll taxes) on costs, while f_t in (12.22) shows the impact of fiscal policy on output through demand management. The interested reader can find an extensive discussion of these points in Dixit and Lambertini (2003a, 2003b) and Lambertini (2006).

of inflation persistence as introduced by Fuhrer and Moore. However, all three generalizations are easily removed without changing our essential results by setting $\lambda = 0$ and abstracting from fiscal policy ($\phi = \chi = 0$). Equations (12.21) and (12.22) then describe the simple standard New Keynesian model.

This model can easily be written in the general form of (12.1) by obtaining the model's reduced form:

$$\begin{bmatrix} \pi_t \\ x_t \end{bmatrix} = \begin{bmatrix} 1 & 0 \\ \kappa & 1 \end{bmatrix} \cdot \left\{ \begin{bmatrix} (1-\lambda)\beta & 0 \\ \sigma & 1 \end{bmatrix} E_t \begin{bmatrix} \pi_{t+1} \\ x_{t+1} \end{bmatrix} + \begin{bmatrix} \lambda & 0 \\ 0 & 0 \end{bmatrix} \begin{bmatrix} \pi_{t-1} \\ x_{t-1} \end{bmatrix} + \begin{pmatrix} \phi & 0 \\ \chi & -\sigma \end{pmatrix} \begin{pmatrix} f_t \\ i_t \end{pmatrix} + \begin{pmatrix} v_t \\ \varepsilon_t \end{pmatrix} \right\}. \tag{12.23}$$

In this case the parameter matrices of (12.1) are defined as

$$A = \begin{bmatrix} \lambda & 0 \\ 0 & 0 \end{bmatrix}; \quad B = \begin{bmatrix} \phi + \kappa\chi & -\kappa\sigma \\ \chi & -\sigma \end{bmatrix}; \quad C = \begin{bmatrix} (1-\lambda)\beta + \kappa\sigma & \kappa \\ \sigma & 1 \end{bmatrix}; \tag{12.24}$$

and $\begin{bmatrix} 1 & 0 \\ \kappa & 1 \end{bmatrix} \begin{pmatrix} v_t \\ \varepsilon_t \end{pmatrix}$ is the vector containing the error terms.

Thus, allowing for the full effects of both policy instruments takes us to (12.23); that is, a model of the form of (12.1) with parameter matrices defined by (12.24). Note that the policy multiplier matrix B is nonsingular if $\phi \neq 0$. Hence we have static controllability, given arbitrary initial conditions and arbitrary values for the terminal condition.

So far the story is the same as in the case of no REs. However, things start to change if we have only one instrument (monetary policy, say) available. To see that, we write the policy problem as a two-period problem with both policy instruments:

$$\begin{bmatrix} \pi_t \\ x_t \\ \pi_{t+1} \\ x_{t+1} \end{bmatrix} = \begin{bmatrix} I & -C \\ -A & I \end{bmatrix}^{-1} \left\{ \begin{bmatrix} B & 0 \\ 0 & B \end{bmatrix} \begin{bmatrix} f_t \\ i_t \\ E_t(f_{t+1}) \\ E_t(i_{t+1}) \end{bmatrix} + \begin{pmatrix} w_t \\ w_{t+1} \end{pmatrix} \right\}, \tag{12.25}$$

which is a particular case of (12.2). For static controllability, we are interested in only the first two rows of (12.25). But we need to use the whole system if we are to go to dynamic controllability in the second period. The policy multiplier matrix implied by (12.25) is, in fact,

$$\begin{bmatrix} \phi+\kappa\chi & -\kappa\sigma & [(1-\Delta)\phi/\lambda+1]\kappa\chi & -[(1-\Delta)/\lambda+1]\kappa\sigma \\ \chi\Delta+\sigma\lambda(\phi+\kappa\chi) & -\sigma[\Delta+\kappa\lambda\sigma] & \chi[\sigma\lambda\kappa+\Delta+\sigma\phi\kappa(\lambda(1-\Delta)+\Delta)] & -\sigma[\sigma\lambda\kappa+\Delta+\sigma\kappa(\lambda(1-\Delta)+\Delta)] \\ \lambda(\phi+\kappa\chi) & -\kappa\sigma\lambda & (\phi+\lambda)\kappa\chi & -(1+\lambda)\kappa\sigma \\ 0 & 0 & \chi & -\sigma \end{bmatrix}\Delta^{-1}, \tag{12.26}$$

where $\Delta = 1 - [\lambda(1-\lambda) + \lambda\kappa\sigma] \neq 0$. The one-period policy multiplier matrix (the top left 2×2 sub-matrix) is nonsingular as noted above. That implies static controllability. But if there is just one policy (monetary policy) available, $\phi = \chi = 0$. In that case, instead of (12.26), we get

$$\begin{bmatrix} 0 & -\kappa\sigma & 0 & -(1-\Delta+\lambda)\kappa\sigma/\lambda \\ 0 & -\sigma(\kappa\sigma\lambda+\Delta) & 0 & -\sigma[\sigma\kappa(1-\lambda)+1]\Delta \\ 0 & -\kappa\sigma\lambda & 0 & -\sigma\kappa(1+\lambda) \\ 0 & 0 & 0 & -\sigma \end{bmatrix}\Delta^{-1}. \tag{12.27}$$

Hence static controllability would be lost at t if only monetary policy, i_t, was available at that time. On the other hand, if we allow for the expectations, held at t, of the monetary policy interventions expected or announced in period $t+1$, we can rewrite the one-period static controllability problem by inserting (12.27) into (12.25) to get

$$\begin{bmatrix} \pi_t \\ x_t \end{bmatrix} = -\Delta^{-1}\begin{bmatrix} \kappa\sigma & \kappa\sigma(1-\Delta+\lambda)/\lambda \\ \sigma(\kappa\sigma\lambda+\Delta) & \sigma[\sigma\kappa(1-\lambda)+1]\Delta \end{bmatrix}\begin{bmatrix} i_t \\ E_t(i_{t+1}) \end{bmatrix} + w_t, \tag{12.28}$$

whose multiplier matrix is easily seen to be nonsingular. In other words, we have static controllability from the point of view of period t, despite having a single instrument and two targets. This is achieved by using both i_t and announcements for the policies to be implemented in period $t+1$. Thus, we can have static controllability even if there are insufficient policy instruments.

The same thing happens when fiscal policy is present but has only one channel of influence ($\phi = 0$). In this case, instead of (12.26), we get

$$\begin{bmatrix} \kappa\chi & -\kappa\sigma & \kappa\chi & -(1-\Delta+\lambda)\kappa\sigma/\lambda \\ \chi(\Delta+\kappa\sigma\lambda) & -\sigma(\kappa\sigma\lambda+\Delta) & \lambda\kappa\chi & -\sigma[\sigma\kappa(1-\lambda)+1]\Delta \\ \lambda\kappa\chi & -\kappa\sigma\lambda & \lambda\kappa\chi & -\sigma\kappa(1+\lambda) \\ 0 & 0 & \chi & -\sigma \end{bmatrix}\Delta^{-1}. \tag{12.29}$$

In such a case, (12.28) will be replaced by inserting (12.29) in (12.25) to yield

$$\begin{bmatrix}\pi_t\\ x_t\end{bmatrix} = \Delta^{-1}\begin{bmatrix}\kappa\chi & \kappa\chi\\ \chi(\Delta+\kappa\sigma\lambda) & \lambda\kappa\chi\end{bmatrix}\begin{bmatrix}f_t\\ E_t(f_{t+1})\end{bmatrix} + w_t, \tag{12.30}$$

whose multiplier matrix is also nonsingular.[11] So again we have static controllability at period t; and for the same reason, credible policy announcements have become a second instrument. In a similar way, we can generate examples that imply static controllability using mixed policies: for example, monetary policy plus announcements about future fiscal policy, or fiscal policy plus announcements of future monetary policies.

The crucial point here is that this example shows that the policymakers need to exercise good communication skills in order to make their announcements credible and have some effect – that is, to make the private sector shift or anchor their expectations of likely future outcomes to values that suit the policymakers' purposes. But obviously, the private agents need to be convinced that the necessary policy changes will actually take place and achieve the said outcomes. They will be convinced if their expectations match the outcomes predicted by Equation (12.2), extended by (12.6) if necessary, when official policy announcements are inserted for $x_{t|1}$. However, if the aims and desired target values of central bankers are unknown, the private sector cannot anticipate the actions of the monetary authorities – even when the bank's targets do not conflict with those of the private sector. Good communication is therefore the crucial factor.

A stark example of explicit announcements and communication about future trends in policy, aimed at influencing expectations of both policy actions and outcomes for the purpose of improving the performance of the economy, comes in the Federal Reserve's attempts to reflate the US economy after the financial crisis in 2008. In a statement summarizing the Fed's approach to unconventional monetary policies (quantitative easing), Williams (2011) identifies "forward guidance" and large-scale asset purchases as the Fed's two main weapons to be

[11] The persistence parameter plays no role in this analysis: setting $\lambda = 0$ alters (12.27) qualitatively, but does not change the rank or non-singularity of the multiplier matrix in Equation (12.28) or (12.30).

used when interest rate changes appear ineffective. Specific instances of the approaches are forward guidance in the form of announcing, in 2011, that interest rates would be kept low until 2014; or, in 2009, how the exit strategy from the Fed's asset purchases would be accomplished; or the large-scale asset purchase programs QE1, QE2 and Operation Twist between 2009 and 2011. Williams (2011) makes it clear that the Fed now regards forward guidance as a major part of its monetary policy arsenal. This section has provided the formal analysis that underpins that type of strategy.

12.6.3 Communication, even without Keynesian fiscal policy effects?

One of the great debates of monetary policy is whether central banks should allow forecasts of future interest rates to be published. Rudebusch and Williams (2008) and Eusepi and Preston (2010) argue this can be used to strengthen economic policy.[12] But others argue that to do so may imply a stronger consensus, or more certainty about future policies, than actually exists; or that doing so may propagate errors and make it more difficult to adjust policies again later in the face of unexpected shocks. In addition, private agents could overreact to noisy public signals, but underreact to more accurate private information (see Faust and Svensson, 2002; Amato, Morris and Shin, 2003; Walsh, 2007).

To resolve this argument, consider an economy represented by the following well-known model:

$$y_t = \rho y_{t-1} + \alpha(\pi_t - E_t\pi_{t+1}) - \beta(i_t - E_t\pi_{t+1}) + \varepsilon_t, \tag{12.31}$$

$$i_t = c_0 + c_1(\pi_t - \pi^*) + c_2 y_t + v_t. \tag{12.32}$$

Equation (12.32) is an elaboration of the standard model that has been part of the theory of monetary policy since the Barro–Gordon model was introduced in 1983. It consists of a short run Phillips curve with persistence ($\rho \neq 0$), set within a standard forward-looking Lucas supply function (a vertical long run Phillips curve) and elaborated to include the effects of real interest rate changes on output. It can

[12] See Archer (2005), Moessner and Nelson (2008), Ferrero and Secchi (2009) for evidence to support this view.

therefore be interpreted as either a dynamic open economy Phillips curve, or as a forward-looking New Keynesian IS curve with dynamics. In that context, y_t is the deviation of output from its natural rate; π_t is the rate of inflation; $E_t\pi_{t+1}$ is the private sector's current expectation for the rate of inflation; and π^* is the government or central bank's target inflation rate; where i_t is the nominal rate of interest, ε_t is a supply shock with mean zero and constant variance, and v_t is a monetary policy shock with mean zero and constant variance. All parameters are positive.

The only policy instrument in this example will be i_t. Equation (12.32) is therefore a Taylor rule: c_0 is a constant term reflecting the equilibrium rate of interest; v_t are the possible control errors; π^* is the inflation target; and determinacy (the Taylor principle) suggests $c_1 > 1$.

To obtain a reduced form for (12.31)–(12.32), we renormalize (12.32) on π_t, set $u_t = \pi^* - c_1^{-1}(c_0 - v_t)$ and solve (12.31) and (12.32). This transforms our system to

$$\begin{bmatrix} y_t \\ \pi_t \end{bmatrix} = \frac{\rho}{\Delta}\begin{bmatrix} 1 & 0 \\ -c_2c_1^{-1} & 0 \end{bmatrix}\begin{bmatrix} y_{t-1} \\ \pi_{t-1} \end{bmatrix} + \frac{\beta-\alpha}{\Delta}\begin{bmatrix} 0 & 1 \\ 0 & -c_2c_1^{-1} \end{bmatrix}\begin{bmatrix} y_{t+1|1} \\ \pi_{t+1|1} \end{bmatrix}$$
$$+\frac{1}{c_1\Delta}\begin{bmatrix} \alpha-\beta c_1 \\ \beta c_2+1 \end{bmatrix} i_t + \frac{1}{\Delta}\begin{bmatrix} 1 & \alpha \\ -c_2c_1^{-1} & 1 \end{bmatrix}\begin{bmatrix} \varepsilon_t \\ u_t \end{bmatrix}, \tag{12.33}$$

where $\Delta = (1 + \alpha c_1^{-1}c_2) \neq 0$. This form of the model does not allow static controllability as it is. However, we can write the two-period policy problem as

$$\begin{bmatrix} y_t \\ \pi_t \\ y_{t+1} \\ \pi_{t+1} \end{bmatrix} = \begin{bmatrix} I & -B \\ -A & I \end{bmatrix}^{-1}.$$
$$\left(\begin{bmatrix} C & 0 \\ 0 & C \end{bmatrix}\begin{bmatrix} i_t \\ E_ti_{t+1} \end{bmatrix} + \begin{bmatrix} A\begin{bmatrix} y_0 \\ \pi_0 \end{bmatrix} \\ B\begin{bmatrix} E_ty_{t+2} \\ E_t\pi_{t+2} \end{bmatrix} \end{bmatrix} + \frac{1}{\Delta}\begin{bmatrix} \varepsilon_t + \alpha u_t \\ u_t - c_2c_1^{-1}\varepsilon_t \\ \varepsilon_{t+1} + \alpha u_{t+1} \\ u_{t+1} - c_2c_1^{-1}\varepsilon_{t+1} \end{bmatrix}\right), \tag{12.34}$$

where A, B and C are the first, second and third coefficient matrices in (12.33). The policy multiplier matrix for this model is

$$\frac{1}{\Phi}\begin{bmatrix} (\alpha-\beta c_1)\Delta & (\beta-\alpha)(1+\beta c_2) \\ \dfrac{\rho(\beta-\alpha)(\alpha-\beta c_1)c_1^{-1}c_2^2+(1+\beta c_2)\Phi}{c_1\Delta} & -c_2c_1^{-1}(\beta-\alpha)(1+\beta c_2) \\ \rho(\alpha-\beta c_1) & \dfrac{\rho(\beta-\alpha)(1+\beta c_2)c_1+(\alpha-\beta c_1)\Phi}{c_1\Delta} \\ -c_2c_1^{-1}\rho(\alpha-\beta c_1) & (1+\beta c_2)\Delta \end{bmatrix}\begin{bmatrix} i_t \\ E_t i_{t+1} \end{bmatrix} \tag{12.35}$$

where $\Phi = \Delta^2 c_1 + \rho(\beta - \alpha)c_2$. Referring back to (12.31) and (12.32) this model tells us that (y_t, π_t) and (y_{t+1}, π_{t+1}) are both statically and immediately controllable using current policies and announcements or projections of future actions. That is because both the upper and lower partitions of the multiplier matrix in Equation (12.35) are nonsingular.[13] And since (y_t, π_t) and (y_{t+1}, π_{t+1}) are current and expected future target variables from the perspective of period t, this means that the policymakers can control not only current inflation and output (in expectation at least); *but also* inflation expectations and growth forecasts for the next period. In other words, they can add to their ability to control inflation (and output) by anchoring those expectations.

This example is therefore in line with our theory of dynamic controllability under REs, and makes the case for publishing conditional forecasts of future interest rates as a regular part of the monetary policymaking framework. Indeed it would become more difficult to achieve successful outcomes if inflation expectations could not be tied down at the same time as inflation itself. There may be other ways of controlling the outcomes for (y_{t+1}, π_{t+1}) in period $t + 1$ of course; for example, using current and past interest rates as implied by (12.32). But that is a conventional backward-looking use of dynamic controllability, and may still fail to tie down/anchor expectations in the terminal period.

[13] Unless the underlying parameters satisfy $\alpha = \beta$ exactly in the upper sub-matrix (for current outcomes); or $\alpha = \beta c_1$ in the lower one (future expected outcomes). These are sufficient conditions; and they cannot both hold simultaneously since we require $c_1 > 1$ for the Taylor principle. So, even in such cases, we can be sure of our ability to control either future expectations or current outcomes through policy announcements or forecasts. Beyond that, there is one particular value for the dynamics term, ρ, which leads to singularity for the whole system – corresponding to the unit root condition identified in Section 11.3.1.

12.6.4 Announcements and fiscal policy (tax cuts)

It is not just in monetary policy that timing and expectations of policy changes may be important for economic activity. House and Shapiro (2006) use a fairly standard model to analyze the announcement and phasing-in effects of the 2001 and 2003 tax cuts in the USA on output (Y_t), investment (I_t), employment/hours worked (N_t) and consumption (Z_t).[14] Their model is a business cycle model with a government sector. Being nonlinear, we can rewrite it in linearized form, as Equations (12.1), (12.2) and (12.3), with partial derivatives replacing the corresponding linear coefficients. The model itself contains nine equations in three fiscal policy instruments as follows (after renormalizing the equations for I_t, K_t, T_t, defined below, and Z_t):

$$
\begin{aligned}
I_t &= K_{t+1} - (1-\delta)K_t \\
K_t &= Y_t^{1/\alpha} N_t^{(1-\alpha)/\alpha} \\
W_t &= (1-\alpha)Y_t / N_t \\
R_t &= \alpha Y_t / N_t \\
Y_t &= Z_t + I_t + G_t + \tfrac{1}{2}\phi K_t (I_t / K_t - \delta)^2 \\
N_t &= [\zeta^{-1} Z_t^{-1/\sigma} W_t (1-\tau_t^N)]^\eta \\
T_t &= \tau_t^N N_t W_t + \tau_t^K K_t \left[R_t - \delta - \tfrac{1}{2}\phi (I_t / K_t - \delta)^2\right] - G_t \\
q_t &= \beta\left[Z_t^{-1/\sigma}\left\{(1+\tau_{t+1}^K)R_{t+1} + \tau_{t+1}^K\delta + \tfrac{1}{2}\phi(1-\tau_{t+1}^K)(I_{t+1}^2 / K_{t+1}^2 - \delta^2)\right\} + (1-\delta)q_{t+1}\right], \\
Z_t &= \left[q_t / \left[1 + \phi(I_t / K_t - \delta)(1-\tau_t^K)\right]\right]^{-\sigma}
\end{aligned}
\tag{12.36}
$$

where it is understood that subscript $t + 1$ means the expected value of that variable in $t + 1$ based on an earlier information set. In obvious notation, I, K, Y, N and Z represent investment, capital, GDP, employment and consumption, respectively; and W, R and q are real wages, the rental price of capital and the shadow cost of capital. Policy targets are therefore Y_t, I_t, N_t and Z_t; and the instruments are τ_t^N, τ_t^K and G_t, i.e., wage taxes, capital taxes and government spending (which necessarily leaves T_t, lump sum transfers and subsidies, as the residual in the government's budget constraint). Thus the model's structural

[14] We use Z_t for consumption instead of C_t, as usual, so that the reader should not become confused with the matrix of coefficients C in the model (12.1).

form implies an endogenous variable coefficient matrix of no particular pattern, hence of full rank and, except for very particular parameter values, with an inverse that is "full" (all entries nonzero). It is then easy to check that matrix B, of order 9×3 in Equations (12.1) and (12.2), is also full with a clear pattern that can be evaluated from the partial derivatives of the original nonlinear model. Likewise, the 9×9 matrices A and C, in (12.1) and (12.2), are $A = 0$ and a matrix of zeros except for elements $C(1,2) = 1$, $C(8,4) = \beta Z^{-1/\sigma}(1 + \tau^K_{t+1})$ and $C(8,8) = \beta(1 - \delta)$. Consequently, Equation (12.2) implies that matrix R in Equation (12.3) is given by

$$R = \begin{bmatrix} B & CB & C^2B & \dots & C^{T-1}B \\ 0 & B & CB & . & . \\ . & . & B & . & . \\ . & & . & . & CB \\ 0 & . & . & 0 & B \end{bmatrix}.$$

Hence, $R_{t,j} = 0$ for all $t > j$, but $R_{t,j} = C^{t-j}B$ if $j \geq t$.[15]

In the general case, even if we do not assign specific numerical values to the parameters and partial derivatives in the model, we can still determine if the policy targets are controllable and expectations managed to achieve specified target values in period t. We can do that by evaluating the appropriate row in R and using Theorem 12.2. Evidently matrix B, when condensed onto four policy targets, has rank 3 at most. Consequently static controllability never was available for these tax reductions, however convincing the policy announcements may have been. On the other hand, matrix BC has nonzero entries in rows 1 and 8, and matrix C^tB nonzero entries in row 8 only (all $t \geq 2$). Thus $\mathrm{r}[R_{t,t}, \dots R_{t,n}] = \mathrm{r}[B, CB] = 4$, except for the cases where specific numerical parameter values happen to reduce $\mathrm{r}[B]$ below 3 or $\mathrm{r}[CB]$ below 1. In other words, these policy targets are *not* controllable by prior announcement (i.e., in period j, using announcements of actions to be taken in period t or later, where $j < t$). *Nor* are they controllable

[15] Note that $A = 0$ implies that the no unit root condition underlying (12.3) is always satisfied. So, for controllability, we are only concerned with rank condition from Proposition 12.1. Notice also that this expression for R ignores the effects of any announced/expected tax changes on q in (12.36). Computing again R to account for those terms only adds one small term in position $C(8,2)$, which does not change the rank condition test in any way. It has therefore been ignored for simplicity.

by immediate action taken in the current period. But they *can* be controlled by contemporaneous action (in period t) plus announcements of actions in the next period or thereafter. So they have to be part of a package that is phased in over time, even if that introduces negative effects of the kind that House and Shapiro (2006) identify. In this model, a phased-in package is unavoidable. All of this can be checked directly, without any need to perform complicated numerical simulations. Moreover, the size of the immediate impact *and* the phasing in effects of any policy changes can be checked by computing the matrices C, CB, C^2B, ... numerically.

12.6.5 Managing expectations in an open economy with low pass-through

We now consider a small open economy model with low pass-through developed by Monacelli (2005). The introduction of incomplete pass-through in an otherwise standard New Keynesian model renders the analysis of monetary policy of an open economy fundamentally different from that of a closed economy because a short run trade-off between the stabilization of inflation and the output gap emerges.[16] By imposing a perfect pass-through instead, one obtains an open economy model that is isomorphic with the New Keynesian closed one already described (see Clarida, Galí, and Gertler, 2001).

The model is described by the following equations:

$$\pi_t = (1-\lambda)\pi_t^h + \lambda\pi_t^f \quad \text{(domestic CPI inflation)}, \tag{12.37}$$

$$\pi_t^h = \beta E_t\pi_{t+1}^h + \kappa x_t + \chi\varphi_t^f \quad \text{(domestic Phillips curve)}, \tag{12.38}$$

$$x_t = E_t x_{t+1} - \sigma(i_t - \pi_{t+1}^h - \overline{r}_t) + \mu\left(E_t\varphi_{t+1}^f - \varphi_t^f\right) \quad \text{(domestic IS curve)}, \tag{12.39}$$

[16] As shown by Monacelli (2005), in such a context a nominal depreciation determines the wedge between the price paid by the importers in world markets and the local currency price in the domestic markets. This wedge acts as an increase in the real marginal cost and therefore increases foreign goods inflation.

$$\pi_t^f = \beta E_t \pi_{t+1}^f + \lambda \varphi_t^f \qquad \text{(imported local currency inflation)}, \tag{12.40}$$

$$i_t - i_t^* = E_t\left(\pi_{t+1}^h - \pi_{t+1}^f\right) + E_t \varphi_{t+1}^f - \varphi_t^f \qquad \text{(uncovered interest parity)}, \tag{12.41}$$

where x_t is the output gap; π_t is the inflation rate, π_t^h and π_t^f are domestic producer inflation and (local currency) imported inflation respectively; and φ_t^f denotes deviations of the world price $(e_t + p_t^*)$ from the domestic currency price of imports (p_t^f), a measure of the deviations from the law of one price. Then i_t and i_t^* are domestic and foreign interest rates; $\bar{r}_t$ is the natural real rate of interest, which depends on domestic productivity and expected growth in world output. We assume that both i_t^* and $\bar{r}_t$ follow some known stochastic processes.

Equation (12.37) just defines domestic CPI inflation. Equation (12.38) is the domestic aggregate supply assuming price stickiness of the Calvo or Rotemberg kind; Equation (12.39) represents the demand side of the economy (a standard IS curve obtained from the consumer's Euler equation); Equation (12.40) describe the dynamics of imported domestic currency inflation; and Equation (12.41) closes the model by imposing the uncovered interest parity. Such an equation results from combining efficiency conditions for an optimal portfolio of bonds held by both domestic and foreign residents.

After some detailed algebra, the model (12.37)–(12.41) can be reduced to the form of the general system (12.1):

$$\begin{bmatrix} x_t \\ \pi_t \\ \pi_t^f \\ \varphi_t^f \end{bmatrix} = \begin{bmatrix} -\kappa & \frac{1}{1-\lambda} & \frac{-\lambda}{1-\lambda} & -\chi \\ 1 & 0 & 0 & \mu \\ 0 & 0 & 1 & -\lambda \\ 0 & 0 & 0 & 1 \end{bmatrix}^{-1} \cdot \tag{12.42}$$

$$\left(\begin{bmatrix} 0 & \frac{\beta}{1-\lambda} & \frac{-\lambda\beta}{1-\lambda} & 0 \\ 1 & \frac{\sigma}{1-\lambda} & \frac{-\lambda\sigma}{1-\lambda} & \mu \\ 0 & 0 & \beta & 0 \\ 0 & \frac{1}{1-\lambda} & \frac{-1}{1-\lambda} & 1 \end{bmatrix} \begin{bmatrix} x_{t+1} \\ \pi_{t+1} \\ \pi_{t+1}^f \\ \varphi_{t+1}^f \end{bmatrix} - \begin{bmatrix} 0 \\ 0 \\ \sigma \\ 1 \end{bmatrix} i_t + \begin{bmatrix} 0 \\ \sigma\bar{r}_t \\ 0 \\ i_t^* \end{bmatrix} + error \right),$$

where $[x_t, \pi_t, \pi_t^f, \varphi_t^f]' = y_t$, $i_t = u$. Definitions for A, B and C are now straightforward:

$$A = 0;$$

$$B = \begin{bmatrix} \mu \\ (1-\lambda)(\mu\kappa - \chi) - \lambda(\sigma+\lambda) \\ -(\sigma+\lambda) \\ -1 \end{bmatrix};$$

$$C = \begin{bmatrix} 1 & \frac{\sigma-\mu}{1-\lambda} & \frac{\mu-\lambda\sigma}{1-\lambda} & 0 \\ \kappa(1-\lambda) & \frac{\lambda^2+(1-\lambda)[\chi+\beta+\kappa(\sigma-\mu)]}{1-\lambda} & \lambda & \lambda^2+\chi(1-\lambda) \\ 0 & \frac{\lambda}{1-\lambda} & \beta-\frac{1}{1-\lambda} & \lambda \\ 0 & \frac{1}{1-\lambda} & -\frac{1}{1-\lambda} & 1 \end{bmatrix}.$$

Thus the model in final form, (12.42), implies an endogenous variable coefficient (or Toeplitz) matrix that is triangular; of full rank (note that $\det(B) = \beta^2$), and with an inverse that is "full" (all entries nonzero). Consequently, (12.42) implies that matrix R in (12.3) is given by

$$R = \begin{bmatrix} B & CB & C^2B & \dots & C^{T-1}B \\ 0 & B & CB & . & . \\ . & . & B & . & . \\ . & & . & . & CB \\ 0 & . & . & 0 & B \end{bmatrix}. \qquad (12.43)$$

Here $R_{t,j} = 0$ for all $t > j$; but $R_{t,j} = C^{t-j}B$ if $t \leq j$. However, even if we do not assign specific numerical values to the parameters or partial derivatives in the model, we can still determine if the policy targets are controllable, and if expectations can be managed to achieve certain specified targets in period t. We can do that by evaluating the appropriate rows in R and using Theorem 12.2.

The first thing to notice is that $r[B] = r[CB] = 1$; so that if we take $T = 2$ (a two-period problem) for illustration, $R = \begin{bmatrix} B & CB \\ 0 & B \end{bmatrix}$, and $r[R] = 2$. This means that we can achieve two of the policy goals at most in the two periods available: a zero output gap, x_t, and low inflation, π_t, in the current period (but not in the future); *or* next year's output gap and inflation targets, but not those in the current period; *or* low inflation this year and a stabilized output gap next year (or vice versa). If we want to achieve all four targets this year, we need both to set current interest rates and make announcements or interest rate forecasts of the next three years[17] (which, given the natural uncertainty of economic events, may stretch credibility too far). But what we cannot do is achieve all four targets – inflation, output, imported inflation and competiveness on world markets – in less than four policy years; or more than one of them in any one policy year; or more than one of them without needing to make credible policy announcements about future policies next year and in the following years.

These conclusions are *radically* different from those in the traditional monetary policy literature because they imply that there is no short term trade-off between inflation and output stabilization when the rate of exchange rate pass-through is taken into account. To get even as far as that trade-off, let alone to resolve it, some interest rate forecasts/forward guidance will be necessary unless carefully coordinated packages of fiscal–monetary policies can be brought to bear. And additional targets mean extending the period of the package of announcements yet further. These results bring a new perspective to the importance of the pass-through problem specifically for performance and policy design, which has yet to be acknowledged in the literature.

It is worth noting that all of these results can be derived directly, without any need for complicated numerical simulations or analytic calculations. Just as well too, because such calculations typically yield expressions that are too complicated to allow us to learn anything.

The simplest case to make that point is an evaluation of the R matrix in (12.43) when $T = 2$. In such a case an open economy with incomplete pass-through is characterized by

$$R = \begin{bmatrix} \mu & -\mu\lambda + \mu - \sigma\chi + \sigma\kappa\mu - \mu\sigma + \mu\chi - \kappa\mu^2 \\ -\lambda\sigma + \kappa\mu - \kappa\mu\lambda - \lambda^2 - \chi + \chi\lambda & \Delta \\ -\sigma - \lambda & \lambda^2 - \chi\lambda - \lambda - \lambda\beta + \kappa\mu\lambda + \lambda\sigma - \beta\sigma \\ -1 & \lambda - 1 + \sigma - \chi + \kappa\mu \\ 0 & \mu \\ 0 & -\lambda\sigma + \kappa\mu - \kappa\mu\lambda - \lambda^2 - \chi + \chi\lambda \\ 0 & -\sigma - \lambda \\ 0 & -1 \end{bmatrix}, \tag{12.44}$$

[17] From the rank of R in (12.43) when $T = 4$.

where

$$\Delta = -\sigma\kappa\mu - \sigma\chi\lambda + 2\kappa\mu\chi + \sigma\chi - 2\chi\lambda^2 - \lambda^2\beta - \chi\beta + \kappa^2\sigma\mu + \kappa^2\mu^2\lambda - \beta\lambda\sigma$$
$$-\kappa^2\sigma\mu\lambda + \kappa\sigma\chi\lambda - 2\kappa\mu\chi\lambda - \kappa^2\mu^2 - \chi^2 + \chi^2\lambda + \beta\kappa\mu + \lambda^2\sigma - \chi + \lambda^3 - \lambda^2$$
$$+\kappa\mu + 2\chi\lambda - 2\kappa\mu\lambda + 2\kappa\mu\lambda^2 + \chi\lambda\beta - \kappa\sigma\chi - \beta\kappa\mu\lambda + \sigma\kappa\mu\lambda$$

On the other hand, the size of the immediate impact *and* announcement effects of any policy changes has to be checked out by computing the matrices B, CB, C^2B, ... numerically.

12.7 Lessons from this chapter

Extending our previous analysis, this chapter has been able to determine the conditions under which policies can affect outcomes, and hence private sector expectations, when economic performance and policy choices are influenced by rationally chosen forward-looking expectations; and, equally, to determine the conditions under which the outcomes cannot be controlled, or when private sector expectations cannot be managed to permit certain objectives.

Our key result is that policy targets can be controlled, and expectations managed consistently with the policy process, as long as the forward dynamics (from private expectations of future outcomes) and the backwards dynamics (from past policies or outcomes) do not interact to imply a unit root; and as long as the rank condition in Theorem 12.1 holds. If no unit root is implied, then expectations can be managed to increase controllability in the conventional sense and to make policies more effective from an earlier date. But if there is a unit root, it means that the forward and backward dynamics exactly offset each other in the *status quo* – so that the anticipated and the feedback effects each other in of a policy change cancel out in their impact on current outcomes. In such a case, no policies could be expected to have an impact.

This provides an explanation of our results: the unit root comes from the matrix product AC in Equation (12.1), where A controls the effect of past decisions and outcomes as chosen by the policy-makers, and C the effect of expected future outcomes as anticipated by the private sector. Only where there is a conflict between the two, such that the influence of the expectations exactly offsets that of the planned changes to the existing state, will policies become ineffective.

The policy neutrality property should therefore be attributed to a conflict between agents and policymakers; a conflict that may take place if the private sector can set their expectations to have a *sufficient* effect on the policymaker's targets (since there is obviously no incentive to align expectations with targets over which the authorities have no control). But that is a special case. Otherwise, if the model satisfies the rank condition in Theorem 12.1 (so that they do have controllability in the usual sense, and expectations are tied down by (12.2)), expectations can be managed: that is, brought into line to assist with what the policymaker intended to achieve.

Thus, although we have shown that REs can make it impossible for the policymaker to affect the outcomes in certain models and situations through policy invariance or time inconsistency, this is not a general result. In fact it will only happen if the matrix product AC has a unit root or the rank condition in Theorem 12.2 fails.[18] Both conditions depend on particular parameter values, so neither can hold in general. Hence REs do not, in themselves, prevent controllability in either its static or its dynamic form. On the contrary, they typically enhance the effectiveness of economic policy.

There are two special cases where REs do create policy invariance: the long run Phillips curve and New Keynesian models without persistence (in both cases where inflation reacts one-for-one to changes in expected inflation, as is conventionally assumed). In the former, $C = 0$ and A is diagonal with a unit element in one position.[19] Although the inverse in (12.2) still exists, it is a companion matrix and the border elements do not decay as $T \to \infty$. Consequently, the policymakers cannot have controllability in the long run, though they will have it in the short term. The same happens in many New Keynesian models. In

[18] There could still be particular values of A and B such that the introduction of $C \neq 0$ makes $(R_{t,1} \ldots R_{t,n})$ have less than full rank, when $(R_{t,1} \ldots R_{t,n})$ would have had full rank with $C = 0$. Although this could happen by chance with certain parameter values, it cannot be a general outcome. In any case, in that situation there would be a further problem of the non-existence of the underlying equilibrium.

[19] This reflects the usual assumption that agents expect inflation at its last observed value. If they expect it at the currently observed value, the inverse in Equation (12.1) becomes block diagonal with $I - A$ on the diagonal, which implies singularity. That means that controllability would be lost in the short term too.

this case $A = 0$, and C is diagonal with a unit element.[20] Again, and for the same reason, policymakers will not have controllability as $T \rightarrow \infty$, although they may have it for shorter horizons.

The implications of our results are important. All dynamic problems that imply the achievement of a given target at a certain moment of time – such as fiscal consolidation, or achieving macroeconomic targets in order to enter a currency union – will find an important ally in the existence of REs if dynamic controllability is satisfied. The policy problem is no longer a matter of how to find a credible commitment, but of when the policy changes should be announced given the economy's lag structure. Similarly, policy announcements ("forward guidance" in Federal Reserve language) have become a useful instrument for stabilizing an economy hit by a temporary downturn since the stabilizability property of backward-looking models generalizes and allows a sequence of stabilizing actions with announcements to become effective from an earlier point.

Lastly, our analysis has generated additional insights into the need for commitment. So long as the no unit root condition and the rank condition of Theorem 11.1 are satisfied, the private sector knows that the policymaker has controllability and can reach their desired target values in any event. There is no point in expecting anything else: the system is fully tied down by those conditions. Thus, time consistency is never a problem for governments with patience or sufficient instruments. But in other cases, if the controllability conditions are not satisfied and/or private sector expectations are capable of offsetting the policymaker's action, then expectations are not tied down and commitment by the policy authorities will be necessary. Hence, time inconsistency and the need for a commitment technology may appear in certain cases, but they are far from representing the typical outcome or a necessary requirement.

This chapter also shows that policy failures only emerge when there are conflicts between public and private information sets, or if there is insufficient time or scope to use the policy instruments to reach all the targets required. Outside those cases, policymakers can harness private expectations to help them achieve their targets.

[20] This will also happen with full persistence if either fiscal policy or monetary policy is absent or unused.

Second, REs are a powerful mechanism, in combination with the chosen sequence of policy values, for influencing the natural dynamics of the economy. It is therefore important to know the conditions under which expectations can be managed to achieve the desired outcomes (recovery path), and to test if they are satisfied before embarking on a policy program that depends on expectations to reach its objectives. In Chapter 11, we obtained a rank condition that defines the circumstances under which REs can be used to increase a policymaker's power to control an economy over time. In this chapter, we have shown how communication and policy announcements can be exploited to supplement and extend the impact or use of conventional policy instruments. This gives us a formal justification for using policies designed to manage expectations, and also defines the circumstances in which private sector expectations cannot be anchored or steered.

One implication of these results is that, in the absence of changes in information, once a policy sequence has been announced there can be no question of revising an announcement for strategic reasons, or of expecting it to be revised, because the policymaker can and is known to be able to reach his first best outcomes. He has no incentive or interest in not following through on his announcements. Not to follow through would predictably make him worse off.

A second implication is that the quality and credibility of communication by policymakers is a key issue. It is important to examine the conditions that permit or require effective signaling and commitment. But it is equally important to recognize that there is a large class of problems for which they are neither necessary nor relevant (although clear communication is still required so that agents can check the consistency of the announced policies and target values with the implications of their own information). This is going to be a large class of policy problems because policymakers can get down to one instrument and still have controllability if their policy horizon is long enough.

This last point leads to four specific conclusions:

(a) Successful communication decomposes into two parts; consistency with the announced targets, and clear priorities/targets to signal credibility when there are too few instruments or time periods for instant success.
(b) Policymakers who are patient can achieve, and can expect to achieve, what goals they want (their first best targets) if they have either the time, $T \geq S$, or enough instruments, $M \geq S$.

(c) Time-inconsistent behavior is therefore a limited phenomenon, but will become a problem if policymakers persuade themselves that they need to reach too many targets in too short a time.
(d) Coordinated fiscal and monetary policy packages, as well as unconventional policy instruments, are typically indispensable if time horizons are short.

13 *Expectations and target coordination: institutional aspects*

Summary. Suitable institutions are always required to support the policymaking process. Instability deriving from the existence of multiple equilibria may require either centralized institutions or some form of formalized coordination to oversee a sequence of policy announcements. Thus, institutional backing must be provided to underpin centralized or jointly taken decisions if no equilibrium exists, or to sequence the announcements/policy selection process if there are multiple equilibria. Moreover, in situations of conflict, credibility issues that might arise can be solved by target bargaining and the formation of implicit coalitions which can lead to better outcomes overall. In that sense, providing the means to arrive at a clear set of target values, and the institutions to support the players' efforts to reach and stick with those values, is more important than the precise form of the policy rules themselves. The effectiveness of both monetary and fiscal policy can also be enhanced by providing information about the policy targets when the private sector has forward-looking expectations. In addition, ensuring transparency about the current fiscal position as well as monitoring its sustainability by an independent authority will not only improve the democratic process, but also contribute to anchoring expectations.

13.1 Introduction

In previous chapters we have concentrated on deriving results that show when policies exist to achieve certain objectives at certain times and when they do not; or the circumstances in which policy equilibria exist in the same sense given multiple policy agencies; or when there are multiple equilibria (requiring announcements to provide an equilibrium selection); and when there are no equilibria (implying that a social planner or hegemon is needed to provide a defined solution to the policy selection problem). Certain other results describing the possibility of implicit coalitions or coordinated policies also emerged along the way.

However, there is also the question of how to implement the policies that might emerge from these scenarios. Having established that the desired goals can be achieved, or that certain policy equilibria exist, or that some mechanism is needed to break the random outcomes or policy paralysis that otherwise follow from multiple equilibria or the absence of an equilibrium, all these cases will require suitably designed institutions to support the policymaking process.

The five cases that we need to provide institutional backing for are:

(1) institutions sufficient to underpin centralized or jointly taken decisions if no equilibrium exists; or to sequence the announcements or policy selection process correctly if there are multiple equilibria;
(2) institutional mechanisms to ensure the consistency, commitment and credibility of individual (fiscal and monetary) policies over shorter time periods before dynamic controllability can be brought to bear, and in general in the cases where controllability might not apply;
(3) institutional mechanisms to provide sufficient information for the markets to check controllability as it applies to themselves or to others, or to ensure that any policy announcements made actually do coincide with their own expectations;
(4) a process for selecting and agreeing target values so that the implicit coalitions we studied in earlier chapters can emerge as an alternative to the traditional cooperative solution where commitment and bargaining, differently from many real-world cases, are related to the policy, not to the goals of the individual policymakers; and
(5) mechanisms sufficient to ensure the consistency, commitment and coherence of policies when there are costs to using policy instruments, or natural or imposed limits to the use of those instruments (for example, because controllability says nothing about what instrument values are necessary to reach the desired target values; those values could be beyond what is economically reasonable or politically acceptable).

Strict controllability never applies in any of these cases.

We deal with the most obvious case, (1), in Sections 13.2 and 13.3; and with case (2) in Sections 13.3, 13.4, and 13.5. In Section 13.3 we also discuss cases (2) and (4); in Sections 13.4 and 13.5, in addition to case (2), we review case (3). Notice those two sections are relevant for the all-important case where policymakers are subject to costs on, or limits to, the use of their instruments: i.e., for case (5).

13.2 Instability, centralized institutions and alternatives

Economic systems are characterized by systemic instability. In a broad sense, instability is related to short run fluctuations and/or the existence of multiple long run equilibria. In the former, given an equilibrium path, instability is manifested by large fluctuations around this path. In the latter case, the economy can be trapped in a sub-optimal equilibrium for a long time with high welfare losses; or may switch between equilibria. The two concepts are also connected: if there are multiple equilibria, the agents face a coordination problem in making their expectations converge toward one of them. Moreover, as we have shown in Part III, it is also possible that, although there may be a clear unique equilibrium for the economy (a unique equilibrium in outcome space), agents might not be able to reach it as there are multiple paths toward it (multiple equilibria in instrument space).

As a result, instability is, even if not exclusively, strongly related to the existence of multiple equilibria in outcome or policy space and the problem of coordinating private expectations. Multiple equilibria, in fact, always depend on uncoordinated actions set at a decentralized level; more precisely on a failure to coordinate private expectations. As a result, the instability associated with multiple equilibrium existence can be naturally solved by a centralized solution: a social planner has no problem of coordinating his action with respect to the expectation of the others as he sets all instruments at the same time. However, this solution has many practical problems of implementation, both in the case of common interest games and in the case of conflicts. In the former, for instance, centralization may have high costs in collecting the information needed and can be subject to costly delays. In the latter, centralization has to solve also the problem of which equilibrium the social planner should converge to, as the conflict among the players does not guarantee a clear answer to this question.

Chapter 7 has offered us a number of scenarios where some kind of institution would be needed to support and promote centralized decision making rather than to leave the field free for decentralized (and self-interested) decision making, and hence a rationale for why such institutions are necessary in a number of rather common situations.

One set of situations where institutions are needed to support centralized or coordinated decisions will involve an agreed institutional framework run on behalf of the common good, and (one hopes) in the common interest, by a hegemon or designated leader; or when a common institution is jointly run by the participants as a social planning device. Nevertheless, a second set emerges when a coordinating institution is needed to oversee a sequence of policy announcements intended to act as an equilibrium selection device and coordinate the information sets that the players need to establish the credibility of these announcements.

The need for this second set of situations derives from cases where there are multiple (and not necessarily equally good) equilibria. By contrast, the need for institutions to support centralized or coordinated decisions may arise both when there is no defined equilibrium and when there are multiple equilibria: in the former case if we have to pick out a sequence of policy positions that are acceptable (the hegemon/designated leader case), and in the latter if we need to choose one equilibrium that maximizes the joint gains to all on a Pareto optimal or optimal bargaining basis (the social planner case).

Numerous examples of where these two types of situation arise appear in practice, and in the literature. Some of the more obvious are trade policy, especially where tariff or non-tariff barrier reductions are concerned; the management of exchange rate regimes (especially with respect to the choice of exchange rate target values of joint stability); common interest games; natural resource (revenue) games; international monetary arrangements; and the management of public goods in general.

Examples of coordinating institutions to jointly manage policy (in the sense of a social planner) in these cases are the WTO for trade policy and the IMF for international monetary arrangements, or the European Commission to oversee Europe's Stability and Growth Pact. There are also many examples of institutions created to allow a hegemon or designated leader to act as a coordinated focal point. Among these we recall the IMF servicing the Bretton Woods exchange rate system which allowed the USA to act as hegemon; or the European monetary committee (as it was) to oversee the European Monetary System of exchange rates which allowed Germany to act as designated leader for EU monetary policies.

More controversially, perhaps, one could argue that the iterative process of national budget plans being monitored and then adjusted in the light of anticipated changes in ECB monetary policies, under the European Commission's convergence and medium term objectives program, is an instance of a sequence of policy announcements leading (if everyone keeps to the rules) to a selected equilibrium point. The same argument could be used more generally for cases where fiscal and monetary policies adjust to each other in a series of policy changes, where the fiscal authorities and central bank both have instrument independence (as in the USA or UK, for example).

The lesson here is that we often need some form of centralized policymaking to devise policies, or to get to a policy equilibrium or to a stable point when the economic system is over-determined or under-determined so that either multiple equilibria or no equilibrium would otherwise prevail. Policies in these circumstances will break down unless suitable institutions are brought into play. This is not an issue of whether the policies are effective or not, but of what to do when there are multiple or no underlying equilibria. Strong supporting policy institutions are then unavoidable.

13.3 Credibility, target bargaining and implicit coalitions

All economies are complex systems of interactions among many actors who sometimes share some interests but are more often at least partially in competition in attempting to achieve their private objectives. Aside from pure coordination problems represented by common interest games, economic activities are in fact characterized by nonzero-sum games, externalities, or a mix of the two. Externalities lead to inefficient non-cooperative equilibria, which can clearly be avoided by cooperative solutions. But those cooperative solutions need to be supported by some institutional framework designed to hold each player to his agreed policies; that is, to prevent individual players deviating from the agreed policies and trying to re-optimize in their own interest.

Cooperation also involves a dialogue between the parties. This dialogue is usually modeled as a bargaining on policies, which implicitly takes account of the wishes and the relative powers of negotiation of the parties. That is to say, it consists in delegating the choices of policies to an imaginary social planner who takes account of both the preferences of the different players and their relative bargaining power. This kind of solution represents many situations of "institutionalized" cooperation (such as monetary policy in Europe through the ECB).

The creation of a customs union is another example of this mechanism: in a customs union some common institution needs to be created to manage the policy vis-à-vis third countries. By contrast, trade agreements are an example of the latter kind of cooperative mechanism. These agreements are usually signed on the basis of some common targets, not common policies. Another example of the two different ways of implementing a cooperative solution is given by the management of fiscal and monetary policy in common currency areas: consider a monetary union compared to agreements on exchange rate setting between China and the United States. Agreements on common targets are rather common. One example would be agreeing a single set of exchange rate target values for all economies in the European exchange rate mechanism. Other examples are the Louvre accord in 1987 on exchange rate target zones; a single inflation target for coordinated monetary policies in the EU; and a system of common target values for the targets of economic policy at the G7 (now G20) summit meetings each year. Evidently, a common secretariat and system of civil service *sherpas* to negotiate this outcome could be enough to achieve what we want. Notice, however, that this is quite different from negotiating a system of common rules, which is usually the favored approach to this type of policy problem. Not only are common rules very fragile with respect to political pressures and unexpected shocks, they are of no use if policymakers cannot agree (or do not take the trouble to agree) on the underlying policy target values.

Summarizing, cooperation can be associated with two main operative mechanisms: dialogues on the policies to be followed, or on the targets to be pursued. Both need a commitment technology in order to be sustainable, but the commitments can be applied equally to different objectives. Our implicit coalition approach can be used to deepen the cooperation mechanisms of the second type; in fact, implicit coalitions no longer depend on a commitment on policies, but on a commitment to the targets.

As an extension to ideas on controllability, Chapter 8 considered the related possibility of coalitions or implicit coalitions between policymakers (where policymakers continue to act non-cooperatively, but appear to operate *as if* they were in a coalition and thereby benefit by appropriating the coalition gains over the fully non-cooperative solution). For the system as a whole, this produces an intermediate position – partly cooperative and partly non-cooperative; or partly centralized and partly decentralized. It is an important case to look at because the gains to the implicit coalition partners will be larger than they could achieve in a fully cooperative solution if the coalition is powerful enough to expropriate some of the gains that would otherwise go to the coalition's non-members.

In short, our implicit coalition approach studies common interest games for *some* of the policymakers. We discovered that there might be no equilibrium if more than one coalition exists and at least one of them has conflicting interests with other coalitions. But, more generally, unique Nash equilibria or multiple equilibria or no equilibrium will exist. These results naturally give rise to the idea of decisiveness, or partially effective instruments. However, the institutional conditions needed to exploit and realize those coalition gains are different from those for the standard centralization case in the previous section.

Implicit coalitions are rather different from explicit coalitions, although the institutional implications are the same, since all players continue to play non-cooperatively, even if they end up behaving as if they were in a coalition and benefit from the absence of internal conflicts. The conditions for existence or multiplicity of equilibria are thus the same as for any examples of non-cooperative policy games. However, the institutional requirements are the same as for explicit coalitions.

Since the coalition outcomes, either implicit or not, will make each participant better off than under purely non-cooperative decision making, and may produce an equilibrium when unfettered non-cooperative decisions do not, we need an institutional framework that allows coalition members to agree on target values. That is largely a matter of trading and agreeing information on the policy targets and expected outcomes for each player, and then modifying those target values as necessary to make it possible to realize the gains of the agreed coalition policies for each participant.

In a broader perspective, implicit coalitions may thus be viewed as a credible operating mechanism to implement cooperation based on *bargaining on the objectives* and reinforced by a commitment technology. Policymakers with different conflicting objectives can agree to pursue sets or sub-sets of common goals that will be bound by the conditions of implicit coalition that, together with the technologies of commitment on the target, will ensure the credibility of the policy. They will agree if the cost of such a policy is lower than the cost associated with the creation of a "common institution" to manage their policy and internalize the externalities from the non-cooperative solution.

The institutional lesson here is that agreeing on target values, not policy rules, is the key to achieving better outcomes overall. Ironically, the history of Europe's Stability and Growth Pact might have been quite different if it had been cast in terms of debt and deficit targets, instead of common policy rules and fiscal limits.

13.4 Monetary transparency, communication and dynamic controllability

Most economists agree that greater transparency in monetary policy is desirable because it allows the private sector to make better – that is, welfare improving – decisions, as well as better-informed decisions (Blinder, 1998). However, not all agree on this. Some argue that incomplete transparency is optimal, as the effect on the central bank's reputation and its consequent ability to control inflation has to be balanced against the private sector's wish to see output, employment and prices stabilized (see for example Faust and Svensson, 2001 or Jensen, 2002). Others argue that certain restrictions on transparency are important for operational reasons. Once again, the idea is to reinforce the credibility of the central bank (Eijffinger and Hoeberichts, 2002) and to separate "the need to know" from "the need to understand" (Issing, 1999).

Since the mid-1990s, there has been a trend toward greater transparency in economic policymaking – particularly with respect to monetary policy. As a result, a number of central banks have actually increased their transparency, using inflation forecasts, extensive explanations of the reasoning behind their decisions, and sometimes voting records on policy decisions or a discussion of the "bias" in those decisions. Prominent examples are found in the Federal Reserve System in the United States; but also in the Bank of England, and in the Central Banks of Canada, New Zealand and Sweden. Yet, on the basis of casual empiricism or circumstantial evidence, one cannot tell whether greater transparency has actually made any factual difference to the policies chosen – or, more exactly, to the impact and effectiveness of those policies. Nor is it possible to determine exactly what kind of effects one should expect, in terms of average inflation, output performance and the stability of these indicators.

In discussing modeling and evaluating the effects of transparency, the main problem is that it has many different dimensions, and may mean different things to different people (Eijffinger and Geraats, 2006). As a result, there are different ways to introduce transparency into theoretical models, and there are different indexes used to measure it in empirical studies.[1]

Kuttner and Posen (2000) list a number of characteristics thought necessary for "institutional" transparency in monetary policy. These are: (1) a numerical goal; (2) an inflation report, explaining the expected effects of changes in monetary policy; (3) an inflation forecast (plus assumptions) explaining why those changes were necessary; (4) a post-mortem evaluation of past policies and their achievements. The same characteristics would apply to other policies, say fiscal policies, where the goals, report and forecasts apply to the target of that policy (output gap, employment, stability, growth).

These attributes cover both the information content and the way in which that information has been used. That distinction is important, but is seldom made. The distinction itself relates directly to the potential for conflict between the ability to control and the need for transparency. As a result, commentators may reach opposite conclusions about the need for transparency.

For instance, Kuttner and Posen (1999) argue that it enhances the central bank's ability to use discretionary policies, while Faust and Svensson (2002) argue the opposite (albeit in particular cases). In fact, both sets of authors agree that transparency will reduce the noise and the imprecision in the private sector's decision making. They only differ as to whether greater transparency would increase the ability of the central bank and private sector to make consistent decisions, or whether it would reduce the central bank's ability to control the private sector's natural tendency to try to avoid monetary discipline.

In model building, the existing literature typically identifies a lack of transparency with (a) the central bank having private information about the nature of the shocks (Cukierman, 1992, 2001) and (b) the public being unclear about what the central bank's preferences

[1] Multi-dimensional transparency indexes have been developed by, among others, Eijffinger and Geraats (2002) and Di Bartolomeo and Marchetti (2004).

or objectives really are (Cukierman and Meltzer, 1986; Nolan and Schaling, 1998; Muscatelli, 1998). In other words, imperfect transparency is introduced in two forms: imperfect "economic" transparency about the conditioning information, shocks and target values, and imperfect "political" transparency about priorities and objectives. In either case, a lack of transparency introduces a disturbance that distorts the private sector's expectations for inflation and changes the decisions they make.

On this view, the lack of transparency always implies, at least as a direct effect, an increase in uncertainty and thus a variability cost (Demertzis and Hughes Hallett, 2007) – as long as agents aim for smooth and predictable dynamics. However, the associated changes in private sector expectations may sometimes offset or partially offset this cost. The effects of changes in transparency are then closely related to the externalities that the central bank and the private sector have to cope with. For instance, if there is a conflict, the central bank can use the lack of transparency strategically as private information à la Canzoneri (1985) and some degree of opacity may be desired.[2] By contrast, if they face a pure coordination problem, as in some cases of multiple equilibria, the lack of transparency may have greater costs.[3] More complex cases emerge when more strategic agents are involved.[4]

The approach developed in Chapter 12 stresses a further dimension in the debate about the pros and cons of transparency and announcements. This dimension is related to the introduction of forward-looking expectations and the property of dynamic controllability.

A large part of the literature has emphasized that the introduction of forward-looking expectations has destructive effects on the policymaker's ability to influence the economy. Prominent examples of this view are the well-known Lucas' proposition of policy invariance or Ricardian equivalence. However, in Chapter 12, we underlined that

[2] Cuckierman and Meltzer (1986), Grüner (2002), Morris and Shin (2002, 2005, 2007), Demertzis and Hughes Hallett (2003), Issing (2005).

[3] See, e.g., Blinder, Ehrmann, Fratzscher, de Haan and Jansen (2008), Faust and Svensson (2001), Ferguson (2002), Woodford (2005), Svensson (2006).

[4] Typically when the government is also considered: for example, see Hughes Hallett and Viegi (2003), Demertzis, Hughes Hallett, and Viegi (2004), Ciccarone, Marchetti and Di Bartolomeo (2007).

these cases, although celebrated for their relevance, are not general but rather special ones. The introduction of forward-looking expectations in fact does not in general reduce the effectiveness of the policymaker's action; on the contrary, under some circumstances, it can even improve it.

The point is simple: the introduction of "new" variables (i.e., expectations) that react to the policymaker's actions does not necessarily offset them. In fact they may even reinforce the policymaker's ability to pursue his targets when the conditions for dynamic controllability are satisfied. In the abstract where, in addition to this controllability condition, also perfect knowledge of both the model and of the policymaker's preferences are ensured, forward-looking expectations actually enhance the ability of the policymaker to reach his targets by guaranteeing controllability in a shorter time. In this case, knowledge of the policymaker's preferred target values becomes crucial to forming "correct" and thus "useful" expectations by the private sector. This knowledge can be spread directly by providing information about the policy targets or indirectly by giving information about future policies through announcements. According to this view, in the case where expectations reinforce policy actions, a good communication system becomes an essential prerequisite for good policy.

As shown in Chapter 12, the crucial point is that the extent to which dynamic controllability can be used to reinforce policy depends on the policymaker's ability to exercise good communication skills. In this, announcements can be made credible and have some effect if the private sector is induced to shift (or anchor) their expectations of the likely future outcomes to values that suit the policymaker's purpose. This is true for any policy problem that depends on policy announcements, or on the management or anchoring of expectations, or on the knowledge of the policymaker's information set. But obviously, the private agents need to be convinced that the necessary policy changes will actually take place and achieve the said outcomes.

They will be convinced if their expectations match the outcomes predicted by their own analysis when official policy announcements are inserted for the policy instruments in their models. However, if the aims and desired target values of central bankers are unknown, the private sector cannot anticipate the actions of the monetary authorities – even when the bank's targets do not conflict with those of the private sector. Good communication about all aspects of the problem is therefore a crucial factor and the institutional arrangements underpinning policy must make sufficient and detailed provision for such communication.

Our vision of the importance of communication differs from the recent trend in the literature. In our framework, the crucial element is to reaffirm the policy targets and why the policies chosen can be expected to reach them; as emphasized by Eggertson and Pugsley (2006), Moessner and Nelson (2008), Ferrero and Secchi (2009) and Libich (2009), and by Woodford's (2003) observation that policy trade-offs will be eased when expectations fall into line. By contrast, much of the recent communication literature has focused on the quality of forecasts, on the degree of divergence or agreement among policymakers, and on transcripts or voting records from policy committees (Ehrmann and Fratzscher, 2005, 2007; Jansen and de Haan, 2006; Visser and Swank, 2007).

As noted before, announcements and communication about future trends in policy, aimed at influencing expectations of both policy actions and outcomes for the purpose of improving the performance of the economy, comes in the Federal Reserve's attempts to reflate the US economy after the financial crisis in 2008. Specific instances are forward guidance in the form of announcing, in 2011, that interest rates would be kept low until 2014; or, in 2009, how the exit strategy from the Fed's asset purchases in the large-scale asset purchase programs QE1, QE2 and Operation Twist between 2009 and 2011 would be accomplished. Williams (2011) makes it clear that the Federal Reserve now regards forward guidance as an important part of its monetary policy arsenal.

13.5 Fiscal credibility and commitment: a Fiscal Policy Commission

Communication is traditionally seen as a problem for the central bank in its conduct of monetary policy, but it is just as much a crucial factor in fiscal policy. Indeed, the Swedish Fiscal Policy Council has an explicit mandate to comment on, and where necessary recommend improvements to, the communication practices for (explanation of, and justification for) changes to the Swedish government's fiscal policies – and it has availed itself of the chance to do so (Calmfors, 2012).

Traditional monitoring procedures of fiscal policy are based on automatic and partial rules, which are backward-looking. As far as fiscal policy could be used to anchor expectations, these characteristics of monitoring procedures are a defect. They do not imply any pressure to modify fiscal plans in the light of predictable future problems. An independent Fiscal Policy Commission (FPC) should have responsibility for (a) reviewing the fiscal outlook for the government and the public; (b) reviewing the revenues likely to be available; (c) estimating current *structural* positions; (d) estimating the likely consequences of current spending plans, including those implied by changing demography and pension costs, and developments in partner economies; and (e) giving advice on possible corrections to the current policy. In particular, tasks (d) and (e) should underpin the role of anchoring expectations.

The tasks of the FPC should thus be designed to provide an informed and independent assessment of the fiscal position and general prospects for the economy as a whole, covering the outlook for public finances and the main targets of policy into the future. This would bring fiscal policy back to a system that safeguards solvency and efficiency, without impairing the policymaker's ability to apply discretion or judgment. More importantly, it would be forward-looking. And by entrusting the analysis and judgment of sustainability to an independent commission, it would solve the basic credibility problem that arises in any fiscal regime: namely, that governments are left to judge the quality and sustainability of their own policies, especially those with financing implications that last beyond the next election. In this regard, a proper balance between long run sustainability and short run obligations can be maintained by making the assessments independent of short term political pressures.[5]

An FPC should be expected to act as referee in the budgeting process. The FPC should judge the compatibility of changes in government

[5] This discussion draws heavily on earlier work: Fatàs, Hughes Hallett, Sibert, Strauch and von Hagen (2003), Eichengreen, Hausman, and von Hagen (1999), Wyplosz (2005), and most recently Hughes Hallett and Jensen (2012). An alternative discussion can be found in Leeper (2009). Many countries now operate a fiscal policy watchdog system, including Belgium, Canada, Chile, Germany, Hungary and Sweden.

debt with the sustainability of the country's public finances. Its assessment would take into account past and current economic performance and the medium-term outlook of the economy, as well as the financial position of its public sector. The FPC would issue a public warning if it concluded that a government's fiscal plans were not sustainable in the longer term. In this case, it would demand adjustments and make recommendations for such adjustments. The FPC would also monitor, and publicly comment on, the development of public debt during the course of each fiscal year to see whether the government had complied with their plans and whether any slippage had arisen that might have damaging consequences for sustainability.

To fulfill its role properly and make unbiased judgments, the FPC would need full political independence. The independence of the FPC also demands a high degree of transparency in its operations.[6]

It is clear that the responsibility for ensuring sustainability, and the choice of fiscal policies, would remain firmly with the government. The FPC warnings would, however, force a government to argue openly about sustainability and signal that sustainability is their responsibility to achieve. Governments would retain full control over all fiscal policy instruments and, hence, control over the adjustments to be made when sustainability is at risk.

As Calmfors (2012) emphasizes, in conceiving the role of an FPC there is a fundamental trade-off between devising an organization restricted to forecasting and commenting on (or recommending changes to) the likely future state of public finances and debt and an organization with a wider remit to monitor the likely implications for the other targets of policy[7] and to recommend changes to the policies that guide the evolution of those targets that would improve the economy's fiscal balances.

The former is a narrow definition that risks turning the council into a statistical audit agency and making it less relevant as an effective policy watchdog (as has happened, some have argued, to the Office of Budget Responsibility in the UK). The latter definition provides for a more effective policy watchdog (like the Swedish Fiscal Policy

[6] For details on a possible articulation of a FPC, see Hughes Hallett and Jensen (2012).

[7] E.g., employment, growth, income distribution, how well the government communicates, explains or forecasts the outcomes of its own policies, and so on.

Council), but risks the council becoming politicized if it inadvisedly enters the policy debate on guidelines, priorities and appropriate targets for policy – and places an important premium on maintaining the independence of the council (for example, by making it report to parliament rather than to the government of the day).

The benefit from a FPC could lie in the fact that its independent assessment can add to the credibility of the government and ensure dynamic controllability. In the case when the FPC finds that government policy is not sound, its advice can help the policymakers to improve their policies, moving them toward a more credible path and a position of dynamic controllability. As a second opinion on the soundness and reliability of the government's policies, the FPC's analysis would complement (reinforce or possibly change) the private sector's own analysis of the likely outcomes – and thereby increase the power of the government's announcements of future policy. It is important in that context that the FPC should be independent of the government and its agencies, should have access to its own forecasts and information, but should accept the government's own policy priorities and target values. Given that, the private sector's evaluation of the government's fiscal health and the likely outcomes for the economy must be a matter of judgment, will likely vary in different cases, but may lead to some changes in behavior.

14 A summary and round-up of the conclusions

The design of economic policy represents, under various different perspectives, an intriguing and complex challenge for both scholars and policymakers. Policies are often implemented based on common or ad-hoc beliefs or preconceived theories. But this process can be enormously damaging to society. In order to avoid misleading decisions, the design of optimal policies needs a logical and consistent general framework in which the effects and the interactions of the policymaker's choices with the decisions or expectations of other agents and their activities are correctly and fully taken into account.

If we fail to create such a framework, policies based on common beliefs may neglect the effects of the decisions taken by others, or the expectations that those policies create; and that in turn could easily offset the policymaker's original intents and lead to outcomes different from those expected. That would render the original policies counterproductive. Moreover, and perhaps even more serious, since optimal policies always depend on certain underlying theoretical assumptions, if those assumptions are not made clear but are sold instead (in a kind of intellectual mystification) as a general methodology to investigate policy problems, then again the limits and reliability of the policy proposals will inevitably remain undefined. In other words, the "muddle" between assumptions and propositions imposed by models based on some kind of orthodoxy creates a foggy area around the trustworthiness or reliability of their policy implications.

The first purpose of this book was therefore to provide scholars and policymakers with a clear and consistent framework with which to analyze problems of economic policy. Our approach was built on the idea that the economic outcomes are the result of (rational) interactions and conflicts between many agents or agencies, both private and public. Our analytic tools are therefore quite naturally based on game theory. However, as a part of that intellectual philosophy, our approach is necessarily and clearly unrelated to any specific school of thought or economic view. In this sense it is general, neutral, and consistent with different views of how the economy works or should be made to work. Thus, having covered any strategic interaction (including cooperation, coalitions, hegemonic behavior, strategic announcements) and endogenous expectations, our techniques and results (though not necessarily all the detailed examples we present) can be applied to and used in any context advocated by any of the standard schools of economic thought.

More specifically, by revisiting the Tinbergen–Theil classical theory of economic policy in a policy game context, we have been able to develop a new theory that takes account of the Lucas critique and that fully explores the deeper meaning of the rational expectations hypothesis. We are able to distinguish the concept of rational expectations in terms of a mathematical description of the expectation formation process, and the mechanical process of solving economic models for their policy implications, from the proposition of policy invariance which can be derived from rational expectationss under certain specific circumstances. We have shown that rational expectations are in fact introduced as a tool to summarize the interactions between agents and not as a constraint to obtain certain implications for policy. As a result we obtain a richer and more general framework, in which the relevance and limits of the public actions can be more readily investigated and discussed.

We also focus on two unusual theoretical issues in policy design: policy invariance, and policy equilibrium existence and uniqueness. For the policymaker, and for society as a whole, these issues can be translated into two crucial debates: the question of the state vs. markets, and the debate on the stability of the economic system. Our results give certain (that is to say, not uncertain or conditional) answers to those fundamental questions.

With respect to the former question, in order to investigate policy neutrality we have provided some simple theoretical tools based on Tinbergen's Golden Rule in a general set-up with expectations and policy games. We showed how the introduction of strategic interactions or rational expectations does not necessarily imply that public policy invariance holds, even if perfect information is assumed. On the contrary, in the majority of cases, rational expectations provide an additional powerful instrument for enhancing the policymakers' policy power in the form of announcements with which governments may be able to influence economic outcomes. From the point of view of practical applications, the importance of taking a neutral approach, as here, is borne out by the fact that the celebrated superiority of markets over public policy has proved to be a fallacy in many important cases.

Concerning the issue of stability, we have provided the tools to investigate the existence of an equilibrium of the policy game and its potential multiplicity. Again our tools are useful not only from a theoretical point of view; but also because they stress the sources of non-existence and/or multiple equilibria, which translated into policymaker terms means that they can provide guidelines for the optimal design of the institutional set-up. It naturally follows, in fact, that our theory has implications for both model building and optimal institutional design. Theoretical economists may be more interested in the former, whereas practical policymakers or political scientists would be more interested in the latter.

Policy invariance and economic stability are perhaps the main issues discussed under different perspectives in both static and dynamic policymaking contexts. However, we used our approach also to explore many other aspects of policy, such as (implicit) coalition formation, policy announcements, credibility and time consistency. For instance, we investigated the conditions under which policymakers can implicitly coordinate their actions and when they cannot. We explored the issue of policy announcements, deriving a theory of their strategic use in situations where there are potentially multiple equilibria and when those announcements may be considered credible or not. We showed that, under a range of conditions, announcements may act as an equilibrium selection device. Alternative mechanisms to solve multiple equilibrium problems have also been investigated: for example, the role of hegemonic leaders, or the imposition of costs on the policymakers' actions (instrument costs). Further, we derived the conditions under which policymakers can manage expectations to enhance the effectiveness of their policy instruments by means of forward guidance indicators of future policies or outcomes – as the Fed and other central banks have so often done (or tried to do) in the recent financial crisis.

In our uncertain times, where some common beliefs are debated and the policy discussions are strongly influenced by preconceived ideologies, a general approach to evaluate the consistency of economic policy suggestions may represent strong value added for both scholars and policymakers. Although many approaches and many valuable theories are available to investigate specific issues, a general benchmark by which we can evaluate these proposals has been striking by its absence from the literature. In developing a new theory of economic policy along the lines originally set out by Tinbergen, Theil and Frisch, but updated to account for all the methodological issues that we now know to be crucial for a realistic evaluation of the policy options in any particular case, we have attempted to fill this vacuum and bridge the gap between theory and practice.

References

Acocella, N. and G. Ciccarone (1997). "Trade unions, non-neutrality and stagflation." *Public Choice*, 91: 161–178.

Acocella, N. and G. Di Bartolomeo (2004). "Non-neutrality of monetary policy in policy games." *European Journal of Political Economy*, 20: 695–707.

(2005). "Controllability and non-neutrality of economic policy: The Tinbergen's approach revised." *Working Paper No 81*, Public Economics Department, University of Rome La Sapienza.

(2006). "Tinbergen and Theil meet Nash: controllability in policy games." *Economics Letters*, 90: 213–218.

(2010). "Convergenza di interessi, conflitto e coordinamento nella fornitura di beni pubblici." *Politica economica*, 3: 389–408.

(2011). "Theoretical issues in the provision of global public goods," in N. Acocella (ed.), *Governance and Distributional Issues in Global Public Goods*, Rome: Università La Sapienza Publishing House.

(2012). "The cost of social pacts." *Bulletin of Economic Research*. In press, first published online: http://onlinelibrary.wiley.com/doi/10.1111/j.1467-8586.2011.00405.x/full.

Acocella, N., G. Di Bartolomeo and D. A. Hibbs (2008). "Labor market regimes and the effects of monetary policy." *Journal of Macroeconomics*, 30: 134–156.

Acocella, N., G. Di Bartolomeo and A. J. Hughes Hallett (2006). "Controllability in policy games: Policy neutrality and the theory of economic policy revisited." *Computational Economics*, 28: 91–112.

(2007). "Dynamic controllability with overlapping targets: or why target independence may not be good for you." *Macroeconomic Dynamics*, 11: 202–213.

Acocella, N., G. Di Bartolomeo, A. J. Hughes Hallett and P. G. Piacquadio (2009). *Announcement Wars as an Equilibrium Selection Device*, CORE D.P. 2009/77, Université Catholique de Louvain.

Acocella, N., G. Di Bartolomeo and W. Pauwels (2010). "Is there any scope for corporatism in stabilisation policies?" *Empirica*, 37: 403–424.

Acocella, N., G. Di Bartolomeo and P. G. Piacquadio (2009). "Conflict of interest, (implicit) coalitions and Nash policy games." *Economics Letters*, 105: 303–305.

Acocella, N., G. Di Bartolomeo and P. Tirelli (2009). "The macroeconomics of social pacts." *Journal of Economic Behavior & Organization*, 72: 202–313.

(2012a)."Trend inflation, the labor market wedge, and the non-vertical Phillips curve." *Journal of Policy Modelling*, in press.

(2012b). "Inflation as a worker disciplining device: EMU vs. US." *Empirica*, in press.

Alesina, A. and G. Tabellini (1987). "Rules and discretion with noncoordinated monetary and fiscal policies." *Economic Inquiry*, 25: 619–630.

Amato, J. D., S. Morris and H. S. Shin (2003). "Communication and monetary policy." *Oxford Review of Economic Policy*, 18: 495–503.

Andersen, T. G., T. Bollerslev, F. X. Diebold and C. Vega (2003). "Micro effects of macro announcements: real-time price discovery in foreign exchange." *American Economic Review*, 93: 38–62.

Andersen, T. M. and F. Schneider (1986). "Coordination of fiscal and monetary policy under different institutional arrangements." *European Journal of Political Economy*, 2: 169–191.

Aoki, M. (1976). *Optimal Control and System Theory in Dynamic Economic Analysis*. Amsterdam: North Holland.

Archer, D. (2005). "Central bank communication and the publication of interest rate projections." Basel: Bank for International Settlements, mimeo.

Athans, M. and P. L. Falb (1966). *Optimal Control.* New York: McGraw-Hill.

Athans, M., E. Kuh, L. Papademos, R. Pyndick, T. Ozan and K. Wall (1976). "Sequential open loop, optimal control of a nonlinear macroeconomic model," in M. D. Intriligator (ed.), *Frontiers of Quantitative Economics*. Amsterdam: North Holland, Vol. IIIA.

Aumann, R. (1974). "Subjectivity and correlation in randomized strategies." *Journal of Mathematical Economics*, 1: 67–96.

(1990). "Nash equilibria are not self-enforcing," in J. J. Gabszewicz, J. F. Richard and L. A. Wosley (eds.), *Economic Decision-Making: Games, Econometrics and Optimization*. Amsterdam: Elsevier.

Backus, D. and J. Driffill (1984). "Rational expectations and policy credibility following a change in regime." *Review of Economic Studies*, 52: 211–221.

(1985). "Inflation and reputation." *American Economic Review*, 75: 530–538.

Balduzzi, P., E. J. Elton and T. C. Green (2001). "Economic news and bond prices: Evidence from the U.S. treasury market." *Journal of Financial and Quantitative Analysis*, 36: 523–543.

Baliga, S. and S. Morris (2002). "Co-ordination, spillovers, and cheap talk." *Journal of Economic Theory*, 108: 450–468.

Barro, R. J. (1974). "Are government bonds net wealth?" *Journal of Political Economy*, 82: 1095–1117.

Barro, R. J. and D. Gordon (1983). "Rules, discretion and reputation in a model of monetary policy." *Journal of Monetary Economics*, 12: 101–120.

Başar, T. and G. J. Olsder (1995). *Dynamic Noncooperative Game Theory*, 2nd ed. London: Academic Press (first edition 1982).

Beetsma, R. M. W. J. and L. Bovenberg (1998). "Monetary union without fiscal coordination may discipline policymakers." *Journal of International Economics*, 45: 239–258.

Beetsma, R. M. W. J. and X. Debrun (2007). "The new stability and growth pact: A first assessment." *European Economic Review*, 51: 453–477.

Beetsma, R. M. W. J. and H. Jensen (1998). "Inflation targets and contracts with uncertain central banker preferences." *Journal of Money, Credit and Banking*, 30: 384–403.

(2003). "Why money talks and wealth whispers: monetary uncertainty and mystique: comment." *Journal of Money, Credit and Banking*, 35: 129–136.

(2005). "Monetary and fiscal policy interactions in a micro-founded model of a monetary union." *Journal of International Economics*, 67: 320–352.

Beetsma, R. M. W. J. and H. Uhlig (1999). "An analysis of the Stability and Growth Pact." *Economic Journal*, 109: 546–571.

Bellman, R. (1957). *Dynamic Programming*. Princeton University Press.

(1961). *Adaptive Control Processes: A Guided Tour*. Princeton University Press.

Benigno, P. (2002). "A simple approach to international monetary policy coordination." *Journal of International Economics*, 57: 177–196.

Benigno, P. and M. Woodford (2005). "Inflation stabilization and welfare: the case of a distorted steady state." *Journal of the European Economic Association*, 3: 1185–1236.

(2006). "Optimal taxation in an RBC model: a linear-quadratic approach." *Journal of Economic Dynamics and Control*, 30: 1445–1489.

(2012). "Linear-quadratic approximation of optimal policy problems." *Journal of Economic Theory*, 147: 1–42.

Ben-Israel, A. and T. N. E. Greville (2003). *Generalized Inverses*. Berlin: Springer-Verlag.

Binmore, K. G. (1987). "Nash Bargaining Theory I, II, III," in K.G. Binmore and P. Dasgupta (eds.), *The Economics of Bargaining*. Oxford: Blackwell: 27–46, 61–76, 239–256.

Blanchard, O. J. and C. M. Khan (1980). "The solution of linear difference models under rational expectations." *Econometrica*, 48: 1305–1310.

Blanchard, O. J. and N. Kiyotaki (1987). "Monopolistic competition and the effects of aggregate demand." *American Economic Review*, 77: 647–666.

Blinder, A. (1998). *Central Banking in Theory and Practice*. Cambridge, MA: MIT Press.

Blinder, A., M. Ehrmann, M. Fratzscher, J. de Haan and D. J. Jansen (2008). "Central bank communication and monetary policy: a survey of theory and evidence." *Journal of Economic Literature*, 46: 910–945.

Blume, A. and A. Ortmann (2007). "The effects of costless pre-play communication: experimental evidence from games with Pareto-ranked equilibria." *Journal of Economic Theory*, 132: 274–290.

Brainard, W. (1967). "Uncertainty and the effectiveness of policy." *American Economic Review*, 57: 411–425.

Brandsma, A. and A. J. Hughes Hallett (1984). "The structure of rational expectations behaviour: an empirical view," in J. P. Ancot (ed.), *The Structural Analysis of Economic Models*. Boston and Dordrecht: Nijhoff Academic Publishers.

Buiter, W. H. and M. Gersovitz (1981). "Issues in controllability and the theory of economic policy." *Journal of Public Economics*, 15: 33–43.

(1984). "Controllability and the theory of economic policy: a further note." *Journal of Public Economics*, 24: 127–129.

Buti, M., W. Roeger and J. In't Veld (2002). "Stabilizing output and inflation: policy conflicts and co-operation under a stability pact." *Journal of Common Market Studies*, 39: 801–828.

Caffé, F. (1966). *Politica Economica. Sistematica e Tecniche di Analisi*. Torino: Boringhieri.

Calmfors, L. (2012). "The Swedish Fiscal Policy Council: watchdog with a broad remit." *CESifo Working Paper 3725*. CES Institute, University of Munich.

Camerer, C. (2003). *Behavioral Game Theory. Experiments in Strategic Interaction*. Princeton University Press.

Canzoneri, M. B. (1985). "Monetary policy games and the role of private information." *American Economic Review*, 75: 1056–1070.

Carraro, C. (2003). *The Endogenous Formation of Economic Coalitions*. Cheltenham, UK: Edward Elgar.

Cavallari, L. (2001). "Inflation and openness with non-atomistic wage setters." *Scottish Journal of Political Economy*, 48: 210–225.

Charness, G. (2000). "Self-serving cheap talk: a test of Aumann's conjecture." *Games and Economic Behavior*, 33: 177–194.

Chen, Y., N. Katik and J. Sobel (2008). "Selecting cheap-talk equilibria." *Econometrica*, 76: 117–136.

Chow, G. C. (1972). "Optimal control of linear econometric systems with finite time horizon." *International Economic Review*, 13: 16–25.

(1973). "Problems of economic policy from the viewpoint of optimal control." *American Economic Review*, 63: 825–837.

(1975). *Analysis and Control of Dynamics Systems*. New York: Wiley.

Chwe, M. (1994). "Farsighted coalitional stability." *Journal of Economic Theory*, 63: 299–325.

Ciccarone, G., E. Marchetti and G. Di Bartolomeo (2007). "Unions, fiscal policy and central bank transparency." *The Manchester School*, 75: 617–633.

Clarida, R., J. Galì, and M. Gertler (1999). "The science of monetary policy." *Journal of Economic Literature*, 37: 1661–1707.

(2001). "Optimal monetary policy in open vs. closed economies: an integrated approach." *American Economic Review*, 91: 248–252.

Cochrane, J. H. (2011). "Determinacy and identification with Taylor rules." *Journal of Political Economy*, 119: 565–615.

Cooper, R. (1999). *Coordination Games: Complementarities and Macroeconomics*. Cambridge University Press.

Cooper, R. N. (1969). "Macroeconomic policy adjustment in interdependent economics." *Quarterly Journal of Economics*, 82: 1–24.

Cooper, R. and A. John (1988). "Coordinating coordination failures in Keynesian models." *Quarterly Journal of Economics*, 103: 441–463.

Cooper, R., D. V. De Jong, R. Forsythe, and T. Ross (1989). "Communication in the battle of the sexes game." *Rand Journal of Economics*, 20: 568–587.

(1990). "Selection criteria in coordination games: Some experimental results." *American Economic Review*, 80: 218–233.

(1992). "Communication in coordination games." *The Quarterly Journal of Economics*, 107: 739–771.

Coricelli, F., A. Cukierman and A. Dalmazzo (2004). "Economic performance and stabilization in a monetary union with imperfect labor and goods markets." In H-W. Sinn and M. Widgrén (eds.), *Issues of Monetary Integration in Europe*. Cambridge, MA: MIT Press.

(2006). "Monetary institutions, monopolistic competition, unionized labor markets and economic performance." *Scandinavian Journal of Economics*, 108: 39–63.

Corsetti, G. and P. Pesenti (2001). "Welfare and macroeconomic interdependence." *Quarterly Journal of Economics*, 116: 421–446.

Crawford, V. (1998). "A survey of experiments on communication via cheap talk." *Journal of Economic Theory*, 78: 286–298.

Crawford, V. and J. Sobel (1982). "Strategic information transmission." *Econometrica*, 50: 1431–1452.

Cubitt, R. P. (1992). "Monetary policy games and private sector precommitment." *Oxford Economic Papers*, 44: 513–530.

(1995). "Corporatism, monetary policy and macroeconomic performance: a simple game theoretic analysis." *Scandinavian Journal of Economics*, 97: 245–259.

(1997). "Stagflationary bias and the interaction of monetary policy and wages in a unionized economy." *Public Choice*, 93: 165–178.

Cuciniello, V. (2011). "The welfare effect of foreign monetary conservatism with non-atomistic wage setters." *Journal of Money, Credit and Banking*, 43: 1719–1734.

Cukierman, A. (1992). *Central Bank Strategy, Credibility and Independence: Theory and Evidence*. Cambridge, MA: MIT Press.

(2001). "Accountability, credibility, transparency and stabilisation policy in the Euro system," in C. Wyplosz (ed.), *The Impact of EMU on Europe and the Developing Countries*. Oxford University Press, pp. 40–75.

(2004). "Monetary institutions, monetary union and unionized labor markets – some recent developments," in R. Beetsma, C. Favero, A. Missale, V. A. Muscatelli, P. Natale, and P. Tirelli (eds.), *Monetary Policy, Fiscal Policies and Labour Markets: Key Aspects of Macroeconomic Policymaking in EMU*. Cambridge University Press.

Cukierman, A. and F. Lippi (2001). "Labour markets and monetary union: a strategic analysis." *The Economic Journal*, 111: 541–565.

Cukierman, A. and A. Meltzer (1986). "A theory of ambiguity credibility and inflation under discretion and asymmetric information." *Econometrica*, 54: 1099–1128.

Cuthbertson, K. and M. P. Taylor (1987). *Macroeconomic Systems*. Oxford: Blackwell.

Dasgupta, P. and E. Maskin (1986). "The existence of the equilibrium in discontinuous economic games I: Theory." *Review of Economic Studies*, 53: 1–26.

Debreu, G. (1952). "A social equilibrium existence theorem." *Proceedings of the National Academy of Sciences*, 38: 886–893.

Demertzis, M. and A. J. Hughes Hallett (2003). "Three models of imperfect transparency in monetary policy." *CEPR Discussion Paper No. 4117*. London: CEPR.

(2007). "Central bank transparency in theory and practice." *Journal of Macroeconomics*, 29: 760–789.

Demertzis, M., A. J. Hughes Hallett and N. Viegi (2004). "An independent central bank faced with elected governments." *European Journal of Political Economy*, 20: 907–922.

Demertzis, M. and N. Viegi (2008). "Inflation targets as focal points." *International Journal of Central Banking*, 4: 55–87.

Dennis, R., K. Leitemo and U. Söderström (2009). "Monetary policy in a small open economy with a preference for robustness," unpublished manuscript, Federal Reserve Bank of San Francisco.

Detken, C. and M. Gartner (1992). "Governments, trade unions and the macroeconomy: an expository analysis of the political business cycle." *Public Choice*, 73: 37–53.

Di Bartolomeo, G. (2002). "Calmfors and Driffill's hump-shaped relationship: a different view," in R. Balducci and S. Staffolani (eds.), *Income Distribution, Unemployment and Growth*. Napoli: ESI, pp. 261–280.

(2005). "Unions' inflation aversion and international competitiveness." *Journal of Policy Modeling*, 27: 137–142.

(2007). "Interest groups and the monetary policy management." *Journal of Current Issues in Finance, Business and Economics*, 1: 71–89.

Di Bartolomeo, G. and F. Giuli (2011). "Fiscal and monetary interaction under monetary policy uncertainty." *European Journal of Political Economy*, 27: 369–375.

Di Bartolomeo, G., F. Giuli and M. Manzo (2009). "Policy uncertainty, symbiosis, and the optimal fiscal and monetary conservativeness." *Empirica*, 36: 462–476.

Di Bartolomeo, G. and E. Marchetti (2004). "Central banks and information provided to the private sector." *BNL Quarterly Review*, 230: 265–297.

Di Bartolomeo, G. and W. Pauwels (2006). "The issue of instability in a simple policy game between the central bank and a representative union." *Public Choice*, 126: 275–296.

Di Bartolomeo, G., N. Acocella and P. Tirelli (2012). "Inflation targets and endogenous wage markups in a New Keynesian Model." *Journal of Macroeconomics*, 34: 391–403.

Dixit, A. and L. Lambertini (2001). "Monetary–fiscal policy interactions and commitment versus discretion in a monetary union." *European Economic Review*, 45: 977–987.

(2003a). "Interactions of commitment and discretion in monetary and fiscal policy." *American Economic Review*, 93: 1522–1542.

(2003b). "Symbiosis of monetary and fiscal policies in a monetary union." *Journal of International Economics*, 60: 235–247.

Dockner, E., S. Jorgensen, N. Van Long, and G. Sorger (2000). *Differential games in economics and management science*. Cambridge University Press.

Eggertson, G. and B. Pugsley (2006). "The mistake of 1937: a general equilibrium analysis." *Monetary and Economic Studies*. Institute for Monetary and Economic Studies, Bank of Japan, 24, S1: 151–190.

Ehrmann, M. and M. Fratzscher (2005). "How should central banks communicate?" *Working Paper No. 557*. Frankfurt: European Central Bank.

(2007). "Communication by committee members: different strategies, same effectiveness?" *Journal of Money Credit and Banking*, 39: 509–541.

Eichengreen, B., R. Hausman and J. von Hagen (1999). "Reforming budgetary institutions in Latin America: the case for a national fiscal council." *Open Economies Review*, 10: 415–442.

Eijffinger, S. C. W. and M. Hoeberichts, (2002). "Central bank accountability and transparency: theory and some evidence." *International Finance*, 5: 73–96.

Eijffinger, S. C. W. and P. M. Geraats (2006). 'How transparent are central banks?' *European Journal of Political Economy*, 22: 1–21.

Ellison, M. and T. Sargent (2011). "A defence of the FOMC." *International Economic Review*, in press.

Engwerda, J. C. (2000a). "Feedback Nash equilibria in the scalar infinite horizon LQ game." *Automatica*, 36: 135–139.

(2000b). "The solution set of the *N*-player scalar Feedback Nash algebraic Riccati equations." *IEEE Transactions on Automatic Control*, 45: 2363–2369.

Eusepi, S. and B. Preston (2010). "Central bank communication and expectations stabilization." *American Economic Journal: Macro*, 2: 235–271.

Evans, G. W. and S. Honkapohja (2003). "Expectations and the stability problem for optimal monetary policies." *Review of Economic Studies*, 70: 807–824.

(2006). "Monetary policy, expectations and commitment." *Scandinavian Journal of Economics*, 108: 15–38.

Fair, R. (2003). "Shock effects on stocks, bonds and exchange rates." *Journal of International Money and Finance*, 22: 307–341.

Farrell, J. (1987). "Cheap talk, coordination, and entry." *Rand Journal of Economics*, 18: 34–39.

(1988). "Communication, coordination and Nash equilibrium." *Economics Letters*, 27: 209–214.

(1995). "Talk is cheap." *American Economic Review*, 85: 186–190.

Farrell, J. and M. Rabin (1996). "Cheap talk." *Journal of Economic Perspectives*, 10: 103–118.

Fatàs, A., A. J. Hughes Hallett, A. Sibert, R. Strauch and J. von Hagen (2003). "Stability and growth in Europe: towards a better pact." *Monitoring European Integration 13*. London: CEPR.

Faust, J. and L. E. O. Svensson (2001). "Transparency and credibility: monetary policy with unobservable goals." *International Economic Review*, 42: 369–397.

(2002). "The equilibrium degree of transparency and control in monetary policy." *Journal of Money, Credit and Banking*, 34: 520–539.

Faust, J., J. H. Rogers, S. B. Wang and J. H. Wright (2007). "The high-frequency response of exchange rates and interest rates to macroeconomic announcements." *Journal of Monetary Economics*, 54: 1051–1068.

Ferguson, R.W., Jr (2002). "Why central banks should talk." Remarks at the Graduate Institute of International Studies, Geneva, 8 January, BIS Review 2.

Ferrero, G. and A. Secchi (2009). "The announcement of monetary policy intentions." *Working Paper No 720*. Rome: Bank of Italy.

Friedman, J. W. (1991). *Game Theory with Applications to Economics*. Oxford University Press.

Friedman, M. (1968). "The role of monetary policy." *American Economic Review*, 58: 1–17.

Frisch, R. (1949). "A memorandum on price–wage-tax subsidy policies as instruments in maintaining optimal employment." UN Document E (CN1/Dub 2). New York: UNO. Reprinted as Memorandum from Universitets Socialokonomiske Institutt, Oslo, 1953.

(1950). "L'emploi des modèles pour l'élaboration d'une politique économique rationnelle." *Revue d'Économie Politique*, 60: 474–498, 601–634.

(1957). "Numerical determination of a quadratic preference function for use in macroeconomic programming." Memorandum from the Institute of Economics at the University of Oslo, No. 14. Reprinted in *Studies in Honour of Gustavo del Vecchio, Giornale degli Economisti e Annali di Economia*, 1961; 1: 43–83.

(1961). "A survey of types of economic forecasting and programming and a brief discussion of the Oslo channel model." Memorandum from the Institute of Economics at the University of Oslo, 13 May.

Fudenberg, D. and J. Tirole (1991). *Game Theory*. Cambridge, MA: MIT Press.

Fuhrer, J. C. and G. R. Moore (1995). "Inflation persistence." *Quarterly Journal of Economics*, 440: 127–159.

Galì, J. (2008). *Monetary Policy, Inflation and the Business Cycle: An Introduction to the New Keynesian Framework*. Princeton University Press.

Galì, J. and M. Gertler (1999). "Inflation dynamics: A structural econometric analysis." *Journal of Monetary Economics*, 44: 195–222.

Gartner, M. (2000). "Political macroeconomics: a survey of recent developments." *Journal of Economic Surveys*, 14: 527–561.

Giannoni, M. (2002). "Does model uncertainty justify caution? Robust optimal monetary policy in a forward-looking model." *Macroeconomic Dynamics*, 6: 114–144.

Gibbons, R. (1992). *Game Theory for Applied Economists*. Princeton University Press.

Glicksberg, I. (1952). "A further generalization of the Kakutani fixed point theorem with application to the Nash equilibrium points." *Proceedings of the American Mathematical Society*, 3: 170–174.

Gnocchi, S. (2009). "Non-atomistic wage setters and monetary policy in a New-Keynesian framework." *Journal of Money, Credit and Banking*, 41: 1613–1630.

Golub, G. H. and C. F. Van Loan (1996). *Matrix Computations*, 3rd ed. Baltimore, MD: Johns Hopkins University Press.

Grüner, H.P. (2002). "How much should central banks talk? A new argument." *Economics Letters*, 77: 195–198.

Guzzo, V. and A. Velasco (1999). "The case for a populist central banker." *European Economic Review*, 43: 1317–1344.

Gylfason, G. and A. Lindbeck (1990). "Wages, money and exchange rates with endogenous unions and governments." *Journal of Policy Modeling*, 12: 469–493.

(1994). "The interaction of monetary policy and wages." *Public Choice*, 79: 33–46.

Hansen, B. (1958). *The Economic Theory of Fiscal Policy*. London: Allen & Unwin.

(1968). *Lectures in Economic Theory II: The Theory of Economic Policy and Planning*. Lund: Studentlitteratur.

Hansen, L. P. and T. J. Sargent (2001). "Robust control and model uncertainty." *American Economic Review*, 91: 60–66.

(2007). *Robustness*. Princeton University Press.

Harsanyi, J. C. and R. Selten (1988). *A General Theory of Equilibrium Selection in Games*. Cambridge, MA: MIT Press.

Heal, G. (1973). *The Theory of Economic Planning*. Amsterdam: North Holland.

Holly, S. and A. J. Hughes Hallett (1989). *Optimal Control, Expectations and Uncertainty*. Cambridge University Press.

House, C. and M. Shapiro (2006). "Phased-in tax cuts and economic activity." *American Economic Review*, 96: 1835–1849.

Hughes Hallett, A. J. (1979). "Computing revealed preferences and limits to the validity of quadratic objective functions for policy optimization." *Economics Letters*, 2: 27–32.

(1981). "Measuring the importance of stochastic control in the design of economic policies." *Economics Letters*, 8: 341–347.

(1984). "Optimal stockpiling in a high-risk commodity market the case of copper." *Journal of Economic Dynamics and Control*, 8: 211–238.

(1986a). "Autonomy and the choice of policy in asymmetrically dependent economies." *Oxford Economic Papers*, 38: 516–544.

(1986b). "International policy design and the sustainability of policy bargains." *Journal of Economic Dynamics and Control*, 10: 457–494.

(1989). "Econometrics and the theory of economic policy: the Tinbergen–Theil contributions 40 years on." *Oxford Economic Papers*, 41: 189–214.

Hughes Hallett, A., N. Acocella and G. Di Bartolomeo (2001). "Tinbergen controllability and *n*-player LQ games." *Economics Letters*, 113: 32–34.

(2012). "A general theory of controllability and expectations anchoring for small-open economies." *Journal of International Money and Finance*, 31: 397–411.

Hughes Hallett, A. J., G. Di Bartolomeo and N. Acocella (2012), "Expectations dynamics: policy, announcements and limits to dynamic inconsistency." *Studies in Nonlinear Dynamics & Econometrics*, 16(2). doi: 10.1515/1558-3708.1918.

Hughes Hallett, A. J. and P. G. Fisher (1988). "Efficient solution techniques for linear and non-linear rational expectations models." *Journal of Economic Dynamics and Control*, 12: 635–657.

Hughes Hallett, A. J. and S.E.H. Jensen (2012). "Fiscal Governance in the Euro-area: institutions vs. rules." *Journal of European Public Policy*, 18: 646–664.

Hughes Hallett, A. J. and H. Rees (1983). *Quantitative Economic Policies and Interactive Planning*. Cambridge University Press.

Hughes Hallett, A. J. and N. Viegi (2003). "Transparency and the strategic use of private information in monetary policy." *The Manchester School*, 71: 498–520.

Hughes Hallett, A. J. and D. N. Weymark (2004). "Independent monetary policies and social equity." *Economics Letters*, 85: 103–110.

(2007). "Fiscal leadership and central bank design." *Canadian Journal of Economics*, 40: 607–627.

Issing, O. (1999). "The monetary policy of the Eurosystem." *Finance and Development*, 36: 18–21.

(2005). "Communication, transparency, accountability: monetary policy in the twenty-first century." *Federal Reserve Bank of St. Louis Review*, 87: 65–83.

James, J. G. and P. Lawler (2009). "Aggregate demand shocks, central bank preferences and macroeconomic outcomes with imperfect information." *Economics Letters*, 105: 208–210.

(2011). "Optimal policy intervention and the social value of public information." *American Economic Review*, 101: 1561–1574.

Jansen, D.-J. and J. De Haan (2006). "Look who's talking: ECB communication during the first years of EMU." *International Journal of Finance and Economics*, 11: 219–228.

Jensen, H. (1993). "International monetary policy cooperation in economies with centralized wage setting." *Open Economies Review*, 4: 269–285.

(1994). "Sustaining policy cooperation between economies of different size." *Journal of International Economics*, 36: 289–307.

(2002). "Optimal degrees of transparency in monetary policy making." *Scandinavian Journal of Economics*, 104: 399–422.

Jerger, J. (2002). "Socially optimal monetary policy institutions." *European Journal of Political Economy*, 18: 761–781.

Johansen, L. (1977). *Lectures on Macro-Economic Planning, Part I.* Amsterdam: North Holland.

(1978). *Lectures on Macro-Economic Planning, Part II.* Amsterdam: North Holland.

Juilliard, M. (2011). "Local approximation of DSGE models around the risky steady state." *Working Paper No. 87.* Department of Communication, University of Teramo, Italy.

Kalman, R. E. (1960). "Contributions to the theory of optimal control." *Boletin de la Sociedad Matematica Mexicana*, 5: 102–119.

Kim, Y. and J. Sobel (1995). "An evolutionary approach to pre-play communication." *Econometrica*, 63: 1181–1193.

Kindleberger, C. P. (1973). *The World in Depression, 1929–1939.* Berkeley and Los Angeles: University of California Press.

Kohlberg, E. and J. F. Mertens (1986). "On the strategic stability of equilibria." *Econometrica*, 54: 1003–1038.

Kohler, M. (2002). "Coalition formation in international monetary policy games." *Journal of International Economics*, 56: 371–385.

Kreps, D. (1990). *Game Theory and Economic Modeling.* Oxford University Press.

Kreps, D. and R. Wilson (1982). "Reputation and imperfect information." *Journal of Economic Theory*, 27: 253–279.

Kuttner, K. N. and A. S. Posen (1999). "Does talk matter after all? Inflation targeting and CB's behavior." *Working Paper n. 99–10*. Washington, DC: Institute for International Economics.

(2000). "Inflation, monetary transparency, and G-3 exchange rate volatility," in E. Hochreiter (ed.), *Adapting to Financial Globalization*. London: Routledge.

Kydland, F. E. and E. C. Prescott (1977). "Rules rather than discretion: the inconsistency of optimal plans." *Journal of Political Economy*, 85: 473–492.

Lambertini, L. (2006). "Monetary-fiscal interactions with a conservative central bank." *Scottish Journal of Political Economy*, 53: 90–128.

Lane, P. (2000). "Asymmetric shocks and monetary policy in a currency union." *Scandinavian Journal of Economics*, 102: 585–604.

Lawler, P. (2000). "Centralised wage setting, inflation contracts and the optimal choice of central banker." *Economic Journal*, 110: 559–575.

(2001). "Monetary policy, central bank objectives and social welfare with strategic wage setting." *Oxford Economic Papers*, 53: 94–113.

(2005). "Central bank inflation contracts and strategic wage setting in a multi-union economy." *Economics Letters*, 88: 323–329.

(2007). "Strategic wage setting, inflation uncertainty and optimal delegation." *European Journal of Political Economy*, 23: 1105–1118.

Leeper, E. M. (1991). "Equilibria under 'active' and 'passive' monetary and fiscal policies." *Journal of Monetary Economics*, 27: 129–147.

(2009). "Anchoring fiscal expectations." *Reserve Bank of New Zealand Bulletin*, 72: 17–42.

Leitemo, K. and U. Söderström (2008). "Robust monetary policy in the New-Keynesian framework." *Macroeconomic Dynamics*, 12: 126–135.

Leontief, W. (1964). "Modern techniques for economic planning and projections," in W. Leontief (ed.), *Essays in Economics, Theories and Theorizing*. Oxford: Blackwell, Vol. 1.

(1976). "National economic planning; methods and problems," in W. Leontief (ed.), *The Economic System in an Age of Discontinuity*. New York University Press.

Libich, J. (2009). "A note on the anchoring effect of explicit inflation targets." *Macroeconomic Dynamics*, 13: 685–697.

Libich, J., A. J. Hughes Hallett, and P. Stehlik (2012). "Monetary and fiscal policy interactions with various degrees of commitment." Paper presented to the American Economic Association 2012 Annual Meeting, Chicago, January 2012.

Lippi, F. (2003). "Strategic monetary policy with non-atomistic wage setters." *Review of Economic Studies*, 70: 909–919.

Lucas, R. E. (1976). "Econometric policy evaluation. A critique." *Journal of Monetary Economics,* Supplement, Carnegie-Rochester Conference Series on Public Policy, 1: 19–46.

Magnus, J. R. and M. S. Morgan (1987). "The ET interview: Professor J. Tinbergen." *Economic Theory*, 3: 117–142.

Mas-Colell, A., M. D. Whinston and J. R. Green (1995). *Microeconomic Theory*. Oxford University Press.

McCallum, B. T. (1997). "Crucial issues concerning central bank independence." *Journal of Monetary Economics*, 39: 99–112.

Milgrom, P. and J. Roberts (1982). "Predation, reputation, and entry deterrence." *Journal of Economic Theory*, 27: 280–312.

Mishkin, F. (2002). "The role of output stabilisation in the conduct of monetary policy." *International Finance*, 5: 213–227.

Moessner, R. and W. R. Nelson (2008). "Central bank policy rate guidance and financial market functioning." *International Journal of Central Banking*, 4: 193–226.

Monacelli, T. (2005). "Monetary policy in a low pass-through environment." *Journal of Money, Credit and Banking*, 37: 1047–1066.

Morris, S. and H. S. Shin (2002). "The social value of public information." *American Economic Review*, 92: 1521–1534.

(2005). "Central bank transparency and the signal value of prices." *Brookings Papers on Economic Activity*, 2: 1–66.

(2007). "Optimal communication." *Journal of the European Economic Association*, 5: 594–602.

Mundell, R. A. (1962). "The appropriate use of monetary and fiscal policy under fixed exchange rates." *IMF Staff Papers*, March; reproduced in Mundell (1968).

(1968). *International Economics*. London: Macmillan.

Muscatelli, A. (1998). "Optimal inflation contracts and inflation targets with uncertain central bank preferences: accountability through independence?" *Economic Journal*, 108: 529–542.

Nash, J. (1951). "Non-cooperative games." *Annals of Mathematics*, 54: 286–295.

Neiss, K. S. (1999). "Discretionary inflation in a general equilibrium model." *Journal of Money, Credit and Banking*, 31: 357–374.

Nolan, C. and E. Schaling (1998). "Monetary policy uncertainty and central bank accountability." *De Economist*, 146: 585–602.

Orphanides, A. and J. C. Williams (2002). "Robust monetary policy rules with unknown natural rates." *Brookings Papers on Economic Activity*, 2: 63–118.

Osborne, M. J. and A. Rubinstein (1990). *Bargaining and Markets*. New York: Academic Press.

(1994). *A Course in Game Theory*. Cambridge, MA and London: MIT Press.

Pappa, E. (2004). "Do the ECB and the Fed really need to cooperate? Optimal monetary policy in a two-country world." *Journal of Monetary Economics*, 51: 753–779.

Persson, T. and G. Tabellini (1990). *Macroeconomic Policy, Credibility and Politics*. Chur: Harwood Academic Publishers.

(2000). *Political Economics: Explaining Economic Policy*. Cambridge, MA: MIT Press.

Petit, M. L. (1990). *Control Theory and Dynamic Games in Economic Policy Analysis*. Cambridge University Press.

Phillips, A. W. (1954). "Stabilisation policy in a closed economy." *Economic Journal*, 64: 290–323.

(1957). "Stabilisation policy in the time-form of lagged responses." *Economic Journal*, 67: 265–277.

Piacquadio, P. G. (2011). "A theoretical approach to strategic policy interactions." Ph.D. thesis, Department of Economic and Social Analysis, "Sapienza" University of Rome.

Pindyck, R. S. (1973). "Optimal policies for economic stabilization." *Econometrica*, 41: 529–560.

Plasmans, J., J. Engwerda, B. van Aarle, G. Di Bartolomeo and T. Michalak (2006). *Dynamic Modeling of Monetary and Fiscal Cooperation among Nations*. Berlin: Springer-Verlag.

Pontryagin, L. S., V. Boltyanskii, R. Gamkrelidze and E. Mishchenko (1962). *The Mathematical Theory of Optimal Processes*. New York: Interscience.

Preston, A. J. (1974). "A dynamic generalization of Tinbergen theory of policy." *Review of Economic Studies*, 41: 64–74.

Preston, A. J. and A. R. Pagan (1982). *The Theory of Economic Policy. Statics and Dynamics*. Cambridge University Press.

Rabin, M. (1994). "A model of pre-game communication." *Journal of Economic Theory*, 63: 370–391.

Rasmusen, E. (1989). *Games and Information: An Introduction to Game Theory*. Oxford: Basil Blackwell.

Ray, D. and R. Vohra (1999). "A theory of endogenous coalition structures." *Games and Economic Behaviour*, 26: 286–336.

Rogoff, K. (1985). "The optimal degree of commitment to an intermediate monetary target." *Quarterly Journal of Economics*, 100: 1169–1189.

Rubinstein, A. (1982). "Perfect equilibrium in a bargaining model." *Econometrica*, 50: 97–110.

Rudebusch, G. and J. Williams (2008). "Revealing secrets of the temple: the value of publishing central bank interest rate projections," in J. Y.

Campbell (ed.), *Asset Prices and Monetary Policy*. NBER-University of Chicago Press.

Salmon, M. (1982). "Error correction mechanisms." *Economic Journal*, 92: 615–629.

Samuelson, P. A. and R. M. Solow (1960). "Analytical aspects of anti-inflation policy." *American Economic Review*, 50: 177–194.

Sargent, T. J. (1987). *Dynamic Macroeconomic Theory*. Cambridge, MA: Harvard University Press.

(1999). *The Conquest of American Inflation*. Princeton University Press.

Sargent, T. J. and N. Wallace (1975). "Rational expectations, the optimal monetary instrument, and the optimal money supply rule." *Journal of Political Economy*, 83: 241–254.

Schelling, T. (1960). *The Strategy of Conflict*. Cambridge, MA: Harvard University Press.

Sims, C. (1998). "Stickiness." *Carnegie-Rochester Conference Series On Public Policy*, 49: 317–356.

(2003). "Implications of rational inattention." *Journal of Monetary Economics*, 50: 665–690.

(2006). "Rational inattention: beyond the linear-quadratic case." *American Economic Review*, 96: 158–163.

Soskice, D. and T. Iversen (1998). "Multiple wage-bargaining systems in a single European currency area." *Oxford Review of Economic Policy*, 14: 110–124.

(2000). "The non-neutrality of monetary policy with large price or wage setters." *Quarterly Journal of Economics*, 115: 265–284.

Stokey, N. L. (1989). "Reputation and time consistency." *American Economic Review*, 79: 134–139.

(1991). "Credible public policy." *Journal of Economic Dynamics and Control*, 15: 627–656.

Svensson, L.E. (2006). "Social value of public information: Morris and Shin (2002) is actually pro-transparency, not con." *American Economic Review*, 96: 448–451.

Theil, H. (1954). "Econometric models and welfare maximization." *Weltwirtschaftliches Archiv*, 72: 60–83

(1956). "On the theory of economic policy." *American Economic Review*, 46: 360–366.

(1958). *Economic Forecasts and Policy*. North Holland: Amsterdam.

(1961). "Some reflections on static programming under uncertainty." *Weltwirtschaftliches Archiv*, 87: 124–137.

(1964). *Optimal Decision Rules for Government and Industry*. Amsterdam: North Holland.

Tinbergen, J. (1936). *Prae-adviezen voor de Vereeniging voor de Staathuishoudkunde en de Statistiek.* The Hague: Nijhoff, pp. 62–108.

(1939). "Statistical evidence on the acceleration principle." *Economica*, 5: 164–176.

(1952). *On the Theory of Economic Policy.* Amsterdam: North Holland.

(1956). *Economic policies. Principles and Design.* Amsterdam: North Holland.

Turnovsky, S. J. (1973). "Optimal stabilization policies for deterministic and stochastic linear economic systems." *Review of Economic Studies*, 40: 79–65.

(1974). "The stability properties of optimal economic policies." *American Economic Review*, 64: 136–148.

van Aarle, B., G. Di Bartolomeo, J. Engwerda and J. Plasmans (2002). "Coalitions and dynamic interactions between fiscal and monetary authorities in the EMU." *IFO Economic Studies*, 2: 207–229.

(2004). "Policymakers' coalitions and stabilization policies in the EMU." *Journal of Economics*, 82: 1–24.

van Huyck, J. B., R. C. Battalio and R.O. Beil (1990). "Tacit coordination games, strategic uncertainty, and coordination failure." *The American Economic Review*, 80: 234–248.

(1991). "Strategic uncertainty, equilibrium selection, and coordination failure in average opinion games." *The Quarterly Journal of Economics*, 106: 885–911.

Vercelli, A. (1991). *Methodological Foundations of Macroeconomics: Keynes and Lucas.* Cambridge University Press.

Visser, B. and O. Swank (2007). "On committees of experts." *Quarterly Journal of Economics*, 122: 337–372.

von Neumann Whitman, M. (1969). "Comment," in R. A. Mundell and A. K. Swoboda (eds.), *Monetary Problems of the International Economy.* The University of Chicago Press.

Walsh, C.E. (2007). "Optimal economic transparency." *International Journal of Central Banking*, 3: 5–36.

Whittle, P. (1982). *Optimization over Time.* New York: Wiley.

Williams, J. C. (2011). "Unconventional monetary policy: lessons from the past three years." *Economic Letter, 2011–31.* Federal Reserve of San Francisco, October.

Wonham, W. M. (1974). *Linear Multivariable Control.* New York: Springer-Verlag.

Woodford, M. (2003). *Interest & Prices: Foundations of a Theory of Monetary Policy.* Princeton University Press.

(2005). "Central bank communication and policy effectiveness." Paper presented at FRB Kansas City Symposium on *The Greenspan Era: Lessons for the Future*, Jackson Hole, Wyoming, August 25–27.

(2007). "The case for forecast targeting as a monetary policy strategy." *Journal of Economic Perspectives*, 21: 3–24.

(2008). "Forward guidance for monetary policy: is it still possible?" *Vox*, 17 January.

Wyplosz, C. (2005). "Fiscal policy: institutions versus rules." *National Institute Economic Review*, 191: 70–84.

Yi, S.-S. (1997). "Stable coalition structures with externalities." *Games and Economic Behaviour*, 20: 201–237.

Index

announcements
  and commitment, 203, 208–210, 287
  monetary, 284, 290–293, 301, 305
  one-sided, 205, 218
  two-sided, 215–218
  war of, 218
asymptotic controllability, *see* controllability

centralization, 119, 168, 186, 309, 313
certainty equivalence, 18, 30–34, 69, 127, 212, 233, 248, 276
  multi-period, 31, 34, 70
cheap talk, 202, 208, 215, 216, 224
χ-game, 191
χ-group decisiveness, 192
coalition controllability, *see* controllability
commitment, 106, 128, 129, 140, 149, 165, 182, 202–204, 208–210, 215, 223, 232, 259, 287–289, 304–305, 312–313
communication, 167, 224, 279, 288–289, 304–305, 317–318
conflict of interest, 167, 183, 184, 189, 230–231
conjectural variations, 94
controllability, 20–22, 24, 36, 59
  asymptotic state, 61, 64
  coalition, 182, 193
  coalitions, 183–186, 188–189, 195–196
  dynamic, 59–61, 62–66, 77–78, 235, 247–249, 251, 259, 270, 272–306, 317
    with forward looking behaviour, 277–306
  multi-period static, 59–60, 66–67, 236, 257, 258, 270
  null state, 61, 63
  path, 60, 64–67, 77
  Q-, 36, 133–137, 145
  state, 61–65, 74
  static, 21, 59–60, 65–67, 75, 77
    in a dynamic setting, 234, 236, 248, 257–258, 270, 279–280, 282, 287, 290–291, 294, 297
    multi-period, 59
    under REs, 257
  target path, 64–67
controllable set, 130, 135–137, 140–142, 144, 145, 150
coordination, 119, 148, 159, 163–164, 167–169, 203, 224
  failures, 202, 207, 218, 222
  implicit, 178, 180, 230, 240
  problems, 68, 158, 163, 179, 218, 224, 309, 311, 316
credibility, 106, 203, 207, 223, 301, 310, 314, 319

decentralization, 168
decisiveness, 127, 151, 196, 313
deep parameters, 85–87
derivatives with respect to vectors, 40
dynamic controllability, *see* controllability

equilibrium
  existence
    in dynamic models, 53, 59, 64, 69, 237, 239, 241, 243, 247, 254, 259–262, 265, 268, 309–310, 324
    in static models, 20, 44, 121, 130–133, 134, 141, 146, 151, 155–157, 162, 168–169, 174, 176, 182, 184, 188, 190, 196, 218
  multiplicity, 67, 117, 156, 158, 164, 168, 176, 189, 313, 324

Nash, *see* Nash equilibrium
uniqueness, 20, 23, 53, 67–68, 157, 174, 185, 191, 205, 216, 220, 323
exchange rate targeting and stabilization regimes, 165
expectations
adaptive, 39, 244, 249
forward-looking. 39, 51, 76–78, 89, *see also* expectations: rational
rational, 72, 87–94, 246–250, 257–270, 275–306, 323, *see also* expectations: forward-looking
and policy games, 90–94, 158, 163
externalities, 148, 163, 311, 314, 316

Feedback Nash equilibrium, 232, 237–239, 243, 249
with REs, 260, 262
fiscal announcements, 214
fiscal policy, *see* policy: fiscal
fixed targets, 24, 25, 52
approach, 27
geometric representation, 25
flexible targets, 23, 149
approach, 22, 23, 24, 29
geometric representation, 28
form
final, 22, 50, 53–55, 59, 65, 77, 78, 91, 254–256, 260, 275–276, 281, 288, 300
quadratic, 41, 204
reduced dynamic, 47–48, 53–54, 57, 58–59, 63–65, 69, 73–74, 77, 245, 254, 263, 265, 275, 290, 294
static, 19, 26–27, 34, 118, 148, 150, 154, 160, 166, 187, 211
structural, 18, 26, 39, 46–48, 57, 242, 244, 297

games
LQ, 100, 103, 133, 150, 154, 158, 168, 172, 195, 200, 237

implicit coalition, 182, 184–186, 188–189, 193, 196, 237, 312–314, 324
information sets, 74, 76, 77–79, 85
closed loop, 71
feedback, 71
open loop, 71
in policy games, 101–102, 104, 107–111, 127, 166, 200, 231, 232, 237, 246, 253–254, 257, 260, 266, 275, 280, 285, 288, 293, 296, 304–305, 309–310, 313, 315–317, 321
instability, 164–165, 286, 309
instrument
costs, 18, 22, 37, 60, 68, 98, 126, 132–133, 151, 154, 158–159, 162, 168–169, 189, 230, 248, 324
partial effectiveness, 171, 179
interaction between fiscal and monetary policy, 113
international monetary system, 160, 169

loss
LQ, 35, 131, 134–136, 181
loss functions, 35, 121, 127, 133, 154, 172, 200, 215, 218, 231, 248
LQ loss, 126
Lucas critique, 85–90, 93–94, 150, 258, 269, 323

matrix
inversion, 23, 43, 92, 94, 255–258, 260, 276, 282, 297, 300, 303
pseudo inverse, 43–44
model, *see also* form
building
implications, 151, 168, 196, 269, 315, 324
multi-lag, 53, 73
New Keynesian, 262, 284, 286, 289–290, 298, 303
monetary announcements, 214
monetary policy, *see* policy: monetary
monopolistic competition and wage setters, 117

Moore-Penrose generalised inverse, 23, 43, 92, 278
multi-period static controllability, *see* controllability
multipliers, *see* policy: multiplier

Nash equilibrium, 99–105, 109, 110–112, 115–116, 119–122, 127, 129–133, 134–140, 144, 146, 150, 159, 161–163, 168, 173–180, 182, 184–186, 188–191, 193–196, 202, 205–207, 215–218, 221, 232, 241–243, 246, 259, 262, 264, 267–269
null state controllability, *see* controllability

objectives
  multiperiod, 52
  strategic, 52
  target path, 52
  target point, 52
observability, 68

Pareto optimality, 175, 237
pass through, 298, 301
path controllability, *see* controllability
point controllability, *see* controllability
policy
  fiscal, 84, 107, 121, 138–140, 150, 200, 210, 263–264, 267, 284, 304, 318–320
  invariance, 141, 182, 184–185, 187, 191, 229, 249, 252, 303, 316, 323–324, *see also* policy: neutrality
  monetary, 39, 86, 104–107, 112–115, 119–120, 138, 165, 210, 251, 264, 267, 284, 290–296, 298, 301, 304, 306, 311–312, 314–315, 318–320, *see also* policy neutrality
    neutrality, 117, 141–142
    non-neutrality, 146–150
  multiplier, 29–30, 46, 49, 54, 60, 77, 154, 181, 183, 200, 235, 256, 278, 280, 290, 294
  neutrality, 19, 23, 98, 112, 114–115, 118, 121, 130–132, 137, 140, 146–149, 151, 185, 188, 189, 191, 196, 237, 252, 265, 268–269, 303, 323
    endogenous, 23, 112, 179
    exogenous, 20, 112, 179
  rule, 63, 69–70, 74, 76, 77, 87, 93, 128, 228, 238, 251, 253, 281–284, 286–287, 314
    closed loop, 71
    feedback, 71, 75, 283
    open loop, 71
preference
  function, 35, 38, 143, 149, 166, 252, 262
  LQ, 36, 117, 133, 137, 144, 148, *see also* loss: LQ; games: LQ
  non-satiated, 130
  not-satiated, 36
prevention of contagious diseases, 166
public good, 160, 310
  global, 160, 166–167, 169
  local, 166

Q-controllability, *see* controllability
quasi-reaction function, 102, 104–105, *see also* reaction function
  coincident, 156

reachability, 75
reaction function, 91–93, 102–105, *see also* quasi reaction-function
  coincident, 176, 180

sparse economic system, 242–243
stabilizability, 63, 64, 72, 74–75, 77, 282–284, 286, 288, 304
Stackelberg equilibrium, 102, 105–106, 116–122, 132, 139, 145–146, 151
state controllability, *see* controllability
state space, 51, 55–59, 61–63, 66, 68, 74, 78
static controllability, *see* controllability
strategic conflict, *see* conflict of interest
sub-game perfectness, 233

target priorities, 24

time inconsistency, 106–107, 258, 266, 279–280, 287–289, 303, 304
trade imbalances
  global, 160
transparency, 262, 314–316, 320
uncertainty, 32, 34, 61, 207, 212, 222, 224, 301, 316
  additive, 18, 30, 31, 108
  multiplicative, 33, 34

wage-wedge, 115

Author index

Acocella N., 7–10, 114–117, 127, 131, 141, 160, 162, 178, 187, 197
Alesina A., 138, 263
Amato J. D., 293
Andersen T. M., 273
Andersen T. G., 119
Aoki M., 3
Archer D., 293
Athans M., 3
Aumann R., 186, 199

Backus D., 273
Balduzzi P., 273
Baliga S., 199, 204
Barro R. J., 4–6, 106, 113, 273
Başar T., 23, 94, 238
Battalio R. C., 199
Beetsma R. M. W. J., 34, 119, 138
Beil R. O., 199
Bellman R., 233
Benigno P., 152
Binmore K. G., 221
Blanchard O. J., 118, 251, 255, 263, 316
Blinder A., 273, 279, 314
Blume A., 199
Bollerslev T., 273
Boltyanskii V., 3
Bovenberg L., 138
Brainard W., 33
Brandsma A., 107
Buiter W. H., 66
Buti M., 119

Caffé F., xii
Calmfors L., 319–320
Camerer C., 199
Canzoneri M. B., 316
Carraro C., 182
Cavallari L., 115
Charness G., 199
Chen Y., 198
Chow G. C., 3, 55
Chwe M., 182
Ciccarone G., 7, 114, 316
Clarida R., 6, 7, 298
Cochrane J. H., 284, 286
Cooper R. N., 152, 178, 198–199, 202, 204
Coricelli F., 7, 116
Corsetti G., 152
Crawford V., 198–199
Cubitt R. P., 113–114
Cuciniello V., 115
Cukierman A., 7, 117, 315–316
Cuthbertson K., 85

Dalmazzo A., 7, 116
Dasgupta P., 130, 267
de Haan J., 273, 279, 316, 318
De Jong D. V., 199
Debreu G., 130
Debrun X., 119
Demertzis M., 121, 138, 186, 316
Dennis R. K., 34
Detken C., 187
Di Bartolomeo G., 7–10, 34, 112, 115–117, 127, 131, 141, 152, 160, 162, 178, 182, 187, 197, 315–316
Diebold F. X., 273
Dixit A., 119–120, 138, 163, 178, 210, 230, 289
Dockner E., 238
Driffill J., 273

Eggerston G., 273, 316
Ehrmann M., 279, 316, 318
Eichengreen B., 319
Eijffinger S. C.W., 314–315
Ellison M., 34

Elton E J., 273
Engwerda J., 152, 182, 238, 241
Eusepi S., 270, 293
Evans G. W., 251, 270

Fair R., 273
Falb P. L., 3
Farrell J., 198–199, 203–204
Fatàs A., 319
Faust J., 273, 293, 314–316
Ferguson R. W, 316
Ferrero G., 293, 318
Fisher P. G., 255, 259
Forsythe R., 199
Fratzscher M., 273, 279, 316, 318
Friedman J. W., 130
Friedman M., 39
Frisch R., 2
Fudenberg D., 102, 130
Fuhrer J. C., 289

Galì J., 6, 7, 249, 298
Gamkrelidze R., 3
Gartner M., 187
Geraats P. M., 315
Gersovitz M., 66
Gertler M., 6, 7, 249, 298
Giannoni M., 34
Gibbons R., 102, 198
Giuli F., 34, 178
Glicksberg I., 130
Gnocchi S., 116
Gordon D., 4–6, 106, 113, 273
Green J. R., 107
Green T. C., 273
Gruner H. P., 316
Guzzo V., 7, 114
Gylfason G., 7, 114–117, 143

Hansen B., 2, 25
Hansen L. P., 33–34
Harsanyi J. C., 198
Hausman R., 319
Heal G., 3
Hibbs D. A., 117
Hoeberichts M., 314
Holly S., 3, 33–34, 232–233
Honkapohja S., 251, 270
House C., 298
Hughes Hallett A. J., 1–3, 8, 10, 22, 33–35, 46, 94, 107, 119, 121, 138, 141, 152, 197, 232–233, 255, 259, 316, 319–320

In't Veld J., 119
Issing O., 149, 314, 316
Iversen T., 7, 116

James J. G., 34
Jansen D. J., 273, 279, 316, 318
Jensen H., 34, 115, 119, 314, 319–320
Jerger J., 7, 116
Johansen L., 3
John A., 179, 198, 202, 204
Jorgensen S., 238
Juilliard M., 277

Kalman R. E., 3
Katik N., 198
Khan C. M., 251, 255
Kim Y., 199
Kindleberger C. P., 163
Kiyotaki N., 118, 263
Kohlberg E., 199
Kohler M., 182
Kreps D., 100, 106, 198, 273
Kuttner K. N., 315
Kydland F.E., 5, 106

Lambertini L., 19–20, 138, 163, 178, 210, 230, 289
Lane P., 115
Lawler P., 34, 114, 117
Leeper E. M., 88, 319
Leitemo K., 34
Leontief W., 2
Libich J., 119, 318
Lindbeck A., 7, 114–115, 143
Lippi F., 7, 117
Lucas R. E., 4, 84, 250–251, 273

Magnus J. R., 1
Manzo M., 34, 178
Marchetti E., 315–316
Mas-Colell A., 109
Maskin E., 130, 267
McCallum B. T., 107
Meltzer A., 316

Mertens J. F., 199
Michalak T., 152
Milgrom P., 273
Mishchenko E., 3
Mishkin F., 284
Moessner R., 293, 318
Monacelli T., 298
Moore G. R., 289
Morgan M. S., 1
Morris S., 199, 204, 293, 316
Mundell R. A., 152–153
Muscatelli A., 316

Nash J., 130
Neiss K. S., 113
Nelson W. R., 293, 318
Nolan C., 316

Olsder G. J., 23, 94, 238
Orphanides A., 6
Ortmann A., 199
Osborne M. J., 97, 215, 219

Pagan A. R., 1, 3, 17, 21, 23, 46, 58, 247
Pappa E., 152
Pauwels W., 112, 115, 187
Persson T., 273
Pesenti P., 152
Petit M. L., 3, 46, 55, 107, 232
Phillips A. W., 72
Piacquadio P. G., 9, 10, 178, 197, 228
Pindyck R. S., 3
Plasmans J., 152, 182
Pontryagin L. S., 3
Posen A. S., 315
Prescott E. C., 5, 106
Preston A. J., 1–2, 17, 21, 25, 46, 58, 247
Preston B., 270, 293
Pugsley B., 318

Rabin M., 199
Rasmusen E., 96, 98, 130
Ray D., 182
Rees H., 3, 21
Roberts J., 273
Roeger W., 119
Rogers J. H., 273
Rogoff K., 6, 30
Ross T., 199
Rubinstein A., 97, 215–216, 219
Rudebusch G., 273, 279, 293

Salmon M., 76
Sargent T. J., 6, 33–34, 112–113, 238, 273
Schaling E., 316
Schelling T., 198, 207
Schneider F., 119
Secchi A., 293, 318
Selten R., 198
Shapiro M., 298
Shin H. S., 316
Sims C., 33
Sobel J., 198–199
Söderström U., 34
Sorger G., 238
Soskice D., 7, 116
Stehlik P., 119
Stokey N. L., 5, 113
Strauch R., 319
Svensson L. E. O., 293, 314–316
Swank O., 318

Tabellini G., 138, 263, 273
Taylor M. P., 85
Theil H., 2, 3, 6, 18, 31
Tinbergen J., 1, 2, 6, 31
Tirelli P., 115, 187
Tirole J., 102, 130
Turnovsky S. J., 55

Uhlig H., 138

van Aarle B., 182
van Huyck J. B., 199
Van Long N., 238
Vega C., 273
Velasco A., 7, 114
Vercelli A., 87
Viegi N., 121, 138, 186, 316
Visser B., 318
Vohra R., 182
von Hagen J., 319
von Neumann Whitman M., 153

Wallace N., 273

Walsh C.E., 293
Wang S. B., 273
Weymark D. N., 119
Whinston M.D., 107
Whittle P., 33
Williams J. C., 6, 89, 273, 279, 292–293, 318
Wilson R., 273
Wonham W. M., 74, 281
Woodford M., 6, 22, 35, 89, 273, 279, 316, 318
Wright J. H., 273
Wyplosz C., 319